Dream the Size of Freedom

POWER, POLITICS, AND THE WORLD

Series editors: Christopher R. W. Dietrich,
Jennifer Mittelstadt, and Russell Rickford

Power, Politics, and the World showcases new stories
in the fields of the history of U.S. foreign relations,
international history, and transnational history. The
series is motivated by a desire to pose innovative
questions of power and hierarchy to the history of
the United States and the world. Books published in
the series examine a wide range of actors on local,
national, and global scales, exploring how they
imagined, enacted, or resisted political, cultural,
social, economic, legal, and military authority.

A complete list of books in the series
is available from the publisher.

Published by
University of Pennsylvania Press
Philadelphia, Pennsylvania 19104-4112
www.pennpress.org

Printed in the United States of America on acid-free paper
10 9 8 7 6 5 4 3 2 1

A Cataloging-in-Publication record is
available from the Library of Congress.

Hardcover ISBN 978-1-5128-2767-5
Ebook ISBN 978-1-5128-2768-2

DREAM THE SIZE OF FREEDOM

How African Liberation Mobilized
New Left Internationalism

R. Joseph Parrott

PENN

UNIVERSITY OF PENNSYLVANIA PRESS

PHILADELPHIA

For Austin and Julie

CONTENTS

List of Acronyms and Abbreviations   ix

Introduction   1

PART I. COLD WAR REVOLUTIONS

Chapter 1. The Angolan Crisis of 1961   19

Chapter 2. A Tale of Two Lobbies   37

Chapter 3. The Limits of Cold War Liberalism   59

Chapter 4. Fighting for Southern Africa   79

PART II. GRASSROOTS SOLIDARITY

Chapter 5. The Religious and Radical Origins of Solidarity   105

Chapter 6. Transforming Established Institutions   131

Chapter 7. Forging Pan-African Solidarity   162

Chapter 8. The Interracial Coalition Politics of the Gulf Boycott   190

PART III. INSTITUTIONALIZING NEW LEFT INTERNATIONALISM

Chapter 9. A Precedent Against Intervention   223

Chapter 10. Cold War Crucible   249

Conclusion   277

Notes   297

Index   351

Acknowledgments   375

ACRONYMS AND ABBREVIATIONS

Liberation Groups in Portuguese Africa

CONCP   Conferência das Organizações Nacionalistas das Colónias Portuguesas (Conference of Nationalist Organizations of the Portuguese Colonies)

Prominent members of the CONCP included:

FRELIMO   Frente de Libertação de Moçambique (Mozambique Liberation Front)
MPLA   Movimento Popular de Libertação de Angola (Popular Movement for the Liberation of Angola)
PAIGC   Partido Africano da Independência da Guiné e Cabo Verde (African Party for the Independence of Guinea and Cabo Verde)

The following three groups were variations of the movement led by Holden Roberto:

UPA   União dos Povos de Angola (Union of Angolan Peoples)
FNLA   Frente Nacional de Libertação de Angola (National Liberation Front of Angola)
GRAE   Govêrno Revolucionário de Angola no Exílio (Angolan Revolutionary Government in Exile)

UNITA   União Nacional para a Independência Total de Angola (National Union for the Total Independence of Angola)

United States Organizations and Movements

AAAA	American-African Affairs Association
ACOA	American Committee on Africa
AFSC	American Friends Service Committee
ALD	African Liberation Day
ALSC	African Liberation Support Committee
ANLCA	American Negro Leadership Conference on Africa
CAP	Congress of African People
CBC	Congressional Black Caucus
CCLAMG	Chicago Committee for the Liberation of Angola, Mozambique, and Guinea
CORE	Congress of Racial Equality
CRV	Committee of Returned Volunteers
CWS	Church World Services
FIM	Frontier Internship in Mission
GBC	Gulf Boycott Coalition
LSM	Liberation Support Movement (Canada and United States)
MACSA	Madison Area Committee on Southern Africa
NCC	National Council of Churches
New Mobe	New Mobilization Committee to End the War in Vietnam
NSCF	National Student Christian Federation
NWRC	New World Resource Center
PACFA	Portuguese-American Committee on Foreign Affairs
PALC	Pan-African Liberation Committee
PASC	Pan-African Solidarity Committee
SAC	Southern Africa Committee
SDS	Students for a Democratic Society
SNCC	Student Nonviolent Coordinating Committee
UCC	United Church of Christ
UCM	University Christian Movement
WOA	Washington Office on Africa
YOBU, SOBU	Youth/Students Organized for Black Unity

Other African/International Organizations and Movements

ANC	African National Congress (South Africa)

FLN	Front de Libération Nationale (Algerian National Liberation Front)
MCF	Movement for Colonial Freedom (Britain)
MFA	Movimento das Forças Armadas (Portuguese Armed Forces Movement)
OAU	Organization of African Unity
PCP	Portuguese Communist Party
PIDE	Polícia Internacional e de Defesa do Estado (International and State Defense Police [of Portugal])
WCC	World Council of Churches

Archives and Collections Abbreviated in the Notes

AAA	African Activist Archive, Michigan State University (online)
ACOA	American Committee on Africa Papers, Amistad Research Center, Tulane University (New Orleans, LA)
AFSC	American Friends Service Committee Archives (Philadelphia, PA)
AHD	Arquivo Historico Diplomatico (Lisbon, Portugal)
AJYP	Andrew J. Young Papers, Auburn Avenue Research Library on African American Culture and History (Atlanta, GA)
BOP	Barrett O'Hara Papers, University of Illinois at Chicago (Chicago, IL)
BRP	Private Papers of Brenda Randolph
CCDP	Charles C. Diggs Jr. Papers, Moorland-Spingarn Research Center, Howard University (Washington, DC)
CFMAG	Committee for Freedom in Mozambique, Angola, and Guinea Papers, Bishopsgate Institute (London, United Kingdom)
DAC, CC	Documentos Amílcar Cabral, Projecto Casa Comum, Fundaçao Mário Soares (online)
DMFP	Donald M. Fraser Papers, Minnesota Historical Society (Saint Paul, Minnesota)
GRFL	Gerald R. Ford Presidential Library (Ann Arbor, MI)
GWMP	Gale W. McGee Papers, American Heritage Center, University of Wyoming (Laramie, Wyoming)

HDL	Harvard Divinity Library (Cambridge, MA)
HH	Hall-Hoag Collection of Extremist and Dissenting Propaganda, Brown University (Providence, RI)
JCL	Jimmy Carter Presidential Library (Atlanta, GA)
JFKL	John F. Kennedy Presidential Library (Boston, MA)
JVTP	John V. Tunney Papers, University of California (Berkeley, CA)
LBJL	Lyndon B. Johnson Presidential Library (Austin, Texas)
MSU	Michigan State University (East Lansing, MI)
NARA	National Archives and Records Administration (College Park, MD)
NCC, PHS	National Council of Churches Papers, Presbyterian Historical Society (Philadelphia, PA)
NWRC	New World Resource Center Papers, Chicago History Museum (Chicago, IL)
NYPL	New York Public Library (New York, NY)
RCCP	Richard C. Clark Papers, University of Iowa (Iowa City, IA)
SADFAA	South African Department of Foreign Affairs Archives (Pretoria, South Africa)
SIHP	S. I. Hayakawa Papers, Hoover Institution (Stanford, CA)
TT-PT	Arquivo Nacional da Torre do Tombo (Lisbon, Portugal)
UKNA	National Archives of the United Kingdom (Kew, England)
WGBH	WGBH Media Archive (Boston, MA)
YDL	Yale Divinity Library (New Haven, CT)

Introduction

How can we tell you the size
of our dream?

Today
our Revolution
is a great flower
to which each day
new petals are added.

The petals are the land
reconquered,
the people freed
the fields cultivated
schools and hospitals.

Our dream has the size
of Freedom.
      —Unknown author, Mozambique

A persistent drizzle failed to suppress the excitement of the fifty thousand people packed into Machava Stadium on the outskirts of Lourenço Marques, soon to be rechristened Maputo. It was midnight on June 25, 1975, the day that Portugal formally dissolved its colony in Mozambique and handed power to the government of a new, independent nation. For over a decade, Mozambicans had waged a military campaign for control of their country, all the while developing education, health, and agriculture

programs that hinted at their ambitious dreams for a free future. At 12:20 A.M.,
the red and green Portuguese flag symbolizing 470 years of European rule
finally lowered, replaced by a new standard featuring a bayonetted gun and
hoe crossed over a book that represented the military and social revolutions
led by the Frente de Libertação de Moçambique (Mozambique Liberation
Front, FRELIMO). The khaki-clad Samora Moises Machel, a forty-one-year-
old nurse turned revolutionary, presided over the festivities. FRELIMO's
second president had led the fight against Portugal since his party began its
armed liberation struggle in 1964, joining the campaigns already under way
in Lisbon's other mainland African colonies of Angola and Guinea-Bissau.
After ten years of fighting, Machel stood ready to accept the presidency of
the nation amid booming cannons of a more joyous variety. The mostly Black
African crowd roared its approval. "We have won our independence by dint of
our struggle," Machel proclaimed in his characteristically animated way, "We
shall make revolution triumph! Long Live FRELIMO! Long Live the People's
Republic of Mozambique! The struggle continues [A luta continua] . . ."[1]

Present in Machava Stadium that morning were dignitaries from the many
countries and organizations that had aided FRELIMO over the prior decade.
Nearby was Portugal's revolutionary prime minister Vasco Gonçalves, who
came to power after a coup toppled the fascist dictatorship in Lisbon the year
before. Representatives of numerous African nations were present, notably
Tanzania, which sheltered FRELIMO during its time in exile, and Algeria,
which armed it. India sent its ambassador, ready to present his credentials
to the government alongside diplomats from other Global South states that
championed the cause of African liberation at the United Nations. Sizable
delegations from the Soviet Union and the People's Republic of China hinted
at the role they played arming the revolutions alongside a smattering of Eastern European partners. Largely absent, however, were the major nations of
the Western alliance. The United States, Canada, France, and West Germany
had no officials at the ceremonies. Britain alone among the greater powers
received an invitation, along with the Netherlands and the Nordic countries.
Machel praised those present, singling out his African and socialist allies, the
Dutch, and the Scandinavians for aiding the revolution in its early stages.
Amid the fanfare, the century-old U.S. consulate located on the other side of
the city lowered its own flag at midnight, since the government of independent Mozambique had not requested it reopen as an embassy.

This is not to say that there were no Americans in the audience. Congressional Black Caucus members Charles Diggs and Cardiss Collins were in the

stadium, and Senator Ted Kennedy had regretfully declined an invitation. A few others represented organizations that aided FRELIMO, including two members of the nongovernmental American Committee on Africa (ACOA).[2] These politicians and activists had supported the liberation struggles, even as their government maintained its alliance with imperial Portugal. American reporters speculated that the absence of U.S. delegates had Cold War implications, worrying that it signaled Mozambique's hostility toward the West and embrace of communism. But those in attendance thought differently. Diggs acidly assured a reporter that the United States would have been invited had it "followed a policy of more than lip service to the independence movements in Africa."[3] The Americans present had spent the previous decade building a domestic network that championed African liberation and aided the social programs that emerged from Mozambican nationalist dreams, earning their positions in the football stadium that rainy night. Five months later, the same individuals and their domestic allies reunited to lobby and legislate against the U.S. intervention that sought to block a similar transfer of power to FRE-LIMO's leftist allies in the Movimento Popular de Libertação de Angola (Pop-ular Movement for the Liberation of Angola, MPLA). The network of U.S. activists and politicians hoped to move their country beyond lip service and toward more collaborative relationships with parties like FRELIMO and the MPLA that were transforming the Global South.

The fact that FRELIMO gave these Americans status akin to national leaders and ambassadors reveals their importance to the revolutionary diplomacy of Lusophone Africa—a value soon confirmed by their success-ful defense of the MPLA. *Dream the Size of Freedom* explores the construc-tion of this solidarity movement in the United States and the role African liberation played in transforming U.S. engagement with the Global South. As revolutionary movements in the Portuguese colonies of Angola, Mozam-bique, and Guinea-Bissau struggled for the independence of their countries, their success depended as much on assembling international support as it did on winning pitched battles. The nationalists were forced into exile in neighboring African states by the Lisbon dictatorship's repressive politics, and they relied on African and Eastern arms to wage militant campaigns for freedom when Portugal refused to negotiate a transfer of power. Attempts to convince Western governments to pressure their North Atlantic ally proved fruitless because African desires for self-determination were less important than Cold War containment and a pyrrhic search for African stability. There were, however, still avenues for support in Europe and North America. The closely allied leftist parties of FRELIMO, the MPLA, and the Partido Africano da Independência da Guiné e Cabo Verde (African Party for the Independence of Guinea and Cabo Verde, PAIGC) believed their global visions of liberation could have a transformative effect on U.S. politics, changing official attitudes toward decolonization and protecting national independence when it was finally achieved. Internationally, this meant assembling a broad anti-imperial front that cut across East-West and North-South divides. The socialist parties paired national reconstruction with military liberation, informing the symbolism of FRELIMO's flag and inspiring Western radicals to adopt similar programs at home. The appeal of these broad formulations of self-determination opened avenues for support among Western populations frustrated by the reactionary Cold War politics of the United States and allied countries. As a result, leftist Lusophone nationalists built networks of support that challenged the alliance with Portugal while raising barriers to reactionary interventions—from the ground up.

Within the United States, African transnational appeals intersected with the broad political reorientation of the 1960s to inform a new approach to Global South politics that contrasted with the prevailing Cold War consensus. As the civil rights movement encouraged the United States to rethink race relations and protests against the Vietnam War challenged policies of militant containment, domestic reformers searched for new models of international relations. Religious humanists, young radicals, and militant African Americans all gravitated to the ongoing revolutions in Portuguese Africa. FRELIMO, the MPLA, and the PAIGC worked with these organizations to justify and promote their platforms in the United States without straining their limited resources. This "grassroots diplomacy" allowed the marginalized African parties, who positioned themselves as governments-in-waiting of future independent states, to amplify their demands via the efforts of American citizens who directly identified with nationalists and their programs. Such transnational collaboration helped the parties to tailor their appeals to specific U.S. constituencies and win additional support, offering an increasingly effective response to the official anti-communist and civilizational attacks used by Portugal and its regional allies, Rhodesia and South Africa. These tailored appeals helped individual American communities imagine their domestic agendas in global terms, with the African nationalist desire for a cohesive political front curtailing the potential for fracture by uniting distinct constituencies behind shared goals. While no singular organization emerged to champion Lusophone liberation, solidarity organizing created interracial, intergenerational, and pan-ideological networks during a period when, historians argue, leftist organizing—and key manifestations of it like the anti-war movement—splintered. The result was a set of collaborative relationships that encouraged more centrist organizations like the American Committee on Africa to embrace assertive New Left ideas of social justice while convincing radical elements to seek practical compromise with established institutions. While diverse and decentralized, this movement cohered around the pursuit of African freedom and self-determination, becoming a model for future organizing on international issues.

The process of building U.S. support for Lusophone liberation promoted the formation and institutionalization of what I term New Left Internationalism. This worldview mirrored Global South revolutionaries in breaking with the Old Left fixation on class conflict, focusing instead on issues of global racial equality, the preservation of authentic cultures, economic development projects, the danger of global wars, and the need for more democratic formulations of policymaking. While emphasizing transnational collaboration and humanist connections, its prioritization of social justice encouraged advocates to identify with militant revolutions in Angola, Mozambique, and Guinea-Bissau. U.S. activists used nationalist reconstruction projects to justify the political violence of armed struggle by pointing to the idealized postcolonial societies that would emerge after the old imperial order was removed by force. This worldview extended beyond Africa, offering a global critique of Cold War priorities while emphasizing the need to work cooperatively with Global South states as they sought to transform the Eurocentric international system. Especially pronounced at the grassroots level, New Left Internationalism made its way into official debates via the U.S. Congress, where Vietnam-era protests defied inherited ideas of foreign affairs and produced a generation of reform-minded legislators. Congress challenged the executive branch's embrace of Portugal and channeled public anger at the 1975 Angolan intervention by passing laws that constrained executive freedom in foreign policy. While New Left Internationalism did not achieve a new consensus to replace Cold War thinking, it did create a powerful grassroots-congressional nexus championing Southern priorities that competed with establishment officials for control of foreign policy. The result was a heated competition over the terms of U.S. involvement in the Global South that extended through the 1980s. It pitted an interventionist executive branch backed by traditional cold warriors against legislators sympathetic to New Left Internationalism, who achieved their greatest victories when transnational grassroots networks mobilized behind specific policies.

Decolonizing America's Cold War

At its core, *Dream the Size of Freedom* contends that decolonization had a transformative effect on the globe, not only reordering the international system but also promoting political, intellectual, and structural transformations within the countries of the Global North. The process deserves equal attention alongside the Cold War as a defining event of twentieth-century international history. The challenge that decolonization presented to the Cold War is well established, but historians of international affairs generally follow Odd Arne Westad's assertion that the ideological competition between the United States and the Soviet Union contextualized and canalized protest politics in the Global South.[4] Anti-colonial movements and postcolonial states received aid for aligning their ambitions with specific ideological camps, tying debates around freedom and modernization into a heavily armed global rivalry.[5] Indeed, the international narrative of Portuguese African decolonization follows the outline of such proxy conflicts, especially in Angola.[6] To be sure, both the liberation parties and their international supporters were cognizant of the Cold War. Their adversaries in Portugal and the white minority regimes of southern Africa relied on anti-communist appeals to maintain support from the West, while nationalists used Eastern arms to conduct their revolutions. Yet FRELIMO, the MPLA, and the PAIGC pursued a political and economic self-determination that transcended the East-West divide, continuously courting Western civil society in hopes of weakening Portugal while pursuing social revolutions that sometimes baffled their Soviet backers.[7]

This fits with trends in Global South studies that are recovering the anti-imperial programs and alliances that existed independently of the Cold War and challenged its primacy in international affairs. Southern leaders adapted concepts of modernization, nationalism, internationalism, and self-determination around the needs of postcolonial societies.[8] To strengthen these alternatives to empire, Global South revolutionaries sought global allies that could help them contest European domination and its intellectual foundations. This "diplomatic revolution," as Matthew Connelly describes the phenomenon, saw non-state revolutionary actors use globalized transportation, economic, and communication networks to transcend colonial borders and address significant power imbalances, magnifying political protests and military defeats into crushing blows against empire.[9] Cold War containment and the West's tendency to conflate radical national projects with communism erected barriers to this anti-imperial movement, but this only served to radicalize many such programs. By the 1960s, postcolonial states extended the logic that drove political independence toward more ambitious forms of economic and cultural self-determination that transformed the United Nations and informed grand programs such as the New International Economic Order.[10] Lusophone organizing fit neatly within this global trend but went beyond Connelly's focus on interstate politics and elite lobbying to reveal the extent to which African nationalists cultivated grassroots transnational movements aimed at transforming Western thought. Intersecting with the deep soul-searching caused by the youth revolt of the 1960s, the process of decolonization challenged core political and cultural assumptions as post-1945 liberal internationalism confronted its own limitations in Indochina, Lusophone Africa, and beyond.

The specific brand of anti-imperialism that the Lusophone revolutionaries used to confront Euro-American hegemony is best understood within the concept of tricontinentalism. Secular, socialist, and broadly anti-imperial, this radical worldview assailed both formal colonialism and the economic and cultural forms of imperialism that sustained Western influence after independence. Such broad critiques of the international status quo inspired ambitious dreams of freedom that would transform both colonies and their people through the process of revolution. I have argued elsewhere that this tricontinental worldview borrowed heavily from Marxist formulations of empire and global capital but downplayed class-based revolution in favor of nationalist struggles that addressed the structural racism and economic inequalities separating the poor South from an increasingly wealthy Global North (including the Eastern bloc).[11] While Cuba championed the term, tricontinentalism captured the common goals and strategies that led revolutionaries across Asia, Africa, and Latin America to see themselves as part of a common struggle. The leftist parties in Portuguese Africa unified around these ideas and became vital components defining the tricontinental revolution, with FRELIMO and the PAIGC's Amílcar Cabral articulating flexible, practical strategies for achieving cultural, political, and economic independence that won global admiration.[12] Among a generation of sympathizers was a vocal minority of Americans whose frustrations with racial inequality at home and foreign interventions abroad led them to question the national mission and its core policies of containment. They identified with Southern-led revolutions like those in Portuguese Africa, making support for parties like the PAIGC, FRELIMO, and the MPLA a form of active participation in global, anti-imperial struggles.

Just as the Cold War canalized postcolonial politics in the Global South, so too did Southern revolts guide and motivate internal challenges to the U.S. status quo. Taking seriously Campbell Craig and Fredrik Logevall's call to consider the "intermestic" construction of foreign policy as a reflection of domestic politics, it is equally vital to consider how external trends reshaped domestic thought, capturing the transnational nature of intellectual debates during this period of fluid borders.[13] Scholars have documented this influence within minority communities and the radical left, but there has been less appreciation for the extent to which these ideas had sufficient universal appeal to reorient American politics and policies.[14] After the Vietnam War, new popular visions of U.S. foreign affairs sought inspiration from movements like those operating in Portuguese Africa as they championed greater attention to global emancipation projects and social justice campaigns.[15] The result was the transformation of the religious, educational, and migratory ties that long supported empire, turning them into conduits through which Southern nationalists injected their concerns into domestic debates in the Global North.[16] While such exchanges initially operated within Cold War boundaries, the radicalization of Southern movements and loosening of domestic restrictions in the 1960s inspired a clean break with this teetering consensus, legitimizing leftist revolutions, armed liberation, youth protests, and more egalitarian visions of foreign affairs.

New Left Internationalism

New Left Internationalism provides an umbrella to discuss the common ideas that operated at the center of this political reorientation. New Left thought emerged in the West from similar motivations as tricontinentalism, with both seeking to redress the deep inequalities that remained amid an era of abundance, decolonization, and rapid if uneven global development. It found useful ideas in traditional socialist and Marxist thought but felt that an emphasis on socio-political matters better explained why disparities persisted along racialized, gendered, and geographic lines.[17] As New Left thinkers searched, they found comparable ideas in tricontinental anti-imperialism. Its emphasis on Global South leadership and identity meant that the direct adoption of this worldview in the United States occurred mainly among minority groups with ethnic ties to Africa, Asia, and Latin America.[18] But a diverse group of constituencies aligned themselves with these domestic revolts and leftist revolutions abroad while learning from the practical ideologies of leaders like Cabral. Together, they sought to reorient U.S. policy toward a more collaborative relationship with the Global South, a restructuring of international institutions, and less interventionist diplomacy. While critical of unbridled capitalism, New Left Internationalism argued that race, gender, and cultural divides drove global antipathies. The hope was that transnational support for communal self-determination, social democracy, and new economic structures would create a more just international system and rebound to reform the most problematic aspects of U.S. society.

The leftist Lusophone parties played an underappreciated role in this movement because they faced a uniquely unpalatable enemy while modeling the creation of anti-imperial societies. Portugal's antiquated colonial policies and the violence used to retain its African possessions fueled broad opposition. Centrist and even pacifist groups accepted the necessity of armed revolt against colonialism, giving the liberation parties a pathway for American support unavailable to other tricontinental groups embedded in the Cold War or directly confronting U.S. power. Yet sustained support required that foreign advocates identify with nationalist parties and their programs. FRELIMO and the PAIGC won allies by promoting the socialist societies that they created in liberated territories, balancing the destruction of war with the constructive goals of Southern revolution. Cabral and FRELIMO's first president, Eduardo Mondlane, used these communities as evidence of practical, egalitarian social orders. Their educational institutions, cooperative stores, reformed gender relationships, and (one-party) local governance captured the imagination of U.S. activists while signaling a governing potential to sympathetic policymakers. As decolonization and popular resistance to the Vietnam War forced a reevaluation of national approaches to the Global South, Portuguese African revolutionaries provided an idealized vision of Southern self-determination that encouraged the formation of a New Left Internationalism as a way of promoting these political programs.

Central to the effectiveness of this solidarity movement was its diversity and decentralization. The liberation parties believed that a broad front was required to isolate the well-connected Portuguese state politically and materially, so they advocated for collaboration across distinct communities. Early supporters from religious and civil rights organizations wary of Cold War tripwires were joined by sympathetic legislators, radical youth, Black Power advocates, and internationally-minded liberals. Prominent organizations like the American Committee on Africa and National Council of Churches shifted to the left as they opened their doors to youthful rebels, who resisted the urge to break with their more cautious elders thanks to encouragement from leftist African nationalists. Groups remained independent in order to maintain their unique identities, ideologies, and goals, but overlapping personal networks and commitments to African independence promoted collaboration in campaigns like the boycott of Gulf Oil's activities in Angola. Lusophone liberation carried distinct connotations for these groups, reflecting what historian Judy Wu calls a "radical Orientalism" in which U.S. activists essentialized Southern revolutions to justify and motivate their own political work.[19] Yet this idea downplays the extent to which African nationalists actively participated in this process of essentialization. They distilled their own struggles to their most aspirational elements as a form of grassroots diplomacy, seeking U.S. collaborators who could translate their revolutions for distinct constituencies and advocate among them.[20] This process promoted strong bonds of solidarity as activists imagined deeply personal connections to African revolts that reflected local emphases and associations. Such personalized understandings of the liberation struggles sustained domestic advocacy through years of inconsistent success while gradually expanding the list of supporters that ultimately proved pivotal to the defense of the MPLA in 1975.

The decentralized nature of this solidarity movement explains its absence from the historical record, but it also hints that narratives of declension attached to sixties-era politics and the New Left are exaggerated. Historians have documented how both the anti-war and Black Power movements splintered as they embraced broader and more confrontational anti-imperial politics, reinforcing an unfortunate tendency to divide the era into the "good sixties" of grand, noble projects and the "bad sixties" of infighting and sectarianism.[21] In the realm of foreign affairs, Petra Goedde laments that the fractious activist landscape encouraged by New Left Internationalism weakened traditional peace movements.[22] Such framing misses the coalitions and institutions that formed in the wake of these very real divisions. Lusophone liberation offers a case study in how revisionist ideas first explored in the sixties were sustained, institutionalized, and integrated into mainstream political discussions via overlapping advocacy networks.[23] There was no new consensus, which disappointed many at the time and more historians since, but changes in ideology, attitudes, and ambitions were substantial. Admittedly, the decentralized nature of New Left Internationalism limited the grandest projects due to the diverging agendas of its constituents, but where some unanimity existed—as was the case in the rejection of colonialism, apartheid, and some of the more problematic Reagan-era interventions in Latin America—the ability to mobilize diverse supporters via tailored appeals strengthened the impact of popular and political organizing.

Routes to Power

Evaluating the impact of New Left Internationalism requires an understanding of how these ideas influenced policy. This came less through the internal deliberations of the executive branch, where most diplomatic and policy histories concentrate, and more through Congress, where sympathetic legislators framed political issues and defined limits on presidential pursuits of familiar Cold War strategies.[24] Scholars like Barbara Keys demonstrate that advocacy networks encouraged Congress to champion influential human rights–based approaches to foreign affairs, while historians of African American internationalism increasingly identify legislators as instigators for changing policies toward the Global South.[25] These arguments fit the experience of the Lusophone African solidarity network, illustrating the variety of international issues spearheaded by a newly active Congress while bridging the gap in the literature between the rising tide of anti-war legislation in the 1960s and clashes over Reagan-era policies in the 1980s.[26] African liberation leaders and their allies found willing collaborators in Congress, where they faced some of the most stalwart supporters of Portugal and the white minority regimes. This created competition between transnational networks as debates over decolonization informed domestic lobbying, with each side seeking not only to influence policy but also to frame national discussions about the proper U.S. role in the Global South.

Social science research on transnational activist networks provides insight into how such grassroots organizing works. According to sociologists Margaret Keck and Kathryn Sikkink, nontraditional international actors like the liberation parties find success by "mobiliz[ing] information strategically to help create new issues and categories and to persuade, pressure, and gain leverage over much more powerful organizations and governments."[27] As it sought greater autonomy in foreign affairs, Congress required expertise beyond the executive departments that traditionally managed knowledge on international issues. Legislators sympathetic to liberation efforts looked to activists and lobbyists with ties to groups like the MPLA and PAIGC that were locked out of official deliberations. The solidarity movement utilized its privileged access to these Global South perspectives to provide new facts and narratives that challenged those offered by dominant state actors, complicating once straightforward debates and encouraging new policies. Visible grassroots action, like the FRELIMO-inspired 1972 African Liberation Day protests and the Gulf Oil boycott, reinforced the authority of activists by mobilizing key constituencies and garnering the attention of vote-hungry legislators.

While information campaigns and mobilization can also influence policy via electoral pressure or the professional bureaucracy, the legislative branch is more accessible and responsive to organizing, given the smaller, idiosyncratic electorates of its members. These and other factors have led political scientist Jeffrey W. Knopf to conclude that the most likely route for activist influence on policy is via "changing coalitions in Congress."[28] This coalition idea is key, because congressional advocates of individual policies or international parties are usually a minority, but they can sway undecided or uninformed colleagues. This is precisely what happened in the case of Lusophone Africa. Portugal and its allies used conventional Cold War and civilizational tropes to win support from both branches of government, but a relatively small group of legislators first aligned with African liberation and then adopted New Left Internationalist ideas as they interacted with the nationalist parties and their grassroots allies. Congressional hearings worked in tandem with activist information campaigns and protests to win over colleagues, which expanded the ranks of supporters in the early 1970s and more rapidly when the Angolan crisis forced decisive action. In this latter moment, the decade of organizing established a critical framing of intervention and information routes that allowed the pro-liberation coalition to control debates and undercut Cold War arguments before they could be made.

Yet the formation of the coalition did not create consensus; instead, it foreshadowed an era in which advocates of the Cold War and aspects of New Left Internationalism competed for control of Congress and national narratives of foreign policy.[29] The result was two rival visions for global affairs and relations with the Global South, with Angola emerging as a catalyst for defining these camps and the nature of their competition. Elections influenced the relative strengths of these opposing sides, but the main battle occurred as invested legislators sought to sway uncommitted colleagues using the information and lobbying of competing transnational networks. This produced inconsistent policies in the Global South as the executive branch reinvested in the Cold War despite intermittent resistance from Congress. The legislature offered broad support for anti-Soviet Afghans while working to isolate apartheid South Africa and place limits on Reagan-era interventions in Latin America. Scholars like Håkan Thörn have seen these transnational contests as evidence of an emergent "global civil society." But the distinctly antagonistic networks that connected domestic policymaking to Africa and the unique worldviews they represented fit more closely with what Jackie Smith and Dawn Wiest have called an "uneven geography" of international relations.[30] Lusophone solidarity was a single example of multiple fragmented networks with divergent resources operating across state borders that pursued contested internationalist ideologies. While falling short of a single global civil society, it points to a fluid transnational exchange in which local politics became globalized across North and South, transforming both regions as interests and individual identities intertwined.

Structure and Chapter Outline

The book explores African nationalist diplomacy in the United States by adopting a multicontinental, horizontal approach that follows Thomas Bender's conceptualization of transnational history as "weaving together of coexisting histories."[31] Instead of promoting a single overarching narrative, the chapters explore the concrete linkages between Africa and North America that created an effective transnational network and promoted the development of New Left Internationalism. The complex nature of the topics makes choices of emphasis necessary. The book is primarily a transnational history operating across national boundaries and showing that substate actors challenged interstate relations via grassroots diplomacy. Secondarily, it is a U.S. history examining how decolonization and new ideas from the Global South informed a protracted debate on foreign policy priorities that established a model for more democratic, participatory visions of foreign affairs. Finally, an African history extends the common timeline of decolonization, using the underappreciated political work of Lusophone African nationalists to connect familiar histories of imperial transfers of power to the transnational narratives of southern African liberation often treated as separate events.

Three sections follow the multilevel diplomacy of the Lusophone revolutions, their official reception, and the development of grassroots solidarity campaigns in support of African self-determination.[32] Part I offers a more traditional international history, considering the development of Portuguese African nationalism and its unsuccessful search for support from the U.S. government via direct appeals and elite lobbying. Chapter 1 highlights the way that the American Committee on Africa (ACOA) and the Angolan nationalist Holden Roberto initially sought to use Cold War ideas to win over the Kennedy administration, which supported gradual decolonization but proved unwilling to rupture relations with its stubborn North Atlantic Portuguese ally. Chapter 2 explores the competing transatlantic lobbies established by Portugal and African nationalists, which saw the nationalists mobilize sufficient liberal-religious support to win brief policy victories before Lisbon successfully leveraged its role supporting Cold War strategies in Europe and Africa to quiet official opposition to its empire. The chapter also delves into the divisions that developed between Roberto and the MPLA, and the latter's formation of the leftist Conferência das Organizações Nacionalistas das Colónias Portuguesas (Conference of Nationalist Organizations of the Portuguese Colonies, or CONCP) with the PAIGC. Chapter 3 introduces FRELIMO, highlighting how its first president, Eduardo Mondlane, made an unsuccessful final push to sway executive policy with the help of ACOA and Black activists, only to join fellow CONCP members in launching an armed struggle in 1964. Chapter 4 considers the impact of Rhodesia's 1965 Unilateral Declaration of Independence on the Portuguese debate, which Lisbon used to reinforce its African position by joining South Africa and Rhodesia as part of the White Redoubt resisting Black self-determination, even as U.S. attempts to undermine this alliance led it to embrace Lisbon as a stabilizing influence in the region. The CONCP parties and their allies abandoned hope of winning over the executive branch after this point, but they found new allies in Congress, like Representative Charles Diggs, who began mobilizing against the successful lobbying efforts of the White Redoubt.

Part II refocuses on grassroots activism, exploring how a diverse set of activists defined a New Left Internationalism as they embraced Lusophone revolutionaries as allies and models for their domestic reform movements. Chapter 5 examines the origins of popular solidarity at the intersection of the radical politics of the 1960s and a rethinking of religious involvement in the

Global South, both of which informed the Zambia Group activist network. Beginning with the American-educated Mondlane, CONCP nationalists cultivated these grassroots allies in hopes that popular organizing might sway policymakers. Chapter 6 explores how these youthful rebels helped transform existing institutions like ACOA and the mainline Protestant denominations represented by the National Council of Churches. With nationalist encouragement, overlapping activist networks collaborated in and around these institutions in ways that convinced them to align with the tricontinental programs of the CONCP parties. Their money and influence expanded grassroots efforts and gave young activists access to sympathetic legislators. Chapter 7 considers the emergence of mass African American support for Lusophone revolutions as the final and most politically potent constituency within this solidarity campaign. It explores efforts to integrate Southern anti-imperialism into a Black agenda that united community organizers and elected officials, culminating in African Liberation Day celebrations in 1972 and 1973. Chapter 8 demonstrates the collaborative nature of this decentralized solidarity movement via the Gulf Oil boycott, which targeted the largest corporate investor in Angola by mobilizing religious, radical, and African American communities in a series of overlapping campaigns. The movement used CONCP critiques of the global capitalist system to link African liberation with domestic movements, demanding the attention of Portugal and elected officials in the process.

Part III concludes with a discussion of the successful constraint of Gerald Ford's intervention against the MPLA in 1975, and the debates it inspired about the future of U.S. foreign policy. Chapter 9 explores how national legislators sympathetic to New Left Internationalism imagined more constructive engagement with postcolonial states after the Vietnam debacle. When Angola invited a Cold War intervention, these congressional representatives—led by Senators Dick Clark and John Tunney—collaborated with solidarity activists to frame the debate, emphasizing the need to respect Southern self-determination while avoiding the misreading of local events that pulled the United States into Indochina. Chapter 10 considers how this grassroots-congressional coalition formalized after the passage of this legislation while inviting a backlash. Mobilization against Ford's intervention provided proof of concept for decentralized, multilevel organizing and a new direction for southern African policy that encouraged leftist activists. At the same time, it helped forge a new coalition of cold warriors. The emerging New Right used Angola to articulate a distinct set of post-Vietnam lessons that prioritized confrontation with Soviet-backed nationalists like the MPLA as a test of U.S. strength. The Conclusion considers how competition between these two forces explains the history of U.S. policy toward the Global South in the 1980s. It uses the fifteen-year history of the CONCP parties' grassroots diplomacy to rethink the nature and underappreciated consistency of the New Left Internationalist challenge to the revived Cold War.

PART I

Cold War Revolutions

CHAPTER 1

The Angolan Crisis of 1961

I t had been five hundred years since the death of the Infante Dom Henrique, the spiritual father of Portugal's overseas empire known worldwide as Prince Henry the Navigator. In 1960, his homeland was celebrating this event with the pomp and circumstance that would remind the world of the country's once and future greatness. The small Iberian state had declined precipitously since its Golden Age in the 1500s, but it retained a far-flung empire centered on the large African colonies of Mozambique and Angola, complemented by coastal and island holdings including the mid-Atlantic Azores archipelago, Guinea-Bissau in West Africa, Goa in India, and Macao in China. Portugal used these colonial artifacts of a rapidly disappearing era to claim equality with its more powerful European neighbors, which had long since surpassed the agrarian dictatorship in economic and political power.

The extent of Portugal's overseas possessions made the celebration of the long-dead prince a global event, even though nationalists in Asia and Africa had spent much of the previous fifteen years reversing the European expansion Henry helped instigate. The quincentenary coincided with the "Year of Africa," when more than a dozen countries declared independence from foreign rule, but such contradictions did not stop allies new and old from celebrating the world's first global empire. In August, thousands watched alongside the presidents of Brazil and Portugal as ten square-rigged vessels from eight European nations rounded the southernmost point of Sagres, trailed by thirty-three flag-bedecked warships representing North Atlantic Treaty Organization (NATO) allies Italy, France, Canada, and a dozen other countries. The United States, Britain, and the neighboring Spanish dictatorship provided an air guard that saluted the old seaside fortress from which Henry organized his voyages.[1] Portugal viewed these commemorations as a tribute both to its past glory and its continuing mission. Almost alone among European empires, it remained determined to preserve its possessions. While most European governments acknowledged the rising tide of Southern nationalism and were grudgingly accommodating Asian and African demands for political self-determination (if not yet economic autonomy), Portugal hoped to halt the clock before the colonial era completely expired.

Portugal seemed an unlikely candidate to be Europe's last great empire. The small nation failed to meet the criteria that bound the majority of Western Europe together in the postwar period; it was economically weak, dictatorial in its politics, and perpetually backward-looking in its colonial policies. The country had little to its credit except an inherited empire and the canny if regimented mind of its long-serving premier, Antonio de Oliveira Salazar. The sickly looking former economist had quietly moved from isolation to membership in NATO by leveraging the strategically located Azores islands and its massive African colonies. Nationalist demands for decolonization therefore threatened to strip Portugal of its last vestiges of international influence. How Salazar dealt with this challenge might have remained a matter of limited global importance, but both the dictator and African nationalists understood their struggles in larger terms. Salazar's challenge to the prevailing trends, tacking like Henry's caravels into what Britain's Harold Macmillan had termed the nationalist "wind of change," operated at the intersection of the East-West competition in the Cold War and the Global South's assault on the international system that prioritized Northern priorities.

When a major rebellion broke out in Angola, Portugal's largest colony, in 1961, Lusophone Africa became a litmus test for decolonization and Euro-American support for this project. This owed much to the fact that Portugal maintained strict control of its colonies, forcing anti-colonial leaders to journey abroad to find support for their movements. As the Cold War stabilized in Europe, the superpowers shifted their competition to the Global South as East and West competed to win the loyalty, or at least fealty, of new Asian and African states. Competing Cold War globalizations offered by U.S. democratic capitalism and the Soviet Union's universalistic communism opened new avenues for nationalists to operate beyond the traditional confines of the metropole-colony relationship. But in many ways, the U.S.-Soviet competition reaffirmed the traditional importance of Europe, even as both sides sought to sell their visions of modernization as the solution to social and economic limitations inherited by postcolonial states.[2] As a result, decolonization and the Cold War became inextricably intertwined, despite actors in the Global North and South working in vain to separate them. The resulting clash between the small Iberian nation and forces backing self-determination tested the Western commitment to decolonization. In the United States, it revealed the extent to which a Cold War strategic worldview colored all events. While U.S. officials often sympathized with the idea of decolonization, the policies that they pursued placed Southern ambitions below Euro-American ones.

Empire of Stability

Unlikely as Portugal's continuing empire may have been in the 1960s, Lisbon's colonies were equally poor candidates for organized revolution. Salazar institutionalized the idea of empire into the fabric of the nation more than any other postwar European leader. Losing the colonies would undermine popular morale and almost certainly topple his regime, so he carefully controlled the influx of goods, people, and ideas. A ruthlessly effective dictator, Salazar nonetheless stood apart from the megalomaniacs and generals with whom he sometimes shares the fascist label. Resembling a patent clerk more than a strongman, he began his career as an economics professor before serving as finance minister after the military coup of 1926. The deeply Catholic, abstemious Salazar—who worked wrapped in a blanket to save on heating costs—restored order to a country wracked by revolution. He balanced budgets and prioritized conservative economic and social practices, parleying public confidence into a virtual dictatorship as president of the Council of Ministers beginning in 1932. His Estado Novo (New State) managed the country through an extensive system of syndicalist organizations, isolationist regulations, and an effective secret police known as the PIDE (Polícia Internacional e de Defesa do Estado—International and State Defense Police). This made Portugal a bastion of stability throughout the Great Depression and World War II.[3] It used the strategically located Azores islands to win entrance into the Western alliance, beginning in 1944 when the war turned against the Axis Powers and then as a founding member of NATO. Unfortunately for most Portuguese, economic modernization and political freedom were sacrificed at the altar of social cohesion and traditional values, meaning the country did not participate in the postwar European recovery. As late as 1950, nearly half the population worked in agriculture, while three-quarters of industrial firms employed four or fewer people.[4] For Salazar, domestic peace came not from material gain or creature comforts but from the preservation of order and tradition. "I do not believe in equality," he once remarked, "but in hierarchy."[5]

Hierarchy is also the best way to understand the Estado Novo's relationship to its African colonies, which Salazar used to provide an economic and ideological foundation for his regime. Overshadowed by the former colony of Brazil and the wealthy Asian enclaves of Goa and Macao, Portuguese settlements in Africa were originally confined to the coasts. Plantations developed slowly in Angola and Mozambique to grow coffee and cotton, respectively, but Guinea-Bissau remained little more than a moderately sized trading center as late as the 1920s.[6] Though initially indifferent, Salazar came to see Portugal's colonies as the salvation of the nation. The economist promoted imperial trade to decrease foreign imbalances, prop up metropolitan industries, and strengthen the Portuguese currency. New laws raised barriers to foreign investment and formalized African labor conscription to expand cultivation.[7] In the postwar period, African coffee plantations provided important revenue for Portugal—whose primary domestic exports remained wine, cork, and people—while ports such as Mozambique's Lourenço Marques (modern-day Maputo) and Angola's Lobito became profitable railway heads for Britain's southern African colonies, South Africa, and the Belgian Congo. Portugal officially redefined its African possessions as "overseas provinces" in 1951, but it was a legal fiction meant to assuage the United Nations and international critics.[8] The Estado Novo effectively established a neo-mercantilist strategy when other nations flirted with the liberalization of their empires, controlling its massive colonies through isolation and increased oversight from Lisbon. According to historian Margarida Calafate Ribeiro, the use of the overseas provinces to prop up Portuguese economics and cultural identity made the regime a "unique singularity fulfilled only in that empire."[9] Therefore, Salazar jealously guarded its borders from the rising tide of African nationalism.

Vigilance was needed, given the poor conditions in the colonies. In both Mozambique and Angola, large European-owned plantations took the best land, leaving many Africans to scrape out a subsistence existence or submit to brutal conditions as laborers. Forced labor in Angola and the island colony of São Tomé produced conditions nearing slavery, while Portuguese authorities profited from the sale of Mozambican workers to South African mines.[10] The colonies received minimal investment in terms of infrastructure and education. With most Portuguese services confined to the coastal cities until the 1950s, schools in the interiors of Angola and Mozambique were left largely to Protestant missionaries, whom the Catholic Portuguese barely tolerated.[11] Only the predominantly mixed-race population of the Cabo Verde islands approached the Portuguese ideal of an assimilated society, receiving special privileges reserved mainly for Europeans. Yet beyond this special status, Lisbon paid minimal attention to the drought-prone islands, doing little to assuage the famines that marked each generation.[12] Given these conditions, the potential for unrest was high, and the Estado Novo used its secret PIDE force and rapid, violent reprisals to prevent irregular protests from escalating into revolts.

As late as 1960, Portugal faced little visible colonial discontent, while other Europeans struggled to respond to calls for greater Black participation in government in such places as Kenya, the Congo, and South Africa. In fact, Salazar's greatest challenge came not from the colonies but from India, which bristled at Portugal's continued presence in the enclaves of Goa, Daman, and Diu.[13] India led the global challenge to Portugal at the United Nations, which focused its attention on Lisbon's empire as postcolonial countries gained membership and established self-determination as a fundamental right.[14] Yet Jawaharlal Nehru was wary of angering Portugal's European allies, and the United Nations was largely toothless without their support, so immediate threats to Portugal's monopoly of power were scarce. "Angola's period of isolation is ending," one British official noted in late 1957 but concluded that "there are no native troubles and no hint that any are brewing for the foreseeable future."[15] Rather, the hostile colonial climate compelled Black nationalists to look abroad as they prepared to challenge the regime. This reality imbued Lusophone revolutions with a distinctly transnational character, but it also hid the slow process of organization from most outside observers.

Portugal's control of its colonies seemed a welcome respite to Western governments that viewed the Global South in the 1950s as a series of crises. Decolonization in Asia and parts of Africa inspired a sense of Third World independence, led by fiery nationalists like Ghana's Kwame Nkrumah and Egypt's Gamal Abdel Nasser, who criticized continuing European influences as they sought to rapidly modernize their countries. The United States recognized that nationalism would not disappear and encouraged its European allies to accept political self-determination to maintain influence in the Global South. But it also feared that postcolonial nations might drift into the Soviet bloc as nationalist preferences for centralized development plans and semi-authoritarian cults of personality provided common ground with the USSR.[16] Events like the independence of the Congo in 1960 fueled such Cold War fears. When Belgium hastily dismantled its colonial apparatus in the sprawling state, it handed power to Patrice Lumumba, who unsuccessfully tried to use the Cold War to obtain much needed aid for his country. Fearful that the mineral-rich state could defect to the communists, the United States and Belgium backed the secession of the mineral-rich Katanga province and approved the murder of Lumumba, causing years of chaos that made the Congo the first casualty of the Cold War in Africa.[17] While the U.S. government in particular hoped that well-managed decolonization could win nationalists for the West, the rapidity of the Congo's collapse gave Western officials pause. During his May 1960 visit to Lisbon, President Dwight Eisenhower could do little but assent when Salazar argued that "giving" independence to Africans before they were ready would be "a crime."[18] Salazar's refusal to consider self-determination for its colonies was inopportune, but Portugal seemed in control, so neither the United States nor its European allies had much interest in forcing the matter given likely alternatives.

Cold War Transnationalism: Holden Roberto and the American Committee on Africa

Beneath the surface of calm, nationalist resistance was cohering, but Salazar's tight restrictions on the colonies limited organizing pathways. Anti-colonials could either operate secretly or work beyond the borders of the empire. Almost all nascent parties adopted some combination of these tactics, but exile was common thanks to PIDE repression. This created a motivation to build transnational movements. Nationalists hoped foreign allies could champion their interests and build international pressure that would compel Portugal to accept decolonization. The United Nations offered some initial hope thanks to the rapid expansion of Global South membership, but nationalists drifted toward more militant alliances when the power of European empires made the supranational route unfeasible. The result was a mixture of covert organizing and international alliance building that militated against unity, with the Angolan struggle experiencing deep and lasting divides. Exile politics forced the resulting competition for leadership to take place on a world stage, inviting in Cold War competition.

Holden Roberto, the leader of Angola's March 1961 rebellion, emerged as the first prominent nationalist by using international forums and Cold War politics to amplify his message. Born in the northern Bakongo region in the early 1920s to a family with Baptist missionary ties, Roberto spent much of his early life in the Congo after tensions between Protestants and Portugal forced his family over the border. While Roberto was working as a low-level bureaucrat in the colonial administration, an uncle launched an ethnic nationalist organization in Leopoldville with ambitions to restore the former Kongo Kingdom, installing his nephew as the international face of the movement.[19] With minimal power within the still-Belgian Congo, Roberto's uncle looked to the United Nations for aid in pressing this claim. The international body was one of the few arenas where substate actors could air grievances to world governments, laying claim to domestic and international legitimacy in the process. In 1956, the nationalists used missionary linkages to request that the American Committee on Africa (ACOA) help champion the Kongo cause.[20] This connection proved pivotal, helping Roberto become the first face of Portuguese African nationalism.

ACOA was the preeminent organization linking the United States to African nationalists, and it provided the foundation for Lusophone liberation organizing. Founded in 1952 to connect domestic civil rights activists with the emerging anti-apartheid movement in South Africa, it quickly shifted to support continent-wide self-determination. By the late 1950s, ACOA was an active broker of information at the United Nations, publishing a regular bulletin on developments related to Africa and directly assisting African petitions to the General Assembly and the Trusteeship Council. Domestically, the committee sought to help Americans understand Africa as more than just the "jumble of unrelated, undigested rumors" created by sensational reporting on the Mau Mau rebellion or half-hearted debates on apartheid.[21] Under the leadership of George Houser, a Methodist minister involved with the Fellowship of Reconciliation and the Congress of Racial Equality (CORE), ACOA developed good relationships with prominent African nationalists, including Kwame Nkrumah, Tom Mboya, Kenneth Kaunda, and Julius Nyerere. ACOA sponsored speaking tours and promoted their anti-colonial perspectives through publications like the monthly *Africa Today*. As a result, it gained unique insight into the nationalist struggles as its members provided assistance and the occasional overnight couch to sub-Saharan Africa's future leadership.[22] ACOA's professed goal was to "keep the conscience of Americans alive to the issues at stake in Africa—to gain sympathetic support for the aims of self-government and equality."[23] It had succeeded well to that point, counting among its backers such prominent figures as First Lady Eleanor Roosevelt, civil rights activists A. Philip Randolph and Martin Luther King Jr., baseball legend Jackie Robinson, lyricist Oscar Hammerstein II, Senator Hubert Humphrey (D-MN), Congressman Adam Clayton Powell (D-NY), and socialist Norman Thomas. Active board members included the associate executive director of the National Urban League Frank Montero and the lawyer Peter Weiss. The latter became a prominent peace and human rights advocate alongside his wife, Cora Weiss, who also worked with ACOA and served as executive director of the African American Students Foundation.[24]

The relative prominence of ACOA and its advocacy work at the United Nations made it an attractive ally for nationalists like Roberto. Houser was skeptical of the Bakongo ethnocentrism Roberto initially championed and his limited contacts in Angola, but there were few other organizations openly agitating against Portuguese colonialism.[25] ACOA therefore offered Roberto small but valuable aid in the 1950s. He used the committee's New York office "virtually as his headquarters" during visits to the United Nations, while Houser facilitated interactions with various African nationalists after Roberto attended the Accra Conference in 1958.[26] Fluent in French and ambitious, Roberto built a network of supporters who looked past the Angolan's limitations to support a revolution in sub-Saharan Africa's second-largest state. Pan-Africanists such as Nkrumah and Frantz Fanon convinced Roberto that his uncle's ethnic movement was flawed, pushing him to create a more inclusive front that led directly to the formation of the União dos Povos de Angola (Union of Angolan Peoples, UPA), with Roberto as sole leader.[27] The UPA opened itself to all nationalists, claiming an anti-colonial position that sought to replace Portugal with a vaguely redistributive Black state, which Roberto made sure did not hint of communism. "We are Angolans," Roberto said in 1960, "and this means that we are not communists or Portuguese. We are Africans who prefer to die to remain African."[28]

This careful political positioning allowed the revolutionary to make diplomatic overtures even as the UPA began quietly preparing an armed revolution. The UPA drew inspiration from the Algerian Front de Libération Nationale (National Liberation Front, FLN) that was forcing France to decolonize, but Roberto continued to appeal to the United Nations and to U.S. politicians with the assistance of ACOA, which included a forty-minute discussion with Senator John Kennedy in January 1960.[29] The goal was to build enough international pressure that Portugal would have few options besides decolonization if confronted by a colonial revolt. ACOA and religious connections also encouraged Roberto's ties to sympathetic officials in the U.S. State Department.[30] The UPA struck upon a formula for advancing the revolution in exile: ACOA became a primary organ for communicating with the West, while Roberto prepared for an extended armed revolution with aid from African states. Vaguely aware of these plans, if not their timing, ACOA

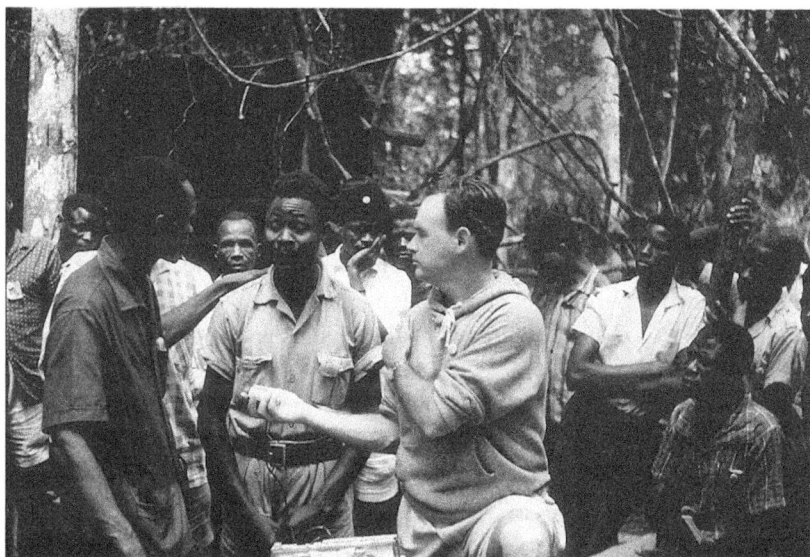

Figure 1. ACOA executive director George Houser meeting with UPA nationalists on a trip into Angola in January 1962. He is likely demonstrating the medicine that he delivered after fundraising efforts in late 1961. Reproduced with permission of Houser Family, African Activist Archive.

understood by 1960 that Lisbon's supposed peace was tenuous. Barely a year before the outbreak of violence in Angola, members of the New York–based committee, relying on personal knowledge of Roberto's activities, publicly warned the U.S. government of brewing unrest.[31]

These African connections provided ACOA with unique perspectives on the Portuguese colonies, but they also revealed the limitations of U.S. solidarity in this period. African nationalists appreciated ACOA's staunch anti-colonialism, but it was by no means a revolutionary organization. An extension of the civil rights movement, it encouraged peaceful transfers of power brought about by diplomacy and, if pushed, nonviolent demonstrations. Houser had been a conscientious objector during World War II and believed deeply in nonviolence. ACOA was also a product of its times, hewing closely to a Cold War liberal view of the world that championed self-determination along democratic lines as the best chance for peace and development. As an early document explained, ACOA aimed "to help in every way the emergence of democratic self-governing states . . . and to free the people on the African

Continent from the exploitation, poverty and racial discrimination under which they suffer. Our committee opposes the fanaticism and totalitarianism of the doctrines of Communism, Mau Mau, White Supremacy and Imperialism and seeks to help the African people to find a democratic peaceful pathway into the new day of the 20th century world."[32] This attitude allowed ACOA to appeal broadly to centrist institutions like the Protestant churches that paid many of its bills while also providing a foundation for building constructive relationships with government officials interested in fighting the Cold War.[33] This produced a wariness of closely aligning with groups like Algeria's FLN, even though ACOA ultimately decided that colonial violence and the end goal of national freedom legitimized forceful African responses. Still, it hesitated to provide direct aid and did not automatically support a provisional government, despite appreciating that the war focused attention on Algeria.[34] ACOA remained uneasy about wars for liberation even if such conflicts did not preclude support for the goals of the belligerent nationalist parties.

Therefore, Roberto—who publicly dismissed communism and urged U.N. action even after the 1961 revolt—was an ideal ally. ACOA's goal in the 1950s was to gain early acceptance of nationalists like Roberto in order to avoid the violence of armed revolution and the drift toward communism that was a logical outgrowth of continued Western support for the outdated imperial model. Changing Western policy—specifically in the United States—was vital. While Roberto was amassing arms from African countries, he understood that international political pressure was necessary to raise the costs of empire sufficiently to shock the empire-addicted Estado Novo. At the same time, this transnational anti-imperial network stood in place of the local organizing made difficult by Portugal's repressive imperialism, contrasting sharply with the way national revolts occurred in many British and French examples.[35] This new formulation of revolution from the outside in—and in some ways from the top down—camouflaged the growing discontent with Portuguese rule.

International Response to Angolan Rebellion

Official ignorance of Lusophone African nationalism ended with a jolt in 1961. In the first three months of the year, a series of popular protests and rebellions shook the tranquility of Salazar's empire. After two months of low-level unrest in the north of Angola over poor wages, a coordinated attack against political prisons occurred in Luanda in February, killing fourteen Europeans and eliciting harsh reprisals from colonial officials and white vigilantes.[36] Then in mid-March, the UPA launched a rebellion in the north, crossing over the Congolese border and taking advantage of the earlier disruptions to begin the first Lusophone independence struggle. During these first months of 1961, brutal Portuguese attempts to restore order left hundreds—likely thousands— of Africans dead. The facade of peace shattered, governments across the globe took notice as Angola seemed on the precipice of collapse just across the border from the chaotic Congo.[37] As the United Nations prepared to respond and Western nations considered their options, African nationalists looked to the United States. "Not only I myself and other leaders, but the whole of the peoples of Angola—and indeed many of the peoples of Africa," Roberto told one Western reporter, "are waiting to see what will be the attitude of the United States towards the crimes perpetrated by Portugal."[38]

The United States became the center of attention because it was Portugal's most powerful ally, and because a new president occupied the White House. The youthful John F. Kennedy had campaigned as a leader for the 1960s ready to address new global challenges, with decolonization high on the list. He believed that the Global South had the potential to become the future battleground of the Cold War and expressed keen interest in Africa. While serving as a somewhat inactive chair of the Senate Foreign Relations Subcommittee on Africa, Kennedy criticized the French handling of Algeria and built personal (if not necessarily close) relationships with several nationalists, including Kenya's Tom Mboya and Roberto. He also backed colonial independence on the campaign trail, scoring points with liberals and African American voters who were understandably unenthused about the Democrat's carefully moderated statements on domestic civil rights.[39]

Kennedy's entrance into the White House encouraged optimism among proponents of decolonization. One of his first appointments filled the position of assistant secretary of state for African affairs, created only a few years before, with Governor G. Mennen "Soapy" Williams. An early backer of Kennedy's presidential run, the Michigan liberal was a vocal civil rights advocate and supported calls for African decolonization, collaborating with ACOA even before taking office.[40] Kennedy's wider national security team—including Secretary of State Dean Rusk and Republican McGeorge Bundy as national security adviser—trended moderate, with strong ties to the Washington establishment, but also featured a few reform-minded liberals such as Chester Bowles. Houser, who received an invitation to serve on the State Department's Africa advisory council alongside ACOA allies like the academic John Marcum, welcomed the possibility of new U.S. policy directions and joined many Africans in believing Kennedy's rhetoric implied a break with past trends.[41] ACOA developed good relationships with Africa Bureau staffers, but an inability to make inroads at the highest levels of policymaking limited its direct influence.[42]

The distance between rhetoric and reality reflected the president's primary motivation for engaging with Africa: the desire to proactively address Cold War tensions. He recognized the geostrategic implications of peripheral independence movements and believed decolonization was inevitable. Not unlike Eisenhower, Kennedy feared that anti-colonialism might lead Global South states to make common cause with the USSR, but he more adamantly believed that public U.S. support for majority rule could win over Southern nationalists.[43] The Congo crisis validated this concern even as it warned of the disorder possible with poorly managed transfers of power. Halting the spread of unrest was especially important, as South Africa's continued resistance to majority Black rule had the potential to transform localized struggles into a regional race war that could invite foreign intervention. Secretary of State Dean Rusk—a Georgia Rhodes Scholar who shared Kennedy's views on colonialism without abandoning a deep sympathy for Europe—argued it was this potential "alliance between Communism and racialism" that most concerned the administration.[44] Facing a relatively weak ally faced with a serious crisis, Kennedy wanted to promote a gradual transfer of power that would stabilize a region on the verge of becoming a Cold War flashpoint. Even before the outbreak of hostilities in Angola, Kennedy had Rusk deliver a blunt warning that Portugal's refusal to publicly consider self-determination threatened regional stability while offering economic assistance to help elicit a change of policy.[45] Salazar accepted the warnings courteously without official response, presuming that the message was the posturing of a new administration and that NATO allegiances would prevent further action.[46]

The aged dictator sorely underestimated U.S. concern about African instability. Still settling into the Oval Office, Kennedy had little knowledge of Salazar but believed he understood events in Angola. The president and his advisers presumed the weakening of central power would expand popular support for independence and military liberation as had happened in Algeria. Prolonged fighting would empower anti-Western radicals. A forced Portuguese retreat would create a power vacuum in Africa, probably toppling the Estado Novo with unpredictable consequences for Europe. With reports that high-ranking officials were open to new policies—notably Defense Minister Júlio Botelho Moniz—Washington hoped that a bold maneuver might convince Salazar to reverse course to preserve power in Angola and within his own cabinet.[47]

On March 15, as reports first began to filter in about the violence in Angola, the American U.N. delegation voted in favor of a Security Council resolution calling for Portugal to move toward self-determination for the colony to avoid "another Congo . . . [and] disastrous consequences." The Liberian-sponsored resolution did not pass, due to a high number of European abstentions, but it represented the first time the United States had voted against a NATO ally (and with the Soviet Union) on a colonial issue.[48] The vote was largely symbolic, since U.S. officials knew it would fail in the face of Franco-British hostility to U.N. involvement in colonial affairs, but the Kennedy administration hoped it would salve Afro-Asian anger while encouraging Salazar to reevaluate outdated policies while he still had time. The Portuguese dictator responded coldly, allowing anti-American protests in both Lisbon and Angola.[49] He consolidated his rule by installing new ministers and ambassadors who shared his view of the colonies while complaining loudly about a NATO ally voting alongside the Soviet Union.[50]

While the Portuguese smoldered, nationalists claimed an early victory. Roberto was at the United Nations when the UPA invasion occurred, taking advantage of the sudden importance of Angola to demand media attention. He made an extended statement to the press that was widely quoted, thanks to ACOA's distribution of it in full. Denouncing "the oppression and racial discrimination which characterizes the Portuguese regime in Angola, a regime of economic slavery and cultural obscurantism," Roberto introduced the world to the UPA. His was a party for freedom, opposed to forced labor, and resisting the "destruction and rape" of the colony.[51] He praised the Security Council vote as an important "reversal in American politics regarding Africa and colonial empires" but reminded listeners it was just a first step, because Portugal was still "exterminating the African population of Angola by forced labor . . . deportations, assassinations and terror."[52] The UPA leader demanded that the world follow the example of the United Nations and "exert pressure on Portugal to bring an immediate end to the atrocities in Angola."[53] Privately, he urged the State Department to continue its activity, warning that inaction could result in the growth of communist sympathies.[54]

This last point was important, because Roberto spent the first months of the revolt reinforcing his image as a useful ally for the United States, even as his party took up arms. Reports, coordinated between Roberto and American allies such as ACOA, framed UPA goals to mesh closely with U.S. priorities. In Roberto's own words, he was fighting imperialism and the regime "that disgraces the name of Portugal," rather than the country or its people. He viewed Portuguese and Angolans as distinct but claimed his revolution sought to establish a democratic Angolan republic, which would integrate all of Angola's people into one nation—including whites.[55] "We do not want to supplant a hatred for the black with a new hatred for the white," Roberto said at his March 15 press conference. "We are Angolans; banish from the land all racism, all forms of oppression, of injustice, all attempts to keep our people in ignorance, and let us work together for the flowering of mankind and the enrichment of humanity."[56] He attempted to create a compelling, attractive vision of Angolan self-determination that could cut through Salazar's fabricated accusations of communism and the graphic reports of revolutionary violence that Lisbon let filter to the press. "If the Portuguese have been accusing us of being communist—it's because it's the only argument they have now," Roberto assured an NBC documentary crew. "We are not communist but are fighting for freedom."[57]

The U.N. vote represented a shift in U.S. rhetoric, but it did not connote the policy change that either the Portuguese or Roberto expected. The CIA had been paying Roberto small sums since the Eisenhower administration, and these continued under Kennedy, but the administration remained wary of aligning with specific nationalist causes.[58] A close reading of documents reveals that the Kennedy administration's view of African independence in Angola was limited in scope, advocating for increased political autonomy while simultaneously seeking to reinforce Lisbon's economic, cultural, and diplomatic control of the colonies as part of a Cold War strategy. Discussions repeatedly highlighted the U.S. desire for Portugal to retain a substantial presence in Africa, albeit in a form that assuaged nationalist demands.[59] Speaking with Salazar in March, Rusk "noted relative success [of the] British in retaining close ties with former colonies after their independence and deplored cases where former profitable relationship broken (Dutch-Indonesia, Belgium-Congo)."[60] The administration believed that it was important for Portugal to retain political and economic relationships with its dependencies, but it worried that the Portuguese commitment to direct rule threatened this very goal.

Portugal on the Defensive

Already feeling isolated as European empires capitulated around his colonies, the dictator perceived American actions as a mortal threat to the Estado

Novo despite the administration's far more ambiguous vision. To Salazar, calls for gradual self-determination meant complete independence for the colonies and the division of multi-continental Portugal. The regime accredited this dissonance to U.S. misinterpretations of the Portuguese situation, either through naivete or ulterior motives. First, the small Iberian state lacked the economic might to tie its colonies to the metropolis after a transfer of power, meaning comparisons with Britain and France were shortsighted at best. At its most conspiratorial, the regime believed that the United States had political reasons for colluding with African countries to oust Portugal in search of political or economic advantages.[61] Second, such shortsighted U.S. actions threatened to undermine the long history of European authority that Salazar believed was key to a lasting peace. The dictator retained strong views on the inherent inferiority of Africans and warned U.S. officials that local peoples would "soon revert to tribalism" without European guidance.[62] Borrowing from the Brazilian sociologist Gilberto Freyre, the Portuguese argued they were uniquely positioned to play this civilizing role. The warm Iberian climate supposedly prepared colonists for settlement in tropical regions, while a lack of formal segregation produced a history of cultural mixing, evidenced in multiracial Lusophone nations such as Brazil.[63] With references to historical documents that Portuguese officials believed showed a history of respect for all peoples, they laid claim to a multiracial, multi-continental society that predated both the Declaration of Independence and the Universal Declarations of Rights.[64]

This manufactured theory of lusotropicalism became the Estado Novo's leading defense of Portugal's imperial role in Africa. It served as the backbone of speeches abroad and at home, and documents expounding on the argument flooded out of Lisbon, helpfully translated into English for U.S. audiences.[65] Illustrated pamphlets showed scenes from multiracial classrooms in Mozambique or Angolan people strolling peacefully in modern cities with a bright Mediterranean flair.[66] Such images showed Portugal in a good light when compared to apartheid South Africa, but they were unrepresentative of the realities in the colonies, where Africans rarely qualified for admittance to state schools and faced labor discrimination. The distance between reality and rhetoric did not stop this propaganda from mobilizing and updating the increasingly outdated idea of the civilizing mission. Rather, proponents insisted that Europe's poorest state would introduce modernity and governing structures to its colonies while demurring that it would take decades or even centuries before Africans were fully prepared for self-rule. A premature separation of Angola and Mozambique from Portugal would directly threaten Western desires for regional stability.[67] Armed with this defense of empire, Salazar rejected what he described as "a self-defeating policy of [the] US with regard to Africa." Portugal would play no part in the dissolution of its African territories and instead positioned itself as an increasingly lonely bulwark against anti-Western intrigue in the region.[68]

The Kennedy administration believed that a joint NATO approach was the best option for cajoling the Salazar regime, illustrating the administration's continued deference to Europe. Yet this strategy proved difficult to achieve. Efforts in March to coordinate with Britian and France on the Portuguese issue won little support, and both countries abstained from voting at the United Nations.[69] The French foreign minister was particularly hostile to requests that NATO criticize Portugal.[70] Franco-American relations, in which periods of strain were not uncommon, were diverging on matters of empire. Eisenhower had humiliated America's ally by opposing the Euro-Israeli invasion of the Suez Canal. The advent of Charles de Gaulle's Fifth Republic amid the Algerian War only amplified this split, as the proud general chafed under U.S. leadership and pushed for greater independence.[71] Though de Gaulle accepted the necessity of decolonization, the how and when of the event in Africa and beyond remained a point of contention. Salazar recognized these tensions and—anticipating U.S. policy and suspecting Britain would fall in line—began courting disaffected European governments in hopes of building a bloc that could resist U.N. and U.S. pressure to rapidly decolonize, with France as the keystone. Portugal and France agreed on the "fundamental importance of Africa in the Western defense system" and expanded cooperation in the 1950s as NATO distanced itself from involvement in the continent. The common bonds and interests boiled down to an interrelated list: "the defense of Africa, close Western solidarity, the problem of NATO, assessment of American policy and incidences of anti-colonialism in defense of the free world."[72] Salazar had worked to reaffirm these ideas as early as 1960, reinforcing the cool reception Kennedy received when he attempted to build a pressure campaign on Lisbon within the Western alliance.[73]

Further undermining U.S. efforts was the fact that Britain was no more eager than France to set any precedents regarding international involvement in European transfers of power. In contrast to de Gaulle, Kennedy developed a bond with Tory Prime Minister Harold Macmillan, who famously backed decolonization in his "wind of change" speech to the South African Parliament in 1960. Britain also had a unique relationship with Portugal, thanks to an alliance that dated to 1386 and long histories of overlapping imperial interests. But while the British shared U.S. concern with Portugal's precarious position, officials felt that attacks on Portugal from the UN or NATO were effectively attacks on all European powers with ties to the continent.[74] Britain expressed sympathy for Kennedy's approach and even joined—over the objections of the foreign minister—in requesting that Portugal supply information on the colonies to the United Nations.[75] But when the Kennedy administration made a final push to coordinate a shared approach to Portugal from NATO's big three, there was little appetite for it. The French preferred to "give the Portuguese a chance to weather the storm both in Angola and in the United Nations," and the British refused to commit to unified action.[76] De Gaulle shut the door on further debate when he bluntly told Kennedy that it would be a mistake to "bully Portugal or place it in the pillory of world opinion."[77] American officials underestimated Portugal's position within the alliance while overestimating allied willingness to advance decolonization, meaning that any U.S. action would likely be unilateral and effectively in opposition to European wishes.

Faced with serious opposition, the Kennedy administration revisited its strategy toward Lisbon. By the end of May, State Department officials recognized that dire predictions of Portugal's collapse had not come true, and they recommended that Kennedy step back to see if Salazar could restore order in Angola, after which the United States could open a less contentious dialogue.[78] Moderating its initial concern with Portuguese collapse and recognizing Salazar's surprising level of support domestically and in Europe, the administration ultimately concluded that it wanted little more, in the words of one diplomat, than to "put the Angola question 'on ice.'"[79] If African nationalist desires for increased U.S. pressure were to become a reality, they would need to find new ways to steel the president's resolve in the face of a cool reception from his most important European allies.

As official shock in the wake of the Angolan rebellion faded, the importance of European alliance politics remained. Roberto and the UPA came to international prominence in part because he was able to use transnational linkages—foreign allies, the United Nations, and even Cold War politics— to promote his cause. ACOA had been an early and important ally in this regard, making sure that when revolution finally began in the first months of 1961 there was at least one U.S. advocate. Yet Roberto's self-promotion along anti-communist lines was a pyrrhic victory, as Portugal was winning the battle of Cold War politics. The risk of losing influence in Angola and

European hostility to any plan that might challenge the right to manage their colonies constrained Kennedy's resolve. Roberto's play won attention but did not assure victory, especially if Portugal could reestablish control of the rogue colony. Yet the Angolan revolt and Portugal's violent response rocketed Salazar's tightly controlled empire to the top of the global agenda in ways that stretched well beyond the superpower conflict. Kwame Nkrumah, Roberto's ally and mentor, captured this reality succinctly: "The issue of Angola is a question of African nationalism and of human liberty and decency. It is in no sense an ideological question. Here no issue of communism arises."[80] Kennedy entered with the goal of giving at least tacit acknowledgment to such Global South perspectives, but he found it difficult to disentangle the Cold War and decolonization, even as this approach became central to another radical strand of Lusophone African nationalism.

CHAPTER 2

A Tale of Two Lobbies

A t the end of the northern summer of 1961, the initial flurry of diplomatic activity began to stall. Portugal dissembled at the United
Nations while coordinating allies within NATO that militated against
strong U.S. action. As the Kennedy administration's enthusiasm waned, the
field of contest shifted to the popular realm. Both Salazar's government and
African nationalists sought to shape public narratives, setting off a contest
that would last for more than a decade. The nationalists lacked resources and
had fewer avenues for challenging Portugal, so they embraced transnational
appeals to civil society groups such as the American Committee on Africa
(ACOA) in advance of the Angolan rebellion. By contrast, Salazar's government scrambled to adapt its diplomacy into a broader campaign to reshape
narratives surrounding Portuguese decolonization. This competition over
the legitimacy of European empire in the U.S. context illustrates the postwar
erosion of strict territorial sovereignty that signaled, according to Matthew
Connelly, a "new, transitional system," in which stateless groups like the Algerian National Liberation Front (NLF) had the ability to challenge European
metropoles at the global level.[1] Yet even more than Algeria, whose Egyptian
allies helped inject these debates into supranational forums and superpower
politics, comparatively weak Lusophone nationalists had to rely on non-state
actors in Western civil society to champion their interests. The nationalists
hoped that sufficient popular support could pressure Euro-American governments to cut ties with Lisbon. At first, this calculation bore fruit, with the
most dramatic U.S. action against Lisbon—a soft arms embargo—reflecting
the demands of a popular transatlantic campaign for decolonization.

While Holden Roberto's Bakongo-dominated UPA lobbied in the United
States, European organizing owed much to a parallel leftist strand of Portuguese African nationalism. The parties that formed the Conferência das

Organizações Nacionalistas das Colónias Portuguesas (Conference of Nationalist Organizations of the Portuguese Colonies, or CONCP) in 1961 represented anti-colonial opposition from Angola, Guinea-Bissau, Mozambique, and beyond. Distinct from—and often opposed to—Roberto in terms of ideology, identity, and political networks, the CONCP parties initially cooperated with the UPA in making international appeals for the general cause of Angolan independence. The result was the construction of a coalition of Western liberal and religious opinion that shifted conversations in the United States and the United Kingdom away from strict Cold War calculations and reflected a powerful confidence in the tide of decolonization. Yet this momentum created its own problem, since the seeming inevitability of imperial retreat—combined with the ambiguous alliance between the CONCP parties and the UPA—divorced the process of independence from the liberation parties that were central to it. Roberto pressed his claim to leadership, but the anti-Portuguese cause lacked a clear figurehead to embody what most Western observers desired: a smooth transition of power. When Portugal launched its own campaign for popular support utilizing anticommunist and Western cultural appeals, nationalists and their allies discovered that building sustained popular support for liberation demanded more than just an enemy; it needed a positive vision of independence for supporters to identify with and mobilize behind. Without a clear alternative, Portugal more readily won popular and political approval because its Cold War framing was more familiar and concrete in the United States, where few had a deep knowledge of African affairs.

Origins of the CONCP

The Angolan rebellion positioned Roberto and his UPA at the forefront of the anti-Portuguese resistance, but he was far from alone in pursuing this goal. Portuguese oppression forced nationalists to organize clandestinely, often in exile, preventing the creation of a mass resistance or a single authoritative party. As a result, there existed several discrete parties with memberships based on ethnic, geographical, and personal connections, with Roberto's Bakongo-dominated UPA being just one example. While most of these parties operated in semi-isolation, a few leftist groups coalesced into a more ideologically coherent alliance that stretched across colonial borders. The CONCP formed in April 1961 as an expansion of an older association between, among others, the Partido Africano da Independência da Guiné e Cabo Verde (African Party for the Independence of Guinea and Cabo Verde, PAIGC) and the Movimento Popular de Libertação de Angola (People's Movement for the Liberation of Angola, MPLA), which became Roberto's primary rival for leadership of the Angolan rebellion. Though leftist in ideology and welcoming to communists, the CONCP parties sought to create a unified front that could mobilize and coordinate opposition to Portugal in Africa and beyond.

The network had its origins in 1950s Lisbon, where a cadre of colonial students reimagined their place within the empire and the wider world. Though educational opportunities were rare in Portugal, even for its white citizens, a handful of mostly *mestiço* (mixed race) and missionary-trained youth gained access to metropolitan universities as part of Salazar's attempts to demonstrate Portugal's civilizing mission.[2] Colonials gravitated together as they confronted life in Portugal, where few citizens had seen Africans from their supposedly integrated empire. The Casa dos Estudantes do Império (House for Colonial Students) provided a refuge for these students while serving as the social, cultural, and political incubator of revolutionary leadership.[3] Trying to make sense of their experiences with racism in Portugal, they studied Marx, French African nationalists, Harlem Renaissance writers, and underground communist literature, which exposed them to revolutionary ideas from beyond the carefully patrolled borders of their colonial upbringings. Members included the Guinean/Cabo Verdean Amílcar Cabral, Agostinho Neto and Mário Pinto de Andrade from Angola, and Marcelino dos Santos from Mozambique. Rejecting a Portuguese identity, these budding nationalists experienced what De Andrade termed "a re-Africanization" of their minds.[4] This was the first step in the development of a leftist anti-colonial movement.

Cabral, the founder of the PAIGC, was central to this network and emerged as its most visible member. Born in Portuguese Guinea in 1924 to Cabo Verdean parents, he began his "long march towards the liberation of our people" while studying agronomy at the Technical University of Lisbon.[5] Cabral grew up on the islands with the relative privileges granted to creolized Cabo Verdeans by Portuguese law, but he also witnessed the famines produced by Lisbon's indifference to its drought-prone colonies. Black revolutionary thought helped explain these dissonances, providing a pathway to escape a sense of alienation via full identification with the "native masses" and a broadly defined African heritage, what Cabral called the "return to the source."[6] He considered this identification and the rejection of privilege as revolutionary acts and the first steps in breaking fully with the Portuguese

Empire. Over the next decade, Cabral worked with the web of associates to turn personal renaissance into political action, gradually informing multiple nationalist movements. De Andrade and Dos Santos settled in France, where they developed unfettered contacts with the European left, but Cabral used his position as a colonial agronomist to travel and expand his local knowledge of Guinea, strategizing all the while how to achieve independence.[7] During one such trip, party histories claim he founded the PAIGC on vaguely Marxist principles in September 1956. Three months later, official histories claim he was in Angola with De Andrade and Neto when they formed the MPLA.[8] Both claims are likely backdated fictions created later to legitimize the parties, but they capture the network and circulation of ideas during this period, if not the precise reality of either organization.[9] The Mozambican element of this triad was the União Democrática Nacional de Moçambique (National Democratic Union of Mozambique, or UDENAMO), founded by nationalist exiles in Southern Rhodesia and led internationally by Dos Santos.[10]

Comparable nationalist philosophies linked these parties, reflecting their common origins. While independence was the primary goal and their inclusive political platforms sought broad appeal, all shared socialist inclinations and commitments to multiracialism. While a handful of founding members—notably Agostinho Neto—had ties to Portuguese communists, the majority aligned more closely with Third World visions of revolution. Communist ideas, notably Lenin's definition of empire and analysis of the international system, provided a toolkit for analyzing the structures of empire, but the parties avoided the communist label, emphasized the need for national independence, and developed unique political programs. The PAIGC, for example, defined itself as a "workers' political organization" (*uma organizaçao politica da classes trabalhadores*), but Cabral rejected the importation of foreign ideologies. He instead stressed the need to adapt socialist worldviews to the mostly agrarian realities of the colonies and provide rapid postcolonial modernization while forging a common national identity in the wake of centuries of divide-and-rule policies.[11] The centrality of national unity was vital to these movements as leaders sought to align with the masses. Not only did they generally represent an educated elite, but MPLA leadership was heavily mestiço (mixed race) from urban Luanda, while the Cabo Verdean–led PAIGC operated in Guinea, where Portugal's use of islanders as imperial middlemen created tensions with less creolized mainlanders.[12] The socialism adopted by these parties sought to overcome these historic divides through the improvement of living standards and the creation of a nonsectarian national identity, which contrasted sharply with the UPA's ethnocentric origins and Roberto's flirtation with Cold War anti-communism. Ultimately, these definitions of socialism aligned with emerging ideas of tricontinental revolution, providing a framework in which distinct national movements made common cause in support of regional, Third World, and ultimately global challenges to the status quo.

The first layer of solidarity existed at the imperial level, with parties coordinating their international efforts through a series of organizations that culminated in the CONCP.[13] The foundational meeting in April 1961 gathered representatives from six colonies and resulted in an organization conceptualized by the Cabo Verdean Amílcar Cabral, headed by De Andrade of Angola's MPLA, managed by the Mozambican Dos Santos, and represented in London by the Goan João Cabral.[14] The CONCP operated as a front and pledged itself to an Afro-Asian anti-imperialism rather than a specific ideology, but Roberto kept his distance, jealously guarding the independence of the UPA. Nonetheless, these groups shared common goals despite operating different transnational networks and focusing on different allies. The CONCP parties hoped to pressure Portugal into transforming its relationship with its colonies, though they also sought monetary and military aid for potential revolutions. Whichever route was taken, the CONCP recognized that it would need to "develop propaganda in order to obtain the effective support of world public opinion."[15]

In contrast to Roberto, the CONCP ignored Cold War boundaries and sought an array of alliances to legitimize its nascent movements. Early support came from African countries. Party leaders built relationships through gatherings like the All-Africa's People Conference of 1960, which launched the CONCP's immediate predecessor, and the independence of Guinea-Conakry that same year provided a refuge for the PAIGC and access to Guinea-Bissau. Leftists like De Andrade and Dos Santos also cultivated relationships with the Eastern bloc, and Soviet satellites like Czechoslovakia became important sources for arms alongside Egypt and Algeria. Yet from the beginning the Lusophone nationalists believed Western support would be important for weakening Lisbon's resolve. "There is less alacrity on the part of the West, it is true," the MPLA's De Andrade admitted, but "it is one of the most important tasks of our diplomats because there is a lot of work to be accomplished in the West itself. We must reach all the Western democratic forces."[16] The CONCP parties believed that support from European allies could isolate Portugal and combine with world opinion to force a liberalization of policies and, ideally, decolonization. Having taken up residence in Paris, De Andrade and Dos

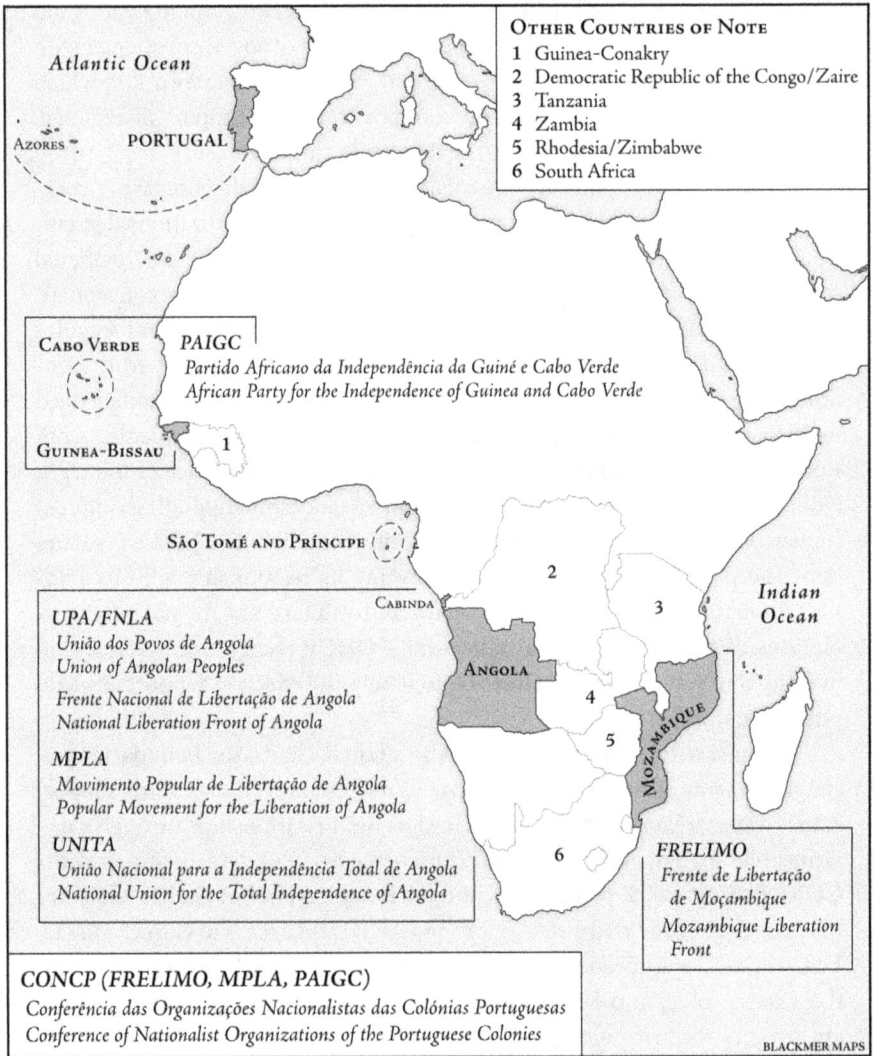

Figure 2. Map of liberation parties and Portuguese Africa. The map lists the active nationalist revolutions across Portugal's three largest colonies, along with the key African countries that aided these revolutions against the countries of the White Redoubt: South Africa, Rhodesia, and colonial Portugal.

Santos built ties to the Francophone left, specifically those associated with the anti-colonial journal *Présence Africaine*. But Roberto's established party and ability to mobilize more freely in the Congo won the support of major figures like Frantz Fanon for practical reasons, representing an early setback for the MPLA and its leftist network.[17]

The United Kingdom emerged as the early center for CONCP efforts thanks to its intertwined history with Portugal's empire. The United Kingdom's strategic decision to champion Portuguese interests during the nineteenth-century scramble for Africa laid the groundwork for extensive economic and political relationships, while Lisbon's refusal to abandon its Goan enclave created tensions with India, one of the British Commonwealth's most important members. When Indian complaints demanded parliamentary (and U.N.) attention, the lawyer João Cabral established an information office for the nationalist Goa League in London around 1960, which also represented the socialist parties that formed the CONCP. Cabral built relations with an informal bloc of mostly Liberal and Labour members of Parliament (MPs) associated with the domestic anti-colonial movement.[18] Organizing gained additional momentum from Portuguese exiles in London with ties to African liberation leaders, who added an important anti-fascist element to anti-colonial condemnations of the Estado Novo. African nationalists hoped the anti-Salazarist alliance could, in the words of MPLA member Lucio Lara, lay the foundations for more active collaboration with "honest Portuguese" based on "common problems."[19]

The CONCP used these connections to announce the coming revolution months before the UPA rebellion. Amílcar Cabral made the first overture in London in early 1960, working with the anti-imperial journalist Basil Davidson to publish a widely distributed English-language pamphlet, *Facts About Portuguese Colonialism*. The brief piece rebuffed Portuguese claims to multiracialism, explaining disparities in economic, social, and political rights operating across the colonies that Cabral described, for the benefit of British audiences, as "Portuguese apartheid."[20] The broadside against Lisbon sought to focus attention on Europe's oldest but least discussed empire. Notably absent was any discussion of party platforms. References to the U.N. Charter and clear approval of the new countries created by the Year of Africa kept the door open to a peaceful transfer of power. Yet on both these fronts, the leftist parties were moving forward. They coordinated their efforts independent of alternative movements like Roberto's, and they increasingly saw armed revolution as the likely solution to the problem of empire.

While there was no formal call for revolt, the implications were clear by the end of 1960. The MPLA—representing Portugal's largest colony—hinted that only the promise of decolonization, the legalization of political parties, and preliminary negotiations with nationalists would "find a peaceful solution to the colonial problem." The party upped the ante when Salazar refused to respond, again relying on its transnational network to make its case. At an unprecedented press conference in December 1960 in the British House of Commons, Mário Pinto de Andrade—as a guest of sympathetic Labour politicians—decried "Portuguese obstinacy" alongside the continued U.S. and British tolerance of Salazar and his claims that the colonies were part of NATO.[21] De Andrade ended with a call for international action to sway the regime to leave all its colonies.[22] The parties did not expect a Portuguese response, but their goal was to build global hostility. Even if it would not sway Salazar, isolating Lisbon would benefit the armed revolutions when they finally occurred.

The MPLA statement clearly asserted the existence of a united, transnational liberation effort within Lusophone Africa, but it received minimal attention from Western officials despite the conference's setting in the seat of British government. There was not even much notice from ACOA, which first made serious contact with the MPLA in 1962 and was slow to build a relationship with the leftist party.[23] Houser's closer relationship with Roberto hinted at the subtle effects Cold War liberalism had on Western links to African liberation, but it also attested to the distinct networks being established by the Congo-based UPA and the CONCP parties developing in Europe's metropoles.[24] In 1960, however, both sides prioritized a Portuguese retreat over their own political projects, making room for front-style politics. This led Roberto to broaden his Bakongo agenda and the expansion of the socialist African alliance into the CONCP. The two sides also shared an ambition to win Western support, with the Angolan rebellion creating new opportunities. The result was that both Roberto and the CONCP launched propaganda campaigns that, in the short term, intersected to establish a clear pro-liberation narrative with transatlantic appeal.

The Anti-Colonial Lobby in the United States and Great Britain

Despite their suspicion of Roberto, the CONCP parties welcomed the UPA rebellion, since it put Portugal on the defensive internationally. Though the

MPLA retroactively claimed that the Luanda prison uprising of February 1961 was a result of their organizing efforts, it was better at building international alliances than developing membership in Angola. The sudden attention to the nationalist plight after March 1961 delivered a welcome opportunity for the leftists to use their networks to pressure Portugal. The creation of the CONCP in April was meant to formalize an expanded set of nationalist revolts, and there were even attempts to create a utilitarian alliance between the UPA and the MPLA that called for a diplomatic and economic boycott of Portugal.[25] The collaboration was brief, but it complemented organizing on both sides of the Atlantic. The MPLA and the CONCP led in Europe—specifically the United Kingdom—where a coalition of leftists and religious humanitarians helped wage one of the first effective solidarity campaigns against the Portuguese crackdown in Angola. This merged with a U.S. movement that ACOA helped organize behind Roberto to embolden the small group of U.S. officials demanding action against Portugal.

New momentum was much needed, because Kennedy's actions in March looked increasingly like outliers as he deferred to European interests and allowed Portugal to mount its brutal offensive in the colony. A minority of officials concentrated in the African Bureau, led by Assistant Secretary of State Mennen "Soapy" Williams, remained interested in pressing matters, but they faced an uphill battle as Portugal's diplomatic and military efforts weakened the alarm that once drove the administration. Even Portugal's diversion of NATO weapons to the African battlefield raised minimal public criticism. Secretary of State Rusk's decisions to cut nearly a million dollars in military aid to Portugal—made as much on budgetary grounds as on principle—convinced many moderates that they had taken sufficient action and faced decreasing returns if they pushed the matter further. The Kennedy White House viewed decolonization as inevitable, but opinion differed as to U.S. responsibilities now that the crisis was past. The tepid European response encouraged advocates of a wait and see approach, notably George Ball and Ambassador Burke Elbrick.[26] Shortly after the aid reduction, the State Department's policy planning staff urged patience: "At this juncture it is doubtful any useful purpose would be served by the United States applying further pressures. . . . We now should give Portugal a reasonable time to see if it can restore peace and order in Angola."[27] Kennedy seemingly accepted this logic after his overtures to France and the United Kingdom proved fruitless.

As the White House's intrinsic interest declined, Roberto and ACOA hoped grassroots organizing could bolster the arguments made by Williams and his allies, steeling the administration to take further action. In the months after the rebellion began, ACOA published a pair of pamphlets on Portuguese colonialism that ended with exhortations for concerned readers to write to the White House.[28] Roberto supported this work, distributing UPA statements and arranging speaking events through ACOA. Emphasis was on Portuguese repression, with vaguer claims to the UPA's plans for future development programs and the creation of a nonracial independent state. These accounts integrated the Angolan cause into domestic agendas, playing to the anti-colonial sympathies of civil rights organizations while using Portuguese forced-labor practices to win over union organizers.[29] The result was the creation of a pro-Angolan sentiment that found ready partners among Democratic constituencies with access to elected officials. In one instance, ACOA arranged for Roberto to share a stage with civil rights organizer James Farmer, Senator Hubert Humphrey (D-MN), and African National Congress leader Oliver Tambo as part of the annual African Liberation Day in April 1961, whose sponsors included Farmer's Congress of Racial Equality (CORE), Americans for Democratic Action, and the United Auto Workers.[30] By May, George Meany, president of the AFL-CIO, cited Angola alongside Algeria, South Africa, Tibet, and (South) Vietnam as proof that "the plain people of the world are determined to win freedom."[31]

Some of the loudest voices within this nascent movement came from Protestant churches, who used their privileged access to information from Angola to push back against press coverage shaped by the information Lisbon allowed to leave the colony. Methodist and Baptist missionaries had been active in Angola and Mozambique since the early 1900s, but tensions with the government arose as Salazar sought to tighten control of the empire. Many Angolan and Mozambican nationalists were educated by missionaries who quietly supported liberalization, including both Agostinho Neto of the MPLA and Holden Roberto, whose namesake was a British Baptist missionary. As a result, the Portuguese associated Protestantism with nationalism and targeted African converts in the early stages of pacification. Missionaries wrote home with stories of government massacres that contradicted Portuguese-fed press coverage of nationalist violence.[32] American Methodist Ralph Dodge, whose central African bishopric included Angola and Mozambique, urged action from the National Council of Churches (NCC). The NCC was an ecumenical bureaucracy based in New York that liaised between mainline Protestant denominations and sought greater communion between the world's Christians. Since its founding in 1950, it prioritized the search for peace over Cold

War politics and developed ties to nearby ACOA through George Houser, an ordained minister. The NCC began protesting Lisbon's actions in May, but Salazar continued to imprison and expel missionaries he blamed for the rebellion.[33] These crackdowns inflamed U.S. citizens even as the rebellion faltered.

As Protestant missionaries returned with harrowing stories of the colonial military response, they became de facto advocates of African nationalism. The NCC supported speaker tours that highlighted Portuguese brutality for congregations across the country, including four Methodist ministers imprisoned for three months in Angola. They urged parishioners to write to the U.S. government. The result was what one Portuguese operative in the United States called "an aggressive publicity campaign against Portugal and its administration of Angola" throughout 1961.[34] The most influential of these missionaries was Malcolm McVeigh, who warned that only a "radical re-thinking" of Portuguese policy could avert an all-out war along racial lines. ACOA, partially funded by church donations, distributed missionary testimonies to its secular mailing list.[35] The reports undermined claims that the nationalists were solely responsible for instigating violence while lending legitimacy to revolutionary claims that their actions were necessary responses to Portuguese oppression. Importantly, these religious initiatives—like most organizing, even from ACOA—were general in their anti-colonialism rather than tied to any one party. At its core, early activism argued for a change in Portuguese and U.S. policy to avert worsening the conflict, diverging in their priorities from the liberation parties that were now tying their fortunes to military campaigns.

While this early solidarity organizing did not fit neatly with liberation party platforms, nationalists benefited because domestic complaints elevated the Portuguese colonial issue just as the Kennedy administration sought to move past it. The State Department could not avoid playing middleman between the churches and Portugal as they discussed remuneration. Both ACOA and the NCC used personal and professional connections to lobby Washington politicians and officials for a more assertive response, concentrating on the executive branch.[36] Civil rights groups, unions, and student organizations also pledged support for African liberation.[37] The gradually expanding coalition pushed for a stronger government response, with ACOA asking in June that Kennedy and Rusk consider expelling Portugal from NATO if violent reprisals continued in northern Angola.[38] These pleas received a friendly hearing in the State Department's African Bureau and from several congressmen. Their effect on the president and his broader set of advisers was less clear.

U.S. organizing therefore benefited from the emergence of a similar movement in the United Kingdom that evolved from greater CONCP involvement. Though not directly involved in the Angolan rebellion, the leftist parties responded to popular British concern with Angola, which the Goan nationalist João Cabral happily noted in June 1961 was largely "in our favor."[39] As in the United States, they worked with a coalition of anti-colonial and religious actors to highlight the repressive tactics that Salazar used to govern both metropole and colonies. The most active support came from the Movement for Colonial Freedom (MCF), founded by pro-independence Labour politicians and headed by the longtime pacifist MP Fenner Brockway. Opposed to British imperialism and apartheid, the MCF adopted the cause of Lusophone liberation because of the historic and geographic closeness of the two empires. At the request of the MPLA, Brockway worked with Portuguese exiles in Britain to form the Council for Freedom in Portugal and the Colonies to lobby the government. It pressured Lisbon to moderate its most repressive actions in Angola, achieving, among other things, the transfer of MPLA President Agostinho Neto from a Portuguese prison to house arrest, from which he eventually escaped.[40] The MCF organized public demonstrations and produced pamphlets linking Portugal's colonies to South Africa. The killing of unarmed protesters in the South African township of Sharpeville barely a year before had earned British scorn, but the MCF argued this paled in comparison to Portugal's military campaign in Angola.[41] These efforts gradually produced political pressure.[42]

Giving added weight to this movement was the mobilization of churches outside London, which demanded attention from a wider array of elected officials. As in the United States, British reports of Portuguese atrocities provided by returning missionaries encouraged strong condemnations of Lisbon from Protestant leadership.[43] In June, the World Council of Churches (WCC), an ecumenical confederation of national Protestant organizations that included the American NCC, delivered a statement it identified as one of its "strongest ever issued" on colonialism, calling for Portugal to accept demands for self-determination. It requested that Portugal avoid violent reprisals and that 176 constituent congregations of the WCC "press upon their governments the urgency of the situation."[44] Encouraged by both the WCC and the national conversation on Portuguese colonialism, British ministers took aim at the presence of NATO arms in Angola. They demanded that Parliament halt all military sales to Salazar's government, collecting more than thirty-seven thousand signatures of support in one day that a Labour MP then presented to the government.[45] Pickets began at the Portuguese consulate, while one concerned Baptist walked 158 miles to protest Portuguese violence at Westminster.[46] "The Churches," one journalist noted, "have not been so 'worked up' since Suez."[47] By July, mainstream organizations such as the War on Want, a development organization with ties to the Labour Party, began making material donations to Angolan nationalists—including the MPLA.[48] Politicians took notice. As religious leaders pressed the Foreign Office for personal meetings on Angola, a clergyman remarked, "On every hand we heard of MP's being inundated with letters until some even pleaded for mercy."[49]

As in the United States, this religious mobilization was indirectly associated with the CONCP, but it dovetailed with efforts by the nationalist parties and drew upon the work they promoted in London. Labour MPs in the House of Commons repeatedly used Angola to attack the Conservative government, demanding a review of the policy for supplying arms to Portugal and its colonies.[50] As parliamentary criticism increased, officials worried how Britain's African allies (and subjects) might view continued inaction. Facing both domestic pressure and African anger, the government began reconsidering its approach in June as deliberations continued in the United States. When Baptist ministers threatened to make the matter a by-election issue, Prime Minister Macmillan felt obliged to act. In late June, the government announced it would not sell or ship military equipment designated for the colonies, though equipment and parts designated for mainland Portugal were still approved.[51] The decision drew the ire of Portugal, but it made few provisions to assure material was not simply transferred from Portugal. And Macmillan had limited options. Popular and political pressure demanded action from a leader who, like Kennedy, publicly indicated that Britain would sail with the "wind of change." In the words of one Tory backbencher, anything less would signal a "lack of moral leadership."[52] The nationalists were rightfully skeptical of the policy but welcomed the popular protests that forced even this small change. "We want them to be isolated in the world," a PAIGC communique argued in 1961, "since an isolated enemy, alone, without support, is easier to defeat."[53]

The adjustment in British policy plus the transatlantic grassroots energy sustained Africanist efforts within the Kennedy administration but struggled to arrest the drift. Leading the charge was Soapy Williams, who chaired a State Department task force that delivered an aggressive report in July demanding the United States either persuade Portugal to grant Angola new levels of self-government or "provide the leadership to compel the achievement of this objective." Recommendations mirrored British policy in denying authorization for the export of arms and equipment to the colonies while maintaining NATO commitments and dissuading African governments from arming Lusophone nationalists. But the report went further in recommending that the United States establish contacts with responsible nationalists and consider bolder steps should the Salazar regime persist in its policies: recognizing an African government in exile and encouraging new leadership in Portugal.[54] Representing the most assertive liberal opinion within the administration, Williams's conclusions drew immediate pushback from the Defense Department and many within the State Department that watered down the final list of recommendations given to the president.[55] Williams's African Bureau deemed these acceptable costs in courting Afro-Asian states but ultimately conceded its most strident suggestions.[56] Facing pressure to act, Kennedy generally approved the recommendations that could be achieved quietly without stoking European tensions.[57] Notable among these was funding for the international education program run by ACOA board member John Marcum at Lincoln University, which hoped to train a non-communist cadre of future African leaders but included only a handful of Angolan and Mozambicans.[58]

Such gradual efforts failed to stem the popular concern with Angola that made inroads into the Democratic Party, focusing especially on the use of U.S. weapons that was similarly animating the British public. Though U.S. officials quietly objected to the diversion of NATO equipment, they hesitated to escalate the matter when Salazar failed to comply.[59] This opened the door for legislators led by Harlem's Adam Clayton Powell to challenge the administration to stop the use of U.S. arms in Angola, referencing reports by missionary Malcolm McVeigh to make their cases.[60] With complaints peaking in July at the same time as Williams's report made similar recommendations, the president relented, in part because he could point to British actions to justify the new policy. On August 16, the State Department announced restrictions on arms exports, which the press described in exaggerated terms as an embargo. This action helped mollify the grassroots while aligning U.S. policy with that of at least one European ally.[61] Kennedy and his administration sympathized with the cause of African nationalism, but they understood decolonization as a process bounded by the geostrategic requirements of the Cold War and Africa's relationship to metropolitan interests. This constrained the options open to the White House. Grassroots interest helped shape U.S. policy, but it was its intersection with agitation in Britain that made change possible.

The arms limitations represented a victory for the nascent solidarity movement with Lusophone anti-colonialism, but it was a small step that required sustained action to benefit the nationalists. Both Britain and the United States continued to supply weapons and equipment as part of Portugal's NATO requirements, with laws limiting them to certified metropolitan needs.[62] But implementation by both British and American authorities was half-hearted at best.[63] Judgment of necessity for all but the largest items was left to Lisbon, which was also responsible for returning NATO matériel to Europe. Salazar ignored or skirted the law whenever possible, continuing to redeploy ordinance to the colonies while using contacts with France and Germany to fill gaps. When the media reported that bombs stamped "Made in America" were found in an Angolan village shortly after the policy began, the government released a statement reiterating its earlier stance without seriously pressing Portugal on the matter.[64] Nationalists complained loudly even as some like Roberto continued to try to woo the United States.[65] Over the next two years, the administration approved the sale of items officials claimed had little value in Africa yet were retrofitted and adapted to become important components of Portugal's imperial wars.[66] This porous embargo and the U.N. vote signaled to casual observers at the time, and many historians since, that the Kennedy administration sympathized with African nationalists, but those closest to the cause understood that further action would be needed to actually isolate Portugal. The question was whether the popular enthusiasm that helped convince Kennedy to act would continue as the tide turned against the Angolan rebellion.

Portugal Pushes Back

The height of American activity—uncoincidentally—aligned with the final weeks of the Angolan crisis. Salazar spent the summer preparing for a long fight for the empire, both militarily and in the realm of international public opinion. The first step was to assure allies that Lisbon retained control in Angola and there would be no second Congo. A massive influx of Portuguese soldiers and matériel set the stage for Operation Viriato, which beat back the UPA rebellion and pacified the countryside. Harsh tactics fueled missionary reports of atrocities but enabled the recapture of key settlements between the capital Luanda and the Congo border. On August 8, a week before Kennedy's declaration of the arms policy, Portugal pronounced the "reconquest of the north."[67] Pessimistic outside observers had underestimated Portuguese abilities and given undue credit to the UPA's poorly trained and outgunned revolutionaries. Roberto wagered heavily that international pressure would bolster his meager forces, but toothless U.N. resolutions and unenforced Anglo-American arms policies proved pyrrhic victories.[68] With the rebellion quieted, Salazar moderated his once combative tone and provided Western leaders with an opening to retreat from prior positions without losing face. Building on a mild reform program begun shortly before the rebellion, the Lisbon government slightly improved labor conditions, created local elective councils, and expanded health and social services in the colonies.[69] At the end of August, the newly installed overseas minister announced a broad package of reforms that made all African subjects nominal citizens of Portugal while also pushing for greater mainland immigration to Angola. Salazar announced plans to expand the colonies' education system, in a seemingly direct response to Anglo-American concerns.[70] The fear of colonial collapse that motivated White House policy waned quickly.

Salazar built on this positive momentum through a multipronged propaganda campaign aimed at Euro-American populations. The goal was to drown the liberation parties' calls for justice and independence with a torrent of appeals utilizing interrelated themes of Cold War containment and an often racialized Western cultural solidarity. Though it took a few months to take effect, the campaign began soon after the March uprising, when a regime-backed assembly of Portuguese businessmen hired the Madison Avenue advertising agency Selvage and Lee. The consultants believed that Lisbon's image problem grew from ignorance about Portuguese Africa. Selvage and Lee sarcastically explained that 99 percent of Americans "did not know whether [Angola] was a country or a goat." When it suddenly became newsworthy, press and experts alike turned to the "hostile propaganda put out by certain committees in this country"—namely, ACOA—that were well positioned to fill the information void.[71] What was needed was an alternative perspective. Selvage and Lee coordinated a propaganda barrage in the United States, quietly bankrolling a private organization to counter ACOA and the churches. Under the leadership of the combative and politically connected New England lawyer Martin Camacho, the Portuguese-American Committee on Foreign Affairs (PACFA) distributed literature that cast Portuguese colonialism in a positive light while vilifying the liberation parties as terrorists and their allies as fools.[72]

The propaganda took a two-pronged approach. The first sought to undermine support for Angolan liberation with grisly reports of anti-colonial violence that went well beyond what had already appeared in newspapers, which Portugal claimed represented an intersection of anti-white racism and international communism. Widely distributed pamphlets featured pictures of white settlers mutilated during the UPA rebellion. "Men, women, and children—white and black—tortured and maimed on explicit directives attributed to Communist-backed leader," one publication of Camacho's PACFA blared, "should the U.S. support the forces behind these unspeakable acts?"[73] The answer was clearly negative, especially as Portugal sought to frame this confrontation in civilizational terms. According to another pamphlet, the violence that accompanied the March 15 uprising demonstrated that the nationalists were unfit to govern and should not "merit the support of the United Nations, or any Christian, civilized society."[74] The intertwining of racial and Cold War fears worked well in the United States as the rising civil rights movement challenged local traditions of white governance and elicited accusations of communist subversion.[75] Portuguese propogandists played to fears of both segregationists and Cold War hawks, positioning Lisbon as a bulwark protecting the West from identarian and ideological threats.

Contrasting with this narrative were positive depictions of Portuguese colonialism that softened traditional tropes of Western superiority in pursuit of global racial equality. Portugal clung to a European civilizing mission, arguing it was preparing its colonies for self-government despite a paucity of overseas investment. It trotted out the pseudo-scientific theory of luso-tropicalism to claim that Portugal's warm climate, historic role in the tropics, and less structured racialism were uniquely suited to produce "multi-racial nations," acting as the ideal interlocuter between Africa and the West.[76] Photos showed Westernized Black Africans interacting with white populations in the city centers of Luanda and Lourenço Marques, which appeared impeccably modern given the recency of major investments.[77] Selvage and Lee recruited Americans to reinforce these messages, sending them on carefully managed junkets that provided specially selected sympathizers with tours of Portugal and its colonies intended to influence press accounts. In one notable example, conservative columnist George Schuyler used his editorials in the African American *Pittsburgh Courier* to praise Portuguese multiracialism.[78] The Lisbon regime juggled issues of race—appealing to tropes of Black savagery while claiming pursuit of a multiracial utopia—with the common thread being its role as guarantor of regional stability.

Lisbon's American advocates proved especially effective at promoting official messages and provided useful domestic counters to ACOA and church activity. Backed by powerful news organizations, the public perceived these men as experts despite paltry experience of Portugal or Angola. In one widely republished piece, Frank Howley, the retired military general who helped rebuild West Berlin, wrote approvingly of Portuguese rule in Angola for *Reader's Digest*.[79] Schuyler used his voice in the African American community to dismiss Roberto as a communist pawn and accuse ACOA of "serving the Soviet purpose" in Africa.[80] Their assessments gained additional credence because Portugal's expulsion of Protestant missionaries robbed pro-liberation elements of their most galvanizing material. ACOA continued to lobby, and Malcolm McVeigh visited churches throughout 1961, but they relied on increasingly outdated revelations that lost ground to efforts by Howley and Schuyler that used recent experience to push Cold War claims.[81] When Roberto tried responding directly to Howley's accusations in *Reader's Digest*, editors rejected his submission saying they had no interest in supporting revolutionary violence.[82] African revolutionaries lacked the resources and standing of Portuguese officials, and their allies struggled to bridge this gap once faced with an organized response. As the northern autumn of 1961 progressed, Houser worried that colonial propaganda was having a greater effect than ACOA's efforts.[83]

This Cold War appeal proved especially important in wooing elected officials. It was an easier sell than forcing decolonization on Portugal given the near consensus supporting NATO and strategies of containment during this period. Selvage and Lee understood that anti-communist appeals provided the bedrock for creating an influential bloc of supporters because it linked disparate constituencies, ranging from Portuguese Americans in the Northeast United States to segregationists with fears of Black self-determination in the American South to Midwestern Protestants with no personal interests in the region.[84] Efforts soon focused on Congress, where both Democrats and Republicans expressed unease with Kennedy's apparent response to Angola. While Roberto and ACOA praised the March U.N. vote, Senate Minority Leader Everett Dirksen (R-IL) lamented that turning on an ally was "hardly a proud moment for Uncle Sam."[85] Shortly after the arms policy went into effect in August, Camacho's PACFA organization began meeting with State Department officials and congressmen to defend Salazar's position in Africa.[86] It sent a barrage of letters criticizing ACOA and the churches from late 1961 into early 1962, asking politicians to investigate their actions and pressuring the board members of organizations to intervene.[87] The rhetoric stressed Cold War national security, with one letter sent to a number of Southern and Midwestern legislators claiming Roberto's real mission was "to make Angola a satellite in the communist orbit . . . for the rich raw materials of that territory to make Russia more powerful against America and the free world."[88] While exaggerated, it was hard for politicians to dismiss the missive in the wake of the Congo debacle. With congressmen rallying to Portugal's defense, even Kennedy's plans to quietly pursue diplomatic pressure became increasingly contentious.[89]

Salazar stoked criticism both within and beyond the executive branch by leveraging Portugal's most important Cold War asset, the Azores islands. By the end of 1961, Salazar rhetorically tied the U.S. position on Angola to the looming bilateral lease renegotiations that had taken place regularly since the 1940s. The Azores facilities were valuable strategic assets for the Americans; the air and sea facilities had proved vital in the transport of troops to Lebanon in 1958, Berlin in 1961, and the Congo in the first two years of the decade, while the communications facilities would prove important during the Cuban Missile Crisis of 1962.[90] All this led the military to claim in the summer report on the Portuguese situation, "The military air base at Lajes in the Azores is the single most valuable facility which the United States is authorized by a foreign power to use."[91] And Salazar was conscious of this value. Having little else with which to bargain, the Portuguese prolonged the negotiations for the base rights that were set to expire at the end of 1962 with the clear goal of quieting White House criticism.[92] Many in the administration believed this a negotiation ploy, and Kennedy questioned the overall value of the islands given advancements in technology and alternative air routes to Europe. The greater fear was always that Salazar would abandon NATO before he would leave Africa, which Portuguese officials had been intimating since March.[93] This tension fueled congressional criticism and empowered executive branch moderates.[94] With a semblance of order restored to the colony by December and a surge of domestic opinion in Portugal's favor, the president had minimal motivation to confront Salazar.[95]

International events reinforced this reevaluation of Portugal. The United Kingdom experienced its own propaganda push that saw Portugal court conservative MPs still smarting over the decline of Britain's empire, which discouraged Prime Minister Macmillan from considering new actions.[96] But it was events in India that fully reoriented transatlantic calculations. After years of unsuccessful diplomacy to resolve Portugal's presence in its enclaves around Goa, the Angolan rebellion encouraged Prime Minister Jawaharlal Nehru to reappraise past tactics, with recently installed UPA foreign policy chief Jonas Savimbi and CONCP leaders like Marcelino dos Santos encouraging a forcible annexation.[97] Operation Vijay saw Indian forces overwhelm the paltry European garrison that was unable to receive reinforcements due to Portugal's military commitments in Africa. Though Salazar ordered his troops to fight to the death, they quickly surrendered, ending Portugal's four-hundred-and-fifty-year-old empire in India on December 19, 1961.[98] In the weeks preceding the invasion, both the United State and the United Kingdom attempted to dissuade India, a member of the British Commonwealth and a major recipient of U.S. aid, from a military solution. But once the invasion occurred, neither was willing to aid Portugal's defense of the territory or block the annexation.[99] Salazar blamed Washington and London for the loss of Goa, sending relations to their lowest ebb. The dictator publicly threatened halting the Azores agreements, ongoing NATO membership, and future cooperation with the British in Africa.[100] Anglo-American diplomats found Portuguese officials increasingly inflexible and unpredictable in early 1962, choosing retrenchment when just a few months before there had been hope for continued reforms.[101]

Events in Goa provided a dramatic impetus for shifting Western discourse on Portugal's colonies and the challenges of compelling decolonization. While few press reports in either the United States or the United Kingdom fully defended Portuguese imperialism, most criticized India for the invasion and the United Nations, along with the Western governments that occupied most of its Security Council, for accepting a brazen violation of international borders. João Cabral noted that reaction in London to Indian actions was almost universally negative.[102] U.K. officials consciously retreated from efforts that might antagonize Portugal, which—when combined with limited news coming from Angola—convinced activists to reprioritize anti-apartheid organizing.[103] Portugal's newfound victimization also accelerated the shifting tenor of American politics begun in the fall. Republicans lambasted the president for abandoning what one Massachusetts congressman called "a bulwark of our European alliances," and some Democrats felt emboldened to demand Kennedy appease Lisbon, citing the Azores-base issue as a clear illustration of Portugal's value to Western defense.[104] The powerful congressman Thomas P. "Tip" O'Neill (D-MA), a staunch Boston liberal who nonetheless counted Martin Camacho among his personal acquaintances, expressed "deep feelings that United States foreign policy and that of the western powers with regards to Angola was wrong."[105]

The nationalists were in a poor position to respond because the collapse of the Angolan rebellion also broke the utilitarian alliance between Roberto's UPA and the leftist MPLA. Roberto repeatedly scuttled talks of union because he feared that the Bakongo-dominated UPA would become a secondary partner in a socialist front. Jealously guarding his personal power, he consolidated control of his party "against all outside groups . . . [and] for others' political ends," and he implied his rejection of the MPLA union was proof of his commitment to the anti-communist cause.[106] Roberto adopted more racist rhetoric domestically. Claiming to represent the true interests of Black Angolans, Roberto contrasted his movement with the educated, mixed-race leadership of the MPLA. Attacks on the "mestiço" leftists were taken up by the UPA's rising star Jonas Savimbi, a political science student in Switzerland whose origins in the large Ovimbundu community of central Angola represented Roberto's attempts to diversify his party base.[107] The MPLA responded with a reaffirmation of its inclusiveness, arguing it opposed Portuguese imperialism while it also "vigorously condemn[ed] tribalism, regionalism, sectarianism, [and] racial and religious intolerance."[108] The shared pursuit of independence collapsed into partisan competition.

This ideological confrontation weakened the nationalist movement just when unity was needed to combat Portuguese success in the United States and beyond. Attempts by the MPLA to infiltrate troops into Angola in the final months of 1961 produced a three-sided war, with UPA forces attacking MPLA columns even as Portugal pressed its advantage.[109] Vicious recriminations from both parties ended prospects for collaboration. In later years, Roberto would even try to set up an identarian nationalist alternative to the CONCP's intracolonial network, unsuccessfully coordinating with Guinea-Bissauan nationalists led by François Mendy, who similarly attacked Amílcar Cabral's PAIGC for its heavily Cabo Verdean, mestiço leadership.[110] Two distinct, opposing nationalist networks were taking shape. These divisions weakened the Angolan rebellion and prevented any coordinated response to Portugal's effective combination of official and public diplomacy. "The aftereffects of our division, of the lack of unity in our underground movements," the MPLA's Mário de Andrade lamented, "naturally holds up the development of our struggle."[111]

With the nationalists in disarray, Portugal's campaign blunted the pro-independence movement that developed over the northern summer. Nationalist allies like ACOA continued to lobby, but even the quiet initiatives Kennedy approved in July seemed to offer limited returns at high costs. The Kennedy administration retained contact with Roberto and refused to abandon calls for decolonization, but little action accompanied the subdued rhetoric coming from the White House. Speaking with Rusk in March 1962, Foreign Minister Franco Nogueira smugly marveled, "It was extraordinary what we [Portugal] had done in the space of a year with American public opinion. There was no doubt that the atmosphere was entirely different and in our favor." Rusk could only agree.[112] Small educational programs for refugees were quietly terminated, according to former Kennedy adviser Winifred Armstrong, "due to political pressure from the Portuguese, or Portuguese government supporters here."[113] Those supporters were concentrated on Capitol Hill. In 1963, African Bureau diplomat George High estimated that two-thirds of Congress were pro-Portugal. Lisbon had achieved this not just by erasing the threat of rebellion but also by transforming the national conversation. Kennedy had pressured Lisbon to adopt a smooth transition lest chaos reign, but many in government now saw Portugal as a vital source of stability. The calculus had changed: "The worse things get for the Portuguese in Angola," High lamented, "the more political pressure will be put on the U.S. Government by conservative groups here not to help the Africans, and to help the Portuguese."[114] Salazar weathered the storm created by the Angolan rebellion by revitalizing a familiar Cold War narrative that would protect the empire for more than a decade.

By January 1962, the surprisingly stalwart response of Salazar's Estado Novo and widening divides between African nationalists erased the momentum for decolonization created by the UPA rebellion. Salazar's offensive—both for Angola and for U.S. popular opinion—proved better organized and funded than the loose pro-independence networks. But most important, Portugal provided a more compelling narrative. Cold War containment was a familiar and ultimately powerful argument, whose concrete impact on U.S. interests won over many politicians. Competing nationalist factions initially united behind criticism of Portuguese empire and calls for independence, but their reliance on humanitarian outrage meant that U.S. organizing was both shallow and dependent on sustained attention to Portuguese actions. As the latter disappeared, the grassroots activism that pressured officials during the northern summer of 1961 faded. Without a clear identification with a specific party or leader, it was difficult to sustain effective interest and action on behalf of Lusophone African liberation. Where Kennedy once had a Congress and media generally sympathetic to his desire to lean on Portugal, he faced a much different situation in 1962. In this first contest for control of the narratives on Portuguese decolonization, Salazar scored a decisive victory. The nationalists needed to offer a clearer vision of African independence, and explain how it intersected with U.S. priorities, to win sustained support in a Cold War–dominated political climate.

CHAPTER 3

The Limits of Cold War Liberalism

The Kennedy administration's retreat from its initially pro-African position was the product of several factors, not least of which was the Portuguese ability to wrest control of narratives around Angola. More generally, the shifting tenor in the executive branch reflected limitations on liberal politics during the Cold War that prioritized pro-Western stability over claims to self-determination, democracy, or global social justice. After the Angolan crisis of 1961 had passed, the Kennedy administration adopted a more collaborative approach toward Lisbon despite Salazar's refusal to make serious concessions around the colonies. The result was a stagnation of both decolonization and U.S. support for it well before the change to the Johnson administration after Kennedy's assassination in 1963. Civil society organizations like ACOA and the newly formed American Negro Leadership Conference on Africa (ANLCA) lobbied the executive branch but were frustrated by their inability to make headway while making their own accommodations to the Cold War. These groups refused to advocate for a radical break with traditions of Western influence in Africa, and as a result they were hesitant to aggressively push the administration and slow to build firm relationships with the CONCP parties that emerged as the most successful challengers to Portuguese rule during this period. Although Kennedy and many domestic supporters championed decolonization, the assertiveness needed to confront recalcitrant states like Portugal proved a harder sell while Cold War considerations remained paramount.

The period witnessed the militarization of Lusophone nationalism as avenues for peaceful transition closed. The turn to widespread revolution transformed the direction, focus, and face of Lusophone African self-determination and laid the foundations for a similar adjustment in U.S. solidarity (see Chapter 5). Roberto's Congo-based party unraveled as military setbacks and internal unrest gradually undermined its claim to leadership of the Angolan revolution. Meanwhile, armed, leftist struggles began in Guinea-Bissau and Mozambique. The newly formed Frente de Libertação de Moçambique (Mozambique Liberation Front, or FRELIMO) became the third major member of the CONCP, opening new opportunities for U.S. engagement under FRELIMO's American-trained president, Eduardo Mondlane. His extensive personal network and careful politics provided domestic officials and activists with a figurehead that allowed them to imagine both direct identification with a socialist party and the positive programmatic aspects of a post-Portugal state. While this idea would be adopted most enthusiastically by grassroots activists whose influence peaked after Mondlane's assassination, one can see the beginnings of later political coalitions in the network that led to his election as head of FRELIMO. These two factors—newly active revolutions and Mondlane's political network—shifted emphasis away from the Cold War conceptualizations of Angola that dominated discussions in 1961 toward the revolutionary, socialist visions pursued by CONCP parties in Mozambique and Guinea. It would be these parties and these countries that inspired effective solidarity, even as Angola remained the strategic prize of the Portuguese Empire for Cold Warriors and—later—their opponents.

Contesting the Kennedy Retreat

African hopes for John Kennedy were high when he entered the White House, but his goals had always been more measured: namely, avoiding the radicalization of African politics that could invite Cold War polarization. Salazar complicated matters by leveraging the Azores lease and Portugal's NATO membership, but the reality was that the U.S. government walked a tightrope between African demands and a desire to operate through its European partners. The end of the Azores lease at the end of 1962 and the tenuous U.S. presence that continued after that date added undesirable drama to transatlantic tensions, but the reality was that, in addition to NATO concerns, the Cold War liberals of the Kennedy administration needed Portugal to manage the transition to independence. As Rusk clarified to his ambassadors in Europe, "Our policy is to encourage Europeans to stay in Africa because they have important interests and contributions to make there which in case of Portugal is almost unique because of language factor."[1] In essence, U.S. officials had trouble imagining the process of decolonization without willing

European partners. As Portugal brutally reestablished control of Angola, it gave them hope that the country might have sufficient time to evolve its policies to avoid the kind of chaos that most felt was inevitable in an unmanaged transfer of power.[2] This tendency toward crisis management meant that U.S. officials focused almost solely on the massive colony of Angola, to the bemusement and perhaps relief of Portuguese officials like Foreign Minister Franco Nogueira.[3] The Americans believed that Angola, as Portugal's largest and most economically important colony, was vital for the future of the continent and that finding a path forward toward self-government would create a pathway for other parts of the empire to follow. With disaster averted in Angola, the Kennedy administration sought ways to compel Salazar to implement reforms without further straining European relationships.

As a result, the Kennedy administration changed its tone in 1962, approaching Salazar with more measured rhetoric and cautious proposals that set the stage for nearly a decade of government policy. The goal was to encourage a restructuring of Portuguese rule without resorting to the frenetic efforts that typified earlier actions. U.S. diplomats seized on every opportunity to praise Portuguese initiatives and promote gradual liberalization. Mild reforms, the appointment of the comparatively liberal Adriano Moreira as overseas minister, and half-hearted talks with conservative nationalists allowed U.S. officials to claim that Portugal was finally taking "steps in the right direction," which one communication to Salazar's government argued would "provide the best assurance that Portugal w[ould] be able to continue in Africa."[4] U.S. officials cooperated with Portugal at the United Nations throughout 1962 and 1963, joining its European allies in turning back African resolutions calling for sanctions while also proposing that a U.N. rapporteur visit Angola and Mozambique in order to comment favorably on government reforms.[5] Several initiatives over the next two years tried to buy out Portugal, offering generous aid packages that would strengthen the metropolis and potentially reinforce its economic ties to the colonies, if only it would move toward their political self-determination.[6] This liberal vision of a managed political transition never swayed the conservative Lisbon regime, but it played into Salazar's propaganda that his government represented a valuable pro-Western influence.

Pro-liberation elements in the United States recognized the official drift and organized in hopes of arresting it. ACOA took the lead, working with liberal and religious allies to provide material assistance as the White House focused on Lisbon. In January 1962, George Houser and John Marcum crossed the Congo border into northern Angola to deliver medicine and supplies to the medical wing of Roberto's party, the Serviço de Assistência aos Refugiados de Angola (the Angolan Refugee Assistance Service, or SARA). Bought with funds raised over the previous months, this aid was the first of an irregular set of material and transportation donations coordinated with Protestant and Catholic relief agencies.[7] ACOA also facilitated the visitation of skilled doctors and a donation of five thousand dollars worth of drugs from the AFL-CIO.[8] Humanitarian assistance continued until at least 1966, but the amounts were always modest.[9] The government was better positioned to provide such aid, but Portuguese hostility to foreign assistance, especially to refugees in countries that harbored nationalists like Roberto, limited official options. ACOA nonetheless continued its campaigns with hopes of compelling official action, supporting the Methodist missionary Malcom McVeigh's speaking events into 1962 and using Houser's trip to the Congo to provide news on the refugee situation there.[10]

These efforts struggled to rekindle popular interest, but they fueled Portugal's continued claims that the United States was hostile to its colonies. As the Kennedy administration sought improved relations, Portugal responded with a series of complaints focused on the activities of nongovernmental groups and the administration's small educational investments, such as Marcum's Lincoln University program. Topping Portugal's literal list of issues were the Congo activities of ACOA and affiliated organizations such as the Methodist Church and the AFL-CIO.[11] Portugal singled out ACOA because the regime assumed that Houser's minor role on the African Bureau's advisory council and its elite membership, which included Kennedy adviser Arthur Schlesinger on its letterhead, gave it special access to policymakers.[12] Salazar was irate that Americans were assisting Roberto in the form of monetary aid, medical supplies, and political networking.[13] The conspiratorial Salazar became convinced that these groups—ACOA in particular—were acting as pro-revolutionary proxies for the government, regardless of official protests to the contrary.[14] Washington could not control independent organizations, but the State Department responded by addressing what it could, limiting educational initiatives and reining in vocally liberal elements of the administration. In one example, it ordered that any speeches by Soapy Williams on Portugal had to receive advance approval.[15] High-level diplomatic negotiations also increased. In June 1962, Secretary of State Rusk paid a personal visit to Salazar, hoping to discuss forthrightly and honestly the issues dividing Portugal and the United States. Little came from the meeting—which the secretary likened to having a séance with a ghost—but it was one more example of the new direction in U.S. policy.[16]

Hoping to arrest the transformation of executive policy, ACOA and its allies tried to replicate the grassroots pressure that arose in mid-1961 but faced far different circumstances. The popular reaction to Angola had been powerful because reports of Portuguese atrocities angered humanitarians, and the use of U.S. arms unnerved Cold War liberals concerned about Soviet criticism. The restoration of Portuguese control took away both these immediate issues, and there was little emotional attachment to the cause or Angolan parties to sustain mobilization. ACOA concluded that the obvious solution was to tie African liberation to the American civil rights movement. After all, ACOA had close ties to civil rights leadership, and Kennedy had used his investment in African affairs to woo Black voters in 1960. Marshaling the collective voice of U.S. Blacks behind Lusophone liberation might win concessions from the president as he looked ahead to the 1962 midterms and his own reelection.

The assumption that Black Americans had a keen interest in events on the continent was a trope clumsily deployed by politicians like Kennedy, but the sentiment was real if inconsistently felt. Scholars such as Jim Meriwether and Brenda Gayle Plummer have documented how decolonization fueled a growth in Black American interest in Africa, which Houser and others hoped to harness to pressure the government.[17] Visible organizing around the Italian invasion of Ethiopia in 1935 and the murder of Patrice Lumumba in 1960 demonstrated communal interest, but Cold War concerns blunted some of the most assertive attempts to articulate a transnational movement for racial equality, notably targeting the global leftist politics most visibly associated with the Council on African Affairs.[18] Individual leaders like Martin Luther King Jr. and major organizations like the National Association for the Advancement of Colored People (NAACP) certainly viewed free Black states as both inspiration and potential allies, but Pan-African collaboration took a backseat to domestic priorities.[19] The result was a tangible African American interest in the continent that remained politically vague.

The potential power of the Black community was not lost on Portugal, which was deeply concerned about the possibility of linking the civil rights movement with anti-colonialism. The fear that criticism from African American congressmen in 1961 might lead to formal organizing motivated several pro-Lisbon activities in the United States. Portugal's American agents courted the African American public, notably winning over Black anti-communists George Schuyler and Max Yergan. Their articles provided a valuable defense of Portugal's claims to multiracial imperialism, though they likely had greater influence among white moderates than among African Americans.[20] Yet Lisbon was most happy with silence, and it achieved its largest gains simply by inhibiting information from leaving Angola. As mainstream media lost interest, Black newspapers lacked the resources to conduct their own investigations or sustain contacts with nationalists, giving Schuyler and other products of Lisbon's carefully managed junkets freer rein to defend Portuguese Africa after 1961.[21] A frustrated Holden Roberto complained that Portugal's "grandiose propaganda machine" effectively silenced Black newsmen.[22] Still, Portugal remained wary of the potential power of African American organizing. As late as 1963, the Selvage and Lee PR firm warned Portugal that the "attitude of black American leaders" represented the greatest danger to improving relations with the United States, especially with Northern Democrats seeking their votes.[23]

The organization of the ANLCA in mid-1962 sought to activate 'this potential. The moment seemed propitious; Kennedy's quiet retreat on Portugal occurred amid the ongoing wave of decolonization that included Tanganyika (now Tanzania) in late 1961 and Algeria in 1962. With momentum still favoring independence, African Americans stood to benefit by aligning their movement with the global embrace of Black self-determination, and they pushed the government to take more decisive action. Civil rights leaders such as A. Philip Randolph, James Baldwin, James Farmer, and Bayard Rustin—all of whom sat on the board of ACOA—realized that the sentiment of the African American community had never been "organized or vocalized completely," effectively acquiescing to the "equivocal position" that typified U.S. policy toward Africa.[24] As a successful labor organizer, Randolph believed that the African American leadership needed to expand the domestic Black freedom movement beyond mere civil rights to a global campaign for political, economic, and individual equality. It could do so by linking itself to the cause of African independence. He pushed for a major convocation to outline a Black agenda for foreign policy and tasked ACOA with organizing the event.[25]

The resulting ANLCA was an attempt to direct the kinship felt by many African Americans toward a concrete political project. The conference's stated goal was to "activize [sic] the political influence of America's 19 million Negro citizens on their government's role in the councils of the United Nations and other diplomatic channels on the critical areas of Sub-Sahara Africa."[26] Gathering at Arden House on the campus of Columbia University in November 1962, the hundred-plus participants were a who's who of the civil rights movement and the Black intelligentsia, including conveners Randolph, Farmer, Martin Luther King Jr., Whitney Young of the Urban League, and Dorothy Height of the National Council of Negro Women. Attendance was heavily African American but included several white experts and African nationalists. The event took a broad approach to Africa and the challenges of postcolonial development, with a focus on regions that were not yet on the path to freedom: Angola and its sister colonies, Southern Rhodesia, and apartheid South Africa. Reports on Portuguese Africa borrowed heavily from the transnational support network that operated around ACOA. John Marcum provided the paper on Angola, while Eduardo Mondlane—recently elected president of FRELIMO (discussed below)—offered another on Mozambique, though the colony's minor status was confirmed by one Black reporter's misidentification of Mondlane's topic as Kenya.[27] Holden Roberto sent a delegation to act as observers.[28]

The gathering of continental and diasporic Africans inspired calls for concerted political action, but it was ultimately limited by a variation of the same Cold War liberalism that constrained the Kennedy administration. Randolph sought to transcend such boundaries by creating a political front dedicated to articulating Black demands as part of a single transnational project. As a first step, he counseled Black Americans to state clearly "the meaning of Africa to them," so that they could "be informed, awakened, aroused, and mobilized to protest, demonstrate, and march for African freedom."[29] Such solidarity would inform concrete initiatives such as a major labor strike protesting apartheid, forcing the U.S. government to take Black demands for the continent as seriously as domestic civil rights. Randolph's radical goal essentially was to link Black American labor, productive capacity, and buying power to larger questions of global Black freedom. African nationalists encouraged such action, but many ANLCA delegates hesitated. As Penny Von Eschen and Brenda Gayle Plummer note, the political success of the civil rights movement came from its ability to leverage the ideological politics of the Cold War, which required movement leaders to sacrifice radical transnational critiques in order to remain within the boundaries of acceptable politics.[30] The NAACP's Roy Wilkins warned, "In developing this activity, we should not relax our prime effort to achieve our proper place in our own country." Rather than adopting Randolph's broad vision of transnational collaboration, Wilkins and his allies championed measured domestic goals like Black participation in the diplomatic corps.[31] They argued that once fully integrated into domestic society and policymaking, Blacks could better align official policy with African self-determination. This was an extension of domestic calls for equal hiring practices, but it also hinted at older ideas of African American leadership of the Black diaspora that contrasted with Randolph's attempts to define a grassroots community of interests.

Strategically aligning with Cold War definitions of Americanism and domestic civil rights, the less ambitious form of cooperation championed by Wilkins won the day, at least for the moment. The ANLCA's final recommendations proved circumscribed. They eschewed Randolph's calls for exploring a transnational identity and engaging in mass protest, instead requesting that the U.S. government act on behalf of the African American community on the world stage.[32] The conclusions on Portuguese Africa are illustrative of the overall program. The conference recognized the need for self-determination and criticized the provision of military equipment to Portugal but avoided the matter of armed revolution altogether. It made no requests for political assistance to the liberation movements beyond nongovernmental humanitarian relief. Essentially, the first ANLCA acquiesced to official diplomacy rather than creating independent structures to pursue global Black liberation and place new pressures on Portugal and Kennedy. There was little effort to expand cooperation with liberation leaders or inject their priorities into national discourse, frustrating nationalists like Roberto and Mondlane, who desired greater exchanges.[33] Picking up this critique, radical activist Daniel Watts argued: "If our brothers and sisters in Africa are waiting or depending on the American Negro Leadership Conference on Africa for aid and support, they might just as well make their peace with [South Africa's prime minister Hendrik] Verwoerd, Salazar, and [the Federation of Rhodesia and Nyasaland's prime minister Sir Roy] Welensky."[34] The ANLCA confirmed African American interest in liberation, but its strategic moderation did little to sway the White House.

Secretary of State Rusk acknowledged the gathering and made feints toward honoring some of its recommendations, especially on issues relating to the diplomatic corps, but the administration's African policy remained unchanged. This included the ongoing balancing act between acceding to Portuguese demands and maintaining its rhetorical support for independence. The Lincoln University education program continued, for example, but the emphasis on Lusophone students lessened as Lisbon's complaints increased.[35] The gradual retreat accelerated as the White House installed more pro-Portuguese voices. In early 1963—just months after the ANLCA meeting—Kennedy changed the tenor of Luso-American relations by replacing career diplomat Burke Elbrick with Admiral George Anderson as ambassador, providing Portugal a military champion of its strategic necessity over the protests of State Department Africanists.[36] By 1963, the department focused its energy on proposals that included heavy economic investment in Portugal and its colonies, which it was hoped would prepare the colonies for self-determination.[37] Yet the timing and ambition of these plans was left deliberately ambiguous. When the unabashed Europhile George Ball personally presented one such proposal to Salazar, the undersecretary of state suggested that Washington would be content if Portugal's relationship with its colonies was "similar to that between the United States and Puerto Rico."[38] The dictator had little interest in the plan and failed to respond before Kennedy's assassination, but the shift in U.S. policy was complete.

ACOA objected to the changing approach to Portugal but found access to the executive branch increasingly difficult and its Africanist allies sidelined. The ANLCA clearly had Rusk's ear and could have raised the domestic costs of the policy shift, but it took no action. Never more than a "part time operation," according to George Houser, it did not reconvene until after Kennedy's death in 1964 and then not again until 1967, by which time its civil rights leadership was falling behind more radical calls for international Black Power.[39] Many African Americans sympathized with nationalist demands for self-determination, but this did not assure meaningful political action. The drift toward supporting Portugal continued unabated.

The Collapse of the FNLA

The Kennedy administration continued to court moderate nationalists via quiet and increasingly small amounts of aid, but the hope for U.S. intervention was gone. This placed Holden Roberto's UPA in a difficult position. Roberto needed to reassert his position as the head of the revolutionary movement at the same time prospects for serious military and international action disappeared. He shifted focus onto local and regional politics, seeking to create a political front to legitimize his movement amid revolutionary setbacks and growing competition with the CONCP-linked MPLA. The goal was to further expand the party beyond his predominantly northern, Bakongo constituency. Ghanaian President Kwame Nkrumah, arguably Roberto's most influential ally, championed political unity as a necessary step for victory in Angola, so such a move might win additional international support.[40] Yet rather than revisiting the elusive alliance with the MPLA, the UPA placed itself at the core of the new National Liberation Front of Angola (Frente Nacional de Libertação de Angola, or FNLA), which included the relatively obscure Kikongo-dominated Democratic Party of Angola (Partido Democrático de Angola) and a handful of Ovimbundu nationalists—notably Jonas Savimbi. A week after its founding in March 1962, the FNLA established the Angolan Revolutionary Government in Exile (Govêrno Revolucionário de Angola no Exílio, or GRAE) in independent Congo. Roberto acted as GRAE president and appointed Savimbi foreign minister, though many of the leadership positions were retained by UPA loyalists. The goal was to demonstrate to the world the continued relevance of the Angolan nationalist movement despite military setbacks. That the FNLA amounted to barely more than Roberto's cronies in Leopoldville and a poorly managed SARA refugee-relief service mattered less than the symbolic gesture of declaring a government. Nearly a dozen African states recognized the FNLA's new government in exile—as did the recently founded Organization of African Unity—followed by a handful of Eastern bloc governments courting Global South nationalists.[41] NATO countries predictably balked, with the United States pressuring Congolese president Cyril Adoula not to recognize the FNLA lest it push Portugal deeper into its defensive position.[42]

Roberto's attempts to maintain leadership of the tenuous revolution only widened the rift developing between nationalists and U.S. diplomats as the White House improved Luso-American relations. Africans were increasingly frustrated with U.S. policies that one ACOA representative working with the FNLA in the Congo described as ambivalent at best.[43] Roberto complained bitterly about the U.S. tendency to pay "lip service to self-determination" while supplying "arms that are used to kill us," hinting at potential overtures to communist states and injecting a tinge of anti-Americanism into his rhetoric.[44] Still more troubling for U.S. diplomats was the FNLA's increasing reliance on racialist rhetoric to reinforce domestic support. Savimbi became the party's attack dog, praising Roberto for leading the "black masses" in opposition to "mulattos or those who marry whites."[45] The State Department reported critically about such attacks on the "mestiço" MPLA but was more alarmed at Roberto's threats to drive out white Portuguese.[46] Officials stationed in Luanda worried that such pronouncements did "not jibe with impression that US policy seeks to create [of] reasonable Negro leadership willing to negotiate and recognition of continued Portuguese Mission in Africa."[47] Rusk began advising U.S. diplomats to maintain distance from Roberto, and even floated building relationships with the MPLA in hopes that its ties to mainland socialists might create ground for negotiations, though there was disagreement on whether the party would even accept scholarships if offered.[48] U.S. and nationalist priorities diverged dramatically after 1962, with Roberto's actions adding additional momentum to the American retreat.

Roberto's combative attempts to maintain control of the revolution ultimately weakened the movement and damaged alliances that went well beyond official U.S. channels. Roberto was unable to parley the FNLA's declaration of its exile government into military or diplomatic success. Instead, he succumbed to intraparty intrigue as he protected his position of authority. Seeking sole leadership of the Angolan national movement, he convinced an MPLA faction under party founder Viriato da Cruz to defect, which Marcum partially attributes to animosity toward Agostinho Neto and the heavily mestiço leadership group.[49] Roberto also used his sway with the Congo government to harass the MPLA, which fled Leopoldville for Brazzaville and the protection of the radical Republic of the Congo. This competition sidelined the MPLA as it rebuilt its strength but failed to aid the long-term prospects of the FNLA.[50] Only Portugal claimed victory, taking advantage of the conflict between the nationalists to establish full control of its most valuable colony.

FNLA tactics soon produced a crisis of leadership. Though more diverse than the UPA, the new party remained dominated by a small cadre of French-speaking Bakongo nationalists loyal to Roberto. Those identifying with other ethnicities and regions of Angola often felt marginalized, most notably the European-educated minister of foreign affairs, Jonas Savimbi. Savimbi had been born in the Ovimbundu region of Angola and received his education through Protestant missions before going to Switzerland. Worldly, charismatic, and ambitious, Savimbi became a key component of the FNLA's international strategy, demonstrating the party's claim to represent all Angola while building personal relationships with African and Eastern leaders.[51] Notably, he developed an affinity for Maoist China, were Roberto looked for assistance after moving on from the United States.[52] But when Roberto continued to appoint corrupt Bakongo allies in regions populated by Ovimbundu refugees, tensions rose, leading Savimbi to build an independent base of political support. When Roberto moved to consolidate his power by removing disloyal followers, Savimbi fled the party with other senior FNLA officers. They accused Roberto of dictatorial and insufficiently revolutionary politics.[53] Savimbi toyed with joining the MPLA but eventually formed the União Nacional para a Independência Total de Angola (the National Union for the Total Independence of Angola, or UNITA) around an Ovimbundu core, and with Chinese aid, in March 1966.[54] Zambia-based UNITA remained the weakest of the major Angolan nationalist parties, but the racial component that Savimbi used strategically in party diplomacy helped it displace the FNLA as a popular international alternative to the MPLA by the early 1970s (see Chapter 8).

Roberto's laser focus on maintaining his personal power also weakened ties to sympathetic U.S. groups, pushing the Lusophone solidarity movement to its lowest point. George Houser tried to keep ACOA above the fray but could not avoid the internal conflicts. As tensions developed with Savimbi, Roberto accused the internationally well-connected SARA medical branch of disloyalty. Working with SARA via ACOA sponsorship was a Canadian physician named Ian Gilchrist, who grew up as a missionary's child in the Congo and strongly supported African independence. Returning in early 1963 to work with the FNLA, Gilchrist offered Houser a firsthand look at Roberto's erratic behavior and the collapse of the once promising movement.[55] He confirmed reports of paranoid and ethnocentric politics that were fracturing the party. Political purges gutted the medical wing of the FNLA to the point that in 1964 the Red Cross ended its refugee assistance, which was one of the party's most important sources of foreign aid.[56] When the head of SARA joined Savimbi in fleeing the party, Gilchrest worried for his own safety.

The period did serious damage to the international reputation of the FNLA, from which it never fully recovered. As he prepared to leave the Congo in late 1964, Gilchrist warned Houser that it had become a party of "bandits, thieves, and scoundrels" and that Roberto no longer represented the Angolan people.[57] Hinting at the Cold War blinders that still constrained U.S. activism, Houser refused to abandon Roberto because he saw "no alternative" to the FNLA, but he had difficulty defending the man he had worked with for nearly a decade.[58] The events of 1964 forced ACOA and its church allies to confront the flaws of Roberto's organization, inspiring a radio silence between the revolutionary and his U.S. partners that lasted two years.[59] Never fully committed to an inclusive Angolan identity, Roberto used racial appeals to sideline the MPLA, only to see his own party splinter. The nationalist movement in the most important and visible of Portugal's colonies was irreparably fractured. And since Angola was the center of international debate over Lisbon's empire, the collapse of the nationalist rebellion implied to all but the most astute outside observers a resounding victory for Portuguese imperialism.

Eduardo Mondlane, FRELIMO, and
the Rise of the CONCP Parties

The decline of the FNLA was offset by the emergence of revolutions in Portugal's other mainland colonies. Both were led by parties associated with the CONCP, with Amílcar Cabral's PAIGC launching a militant struggle in Guinea-Bissau in January 1963 and the Frente de Libertação de Moçambique (Mozambique Liberation Front, or FRELIMO) following in September 1964. African and Eastern states provided the weapons needed to wage these struggles, but the parties never abandoned their attempts to win over Western opinion. They continued to see the isolation of Portugal as a vital component in addressing the power discrepancies between metropole and colonies. The formation of FRELIMO in 1962 and the selection of U.S.-educated Eduardo Mondlane opened a new era in constructing transatlantic relations, gradually building an identification with the socialist parties. These efforts—both military and diplomatic—elicited limited contemporary and scholarly attention given the global focus on Angola, but it would be these struggles and international identification with them that weakened Portugal and built an effective political movement.

FRELIMO became the vital link connecting the CONCP to U.S. activists and, in the process, undermining dominant Cold War political narratives. It formed in the Tanganyikan capital Dar es Salaam in 1962 as a merger of multiple exiled nationalist parties that were established outside Mozambique. The president of newly independent Tanganyika (Tanzania after 1964), Julius Nyerere, supported independence in his southern neighbor but insisted that any Mozambican independence movement operating within his country represent a united front. Among the founding parties was the National Democratic Union of Mozambique under the leadership of Marcelino dos Santos, a veteran of the Casa dos Estudantes do Império (House for Colonial Students) and the longtime secretary of the CONCP.[60] He was a key figure in the new party, serving as foreign secretary and helping to instill a strong socialist sentiment that became progressively more prominent over the years. Dos Santos's membership also aligned FRELIMO with the CONCP, completing the core triumvirate alongside the PAIGC and the MPLA. Yet FRELIMO's founding parties looked outside their ranks when they chose their new president to avoid the internecine conflicts that scuttled Angolan unity while seeking new sources of international support.

The solution was Eduardo Mondlane, a tall, balding Mozambican who worked with the United Nations and as a professor of sociology at Syracuse University. A natural leader with a genial personality, he was respected by many within FRELIMO's founding parties but tied narrowly to none. Of equal if not greater importance were his diplomatic credentials developed during the ten years he spent living in the United States. As Dos Santos recalled, the party elected the "American" professor due in no small part to his "connections and influence abroad."[61] Like its CONCP allies, FRELIMO understood the revolution as a global struggle that demanded the participation and assistance of outside actors, and Mondlane was the best resource for navigating competing international rivalries.[62] Outreach to the East and Global South were aided by shared histories of anti-imperialism, but the West required a different approach, at least at first. Mondlane thus helped FRELIMO translate its goals for militant, anti-imperial revolution into terms more amenable to Western audiences—global justice, equality, and even human rights. Mondlane "was able to speak for us the language of other men," one party member later explained, "the language of the diplomats, the language of the universities, and the language of power."[63]

Mondlane understood how to operate in the United States and the broader Western world because he was deeply familiar with U.S. culture, down to a personal affection for baseball and Sunday football. Born in 1920, the son of a Tsonga chief, Mondlane came to the United States for training as a religious leader in 1951.[64] Educated in a Swiss Missionary School, he had drifted toward nationalist agitation while studying social work in South Africa, where he was "struck by the contradiction between the Christian training I had received and the cruelty of the whites."[65] Forced to leave after the implementation of apartheid, Mondlane's activism in Mozambique invited unwanted colonial attention.[66] In response, Swiss missionaries worked with the National Council of Churches (NCC) to arrange for Mondlane to spend a year studying in Lisbon, where he met many future CONCP members, then finished his undergraduate education at Oberlin University in Ohio. Mondlane married a young American woman he met at a religious retreat before earning a doctorate from Northwestern University under anthropologist Melville Herskovits. After rejecting an offer to teach in Lisbon that reeked of imperial co-optation, he researched trust territories for the United Nations from 1957 to 1961, which allowed him to freely travel as he worked on anti-colonial issues—including a return to Mozambique.[67]

Mondlane spent his time in the United States cultivating anti-colonial solidarity. He used Protestant networks to champion African independence, addressing conferences, congregations, and spiritual retreats throughout the 1950s. His speeches connected domestic struggles for equality with international ones for self-determination.[68] Mondlane believed that personal testament and careful framing provided the foundations for meaningful popular support, remarking, "American public opinion tends to be predominantly sympathetic to almost any desires for political freedom manifested by the colonial peoples of empire other than their own." While he understood that there were limitations to the U.S. commitment to decolonization, Mondlane believed that the country's anti-colonial heritage, democratic traditions, and reverence for an often secularized Christian ethic provided the foundations for transnational cooperation. He argued that the domestic movement for equal rights should adopt a more international perspective that integrated support for Portuguese African self-determination.[69] Mondlane's global vision of social justice resonated with Western audiences, and he moved beyond the churches to form strong relationships with ACOA and civil rights leaders.[70]

Mondlane's conception of national liberation bridged the gap between Christian activism and the socialist nationalism that informed FRELIMO's political program. His ideas of social justice evolved from a universal understanding of Christian ethics paired with an African communalist tradition, which provided the foundation for his belief in nationalism and economic equity.[71] He valued democracy, but his communalist notions made him deeply skeptical of capitalism, which he viewed as the foundation for exploitation and empire in ways that paralleled Marxist worldviews. He sympathized with socialism even if he remained wary of Soviet communism, and he dismissed U.S. anti-communism as reactionary. His socialist leanings grew over time, but he identified from the beginning with the strong anti-imperial programs developing in independent Africa. "We want our government to reflect the spirit of modern Africa ... based on the principle of one man, one vote," he told one Western researcher. "If you look at the structure of Tanganyika and Ghana you will have some idea of the economic system of the new Mozambique."[72] While revolutionary in the sense that he wanted rapid transformation to self-rule, Mondlane initially embraced Gandhian nonviolent activism, arguing with a youthful Andrew Young that it was a powerful tool in the activist arsenal despite the future civil rights leader's own misgivings.[73] His hope that international pressure could compel Portugal to negotiate lasted well into the

1960s, but Salazar's intransigence compelled him to approve preparations for a military campaign shortly after FRELIMO's formation. Mondlane's success operating in the United States and Europe owed much to this ability to articulate a radical vision of liberation in a language accessible to U.S. audiences, providing an alternative to Portuguese rule based on an expansive vision of human rights at a time when the term remained fluid in Western discourse.

Mondlane believed that the key to gaining Western support was to disconnect decolonization from the Cold War. FRELIMO made "a tremendous effort," a party member later recalled, "to depolarize the issue of the liberation struggle."[74] The pertinent issues were ones of racial and international justice rather than geopolitics. Cold War neutrality and independence were common strategies used by the CONCP parties, but FRELIMO kept a greater distance from the Soviet Union even as it worked with independent communist states such as China and Yugoslavia.[75] This positioned FRELIMO to sell itself as the kind of nationalist party that U.S. officials desired. Here was a united front representing peoples from across Mozambique, led by a moderate, rhetorically judicious leader with a commitment to nonviolence who seemed willing to negotiate with Portuguese authorities. Mondlane was such a model nationalist that the State Department produced a fawning profile while he was still a professor at Syracuse.[76] His relations with Washington officials were sufficiently close for him to give them warning of his plans to enter nationalist politics, assuring them months before his election as FRELIMO president that he remained committed to a negotiated transition of power.[77] If the United States was ever going to pressure Portugal to accommodate nationalist demands, FRELIMO was the ideal partner.

Yet even Mondlane could not arrest the American slide. Using his connections, he was able to arrange a secret meeting in 1963 with Attorney General Robert Kennedy, who praised the Mozambican as "a terrifically impressive fellow."[78] Mondlane's requests for official assistance for FRELIMO's educational and medical efforts in Tanzania aligned with U.S. priorities, but President Kennedy wanted to avoid making a grand gesture when Mozambique remained a tangential issue in U.S.-Portuguese relations.[79] Instead, the Ford Foundation provided a hundred thousand dollars to found the Mozambique Institute in Tanzania, likely as a result of unofficial government requests to the foundation's director, former diplomat and Kennedy adviser John McCloy.[80] The institute was the first substantial FRELIMO institution and became an exile hub for education and social services that informed later efforts in liberated territories, but the way in which it was indirectly funded fell far short of Mondlane's hope that the United States would reassert its official position favoring Portuguese decolonization.[81] Only months after Mondlane met with Bobby Kennedy, he was complaining to American friends, including George Houser, about his deep frustrations with U.S. policy, which he considered barely different from that of European allies.[82] "All along these powers have been expressing their sympathies for the rights of self-determination of the colonial peoples of Africa, but when occasion was offered for demonstrating this in a concrete form they balked," Mondlane complained to a U.S audience in September 1963. "[Britain, France, and the United States] hide behind a screen of pretty words when they should be taking positive action in support of the people's struggle for freedom."[83]

With possibilities for meaningful Western support disappearing, Mondlane accepted the necessity of armed revolution, bringing him into closer coordination with his CONCP allies. The PAIGC pioneered this path in January of 1963, when it infiltrated troops into the northern part of Guinea-Bissau after three years of training and preparations led from the party's exile headquarters in neighboring Guinea. Like Mondlane, Cabral claimed to prefer a negotiated route but felt obliged to pursue armed revolution because Portugal and her allies made it necessary. Bracketing events in Angola, Lisbon's violent crackdown of striking workers at Bissau's Pidjiguiti docks in 1959 and the success of the Algerian Revolution convinced Cabral that "armed struggle is the necessary corollary to the impossibility of resolving this conflict through the ballot (voix politique)."[84] While the FRELIMO president's nonviolent principles were more deeply ingrained, he ultimately concluded that the events surrounding Angola and Goa in 1961 "harden[ed] the Portuguese government."[85] Negotiations and the eventual transfer of power would occur only if the nationalists could lessen the power disparities between themselves and Portugal, which allowed Lisbon to dictate terms. Mondlane therefore approved FRELIMO preparations for armed revolt, even as he exhausted alternative options. With their CONCP ally fighting in Guinea and Western states making their peace with Lisbon, FRELIMO militants agitated for action in Mozambique. Mondlane finally relented in September 1964, sending a small band of guerrilla troops into Cabo Delgado, the northernmost coastal province in the Y-shaped colony. While the FNLA collapsed and the MPLA regrouped in Brazzaville, the CONCP parties forced Portugal into a three-front war.

African nationalists like Mondlane were clearly growing disillusioned with the United States even before John Kennedy's assassination placed Lyndon Johnson atop a largely identical administration that continued old policies

Figure 3. Nationalist leaders address the Second CONCP Conference, held in Dar es
Salaam in October 1965. From left to right are Amália Fonseca (PAIGC), Amílcar Cabral (PAIGC), unclear (listed as Aquino de Bragança), Eduardo Mondlane
(FRELIMO), Agostinho Neto (MPLA), and Marcelino dos Santos (FRELIMO). To
highlight connections with leftist revolutions across Africa, other sessions included
participation by Congolese rebel Gaston Soumialot, Zanzibar's Mohamed Babu, and
Algeria's Houari Boumediene. FMSMB/Arquivo Mário Pinto de Andrade.

with fewer rhetorical flourishes. Less personally invested in foreign policy than
his predecessor, Johnson nonetheless revisited the economic inducements that
the State Department hoped would woo Portugal toward greater reform but
did not commit much energy to new initiatives while Salazar remained difficult and Angola quiet. The administration formalized the Kennedy desire to
effectively wait out the aging dictator, seeing little likelihood of changing the
status quo even with the emerging colonial revolutions. Intelligence reports
dismissed FRELIMO's struggle as "limited and ultraclandestine" due to "public apathy" and a disparity of military forces, citing an earlier argument from
Mondlane that such a struggle was practically hopeless.[86] On the other hand,
the CIA marveled at the "surprising" health of the Portuguese economy and

the stability of Salazar's regime, contending that while decolonization was inevitable it would not happen in the near term.[87] Ceding greater authority to Europhile geostrategists like National Security Adviser McGeorge Bundy and Undersecretary of State George Ball, the Johnson administration urged moderate African states to avoid supporting nationalist revolutions and criticized countries like Guinea and Congo (Brazzaville) that openly aided them.[88]

These frustrations did not mean that the CONCP nationalists abandoned their appeals to the West even as they reconsidered the best approach for building U.S. support. In one example, the lack of official response to Cabral's cable urging Kennedy to denounce Portugal's use of napalm bombs fabricated in the United States, sent just days before Kennedy's assassination, did not erase the PAIGC leader's belief in the "great people of the USA principles of liberty, democracy, and anti-colonial, anti-racist policy."[89] The CONCP party leaderships continued to believe that popular Western opinion leaned in their favor.[90] The problem was convincing countries like the United States to adopt policies that would actually weaken Portugal without a crisis demanding national attention. The nationalists needed a concerted effort to change the strategic calculation of the U.S. government, a popular or congressional campaign that could overcome the Cold War mindset and embrace decolonization as positive action and the CONCP parties as the necessary agents of change.[91] Mondlane and his allies therefore urged "all Americans who are concerned with freedom and democracy not to wait until all is confusion, but to act ahead of events."[92] Yet the events of the previous years demonstrated that the same liberal Cold War view of the world that led government officials to make peace with Lisbon also constrained sympathetic activists from launching a more assertive campaign in support of Lusophone African freedom. As an exasperated Mondlane told the ANLCA, U.S. policy would only change if pro-liberation sympathizers stopped "acting within the acceptable lines, typical of the American bourgeois."[93]

The period from 1962 to 1965 witnessed the decline of official U.S. interest in promoting decolonization in Portuguese Africa but also began a dramatic shift in the global image of Lusophone African nationalism. The White House reluctantly accepted Portugal after the Lisbon government demonstrated its ability to hold its position in Africa. Pro-liberation allies in the United States such as ACOA tried fruitlessly to stop this drift, but vague sentiments favoring decolonization proved insufficient after the moment of crisis passed. The Pan-African solidarity that motivated the ANLCA proved too shallow to mobilize serious support. By 1965, the generally optimistic George

Houser advised African nationalists to save their meager resources rather than traveling to Washington, since the likelihood of successfully lobbying the government was almost nil.[94] This confirmed nationalist frustrations with Western politics. With Portugal refusing negotiations and its allies unwilling to pressure the Salazar government, extended guerrilla wars became the only method to end Portuguese colonialism. Angola remained the most widely recognized Portuguese colony and the economic powerhouse of the empire, but the center of liberation shifted to Guinea-Bissau and Mozambique. The CONCP's political and social revolutions depended on support from Eastern states and radical African states, but they kept avenues for Western support open. Mondlane's FRELIMO took the lead even as the moderate instincts that made him so attractive to government officials gave way to more assertive visions of revolution that more closely aligned him with the CONCP leadership. Importantly, the social aspects of the revolution gained greater attention as the PAIGC and FRELIMO liberated new territories, allowing for continued humanist appeals across the North-South divide that gradually expanded U.S. support as new events focused political and popular attention on southern Africa.

CHAPTER 4

Fighting for Southern Africa

By 1964, the armed struggles in Guinea-Bissau and Mozambique had opened two new fronts in the contest over Portuguese imperialism, and the right to majority rule in southern Africa more broadly. Portugal and neighboring white minority governments did not meekly accept events, forging a clandestine alliance to stanch the spread of African independence. This powerful resistance was dramatized by the Unilateral Declaration of Independence (UDI) of Southern Rhodesia from Britain in 1965. The new white minority government in Salisbury (now Harare) used its position between colonial Mozambique and Angola to erect a barrier against decolonization along the Zambezi River. The result was a stark demarcation of two competing camps, with revolutionary African independence struggles headlined by the CONCP parties combating Portugal, South Africa, and what was now simply called Rhodesia—an alliance popularly known as the White Redoubt.

Both sides recognized the necessity for international support. The White Redoubt states promoted the same anti-communist defense of Western culture used by Portugal, bolstering support among U.S. segregationists thanks to the white racial appeal of the minority regimes. Portugal proved a double beneficiary of these efforts, seeing an expansion of grassroots energy thanks to its association with the White Redoubt while receiving favored treatment from government officials who tried desperately to pry Lisbon away from the rogue Rhodesian government. The result was a gradual normalization of relations with Portugal that peaked after the election of Richard Nixon as president in 1968. The CONCP parties relied on African and Eastern arms to wage their wars, but they maintained an interest in weakening Portugal's Euro-American base of support. Recognizing that Westerners were uneasy with the tactics of militant revolt, they emphasized the constructive aspects of their revolutions that pioneered new social relations in liberated territories. These efforts were meant primarily to sell the revolutions to local peoples, but they positioned the parties as governments-in-waiting that could appeal to Westerners eager for alternatives to Portuguese colonialism and white minority governance. The result was an expansion of official interest at the margins, notably among legislators eager to rethink U.S. foreign policy as it stumbled into the quagmire of Vietnam. Familiar Cold War tropes and unsubtle appeals to Western cultural superiority won early support for the White Redoubt, but the liberation movements found sufficient interest from a handful of officials to maintain their belief that grassroots diplomacy might eventually change U.S. policies.

Revolution at the Margins

With Angolan nationalists feuding, it was the struggles in Guinea and Mozambique that challenged Portuguese rule, but the parties needed to show success to expand their revolutions. While progress was not linear and internal dissent flared intermittently, both the PAIGC and FRELIMO made headway as the 1960s progressed. They did so by utilizing assistance from African and Eastern countries. As they began liberating territory, their revolutions became the leading edge of the tricontinental challenge to the international system, aligning them with similar leftist revolts in Cuba, Vietnam, and elsewhere. These revolutions gained additional legitimacy thanks to the formalization of the White Redoubt after Rhodesia's UDI halted the momentum of decolonization. The unprecedented actions by Rhodesia, and the tacit support it received from Portugal and South Africa, demonstrated why armed struggle was necessary in Africa. As the most active revolutionary parties on the continent, FRELIMO and the PAIGC became the standard bearers opposing this White Redoubt, helping to define two opposing camps who battled militarily and diplomatically for the future of majority rule in Africa.

Central to growth of diplomatic success of the PAIGC and FRELIMO was their ability to wage successful revolutions. They used exile bases in Guinea-Conakry and Tanzania to infiltrate troops into Guinea-Bissau and Mozambique, respectively. Initially, military assistance came from revolutionary African states, with Egypt and Algeria providing arms and training. As the revolutions showed signs of success, additional aid came from the East. Arms-exporting Czechoslovakia provided early assistance to the PAIGC, with Soviet aid increasing after 1965 as the armed struggle gained ground. FRELIMO depended more on China due to shared relationships with Tanzania, but it eventually developed relationships with several Eastern bloc states. While Mondlane and the Soviet Union held mutual suspicions of each other, FRELIMO received arms and other military support from Bulgaria, Czechoslovakia, Hungary, and—in all likelihood—Romania.[1] Still, the nationalists remained independent, seeing themselves not so much as part of a world communist revolution as a tricontinental one that extended and expanded upon this older formula to meet the needs of the Global South. As Cabral explained to a Soviet audience, "We changed the names and adapted the discourse to the essential reality of the history of our day: the struggle for life against imperialism."[2] This placed the CONCP parties at the forefront of a new kind of revolutionary movement in Africa.

The PAIGC rapidly gained territory after launching its armed struggle in 1963, mostly in the rural inland areas between the Guinea-Conakry and Senegalese borders, where Portuguese settlement was light. The army consisted mostly of Guineans armed with Eastern weapons, led by a heavily Cabo Verdean leadership trained abroad in China, the Soviet Union, Ghana, and North Africa.[3] Guinea was not the most important colony, but Salazar built the Estado Novo on the idea of an indivisible multi-continental state, so any defeat would echo across the empire. This was in fact part of PAIGC strategy. While aiming to liberate both Guinea and the islands of Cabo Verde, the mainland offered better military prospects than the isolated archipelago, and the hope was that a victory there would force a broader reassessment of Portuguese imperialism. This was the general logic of the CONCP alliance: progress in one or two theaters of war would improve the prospects for freedom for all the member parties. The PAIGC's success therefore made it a rallying point both for Lusophone and southern African freedom struggles more broadly. Historian Patrick Chabal estimates that PAIGC liberated roughly half of Guinea by 1966, with pressure on Portugal's increasingly isolated holdings building as the decade wore on.[4] Portugal responded by sending a large, comparatively well-equipped army to fight a protracted guerrilla war in the tiny colony. To combat the influx of Eastern arms, Portugal—unable to "even manufacture toy airplanes," Cabral quipped—skirted the porous Anglo-American embargoes by buying matériel from Western allies on the open market and quietly transferring resources earmarked for NATO commitments.[5] American-made boats and planes, French helicopters, and German small arms defended the empire against a slowly emerging alliance between Global East and South.[6]

In Mozambique, FRELIMO also made substantial gains, though less consistently than the PAIGC. After a failed nationwide revolt, the party focused its efforts in Niassa and Cabo Delgado, the less densely populated north-eastern provinces of the colony, which lay closest to its bases in Tanzania.[7] FRELIMO faced internal struggles as it managed this effort, with notable examples revolving around frustration with Mondlane's constant diplomatic travel and the role played by his white American wife, Janet, at the Mozambique Institute. A brief upheaval in 1967 strained relations with Tanzania, but Mondlane's consolidation of party leadership eased tensions and strengthened military efforts, including opening a new front in the northwestern province of Tete. By 1968, FRELIMO claimed to hold 20 percent of the country, home to one in seven Mozambicans.[8] That same year, Mondlane held FRELIMO's Second Party Congress in liberated territory.

The loss of ground in Portugal's second-largest colony and its difficulties pacifying tiny Guinea-Bissau threatened the narrative of a stable empire but did not destroy it. Lisbon controlled the major cities and airspace across its colonies, and Angola remained quiet, thanks in large part to FNLA-MPLA infighting. Because Western diplomats judged conditions primarily through an Angolan lens, with some attention to the colonial capitals, they judged any transfer of power unlikely in the short term.[9] But the liberation parties were winning and holding territory, while Portugal's debts ballooned with no end to the fighting in sight. Equally troubling to Lisbon was the fact that as FRELIMO and the PAIGC freed territory, they built new social, educational, and economic programs that contrasted their socialist programs with the underdeveloped imperial infrastructure that offered few benefits in the rural areas where the parties wielded power. The parties used these activities to claim status as governments-in-waiting, providing a concrete articulation of their socialist ideologies that they sold to international audiences (see below).

Military success raised the profiles of the CONCP parties as they became the African embodiments of the revolutionary impulse spreading across the Global South. This fact helps explain why these struggles fit awkwardly into the historiography of African decolonization; they were bridges between the first generation of Global South nationalists that feature in most histories and the radical tricontinental generation that took aim at broader imperial practices associated with U.S. hegemony and neocolonialism.[10] While the parties depended on the postcolonial governments of Guinea and Tanzania for refuge, their leaders identified with countries like North Vietnam and Cuba, who found themselves in conflict with the United States and other Western nations in pursuit of broader definitions of ideological and economic self-determination.[11] This made particular sense from the nationalist perspective given Portugal's dependence on its NATO allies for military and financial support. Rather than simply combating Portugal, the parties were fighting the wider Western alliance and the international system it underwrote. These tricontinental connections earned the CONCP parties new recognition and invitations to major international conferences, establishing their identity as "authentic" revolutionary movements in contrast to U.S.-associated groups like the FNLA. In one notable example, all three sent representatives to the January 1966 Tricontinental Conference hosted by the Cuban government in Havana, where Cabral presented his famous "Weapon of Theory" speech that articulated a practical relationship between political and cultural anti-imperialism. The event dramatically raised the PAIGC's status while defining a broad vision of Lusophone revolution in which military struggles would construct new national identities that could achieve political, economic, and cultural independence from Euro-American influence.[12]

The increased prominence of the PAIGC and FRELIMO benefited the MPLA. Despite lacking the military success present in other colonies, the Angolan party's profile grew in tandem with those of its CONCP allies. One notable example was recognition from the Organization of African Unity's (OAU) Liberation Committee, which provided funds to the individual nationalist groups that it felt were best positioned to challenge European imperialism and govern independent states. At the OAU's founding in 1963, its preferred partners included the PAIGC, FRELIMO, and the FNLA. After the CONCP parties and their state benefactors lobbied on its behalf, the MPLA received recognition in late 1964 alongside the increasingly unstable FNLA.[13] Donations to the MPLA increased in each subsequent year as respect for the CONCP alliance grew and Roberto's party faded. As international support grew, the MPLA sought to restart its revolution and prove its bona fides. It used Eastern arms to launch new operations, building a small but effective military group in Angola's oil-rich exclave of Cabinda. In 1968, the FNLA received no funds from the OAU, and three years later the African organization withdrew its recognition of the party's government in exile.[14] As revolutionary success expanded international recognition, the MPLA expressed confidence that the nationalists would continue gaining "sympathy from governments in Africa and the world, while Portugal gets more and more isolated and aggravates the contradictions between the NATO countries that support the fascist government of Salazar."[15] By the late 1960s, much of the world considered the CONCP parties as synonymous with Lusophone African nationalism and—as the most successful ongoing revolutions in the region—the leading resistance to colonialism and minority rule that afflicted the southern third of the continent.

The White Redoubt

The CONCP parties' active opposition to European rule became especially vital as events challenged the presumed inevitability of decolonization. In November 1965, the white-led government of Southern Rhodesia unilaterally declared its independence from the United Kingdom, completing a barrier of white resistance that stretched almost uninterrupted across the continent from Angola to Mozambique. The event was the product of more than a decade of tensions between Britain and its land-locked settler colony, which looked on suspiciously as the metropole dissolved its imperial holdings. With racial tensions worsening, Britain's repeated attempts failed to find a solution acceptable to Rhodesia's white settlers and the Black majorities that surrounded them.[16] The U.K. government finally bowed to pressure, granting independence to Nyasaland (Malawi) and Northern Rhodesia (Zambia) in 1964 and beginning the process for its southern African protectorates. Nestled between these states, the minority government in Salisbury (modern Harare) broke with Britain in an attempt to preserve white control of Southern Rhodesia. This decision occurred with the tacit understanding that independent Rhodesia had regional allies in Portugal and South Africa. For nationalists like Amílcar Cabral, Rhodesian UDI showed the "complicity of the old and new enemies of the people of Africa and [was], in effect, a declaration of war."[17]

UDI effectively formalized a tripartite bulwark against decolonization. Vital rail links and regular labor exchanges already linked Portugal's colonies with the white settler states. In the 1950s, Salazar identified these relationships as potential refuges in the face of rising African nationalism, doubling down on them when Britain and the United States proved unreliable allies in 1961. He secretly expanded ties with the settler governments while keeping enough distance to convince Anglo-American diplomats that Portugal did not hold a formal alliance. From early 1962, Portugal embraced "the possibility and the advantage of concluding with these countries secret military pacts local, mutual assistance, and forms of economic co-operation to be regulated by bilateral treaties."[18] Salazar also indirectly defended Southern Rhodesia as early as 1963 while praising its leaders for rejecting Black nationalist demands.[19] Both South Africa and Portugal had good reason to keep these relationships quiet: Pretoria avoided outright alignment with Europe's last empire (and later rogue Rhodesia) as it sought to claim identity as an African state, while Lisbon distanced itself from apartheid and minority rule. Yet such independence was a diplomatic fiction. Military historian Luís Barroso notes that Portuguese informational and military cooperation with Pretoria accelerated after the Angolan rebellion, and discussions of sharing information across all three states increased after FRELIMO launched its revolution in Mozambique, which bordered Southern Rhodesia and South Africa. Cooperation became more institutionalized in the early 1970s as rebellions against Portugal and Rhodesia grew.[20]

The formalization of this White Redoubt after Rhodesian UDI triggered deep anxieties within the United States, providing Portugal with an opportunity. Since 1961, government officials had worried that central and southern Africa could devolve into racial conflict, and part of American hesitance to openly criticize Portugal had been an attempt to avoid pushing it "into the arms of South Africa," as Prime Minister Macmillan had warned Kennedy.[21] The United States therefore joined Britain in attempting to rein in Rhodesia without exacerbating the regional situation. The countries encouraged the U.N. Security Council to pass a pair of resolutions in November 1965 condemning the "usurpation of power by a racist settler minority," which called on member states to break economic relations with Rhodesia, especially the importation of oil and petroleum.[22] But Britain feared stoking confrontation with South Africa, so the resolutions lacked coercive power, and enforcement of the economic embargo depended on the cooperation of the surrounding states.[23] Portugal, which controlled the vital oil-importing ports of Beira and Lourenço Marques, joined Pretoria in resisting U.N. actions. Unwilling to start a shooting war with either state, Prime Minister Harold Wilson wagered the future of British policy on the slight possibility that he could convince Portugal or South Africa to change policies, with the former being seen as the most likely candidate.[24] This tactic became central to an Anglo-American courting of the Lisbon government that further improved relations even as it did little to clamp down on Rhodesia.

Portugal played a double game, protecting Rhodesia while winning concessions from the United States and the United Kingdom. In January 1966, Portugal announced that it would keep Mozambican ports open to Rhodesian traffic despite international condemnation. Weeks later, a South African special envoy reported on Salazar's logic: "It is important that Portugal and

South Africa form and present a 'united front.' He did not properly suggest an alliance. But a firm solidarity by both on the Rhodesian question, discouraging those who would take drastic actions against [our] two countries. . . . We should be prepared for a conflict with England and the United States; not an armed conflict, but an open conflict with these two countries."[25] Still, Portugal publicly opposed "white racist" governance when corresponding with Western diplomats, giving them false hope that Salazar might be swayed.[26] Though frustrated by Portugal's two-faced diplomacy, Anglo-American officials agreed that wooing Portugal was the best in a series of bad options. London wholly abandoned its already muted pressure for Portuguese colonial reform, while President Johnson's speech in 1965 positioning the United States against minority rule in Africa pointedly avoided mention of Portugal's colonies.[27] As Dean Rusk explained a year into the standoff, "We need Portuguese assistance in order to help the British achieve success in restoring constitutional rule in Rhodesia."[28] While nationalists fumed over U.S. ambivalence, there was less consternation from independent African states, who worried more about the expansion of white minority rule than the continuation of an anachronistic colonialism.[29] Portugal actually gained diplomatic breathing room at the moment when early success for the revolutions in Guinea and Mozambique began raising pressure within the empire.

While Johnson's strong stand on Rhodesia seemed to maintain or even expand U.S. alignment with decolonization, the reality was more complicated. It evolved from support for the policies of a European ally and assiduously avoided serious confrontation. By the time of Rhodesia's UDI in 1965, the U.S. commitment to the Vietnam War was rapidly mounting and monopolizing White House attention. At the same time, the last vocally pro-African members of the administration either left or were reassigned, with Soapy Williams finally departing in early 1966 after years of increasing marginalization.[30] With troops deploying to Southeast Asia, a new Cold War battlefield in Africa would tax U.S. resources. Johnson's advisers recommended a swift diplomatic conclusion to the Rhodesian crisis and increased reliance on European partners to manage the region.[31] While Portugal was a problematic partner at best, there was little appetite to push the envelope. When the United Nations approved coercive measures, including the right to blockade Beira in April 1966, Britain consciously avoided hostilities, with full U.S. support.[32] Both countries, along with key allies like Zambia's Kenneth Kaunda, prioritized avoidance of regional war over Rhodesian compliance. As Portuguese diplomats wryly remarked to their South African allies, the United

States understood that "Vietnam was enough."[33] Having decided to embrace Portugal as an ally in managing the tense politics of southern Africa, U.S. diplomats could do little besides make excuses. "The multiracial ideal as an ideal (rather than as an established reality—which it is not)," the American ambassador in Lisbon concluded in mid-1967, "would seem to be a healthy alternative to black racism or apartheid."[34]

After beginning with the *annus horribilis* of 1961, Portugal ended the decade in a position of surprising strength. This was most dramatically illustrated by the smooth transition of power from Salazar to Marcello Caetano after the aging dictator was incapacitated in September 1968, dying two years later at the age of 81. A onetime Salazar protégé with a reputation as a reformer, Caetano softened some of his predecessor's harder edges, but the empire remained central to his renamed *Estado Social*. Decisions to reorganize the PIDE secret police and allow nominal electoral participation for opposition parties sought to change foreign perceptions of the regime. But rather than making serious reforms to colonial administration, Caetano doubled down on the lusotropical justification of empire while making overtures to the West.[35] He wanted to reposition Portugal as a willing partner in the Western political project without sacrificing the empire. The surprisingly smooth transition to the post-Salazar Estado Social and Caetano's amenable leadership fed U.S. desires to work with Portugal after the Rhodesian crisis, setting the stage for an era of increased cooperation just as Richard Nixon prepared to enter the White House in January 1969.

U.S. critics were shell-shocked by the Portuguese transition. The assumption that Salazar's passing would remove the final roadblock to decolonization allowed many pro-African policymakers to avoid making what Senator Edmund Muskie called the "tough choice" between their Portuguese ally and its alternatives.[36] Caetano's quick succession and unwavering commitment to the colonial wars created an inflection point that caught pro-African officials flat-footed while providing a willing partner for Europhile proponents of a more managed transition. Caetano cultivated this support by opening negotiations on the Azores and loosening restrictions on foreign economic investment in the colonies. Portuguese officials believed that such investment opened new income streams to support the costly wars while entangling Western allies in the colonies, but U.S. officials heralded such ties as a path to winning Portugal away from the minority regimes.[37] This American logic eventually evolved into Ronald Reagan's constructive engagement policy toward South Africa more than a decade later. By 1970, Portugal was profiting from Gulf Oil's discovery of offshore deposits near Angola and began working with European firms to construct a massive hydroelectric dam in Mozambique.

As the 1960s drew to a close, there was a clear division emerging between two competing forces. On one side, the merger of Portuguese colonial interests and the expansion of white minority governance from South Africa to Rhodesia created a White Redoubt that provided a powerful check on decolonizing momentum. Anglo-American diplomats differentiated Portugal from the minority regimes—and offered concessions to reinforce this hoped-for divide—but there was little doubt where Portugal cast its lot. This White Redoubt collaborated against liberation movements in Africa while coordinating diplomacy to win over distracted, divided Western governments. On the other side, the leftist liberation parties of the CONCP were committed to military struggles and were integrating themselves within broad anti-imperial networks that focused on Southern revolution but depended on Eastern arms. Their positions fighting the White Redoubt allowed them to claim the mantle of African revolution better than South Africa's exiled African National Congress (ANC) or the nascent Zimbabwean revolts, with the West African PAIGC earning regular inclusion among discussions of southern African liberation. These parties offered alternatives to Western officials, who chose more familiar allies to preserve a regional stability that proved increasingly elusive as the two competing camps entered a global competition for hearts and minds.

Beyond the Tar Baby Option

The end of the decade represented the nadir of U.S. Africa policy. The Nixon administration that entered the White House in January 1969 sidelined the ideological promotion of decolonization in favor of a realist view of power politics, in which the African continent was at best a distraction. In collaboration with influential National Security Adviser Henry Kissinger, Nixon sought to use problematic allies to assure regional stability. Nixon viewed South Africa as reliable check on Soviet ambitions on the continent and was openly sympathetic to Portugal, having assured Minister of Foreign Affairs Franco Nogueira amid his wilderness years in 1963 that independence was "not the best thing for Africa or the Africans."[38] Outwardly, State Department diplomats continued to speak of self-determination, but their policies aimed to shore up the alliances with Portugal and South Africa while accepting the status quo with Rhodesia. Shortly after Nixon was inaugurated in January 1969, the White House issued a directive ending all contacts with nationalists, though the CIA defended Roberto's retainer. Nixon also sought to encourage improved high-level dialogue, meeting with both Caetano and Nogueira in his first few months in office. Both conversations sought to assure the Portuguese that Luso-American relations had finally turned the page.[39] At one White House celebration in honor of the twentieth anniversary of NATO, Nixon (possibly intoxicated) grasped Nogueira by the shoulders and promised, "I'll never do to you what Kennedy did."[40]

It was in this context that the Nixon administration formalized its southern African policy, articulated most famously in National Security Study Memorandum (NSSM) 39, the document that diplomat Anthony Lake critically dubbed the "Tar Baby Option."[41] Faced with a variety of options, Kissinger and Nixon chose to extend the logic that justified cooperation with Portugal and South Africa to the entirety of the region. In a global context where the United States faced a great-power conflict with the Soviet Union contextualized by myriad regional crises, Portugal and the southern African white minority regimes were invaluable pro-Western resources on a continent where U.S. interests were secondary at best. With parties like FRELIMO and the ANC weak or exiled, Lisbon and Pretoria seemed unlikely to suffer defeat, even if the wars showed no signs of abating. Kissinger and Nixon embraced the predictability of unpopular stability, concluding that the increased corporate and diplomatic ties that the Johnson administration accepted offered paths for encouraging political and economic liberalization while maintaining good relations with the regimes. The United States therefore began a "relaxation" of existing policy, "broadening the scope of [its] relations and contacts gradually and to some degree in response to tangible—albeit small and gradual—moderation of white policies."[42] Nixon would not align openly with the outmoded value systems of his allies, but neither was the president's team interested in expending limited diplomatic capital to achieve moral victories with few immediate geopolitical benefits. Nixon summarized his view succinctly in a staff meeting in late 1969: "It is obvious that we have to avoid the colonialist label but we must analyze where our national interest lies and not worry too much about other peoples' domestic policies."[43] Domestic policies in this case included not only the actions of the white minority regimes but also Portuguese rule over its colonies.

While diplomatic histories regularly focus on executive decisions during this period, these concessions were made possible in part by the grassroots

support for the White Redoubt that welcomed Nixon into office. Facing isolation due to Anglo-American initiatives at the United Nations, the Rhodesian
government under ex–Royal Air Force fighter pilot Ian Smith launched an
aggressive public relations campaign aimed at winning over Western populations through a mixture of grassroots organizing and high-level lobbying
that recalled Portugal's efforts in 1961. Denied official diplomatic recognition, the Rhodesian Information Office depended heavily on recruiting U.S.
allies to champion its interests with quiet help from Portugal and South
Africa. Friends of Rhodesia groups proliferated beginning in 1966, peaking
at around a hundred individual groups stretching from California, through
the South, and into parts of New England.[44] Cold War anti-communism was
central to these linkages, but so was an explicitly Western, implicitly white
identity. Rhodesian propaganda drew direct linkages between UDI and the
American Revolution while parroting South Africa and Portugal in claiming
its position as an oasis of capitalist modernity in a sea of hostile, backward
states.[45] These appeals won over U.S. segregationists deeply disturbed by civil
rights advances while also appealing to far west conservatives who sympathized with Rhodesia's settler ethos.

Pro-Rhodesian lobbying expanded the coalition forged by Portugal in
1961. Anti-communism was the common thread linking hawkish Northern and Western politicians with Southern segregationists, anticipating the
new conservative coalitions that drove the rise of the New Right in the late
1970s.[46] After Lyndon Johnson placed an embargo on Rhodesian chrome
in 1967, leading to increased imports from the Soviet Union, domestic supporters motivated by cultural and racial affinity found a clear Cold War
rationale that could integrate Rhodesia into existing defenses of the White
Redoubt.[47] A leading example was the American-African Affairs Association
(AAAA). Founded in 1965 by conservative activist William Rusher and ex-
communist Max Yergan, the AAAA published a series of pamphlets praising the cultural and political value of the African minority governments.[48]
These efforts helped shape public opinion on Rhodesia while expanding
support for Catholic, Latin Portugal in areas where it had few cultural ties,
notably the West and the Deep South. In one example, the Southern columnist James J. Kilpatrick, a onetime proponent of Massive Resistance against
integration in Virginia, penned a pamphlet situating colonial Portugal within
the frontier imaginary that linked the United States, South Africa, and Rhodesia by describing Lusophone Africa as "a place for pioneers."[49] Congressional
attempts to roll back Johnson's executive policy, bolstered by renewed interest

in protecting Portugal and South Africa, worried African nationalists and their domestic allies, who credited the White Redoubt's effective lobbying.[50] At the third ANLCA meeting in 1967, where African American attendees praised Johnson's policies on Rhodesia, FRELIMO's Eduardo Mondlane argued that the anti-colonial cause had weakened, with congressional politicians sympathetic to the white minority regimes "contribut[ing] a great deal to the strength and power of the Portuguese."[51]

Narratives about the solidity of the White Redoubt gained credence as its ability to weather international condemnation contrasted with the precarious positions of the liberation movements. The most dramatic example of this latter reality was the assassination of Mondlane in February 1969. It robbed pro-liberation activists in the United States of their primary interlocuter at a crucial moment and boded ill for revolutionary prospects in Portugal's second-largest colony. The FRELIMO president died in Dar Es Salaam when he opened a package bomb delivered to his residence. Evidence suggests that Portugal lay behind the assassination, hoping to decapitate FRELIMO and fuel internal tensions as disparate factions jockeyed for control.[52] With no clear succession plan, the party spent months mired in bickering until the charismatic nurse-turned-general Samora Machel gained control, backed by Foreign Minister Marcelino dos Santos. The new leadership righted FRELIMO and maintained the armed struggle, but the diplomatic damage had been done. U.S. officials pointed to Mondlane's death as proof of nationalist weakness at a moment when Nixon's White House was deciding on policy for the region.[53] The more overtly Marxist rhetoric used by Machel and Dos Santos also reinforced white minority claims they were resisting communist movements. If the smooth transition from Salazar to Caetano strengthened Western perceptions of Portugal's longevity, the turmoil that followed Mondlane's assassination convinced these governments to discount FRELIMO's prospects. In 1970, a State Department official told religious activists that the government preferred "Portuguese 'order' and present regime in Africa" and "did not consider there were viable alternatives to the regime in the near future."[54]

The combination of vocal support for minority governance and apparent setbacks for the nationalists enabled the White House to ease relations with Portugal—the least problematic member of the White Redoubt. Nixon maintained the embargoes against Portugal and South Africa to avoid the colonial label but issued an order allowing the export of "non-lethal equipment which ha[d] dual civilian and military [application]."[55] This blanket permit opened the doors for large items forbidden under the case-by-case practice of previous administrations, including the sale of two Boeing 707s that the Portuguese configured to carry troops and cargo. Made with reinforced undercarriages specifically for landing in war zones, the long-distance planes became the workhorses of the Portuguese military—almost doubling air transport capacity by flying 299 missions in 1973 alone.[56] With bilateral relations improving, Portugal finally took its last trump card off the table. In December 1971, it reached an agreement with the United States on the Azores lease for three years, which provided a $400 million export-import line of credit for infrastructural improvements, millions more worth of surplus agricultural commodities, and a smaller amount of non-offensive Defense Department supplies.[57]

Legislators sympathetic to the nationalists objected vociferously but failed to wreck the agreement. Detroit Congressman Charles Diggs complained, "The Africans regard the Azores agreement . . . as the crux of the U.S. hypocrisy on Africa issues, as a forthright announcement of U.S. support for . . . the minority-ruled countries of southern Africa and Guinea-Bissau."[58] Attempts by a minority of legislators to reclassify the agreement as a treaty, and therefore subject it to a Senate vote, failed due to pro-Portuguese efforts in Congress. While most of the funds from the completed agreement went to mainland Portugal, they did much to free government spending for use in the colonies. All this occurred as Portugal expanded its African wars, committing more troops to Mozambique and briefly invading the Guinean capital of Conakry in 1970 in a failed attempt to capture Amílcar Cabral and overthrow the government of Ahmed Sékou Touré. Lisbon's actions drew international condemnation as a gross violation of postcolonial African sovereignty but proved a minor obstacle to improving U.S.-Portuguese relations.[59] A decade after the Angolan revolution threatened to sever Luso-American relations, Portugal returned to the Western fold.

Liberation Allies in Congress

While the expanding influence of the White Redoubt helped Richard Nixon justify thawing relations with Portugal, the congressional attempts to block the Azores-base deal hinted at another reality: the revival of pro-liberation sentiment among politicians. As was the case with Portugal in 1961, this revival grew from the same Rhodesian crisis that focused conservative attention on southern Africa. In part because so few politicians knew about the continent, sustained attention tended to require crises and waxed and waned depending on political perceptions of executive handling of African politics. Johnson's attempts to isolate Rhodesia created a sense of crisis for the rogue state's domestic defenders, but they found both congressional support and room to maneuver as the Vietnam War demanded more of the president's time. ACOA, the National Council of Churches (NCC), and other groups championing Black majority rule recognized the emerging competition from the White Redoubt's American advocates, but their executive focus meant that congressional lobbying remained a secondary or tertiary priority, and they found themselves losing the competition for political support—as they had in 1961—especially after Nixon entered the White House. Many legislators on both sides of the aisle were sympathetic to African decolonization, but few were willing to spend time or political capital to aid it. Those who did prioritize the matter were few in number and generally minor in importance, but their existence provided opportunities for ACOA and its allies to shift the solidarity movement's strategy as southern African crises—and lobbying efforts by the White Redoubt—manufactured a more sustained interest in the region.

Rhodesia's UDI spurred a handful of legislators to prioritize African issues, but they needed information. The State Department traditionally served this role, but its drift toward Portugal and South Africa, combined with the loss of its most ardent Africanists, limited its usefulness. Individual legislators turned to ACOA and African American groups like the NAACP, but the first coordinated collaboration emerged from the Anglo-American Conference on Africa. This informal gathering of British and U.S. legislators began in 1965 as Anglo-Rhodesian tensions stalled decolonization's momentum and created the conditions for UDI. The conference was organized by Johns Hopkins University's Vernon McKay with a grant from the Carnegie Foundation and assistance from the Africa Affairs Institute (AAI).[60] The AAI was an informational group with a predisposition for nationalist causes, but it eschewed ACOA's overt advocacy for liberation. Targeting "younger members" of the political establishment sympathetic to decolonization, the conference hoped to develop strategies to support development and majority rule on the continent.[61]

The joint Anglo-American response to UDI dramatized the need for such a conference, shifting its focus to southern Africa at subsequent sessions held annually into the 1970s. Legislators researched position papers for discussion on how the United Kingdom and the United States might usefully collaborate, with an emphasis on the challenge of colonialism and white minority governance. While the organizers were nominally apolitical and had weaker connections to African nationalists than did ACOA, most attendees expressed support for decolonization and self-determination, though rarely for specific liberation parties or programs—at least at first. The success of the Anglo-American Conference inspired a similar constellation of legislators, academics, and representatives from the AAI to meet monthly in the United States.[62] While all meetings were informational in nature, the hope was this Africa Group would mobilize politicians, in Congressman Don Fraser's words, to "counteract the pro-Smith, anti-majority position being taken by a vocal minority of right-wingers."[63]

At the center of the Africa Group in its early years were two figures who gained prominence as the decade wore on: Congressmen Charles C. Diggs Jr. (D-MI) and Donald M. Fraser (D-MN). The first African American politician to represent Michigan at the national level, Diggs came from a prominent Detroit family of morticians and was an early advocate of the civil rights movement after his election in 1955, gaining national attention for being the lone congressman to attend the trial of Emmet Till's killers. He was among the most active members of the House Subcommittee on African Affairs in the early 1960s, encouraging hearings into Portuguese Africa and apartheid as early as 1962. Fraser, another member of the committee, supported Diggs in these efforts after he was elected to the House in 1963. The thirty-nine-year-old Minnesota lawyer likely found his way onto the minor subcommittee due to lack of seniority, but the issue of decolonization intersected with his deep-seated interest in human rights and international law.[64] The pair drove the work of the subcommittee in the 1960s and promoted new approaches to the region as they acquired seniority.

The bipartisan Africa Group initially included roughly a dozen members concentrated in the House, with numbers growing over time. Beyond Diggs and Frazer, the group's most consistent members included liberal Massachusetts Republican Bradford Morse and ex-marine John Culver (D-IA). Heading Culver's staff was a political scientist named Dick Clark, who earned his own spot in the Senate in 1973. California Democrat John Tunney and a rotating selection of African American congressmen also attended intermittently. So did a small number of senators, such as Ted Kennedy (D-MA) and Senate African Subcommittee Chair Gale McGee (D-WY), though McGee was less interested in African freedom than in upholding the U.N. charter against the Rhodesian challenge.[65] The group sought proactive, constructive approaches to African problems, rather than following the tradition of reactive policies that Fraser derisively described as waiting "until we are pushed

Figure 4. Representative Charles Diggs in September 1960. Diggs is addressing East African students sponsored for study in the United States by the African American Students Foundation, whose executive director was ACOA associate Cora Weiss. Photograph: Cora Weiss. Reproduced with permission of Cora Weiss, African Activist Archive.

by the African and Asian nations and then try to achieve the weakest possible compromise."[66] Johnson broke with this tendency in Rhodesia, but these congressmen worried about the drift in the administration's regional policy toward Portugal and South Africa, along with the effects of conservative organizing on the White House's resolve. Until the Nixon years sent it into full-on opposition, the Africa Group identified its role as maintaining "gentle pressure and vigilance" on the executive branch to make sure the United States pursued a "principled and effective policy in Africa."[67]

The emergence of a wider interest in Africa among Washington politicians intersected with the clarifying position of Rhodesia to revive and reorient pro-liberation activism. Highlighting this shift was the leadership of the NCC, which worried about the thorny moral questions created by the relationship between sociopolitical change and liberatory violence created by the turn to revolution in Portugal's colonies. Yet the success of the White Redoubt states in building U.S. support demanded a response, which was further encouraged by Eduardo Mondlane's active promotion of the liberation cause in the years before his death (see chapter 6). "[The] southern African lobbies are working very well," a diplomat told church officials in 1968. "The only way to combat this . . . was by sustained concentrated staff work."[68] The NCC began a few modest initiatives, notably providing logistical and financial assistance for ACOA to establish a modest Washington office in 1967.[69] Both groups recognized that competition had shifted to Congress, where the larger membership and extended legislative process demanded a more consistent presence from interested organizations. These efforts expanded the influence of the traditionally New York–based and U.N.-centered decolonization lobby as it built working relationships with congressmen such as Diggs, Fraser, and (on Rhodesia) Senator McGee.[70]

This emerging coalition faced headwinds, especially once Nixon entered the White House. The mostly young, liberal legislators who sympathized with self-determination lacked the institutional power in the seniority-driven Congress to achieve policy changes. With notable exceptions such as Ted Kennedy, whose involvement in an array of issues limited the attention he could give to Africa, most of the pro-independence coalition claimed membership in the crowded House Foreign Affairs Committee, with none holding even subcommittee chairs until the late 1960s. Supporters of the White Redoubt—many drawn from the safely Democratic districts of the U.S. South that racked up seniority—had control of committees on both sides of Congress and were well positioned to manipulate legislation and sway undecided votes. The need to attend to constituent concerns further discouraged pro-liberation legislators from spending extended amounts of time on African affairs; even representatives from areas with substantial Black populations rarely saw Africa atop constituent concerns. As Fraser remarked after Africanist colleagues did well in the 1966 election, "This is probably due to the public's indifference rather than their support of our position."[71] Motivation came from individual conviction more than clear policy platforms or as a response to public opinion, which—when registered—generally favored Rhodesia, Portugal, and South Africa during this period. This meant attitudes toward the issues connected with African liberation varied, especially when it came to NATO ally Portugal. McGee, the Senate's Africa Subcommittee chair, worked closely with ACOA on Rhodesia but warned, "The United States has to be extremely careful to avoid any involvement whatsoever in Portugal's difficulties with its African territories."[72] Even Don Fraser wavered at times, prioritizing the problems of Rhodesia or apartheid that directly related to his interest in human rights, most notably when Portuguese reforms hinted that a negotiated settlement might be possible.[73]

Yet this congressional interest proved to liberation leaders and their allies that there was political potential in the United States. Members of the Africa Group developed working relationships with ACOA as the committee focused more energy on legislative lobbying.[74] Houser's work with the House Subcommittee on African Affairs dated back to the late 1950s, but the committee's relationship with young legislators like Diggs and Fraser was closer. Fraser's office listed ACOA alongside groups like the NAACP and the Congress of Racial Equality in its directory of organizations able to address issues related to apartheid, and it used information provided by ACOA to craft public statements on Africa[75] Diggs did the same while taking increasingly visible actions as his profile rose, notably resigning his seat on the American U.N. delegation over Nixon's treaties with Portugal.[76] Congressmen also gained opportunities to interact directly with liberation leaders. When Fraser visited Tanzania in 1967, for example, he met personally with Eduardo and Janet Mondlane, accepting a sheaf of documents on FRELIMO's political and social programs.[77] These connections were not as well organized as the professional lobbying undertaken by Portugal and its White Redoubt allies, but it illustrated an attempt to better connect congressional actors to solidarity activities. When Africa Group members finally amassed power, highlighted by Diggs's acquisition of the House's Africa subcommittee chairmanship in 1969, they—unlike members of the executive branch—were predisposed to see liberation leaders as future diplomatic partners.

The CONCP parties responded to these political openings by promoting the constructive aspects of their revolutions to win Western support. The rudimentary socialist states established in liberated territories became international showpieces for their postwar goals and provided a different perspective on liberation for those uneasy with revolution. The PAIGC led the way in Guinea, with social services being central to the local conception of the struggle. Never assuming—as Roberto had—that a mass insurrection would arise spontaneously, Amílcar Cabral understood that locals were "fighting to win material benefits, to live better . . . to guarantee the future of their children."[78] Social programs accompanied military campaigns to legitimize the party and win popular support. "National liberation means, for us," Cabral explained, "the liquidation of foreign domination, and the assumption of all the responsibilities on the national and international planes, gradually

Figure 5. Amílcar Cabral meets with female students at a PAIGC school, circa 1971. The provision of education was a central component of the PAIGC revolution and its representation abroad, first in Guinea-Conakry and then through schools in the liberated territories. Photograph: Bruna Polimeni, FMSMB/Arquivo Amílcar Cabral.

building the economic, social, and cultural progress of the people of Guinee and Cabo Verde."[79] Beginning in 1964, PAIGC established medical clinics, schools, and cooperative "people's stores" where locals bartered produce for consumer goods. Though the quality of these institutions varied, and their numbers were surely exaggerated for propaganda purposes, they offered public services to Africans in rural regions where Portuguese investment was absent. Historian Mustafah Dhada estimates that by 1970 the PAIGC operated more than 160 schools, 120 clinics, and four regional hospitals.[80] These efforts necessitated the acquisition of medical supplies, educational materials, and goods for barter, which became an important component of Cabral's diplomacy—and his appeals to the West.

The common CONCP commitment to undertaking social revolution alongside armed struggle became a way of selling the revolutionary parties as future postcolonial partners. Mondlane explained that "liberation does not consist merely of driving out the Portuguese authority, but also of constructing a new country."[81] Like the PAIGC, FRELIMO identified the provision of schools and health centers and the promotion of trade as the only way to "[prove] to the people that a better life [was] both really possible and worth struggling for."[82] The party pursued this strategy even before the revolution, establishing the Mozambique Institute in 1963 with a Ford Foundation grant, which propaganda pointed to as an early demonstration of Western willingness to engage with the constructive elements of party philosophy. The Tanzania-based institute provided educational and relief services to Mozambican refugees, with the goal of training educated cadres who would manage the country after independence. The Johnson administration cut off assistance to it after Portugal complained and the armed revolt began, but aid from the Swedish government and ACOA helped it expand to meet FRELIMO's growing needs.[83] As the war advanced, the Mozambique Institute became the primary coordinator of social programs in the liberated territories. Services included basic schooling and health clinics, and FRELIMO worked to shift agricultural production from cash-crop methods to socialist models.[84] While never as extensive as the PAIGC infrastructure, FRELIMO was exceptionally good at promoting these activities as proof of concept for its vision of cooperative, social revolution. By providing the services that Lisbon's civilizing mission promised but never delivered, the CONCP parties portrayed themselves as governments-in-waiting that deserved the support and trust of Western officials. As one British parliamentarian remarked at an Anglo-American conference, efforts like the Mozambique Institute served as "a shop window for the constructive preparations of FRELIMO for the post-independence tasks."[85]

Building this infrastructure required external assistance, and it was in this arena that Western aid proved irreplaceable. As with military supplies, assistance originally came from the East. Cuba and East Germany donated medical supplies and educational training, while Yugoslavia provided FRELIMO with scientific instruments, technical assistance, and at least one educator.[86] But Western goods were considered superior, especially when it came to medicine. The parties believed that such civic assistance offered an opportunity to align Euro-American organizations and even governments with party goals. While Mondlane pioneered pathways to the United States, the PAIGC and the MPLA used their personal networks to win support from leftists in France and Italy. These relationships offered proof of concept, but real success came when the CONCP parties earned aid from Scandinavia. Countries like neutral Sweden and NATO member Norway had missionary ties to Africa, but they lacked colonial baggage and more actively supported decolonization.[87] As some of NATO's earliest critics of Portuguese imperialism, the Nordic countries proved amenable to nationalist goals. Notable among these early allies was Swedish politician Olof Palme, a critic of Cold War interventionism in the Third World who believed Cabral's philosophy overlapped with that of his Swedish Social Democrats. After he was elected prime minister in 1969, Sweden became the first Western country—albeit outside NATO—to materially support the social programs of the liberation parties. Official assistance from Norway and Denmark soon followed. Success with the Nordic countries gave the CONCP leaders hope that this could be replicated in other Western countries.[88]

While the CONCP parties knew that replicating such success would be difficult in the United States, they felt an urgency to act while the White Redoubt built its powerful lobbying structure. FRELIMO continued to lead in the United States—as well as Britain and the Netherlands—thanks to Mondlane's English fluency and the active role played by the American-born Janet Mondlane. In 1967, as the Rhodesian situation focused interest on southern Africa and eased pressure on Portugal, FRELIMO established a permanent U.S. presence. It sent former Cairo representative Sharfudine Khan to New York, where ACOA helped him operate an office as the first CONCP official stationed in the United States. He had the dual mission of lobbying the United Nations and publicizing FRELIMO and its allied revolutions. Khan and visits by the Mondlanes expanded popular support, explored in detail in the next section. While Mondlane's assassination was shocking, it did not derail these efforts, instead spurring wider CONCP engagement. Khan remained the consistent face of FRELIMO with support from its new president, Samora Machel, while Cabral filled the gap left by Mondlane by increasing PAIGC activities in the English-speaking world. This included appointing the party's own roving ambassador to the United States, the Lincoln University–educated Gil Fernandes. Cabral also took his first American trip beyond the United Nations in 1970, giving a memorial lecture for Mondlane at Syracuse University before testifying to Diggs's House Subcommittee on African Affairs about the wars of liberation and their efforts to construct new societies behind the lines.[89]

This expanded nationalist diplomacy coincided with the final closing of the door to the Nixon White House, meaning the contingent of congressional sympathizers offered the best chance to change policy. The Africa Group remained small, but its most active members were gaining the ability to make noise. Like Diggs, Fraser earned sufficient seniority in 1969 to chair a subcommittee on foreign affairs. Increased authority allowed Africa Group members to mobilize information from activist organizations such as ACOA and integrate it into congressional debates, while publicly opening government deliberations to nationalists like Cabral in a way that the White House never had. Still, these legislators remained in the minority, and even their colleagues who chafed at Rhodesian independence or Nixon's embrace of imperial Portugal gained few benefits from attacking Cold War security structures in support of African independence. If they were going to convince their colleagues to join them in forming a new, pro-liberation coalition, they needed help recasting the dominant political narratives that took root after 1961. One NCC lobbyist explained succinctly: "Some congressmen will be unable, and others will be unwilling to support southern African concerns without some expression of concern from their constituents."[90] Public displays of support would be useful for encouraging quieter members of the Africa Group to prioritize liberation politics while providing ammunition to win over undecided legislators.

Herein lay the hope for CONCP foreign policy in the United States. The development of a sympathetic cohort in Congress promised new possibilities for the parties, especially as key advocates like Diggs gained institutional power. The social infrastructure developing behind the front lines provided a way to sell the revolutions while emphasizing nationalist claims that they were governments-in-waiting. Domestic allies such as ACOA disseminated these narratives domestically and provided a useful alternative to executive branch information. For individuals like Diggs and Fraser, aligning with the nationalists offered an opportunity to address southern African crises without following the White House in embracing continued minority governance. The problem was that Africa remained a minor issue, especially as vitriolic divides over the Vietnam War monopolized foreign policy debates. The Africa Group needed additional help if it was to expand its ranks and convince its colleagues that its break with traditions of foreign policy offered more attractive policies than the familiar Cold War, narratives about defending Western civilization skillfully offered by Portugal, and the powerful domestic lobby created around the White Redoubt.

Yet attitudes were beginning to change, accelerated by the national reckoning over U.S. foreign policy induced by the Vietnam War. Members of a generation frustrated by the national status quo were becoming politically active, and they looked abroad for inspiration as they sought to transform their country and challenge its tendency toward reactionary interventions in the Global South. Many were attracted to the constructive social revolutions of the CONCP parties, even working with the Mozambique Institute in Tanzania. These grassroots supporters renewed nationalist confidence that they could overcome the Cold War mindset that Portugal and the African minority regimes used to buy Western complacence. "The whole problem basically is a lack of information . . . ," explained PAIGC representative Gil Fernandes. "I think that, if Americans were informed about what is happening, they would very likely come and help us. . . . There is always the possibility of getting some amount of aid from the United States—not the government, of course."[91] Over the prior decade liberal internationalists, civil rights activists, African Americans, church groups, and even congressmen provided aid, but their efforts were repeatedly thwarted by domestic unease with international revolution and the organized responses of the White Redoubt. What was missing from the pro-independence solidarity movement was the foundation to sustain, connect, and expand popular efforts, which required clear identification with the liberation parties, propagation of carefully tailored information that aligned party platforms with domestic values, and coordination across community lines. Interest arose intermittently throughout the early 1960s in response to crises, but it was difficult for groups like ACOA— struggling with their own Cold War tendencies—to maintain momentum when news about the colonies faded from the headlines. The CONCP parties struck upon a winning diplomatic strategy to promote their revolutions as constructive agents of social justice, and now they needed to communicate these ideas to Western audiences despite their opponents controlling much of the information entering public debates. Elite educational and lobbying groups like ACOA and the NCC needed to align with grassroots activists to dramatize African freedom struggles, inject the solidarity movement with a new energy that could survive periods of frustration, and pressure politicians to reexamine their assumptions about policy on Africa.

PART II

Grassroots Solidarity

CHAPTER 5

The Religious and Radical
Origins of Solidarity

G rassroots energy was needed to encourage a change in U.S. policy and to shift the popular debate from liberal support for African political independence to the revolutionary liberation envisioned by the CONCP parties. The solidarity movement became a vital component facilitating this process thanks to the intersection of religiously inspired youth activists and pragmatic radicals. Both were heavily influenced by personal connections to southern Africa, with the CONCP's leftist liberation leaders emerging as central influences on their evolving ideologies. On one side, church youth interested in pursuing issues of racial equality participated in programs that positioned southern African liberation as an international complement to the domestic civil rights movement. Their broad emphasis on social justice challenged traditionally hierarchical church relations with the Global South, gave new weight to African ideas promoting leftist political projects, and transformed youth conceptions of global equality and the tactics needed to achieve it. This expansive anti-imperial worldview created connections with secular leftists who also gravitated toward the practical examples of tricontinental revolution in Lusophone Africa, which opposed global capitalism and the racial hierarchies that justified it. These two trends aligned initially with different parties—Christians and progressive internationalists with Eduardo Mondlane's FRELIMO and leftists with the MPLA—but the political front envisioned by the CONCP encouraged collaboration. Distinct personal networks and ideologies meant small groups proliferated, but each saw themselves as components of a broad, complex solidarity movement. They shared goals of supporting the CONCP parties as a way of resisting Western imperialism from within its most powerful source, seeking to redefine traditional relations between Global North and South in the process.

Without abandoning the churches or groups like the American Committee on Africa (ACOA) that first introduced them to southern Africa, the activist youth diverged from their elders in their clear deference to assertive African revolutionary ideas emerging from Portuguese Africa. As campaigns for civil rights and the liberal push for the Great Society fueled a social backlash and then faltered amid the political disruption of the Vietnam War, young Americans looked to the Global South as they sought authentic, revolutionary ideologies to critique their flawed society. The liberation parties introduced the disaffected youth to new ways of thinking about the world as more than extensions of domestic campaigns for racial equality or beneficiaries of Western expertise. This phenomenon is well known in the context of major Cold War flashpoints such as Cuba and Vietnam, but support for the CONCP revolutions reveal that such identification went well beyond headline areas, often with more nuanced and lasting impacts. The practical socialism and multilevel revolutions envisioned by parties like FRELIMO and Amílcar Cabral's PAIGC created broad coalitions because support for the liberation movements proved less contentious than support for other tricontinental revolutions like the one in Vietnam, while highlighting many of the same issues. The result was a New Left Internationalism that identified heavily with the worldview and goals of Lusophone leftists and accepted the necessity of armed violence as a legitimate response to reactionary white governance. The Southeast Asian conflict—and the powerful domestic reaction to it—enabled the growth of this activism by weakening the rigid anti-communism of the Cold War, but the positive visions of liberation promoted by the CONCP parties won youth adherents and integrated concrete Global South visions of anti-imperial resistance and global equality into domestic organizing.

Religious Radicalism: New Left Missionaries and the Zambia Group

The origins of religious support for Lusophone revolution lay in a rethinking of traditional missionary linkages with southern Africa. It was, after all, missionary ties that first inspired activism around Angola in 1961. This sentiment was tied closely to humanitarian impulses, opposing Portuguese colonialism and the crackdown on dissent that swallowed up both African converts and foreign missionaries. Despite Roberto's missionary connections, there was little direct identification with the UPA beyond a handful of personal acquaintances, and religious leaders remained wary of actively supporting armed revolution. Donations to the party went primarily to refugee services.[1] Central to early organizing efforts was a hope that further violence could be averted, hinting at an omnipresent liberal paternalism and a futile hope for negotiated settlements that Portugal never justified.[2] After public sentiment faded, religious leaders retained an interest in southern Africa, but it became subsumed within a broader debate over the proper role of Protestant institutions in the Global South.

The proliferation of new nations at the same time the civil rights movement forced a reckoning on the global nature of racial inequalities deeply affected many churches. As events in Angola demonstrated, missions concentrated in what was then known as the Third World could not avoid changing politics. Even where transitions of power went smoothly, newly independent and assertive states challenged missionary relationships that posited Western culture and morality as inherently superior to local tradition, compelling internationally minded Christians to reconsider their missions in the 1950s. Among the leaders of this movement was Margaret Flory, the dynamic Presbyterian secretary for student work of the Commission on World Mission of the National Student Christian Federation (NSCF).[3] She believed that Protestant churches had to rethink their patriarchal, Eurocentric forms of international engagement, but exactly what should replace the tradition was not clear. The question, as one of Flory's programs put it, was "How can the movement of missions be shifted from the pattern of the West sending to the East, the older sending to the younger churches, to one of the whole Church—the churches together as peers—going together to live and work in the midst of frontiers that exist in every part of the world?"[4] A few years before President Kennedy adopted similar rhetoric and created his own missionary institution with the Peace Corps, Flory hoped to find the answers by helping young people explore the frontiers created by the intersecting challenges of revolution, global demands for racial equality, and the East-West conflict.

Flory's vision of a just, collaborative church depended heavily on listening to and learning from frontier populations rarely represented in high-level decision-making. The Eighteenth Ecumenical Student Conference on the Christian World Mission held in Athens, Ohio, in the closing days of 1959 gives a sense of changing attitudes. Under Flory's leadership, more than thirty-six hundred students from more than seventy-five countries gathered to discuss how they could navigate these new "frontiers." Topics ranged from technological upheaval to the growth of a "university world," but the majority addressed matters deeply entwined with North-South relations: racial tensions, new nationalisms, responsible statesmanship, displaced peoples, and communism.[5] Leading the discussions was a diverse, international collection of frontline activists. Martin Luther King Jr., recently returned from a sojourn in India, drew the most attention, but there were also many continental Africans. Among them was someone Flory had known since 1953: Eduardo Mondlane.[6] As young Christians reoriented their relationship with the changing world, the thirty-nine-year-old Mozambican became a pivotal voice guiding their transformation.

The 1959 Ohio conference hinted at growing religious interest in decolonization, but Mondlane had spent nearly a decade encouraging this shift. While his studies at Oberlin and Northwestern were assisted by the National Council of Churches (NCC), he spoke regularly at churches, introducing parishioners to a strident but carefully measured African nationalism.[7] He also became a regular presence at Christian youth gatherings and camps, where he met his wife, Janet.[8] In these sessions, Mondlane spoke powerfully about the need for action and identified strongly with Gandhian models of nonviolence, impressing a still skeptical Andrew Young—the future King confidant, congressman, and U.N. ambassador—with his confidence in the strategy when they first met in 1951.[9] Mondlane played an important role internationalizing visions for Black social justice during the formative years of the civil rights movement.

This youth culture had an early test in Africa when the Angolan revolution and the persecution of Protestants demanded church attention. The Methodist and Baptist missionaries who raised relief funds with dramatic accounts of atrocities, torture, and imprisonment deeply affected students. They wanted to hear directly from Africans with knowledge of the colonies, and Mondlane was readily accessible. He spoke widely in the wake of the Angolan revolution to youth and church organizations.[10] When the Methodist Student Movement focused its 1961 annual conference on the plight of Portuguese colonies, Mondlane helped organize it, providing a bridge to nationalist Africa. One staff member recalled: "[Mondlane] worked side by side with [students], relaxing over coffee, talking far into the night, explaining fine points of political or economic analysis, telling stories of his people, their suffering, and their victories."[11] Discussion bred action. The NSCF—a coalition of campus church groups—urged its members to lobby the U.S. government and the United

Nations on Angola, distributing resolutions drafted by Union Theological Seminary in New York and ACOA to build support.[12]

These interactions inspired many students to expand their personal involvement with Africa even after Angola disappeared from the news, feeding into the active programs Margaret Flory hoped to create.[13] Importantly, support for African independence paired with a critical reading of U.S. international affairs, which Mondlane believed was vital to motivate domestic activism. At the forefront of this movement was Henry "Hank" Crane, the son of Congo missionaries who met Mondlane in the 1950s and roomed with him at the Ohio conference. In long conversations about African politics, Crane remarked, "[Mondlane] unmask[ed] the vagaries, inconsistencies, and hypocrisy of U.S. foreign policy in relation to Africa, exposing the vast chasm between the ideals we profess publicly as a nation and the narrow self-interest which actually determines our relations with the black people of Africa." These conversations, Crane later recalled, "largely shaped my own attitudes toward events in Africa since."[14] While Mondlane's return to Mozambique and the Portuguese reassertion of power dampened widespread activism, 1961 was an awakening for individuals like Crane. This new understanding of the United States as complicit in imperialism combined with this newfound individual attachment to African nationalism to inspire a small but determined movement within the church. As one young adherent remembered, "This exposure to the situation in Angola was unforgettable. Students discovered a part of the world they had hardly heard of before and were drawn into personal connections with it."[15]

Flory believed that such personal connections and understanding of life on the global frontiers would transform church relations with the Third World. While Angola was still grabbing headlines, she formulated an innovative experiment in missionary activity that put Christian youth on the conceptual frontiers explored at the Ohio conference: the Frontier Internship in Mission (FIM). Beginning in 1961, the program recruited politically active young people—Christian and non-Christian alike—to spend two years abroad, engaging daily with issues of poverty, urbanization, racial tension, and nationalism, among others. All interns lived at a subsistence level to provide perspective on the realities of life in their adopted communities, most of them in Global South countries undergoing what one FIM publication called the global "revolutionary upheavals . . . based in large part on the Christian belief in the worth of the individual."[16] The FIM broke with traditional practice and the concurrent efforts of the Peace Corps by deemphasizing the dissemination of Western knowledge. Rather, interns learned from peoples in the Global South as they challenged old borders and sought greater North-South equality. They sought to explore "the mission strategy of tomorrow: to come not as one having answers, but as one deeply desiring to discover the ultimate questions."[17] The FIM's goal was to encourage young people to connect with foreign peoples, then "be present, to listen, to study, to try to understand and to discover what new patterns might emerge to give guidance to the whole Christian community in its mission in that [frontier]."[18] With backing from the NCC, Flory recruited participants who were active in domestic race issues, poverty relief, and campus activism.[19] Their time abroad was meant to help these activists think and act more globally, creating a new religious internationalism that made Global South concerns integral parts of daily life.[20] The FIM institutionalized the kind of interpersonal exchanges built by Mondlane and became a pipeline for connecting American youth with African nationalists.

The merging of domestic and international activism is typified by the experience of two of the FIM's first class of members who played important roles building southern African activism in the United States.[21] David and Marylee Wiley first explored issues of race and power while organizing for African American candidates in regional elections when David was chaplain at the University of Delaware.[22] In 1961, the FIM sent the couple to Salisbury (modern Harare), the capital of Southern Rhodesia (now Zimbabwe). David taught night school, and they led work camps to promote interracial learning, discovering the liberation ideologies taking root under the minority government.[23] The experience helped progressive young people like the Wileys see the world from a new angle. It also led them to question the role that Western powers, specifically the United States, played in supporting governments like the one in Southern Rhodesia. As the pair explained at the time, "The universal fact is that all of us learned to open our eyes and ears. We thought we had the ideas and techniques, but we learned that we had only knowledge—others had the wisdom. . . . We uncovered our hidden prejudices about the superiority of Western or American knowledge and techniques."[24] Flory's FIM upended the traditional goals of Christian mission by converting progressive Americans to Global South ideas.

When the Wileys returned to the United States in 1963, they refocused their activism on the broad problems of empire and minority rule in Africa. Open revolution and the violent response from both Lisbon and Pretoria forced young Christians to reassess how they viewed nationalist revolutionaries, placing them at odds with their religious elders. The church leadership rallied against Portugal due to their missionary connections but blanched at the idea of directly supporting armed freedom movements, quietly using funds to bankroll refugee services in the Congo and Tanzania without fully aligning with the revolutions. Most church members believed violence was unacceptable no matter the perpetrator and drew assurances from U.S. civil rights leaders. Yet nationalists increasingly understood that this avenue was closed in the wake of the harsh responses to protests at Pidjiguiti in Guinea-Bissau and Sharpeville in South Africa, and the military reprisals in Angola in 1961. This was the common justification for militant revolution across the CONCP alliance, but FRELIMO's change in tactics earned greater U.S. attention thanks to Mondlane's well-known aversion to violence. After two years of fruitless lobbying for increased pressure on Portugal, the Mozambican leader concluded in the party's English-language publication, "There was no other path open to us" besides armed struggle.[25] ACOA preferred peaceful negotiations but made the decision to align with armed movements after Angola and Algeria, though it remained careful about confining aid to peaceful projects. The NCC and Protestant leaderships held deeper reservations, with Quakers being especially uneasy. This created a distance with youth activists like the Wileys, who were inclined to accept African perspectives and therefore questioned the universality of nonviolence as nationalist parties took up arms.

The shift in the tenor of youth discussions of decolonization was clear by 1964. While the NSCF made apartheid a key issue of its Civil Rights Committee in the early 1960s, Angola and tensions in Rhodesia expanded the focus of activism while hinting that new forms of action were needed.[26] At the Student Conference on the Christian World Mission convened in Ohio in 1964, a young South African exile named Kenneth Carstens hinted at the generational shift when he challenged Angolan missionary Malcolm McVeigh's denial of violence as a legitimate nationalist tool. Carstens asked the audience, "If a change is necessary because of the injustice and cruelty of the status quo—now these are big 'ifs'—and the only change that is foreseeable is a change by means of violence, then what are we saying about the native air of the Christian faith if we condemn revolution on both sides?"[27] Seeking to answer this question, the NSCF sent Hank Crane on an extended fact-finding mission to the African continent at the same time domestic activists launched the Freedom Summer. He reconnected with Mondlane during the World Council of Churches (WCC) Consultation on Race Relations in Southern Africa. The FRELIMO president—by then readying to launch the armed revolution in September—joined with other nationalists in urging an expansion of support work that accepted violent resistance. Crane remembers that Mondlane explained that what FRELIMO and the other liberation groups needed was "the help of the Christian community in learning how to use violence without hate, with maximum restraint and discipline, and with the clear goal of the establishment of a non-racial society guaranteeing justice and dignity for all men."[28] Facing persistent state repression, colonized Africans had few alternatives but to match force with force, and Mondlane begged his Christian allies to see the humanity at the core of the revolutionary program.

At the center of Mondlane's appeal was an attempt to challenge the universal application of nonviolence. The Gandhian imprimatur gave notions of active Christian pacifism an ecumenical, global gloss that appealed to legalistic liberals in the postwar United States. Yet Mondlane and Carstens recognized that contexts were not equal; nonviolence worked in some British colonies and domestically in the United States because public and international opinion placed limits on state violence.[29] By contrast, the same rules did not apply to the White Redoubt states, where the threat that Black nationalists posed to core identities made state killings and even vigilante justice acceptable. While it was only obliquely referenced, Christian doctrine made room for states to wage just wars, so Mondlane and his student allies redeployed these ideas about the defensive use of force in the name of stateless peoples claiming the right to self-determination enshrined by U.N. doctrine in international law.[30] The goal was to subsume the abhorrence of violence within the broader, and more pressing issue, of global racial inequality. While youth activists promoted nonviolence in the U.S. context, where change was possible through democratic means, they learned from their experiences abroad and interactions with nationalists like Mondlane that this reality was not universal.

Crane brought these ideas back to the United States and urged fellow youth to engage with Mondlane's vision of a non-paternalistic solidarity, merging the domestic fight for racial justice and the African revolutions into a single struggle with distinct tactics. In the same way Northerners helped advance the Southern civil rights struggle in the United States, youth from the Global North could advance the campaigns waged by nationalists in Africa. The product of these calls to action was the expansion of the Civil Rights Committee's initial concern with South Africa into the independent Southern Africa Committee (SAC) of the NSCF, which formed around the core of Crane, Carstens, the Wileys, and FIM alumnus David Robinson.[31] Housed within Union Theological Seminary, the SAC found a rich ground for recruiting members dedicated to global justice. Members also came from Columbia University and the ranks of recent college graduates who flocked to New York. There were also valuable allies nearby; the headquarters of the NCC, cheekily termed the "God Box," was in neighboring Morningside Heights, and ACOA a mere train ride away.[32] Despite their work within church institutions, many members were not religious or soon drifted away from their faith. What united these activists of differing commitments, backgrounds, and politics was the cause of southern Africa and especially solidarity with freedom struggles—no matter the method.[33] Within a few years the SAC became the locus of an increasingly radical solidarity that outlasted the university Christian movement while maintaining access to influential religious institutions.

While the SAC became a leading source of organizing, its earliest incarnation was a kind of activist study group. Unlike the elder pair of Carstens and Crane, few of its early members had extensive personal experience in Africa. Rather, they had brief encounters through study abroad or conceptualized African independence as a complement to domestic civil rights work. Members sought to understand regional politics and devise strategies for supporting change, particularly in South Africa.[34] It was events in Africa that transformed this initial focus into a broader, more radical approach. When Southern Rhodesia declared independence in November 1965, David and Marylee Wiley spearheaded the publication of a special NSCF newsletter to disseminate information on the event. The bulletin transitioned to a regional lens within six months, finally becoming the long-running *Southern Africa* magazine in 1967. As the most active revolutions, the Lusophone struggles featured prominently in this final iteration, encouraged by connections to Mondlane. The publications became important parts of the SAC identity, providing a consistent source for news on Africa aimed at youth audiences. From the outside, the SAC became a youthful ACOA, merging religious backgrounds, progressive politics, educational outreach on African liberation, and a critical view of U.S. involvement in the region.

The SAC most clearly set itself apart from ACOA by adopting the increasingly radical positions associated with the New Left. In the mid-1960s, civil rights activism and campus free-speech movements laid the groundwork for mass anti-war protests against the escalating conflict in South Vietnam. Students for a Democratic Society (SDS) emerged as a prominent national organization within these efforts, but the proliferation of diverse, local organizations became a hallmark of the era. These groups cohered around the New Left, in which a generation largely raised without the material deprivation that motivated old working-class social democrats defined what Doug Rossinow calls a "post-scarcity" radicalism to address the moral shortcomings of affluent, global societies. New emphases on humanism and participatory democracy sought to address the problems of racial inequality, wealth disparity, and nuclearized militarism that divided nation and world despite rising quality of life. A search for authenticity amid this sense of political and personal alienation drove New Leftists to align with groups at the margins of national and global society—the poor, domestic minorities, and imperial subjects—in pursuit of social justice and personal freedom.[35] Tricontinental ideas promoted by FRELIMO and its CONCP allies influenced and overlapped with the New Left, encouraging the SAC to move in this direction and providing a secular intellectual home for those members drifting away from their religious origins. SAC members joined the opposition to the war, believing U.S. cooperation with South Africa and Portugal paralleled reactionary U.S. strategies in South Vietnam. As groups like SDS adopted broad anti-imperial programs, they expanded their criticism of U.S. policy beyond Asia to intersect with the SAC as it undertook its own leftward drift.[36] While scholars of the 1960s such as Charles DeBenedetti rightly point out that such multi-issue programs distracted SDS from taking a leadership position on Vietnam, it enabled joint action that publicized issues at the margins of the popular consciousness, integrating African solidarity activism into the New Left.[37]

The first major example of this emerging coalition was the joint SDS-SAC protest of Chase Manhattan Bank in 1965. The SAC explored a number of strategies to advance the liberation struggle, including polite discussions with the State Department, but it gravitated toward the confrontational politics of its era.[38] Seeking an issue that could dramatize U.S. complicity with South Africa, it responded positively when the New York SDS chapter approached it with information on Chase.[39] The bank led a consortium that extended credit to the South African government, a necessity after international reactions to the Sharpeville Massacre produced an economic downturn. The use of U.S. deposits to prop up the apartheid regime upset SDS and SAC, and they believed many Americans would withdraw their funds if they realized how Chase used them. From this youth core, the goal was to create a broad coalition to pressure Chase using grassroots tactics popularized by the civil rights movement. The groups launched the boycott alongside the Congress of Racial Equality and the NAACP with a sit-in at the bank headquarters in downtown New York. Seeking to broaden the movement, the SAC worked with ACOA to create the Committee of Conscience Against Apartheid under the chairmanship of

A. Philip Randolph.[40] It also reached out to the NCC and the churches, whose sizable investments would amplify the threats to Chase, but denominational leaders—many deeply ensconced in the corporate world—were divided over the moral implications of normal business practices and did not respond decisively. The SAC and ACOA continued to work on adjusting religious opinion even as SDS participation declined amid internal strife. It was slow going, and by the time the churches began divesting in the late 1960s, the Portuguese colonies eclipsed South Africa as the focus for activism.[41] The Chase campaign was a first step for the southern African solidarity movement but illustrated the difficulty of translating local activism to global politics. It also highlighted the distance separating left-leaning youth and the established institutions that could enhance the impact of their organizing.

The reality was that this more radical anti-imperial philosophy was still defining itself against the left liberalism of organizations like ACOA and the NCC in the mid-1960s. As Hank Crane had shown a year before, it took the influence of trusted African leaders like Mondlane to convince even ardent activists to accept the realities of African revolution. These personal linkages and experiences were invaluable in creating solidarity, and to find them many SAC members looked to Margaret Flory's FIM. Over the next five years, the two organizations constructed an almost symbiotic relationship. Young activists approached Flory with plans for exploring the frontiers of revolutionary nationalism based on their research in New York, while FIMers in Africa developed relationships with the SAC and its alumni through the community that Flory created. The influx of new people and ideas expanded the movement and helped prepare young activists to transform the same institutions that funded the FIM.

One example of this process was William "Bill" Minter. Minter first encountered this new Christian internationalism when he attended the 1959 Ohio conference. He became interested in Africa while spending his junior year in Nigeria as part of another of Flory's programs. When he enrolled at Union Theological Seminary in the mid-1960s, he joined the SAC and soon became its president. Minter met Mondlane when he spoke on FRELIMO's vision of a new, multiracial Mozambican society. Minter and his wife, Ruth, who also participated in the southwest Georgia project of the Student Nonviolent Coordinating Committee (SNCC) in the summer of 1965, were inspired by Mondlane's mission of merging the liberation struggle with the wholesale reconstruction of the colonial nation and wanted to help. This began an exchange of ideas about how the young activists could support FRELIMO;

two years later, they approached Flory with a proposal that they work directly in the secondary school run by the movement in Tanzania. Flory agreed, and Bill and Ruth Minter found themselves among a multinational group of teachers at the school, with Janet and Eduardo Mondlane and much of the FRELIMO leadership working nearby.[42] This experience gave the Minters a deep personal understanding of the African revolution and positioned them to be experts on the topic upon their return to the United States.

In addition to the Minters, Flory sent several activists to southern Africa, including early SAC members Don and Gail Morlan and in later years Tami Hultman and Reed Kramer, who later founded the Africa News Service.[43] But the FIM was also an important program for introducing motivated young activists to ideas of revolution even when the volunteers did not intern in southern Africa. Flory's progressive politics had become increasingly radicalized under the influence of past and present volunteers and the social pressures of Black Power, Vietnam, and women's liberation. "There has been a growing conviction within the program," one FIM pamphlet explained, "that, in the face of Western dominance in the world, Christians must expose exploitative relationships and struggle for just and humane relations through interchange and interdependence."[44] Political and spiritual liberation became a defining element of the FIM, and Flory wanted to introduce volunteers in Africa to the movements seeking this goal—through violent and peaceful means alike.[45]

Eileen Hanson's experience provides an example of this process. The young Lutheran from the Midwest had only a vague knowledge of the African continent when she began preparations to serve in independent Cote D'Ivoire in 1966. She had worked with the NSCF in Chicago and briefly helped organize activities on southern Africa there, but it was two months of travel as part of the Southern Africa Seminar before her FIM service began that opened her eyes to the liberation cause.[46] Spending time in Dar es Salaam and South Africa, she was shocked at the depth of segregation in the apartheid state. Her upbringing in Minnesota and Illinois had shielded her from the worst kinds of racial discrimination, and she did not truly understand the challenges of life in South Africa or the colonies until she witnessed them. In Zambia and Tanzania, she spoke with several liberation leaders, who encouraged her to act in whatever way she could.[47] This formative event shaped the way she understood her two-year mission in independent Cote d'Ivoire, and—like the Wileys and Minters—it inspired her to expand her work on behalf of the liberation movements when she returned home.

Figure 6. The members of the Zambia Group at their first meeting, at Hank Crane's house in Zambia, 1967. From left to right are Dave Wiley, Gail Morlan (Hovey), Don Morlan, Carolyn Wilhelm, Charles Wilhelm, Ruth Minter (Brandon), Bill Minter, Dave Robinson, Marylee Wiley (Crofts), and Hank Crane. The group met almost annually for several years, with Anne Crane and Eileen Hanson joining by 1970. Reproduced with permission of Gail Hovey.

The FIM's most important role, however, was cultivating an activist community, cementing and expanding the network begun with the SAC. While the Minters and the Morlans were on the continent in 1967, Flory facilitated a gathering of African Frontier Interns at the home of Hank Crane in Zambia. Also attending were the Wileys, who were in Zambia while Dave conducted his doctoral research.[48] Most knew one another through the SAC (now part of the recently renamed University Christian Movement, or UCM), but this meeting was a watershed. The attendees wrote a document that integrated their activist experiences, close associations with the socialist nationalist parties, and immediate knowledge of life under minority rule into a common set of goals and strategies.[49] The paper captured an emerging consensus among activists on the relationship between the United States and southern Africa, expressing ideas that influenced U.S. solidarity organizing for decades.

The group reaffirmed the regional definition of solidarity work but expanded it to include a wider critique of Cold War policies, notably the reactionary anti-communism that sustained the White Redoubt. It recognized that South African apartheid differed from colonialism in Mozambique and Angola, but they shared a common logic and would require overlapping strategies to undermine support for them in the United States. The group pledged to champion the creation of new societies on the "basis of majority rule and an equitable distribution of wealth." The young Americans accepted the three-pronged vision of revolution championed by the CONCP parties that envisioned internal change, military revolt, and external pressure—dedicating themselves to the final element. The goal was not just to change U.S. policy toward Portugal, Rhodesia, and South Africa but also to eliminate the dominant official mindset that viewed the region through a narrow Cold War lens. Conditioning the U.S. government to accept southern African independence—which they assumed included socialism—would influence other NATO powers. This shift in thinking was essential, the group wrote, "if Western response in the future, when it is forced to act, is to be a positive contribution rather than unthinking counter-revolution on the model of Vietnam."[50] Beyond rejecting colonialism and minority rule, the young activists sincerely supported the socialist nation-building projects developing in southern Africa, which needed protection after independence as much as assistance before it.

The attendees understood this would be a herculean task, so they established a five-part strategy for forcing southern Africa onto the national agenda alongside more pressing issues like Vietnam. First, sympathetic Americans needed to improve communications, both among themselves in the organizing of solidarity activities and with the nationalists who led the revolutions. Second, research was necessary to reveal the nature of U.S. involvement in the region and provide an alternative to official narratives that promoted continued collaboration with Portugal and the minority regimes. Third, publications "geared to a wide variety of audiences" were necessary to promote nationalist appeals and critical readings of U.S. foreign policy. Fourth, activists had to use this foundation as a platform for fundraising, providing material and monetary support for nation-building projects and military campaigns. Finally, each of these efforts would fuel constituency building and expand the power of the solidarity movement. The Zambia collective believed that small, local groups drawn from the broad base of universities, churches, labor unions, African exile communities, and Peace Corps alumni would inform a decentralized grassroots political-solidarity structure. Contrasting their vision of what they called a "catalytic membership organization" with the more "elitist, single strategy" ACOA, the youth hoped their vision would produce a mass anti-imperial movement "concerned about constituency and supple and alert in its application of appropriate strategies."[51] They pursued goals similar to those of ACOA, but they did so in a way that privileged the needs of the CONCP nationalists and relied on the participatory politics of the New Left.

Creating the Solidarity Movement: Education and Activism in the Youth Left

"The Zambia Group" or simply "the Group," as its members referred to themselves collectively, was not a formal organization but a network of like-minded individuals determined to build an American solidarity movement with progressive African nationalists. As they returned to the United States, the members took advantage of an auspicious moment to establish a web of organizations to aid the liberation parties. Antiwar protests grew rapidly in the same year they gathered in Zambia, while the Black Power movement continued to strengthen in the late 1960s. The Zambia Group took advantage of this radical turn, building new alliances by linking its opposition to U.S.-backed minority regimes with popular anger at seemingly undemocratic domestic institutions. This work expanded on the previous activity of the SAC, providing forums where antiwar activists could learn how southern Africa related to Vietnam, while new recruits could discover the racial inequalities that plagued the international system. This network expanded beyond the religiously affiliated Zambia Group to include radical organizations and organizers that used Marxist theory to justify African liberation. The transition from the 1960s to the next decade saw these constituencies intermix and unite in a common movement supporting African liberation, specifically the CONCP parties.

The creation of these myriad, small, and often idiosyncratic organizations hid the vitality of the movement, leading historians to lament the fracturing of the U.S. political scene, but in fact they served a vital purpose in translating the Lusophone struggles. Mondlane sought support across multiple constituencies, and FRELIMO continued these efforts. After the party sent Sharfudine Khan to act as its emissary to the United States in 1967, he expanded the network created by Mondlane to tap into this new grassroots energy. Khan

argued that U.S. activists needed to "inform and educate" the new generation of sympathetic Americans about the realities of the revolutions, so they
could intensify "pressure on Portugal and the governments supporting her."[52]
This involved presenting their struggles—particularly in Guinea-Bissau and
Mozambique—as direct confrontations with a Euro-American imperial system. But the parties understood that the creation of an effective solidarity
movement required Americans to translate the cause for popular consumption in their specific contexts, so they accepted supporting roles that allowed
groups to articulate their own interpretations of the revolutions that would
resonate with local audiences. Khan explained at one point, "You know better
than ourselves the situation in which you work, so we can only suggest ways
in which you might celebrate [solidarity] with us."[53] ACOA successfully fulfilled this task for years among civil rights leaders and well-to-do liberals, but
the Zambia Group and other youth activists felt that the committee was not
necessarily speaking to them. As a result, it became the mission of this loose
network and a growing number of radical allies to broaden the movement by
addressing the antiwar generation.

As FIMers returned to the United States, life took them in different geographical and tactical directions, even as they remained committed to a
common strategy. The SAC continued as an important node in this network.
Though most of its earliest members, including the Wileys and the Minters,
left the East Coast for professional reasons, the committee continued to operate around a core that included Gail Morlan (now Hovey), Tim Smith, and
antiwar activist Robert Maurer. The group remained on Riverside Drive in the
complex of religious organizations clustered around Union and the NCC, but
it outlasted the UCM and slowly became independent of the church structure. Most important, the SAC expanded its influence with the publication
of *Southern Africa* in 1967. Its news did not come via Associated Press wire
but through personal relationships and information exchanges in the nascent
solidarity network. Along with the Dutch *Facts and Report* that began repub-
lishing carefully selected articles from around the world shortly thereafter, it
became a primary source of information on events in the region.

While the SAC expanded its influence, many of its former members con-
tinued promoting the cause of African liberation after they left New York.
There were two main options: launch new organizations or join existing anti-
imperial groups evolving in concert with the antiwar movement. FIM and
SAC alumni helped found organizations in Chicago, Toronto, Durham, North
Carolina, and elsewhere. One example was the Madison Area Committee on

Southern Africa (MACSA), which played an important role linking African issues to the emerging New Left. Dave and Marylee Wiley launched MACSA in 1968, when Dave took a position as assistant professor at the University of Wisconsin. They were joined later by Bill and Ruth Minter, other Africanist graduate students such as Allen and Barbara Isaacman, and several Black South African exiles.[54] The small organization formed because there was growing interest in southern Africa but little formal organization outside New York. The Wileys argued that "'liberal,' 'student,' and 'civil rights' organizations" had failed to maintain solidarity programs because of the tangential relationship to core domestic concerns. MACSA justified its focus on Africa by taking an anti-imperial approach, which presented the liberation movements as fighting global structures of racism and exploitation that also sustained domestic inequality. It encouraged participation by "any person or group" committed to the "weakening of the southern African systems," and sought to cultivate relationships with Wisconsin politicians and other Midwestern congressmen, including Charles Diggs and Donald Fraser.[55] Though never numbering many more than twenty or so active members at any one point, the committee cooperated with Black, religious, and antiwar groups to engage hundreds on campus and became a pivotal element of the Madison and Midwest political culture.

MACSA focused on three activities: research, education, and coordination of activism in the Midwest. Taking a page from the SAC's bank campaign, and the embryonic boycott of Gulf Oil's activities in Angola discussed in chapter 8, the committee explained in concrete detail how U.S. business activities in southern Africa sustained the minority regimes, with an emphasis on Wisconsin firms. It also linked liberation in southern Africa with that in the Middle East by investigating Israel's ties to the repressive regime in South Africa.[56] Other research informed articles appearing regularly in the bimonthly newsletter distributed throughout the Midwest in the early 1970s, small pamphlets, and educational outreach. MACSA used solidarity days and teach-ins to publicize their work and mobilize support in schools, universities, and religious institutions, while cooperation with local fundraising activities allowed it to send tens of thousands of dollars to FRELIMO's Mozambique Institute and smaller amounts to other parties.[57] Under the influence of former FIMers and other members, the committee emphasized direct contact with African revolutionaries, making Madison a waypoint for nationalists traveling the country on speaking tours ,including Sharfudine Khan, FRELIMO's Armando Guebuza, and Oliver Tambo of the ANC. Marylee Wiley developed the outreach program for the university's African Studies Center, which encouraged local schools and religious organizations to invite students from Africa studying in Madison to translate their personal experiences for local people.[58] By appealing to a diverse array of regional constituencies, MACSA acted as a coordinating point for the various groups as they entered alliances across social and political fault lines.[59] It became a significant conduit, feeding information on African issues into the New Left while also promoting activism in a section of the country distant from existing groups like ACOA and the SAC that operated on the eastern seaboard.

In expanding solidarity efforts to the interior of the country, MACSA cooperated with a broader anti-imperialist collective that involved other members of the Zambia Group: the Committee of Returned Volunteers (CRV). CRV membership consisted primarily of Peace Corps volunteers who had become disillusioned with U.S. policy during their time abroad. They were joined by a handful of other volunteers and missionaries who spent time in the developing world, notably former FIM member Eileen Hanson.[60] In contrast to MACSA, the CRV did not form with the specific intention of publicizing the issues of southern Africa in one location. The CRV's critique of the U.S. system was broader, and its membership numbered in the thousands across nearly a dozen major cities.[61] It aimed at combatting what it understood as a pernicious U.S. imperialism that was manifested in the Global South as predatory capitalism, reactionary militarism, and indifference to deep political inequalities. Service abroad disillusioned members with development strategies they felt were paternalistic and incremental at best.[62] The organization believed that a global revolution was necessary, including drastic structural changes and perhaps emancipatory violence undertaken by Global South peoples.[63] The CRV sought to challenge the reactionary popular mindset at home by explaining the relationship between international and domestic structural inequalities and by building solidarity with revolutionary groups abroad. As one member explained bluntly, "We are bound together by our belief that great domestic changes are needed in the U.S., and our conviction that the United States is screwing the underdeveloped countries."[64] The CRV demanded the abolition of the Peace Corps and programs they believed constrained such foreign revolutions, and it focused secondarily on opposing the Vietnam War as the primary example of U.S. overreach. Yet few of the returnees had actually served in Southeast Asia, so the committee soon adopted a different regional focus: southern Africa and the Portuguese colonies.[65]

Most of the CRV leadership worked either in Africa or in Latin America, and they felt that U.S. involvement in these nations should receive attention alongside opposition to the Vietnam War.[66] The result was the creation of a number of regional committees that objected to, in the CRV's words, a U.S. government that maintained "the status quo of wealth and privilege for the few and poverty and ignorance for the many" around the globe.[67] CRV Africa Committee members served all over the continent, but the immediacy of the Portuguese wars and the influence of individuals like Hanson and Nancy Free-hafer, who worked with FRELIMO in Dar es Salaam, focused action on the outstanding issue of colonialism.[68] Freehafer had the support of Sharfudine Khan, whose presence in New York, accessibility, and encouragement made the focus on Mozambique seem almost "automatic," as Peace Corps alumna Mimi Edmunds remembered.[69] At the first CRV congress in 1969, the group voted to focus on southern Africa as one of two primary campaigns alongside the war in Southeast Asia. The ongoing revolutions represented to the young radicals an example of Che Guevara's widely cited tricontinental dictum that there must be "1, 2, many Vietnams" in order to undermine the "international system of oppression and exploitation" that linked the United States to colonial institutions.[70] With this predilection for revolutions in mind, the struggles in Mozambique and Angola quickly became the focal points of the campaign, informing two of the committee's most ambitious research studies. Mirroring closely the FRELIMO party doctrines that influenced them, CRV activists hoped to isolate Portugal and prevent new countries—specifically the United States—from asserting power after decolonization.[71]

More overtly radical than MACSA, with whom it collaborated, the CRV Africa Committee used research and education to engage with a consciously New Left audience. The CRV developed an aggressive plan of action that included letter-writing campaigns, informational sessions, protests, and direct support for the liberation movements.[72] Pamphlets like *Mozambique Will Be Free* aimed to make leftists "aware of what [was] happening in another part of the world" so they could organize in its defense.[73] In so doing, the group acted as a surrogate propagandist for FRELIMO. The CRV took many of its ideological and rhetorical cues from the party, but they followed Khan's call to tailor their activism for U.S. readers entrenched in a specific culture. The group equated Vietnam with the Portuguese colonies, predicting that they would follow a similar path from being colonies to Cold War battlefields.[74] In so doing, the CRV made the powerful argument that southern Africa might "become another Vietnam," using its network of more than two dozen local branches to inject the Lusophone colonial wars into the discourse of the antiwar left as troop levels declined in Southeast Asia.[75] After it moved its headquarters from New York City to the heartland capital of Chicago, the committee became the center of a new radicalism that encompassed disillusioned youth, religious radicals, and myriad other constituencies under a single anti-imperial umbrella. In so doing, it reinforced the creation of a New Left Internationalism by merging the priorities of the antiwar and solidarity movements.

The leftward drift of solidarity organizing brought the extended Zambia Group network into the political orbit of like-minded organizations with origins in more traditional leftist thought, notably the Marxist-inclined, border-crossing Liberation Support Movement (LSM). LSM emerged from the work of anthropologist Don Barnett, whose dissertation at UCLA had been among the first to provide a sympathetic account of Kenya's Mau Mau rebellion based on extensive local interviews.[76] The activist scholar traveled widely in East Africa, spending more than a year living in Dar es Salaam, where he made contacts with various liberation movements. Barnett's strongest bonds developed with the MPLA thanks to its clearer commitment to Marxist politics.[77] As Barnett explained later, he was impressed by the MPLA's plans for rebuilding the country and hoped it could use its national riches and geopolitical position to become "Africa's Cuba . . . or perhaps its 'Vietnam.'"[78] For its part, the Angolan party welcomed interest from an enthusiastic American who seemed willing to work on behalf of its cause in North America. It granted Barnett access to senior leaders, who explained their goals and methods. Agostinho Neto even invited the anthropologist into Angola to document the first party assembly held in liberated territory in August 1968, in the temporary camp aptly named Hanoi II, roughly 175 miles from the Zambian border.[79] Barnett wrote approvingly of these experiences in several articles for left-wing periodicals such as the New York-based independent weekly *Guardian* (formerly *National Guardian*), introducing American audiences to the individuals and ideologies motivating the MPLA.[80]

Barnett returned to the United States with the goal of building a solidarity movement while assuming various university professorships. At the University of Iowa, he cultivated a following among radical students that became LSM. His politics won few admirers in late 1960s farm country, so in 1968 he moved to Canada's Simon Fraser University, which was a hotbed of activist scholarship. The professor, whom LSM member Ole Gjerstad remembered as an "extremely charismatic, demanding, disciplined person," pushed his students to understand world events in the context of Marxist ideology. His academic position was less about career advancement than a location to recruit dedicated youth to his movement. Politically minded students gravitated to the practical academic, particularly older students who had taken more circuitous paths to collegiate studies and had less patience with the ideologically diffuse, sometimes chaotic protests that typified some student actions later in the decade. By 1970, Barnett's LSM stretched from Vancouver, through Seattle, to its headquarters in the Bay Area, with a small amount of support remaining in the Midwest. Barnett envisioned this professional cadre as the radical center of a larger movement, mobilizing action through educational outreach, publishing, and material aid to foreign revolutions.[81]

From its founding in 1969, the LSM emerged as a major national organization providing a radical informational alternative to groups like ACOA, skewing even further left than MACSA. While never openly hostile to more centrist perspectives, its avowedly Marxist anti-imperialism and solidarity with the MPLA set the group apart. So did its emphasis on presenting the stories of liberation leaders in their own words, highlighted by a series of pamphlets featuring MPLA revolutionaries explaining their goals to foreign audiences at length. Later publications featured leaders of other southern African movements, including FRELIMO's most outspoken Marxist, Marcelino dos Santos.[82] These "life histories" provided conversational overviews of party philosophy and strategy that proved invigorating, educational, and broadly appealing. LSM member Rick Sterling remembers that they were seen by many as "a testament to what the realities were in that time and place."[83] While self-consciously political, they cut through ideological debates by giving the liberation movements their own platform, highlighting the search for political authenticity and deference to Global South ideas that typified the emerging New Left Internationalism. This "first person" approach defined LSM publications, from the reproduction of documents and speeches by Agostinho Neto to the popular liberation calendar that featured quotes, noteworthy dates in liberation history, and photos, primarily of the Portuguese movements.[84] These publications created personal connections with the liberation movements for activists who never left the United States, with the calendar providing a daily reminder of the need for solidarity.

The LSM promoted an integrated strategy of information dissemination, aided by consciousness-raising protests locally and at the national level. Articles in nationally distributed New Left journals, notably the *Guardian*, raised the group's profile, and it was soon in high demand as the voice for Africa on the left.[85] From 1971 to 1977, the movement conducted national educational tours featuring slide shows and films on the African liberation movements. Appearances at college campuses and community centers from the Midwest to the East Coast reinforced the growing knowledge of southern Africa. Forays into the American South with a mobile film unit introduced hundreds in such states as Mississippi and Alabama to assertive Black revolution. The predominantly white LSM members were overwhelmingly welcomed by Black communities there, though visits were cut short by hostile authorities on several occasions.[86] The LSM also became an important channel for connecting domestic audiences with radical African voices, working with familiar personalities like FRELIMO's Khan while championing outspoken Marxists who rarely found themselves invited to the United States. In 1970, for instance, the Seattle branch arranged for a tour by Angolan guerrilla fighter José Condesse, who spoke at local universities and met with Black Panthers before visiting Iowa City, Detroit, Reading, Harlem, and Ontario with LSM support.[87] As the group's reputation grew, orders for publications and requests for aid came in from across the United States and Western Europe.[88] The publications, events, and personal appearances collected tens of thousands of dollars, funding propaganda training for MPLA cadres, the production and distribution of medical textbooks, and the shipment of medical supplies, radio equipment, surplus military gear, and a printing press.[89] By late 1970, the LSM's network of connections led the liberation movements and their European allies to identify LSM as a "priority centre" for coordinating literature distribution and solidarity activities in North America.[90]

Despite the centrality of Marxism to the LSM, it adopted the same cooperative attitude as other solidarity organizations and avoided the political infighting that hobbled antiwar coalitions. The MPLA was itself a front, filled with a diverse array of perspectives. It embraced a Leninist communism more readily than any of its CONCP allies but still refused to adopt a single label. This meant that activists who understood the situation in the Portuguese colonies eschewed taking strong ideological lines. Rather, activists in the LSM and other groups "always followed [the African parties'] lead" in casting a wide net to build solidarity, rejecting only advocates of Roberto's FNLA that they associated with U.S. imperialism. The LSM was willing to work with any group seriously dedicated to promoting the CONCP revolutions. As Rick Sterling remembers, "We tended to work well with the groups that were actually doing things on the ground, either through material support or really good effective outreach activity." This included ACOA, MACSA, the SAC,

Youth Against Fascism and War, the Dutch Angola Comité, and even U.N. subcommittees.[91] The LSM also made critical inroads into the Black community thanks to its emphasis on African voices, becoming one of the first nonblack domestic organizations to print articles in the *Black Panther* and collaborating with Newark's Black Power sage, Amiri Baraka (discussed in Chapters 7 and 8).[92] Though the LSM occupied a position on the far left, its willingness to listen to the African liberation struggles convinced it to pursue connections across the political spectrum. The result was good working relationships with the organizations that came out of the Zambia Group network. These groups adopted different approaches and catered to different audiences based on their individual identities, locations, and ideological proclivities, but they collaborated with the common goal of supporting the liberation movements and challenging reactionary U.S. foreign policy.

The combined membership of Lusophone solidarity groups was modest in comparison to other causes of the era, but their work raised the profile of the Portuguese African wars—and southern Africa generally. The Lusophone revolutions never displaced Vietnam as the preeminent radical cause, but they became complementary, secondary fronts in the domestic war against U.S. imperialism. In 1968, the Portuguese colonies would be cited along with Vietnam during the occupation of Columbia University, where many of SAC's secular members worked.[93] Activists also convinced major national campaigns to pay greater attention to the Portuguese colonies, most notably the New Mobilization Committee to End the War in Vietnam (New Mobe).[94] Activist Bill Ayers looked back at the Lusophone struggles as integral parts of a global revolution, explaining: "The world is in flames, we thought, the people of the world rising against the octopus of imperialism and cutting off its tentacles one by one. It was a compelling image, apocalyptic: Cuba, one, Korea, two, Guinea-Bissau, Mozambique, Angola, Algeria, Ghana, and Viet Nam, of course, number eight, where the monster had overextended itself once and for all."[95] Groups like LSM, CRV, and MACSA helped tear down regional barriers and integrate southern Africa into a radical critique that had focused overwhelmingly on Southeast Asia. When Mondlane had traveled around the United States, he needed to explain Mozambique's situation and the logic for revolution. After 1970, Khan found himself speaking to well-informed crowds who no longer required justifications but instead requested guidance on how they could support FRELIMO's struggle.[96]

The growth of the solidarity movement did not proceed smoothly on all fronts. Groups cooperated, but they faced internal issues. Most prominent was the continuing issue of racial diversity—or a lack thereof—within the movement. All the groups were multiracial, but most were predominantly white in their leadership and membership. Activist Robert Maurer remembers being troubled by the fact that the New York City–based SAC had no Blacks attending meetings in the 1960s; the lone African American associated with the committee—Prexy Nesbitt—resided in Chicago.[97] Whites and Africans constituted much of MACSA's membership, though the organization worked regularly with African American student groups.[98] Some, like Maurer, felt that Black leaders had simply failed to fully articulate the linkages between the international and domestic freedom struggles. Given the difficulties experienced by the ANLCA, there was some truth to the idea, but the problem also reflected Cold War trade-offs demanded of Black activists and ultimately served to reinforce the Black Power movement's wariness of multiracial alliances. Where groups had Black memberships, tensions sometimes developed over the perceived inappropriateness of whites leading an anticolonial solidarity movement with Black African revolutions. This led one leftist news organization, the Boston-based Africa Research Group, to voluntarily dissolve in 1972 and pass its materials to the newly formed Africa Information Service, whose leadership included two prominent African American activists – Prexy Nesbitt and Robert Van Lierop – discussed in later chapters.[99] Such tensions were never fully resolved, but they informed the creation of Black-led organizations that could work collaboratively on African issues with existing groups while maintaining distinct identities and priorities.

The left wing of the solidarity network was well established by 1972. The SAC, LSM, and organizations with ties to the Zambia Group like MACSA acted as the informational center of the movement. Most drew heavily on a core of activists composed of veterans of the religious youth, supplemented by an overlapping population of anti-imperial leftists from various backgrounds. *Southern Africa* provided the monthly news on the region that rarely appeared in mainstream newspapers. LSM gave voice to the revolutions themselves, disseminating their Marxist-inspired analysis and presenting the realities of their wars and national reconstruction projects. CRV and MACSA research provided critical analysis of U.S. activities in southern Africa, as did other organizations such as the short-lived but impactful Africa Research Group, which was founded with the assistance of SAC members and had a regular column in the *Guardian* before its dissolution. Each of these groups, their branches, and others like them around the country undertook varying levels of grassroots protest to dramatize their findings for the public and government officials. The main purpose of this activism was to spread awareness of the liberation movements, provide avenues for personal identification with them, dramatize the issues to win attention from new audiences, and increase public pressure on government and businesses to reassess their ties to Portugal and the minority governments.

At the center of this movement was not a single ideology but rather a more general internationalist outlook that aligned with New Left politics and tricontinental visions of Global South revolution. The Marxist LSM, radical CRV, and academic MACSA all rallied behind a criticism of Western policy that backed a deeply unequal status quo and unrestrained global capitalism. Many activists were originally influenced by Christian moralism, but this quickly gave way to leftist critique of an international structure skewed against Third World peoples. This provided common ground for collaboration with more traditional Marxists like those in the LSM, but these religious origins played an important role in maintaining connections to earlier pro-independence activists like George Houser and Margaret Flory. Central to this emerging New Left Internationalism was a common belief that change would emerge from the periphery, where the preponderant power of the Global North was fraying under the weight of colonialism and Cold War interventionism. Activists believed that taking cues from the Global South was necessary to move beyond the Western tradition of limited political reforms that maintained and even reinforced the racial, economic, and social inequalities of the Eurocentric international system.[100] This hostility to the status quo and commitment to empowering South Global actors led U.S. activists to focus on two activities: providing what material support they could and building a domestic movement against U.S. support for Portugal and the White Redoubt. This latter issue proved vital for integrating African activism with the burgeoning antiwar movement and for contributing to the creation of a New Left Internationalism.

Yet for the most part the expansion of the solidarity movement did not lead to the bickering and collapse that affected anti-Vietnam organizing. The network of personal relationships that produced the student activists led them to maintain relationships with the liberal organizations that preceded and inspired them. Above all there was ACOA, which through Houser's stewardship maintained the largest research files, the best contacts, and the most extensive (though still meager) resources. The major activist groups from the Marxist LSM to the more moderate SAC recommended fact sheets and letters from ACOA while mining ACOA's sources to agitate for African priorities within communities that sometimes viewed the old guard with suspicion. Moreover, so long as both the churches and ACOA voiced criticism of government policy in some way, the activists were not going to break with them. All were opposed to the same U.S. structures that were inhibiting independence, and, as CRVer Mimi Edmunds remembered, it was important to maintain "somewhat of a united front."[101] By continuing to work with ACOA and church organizations, the radical youth activists maintained access to information, funding, foreign contacts, and the handful of policymakers interested in Africa. Their presence both in and alongside these established organizations provided the opportunity to help guide their actions, pulling what were once consistent if reluctant adherents to Cold War liberalism in increasingly revisionist and internationalist directions.

Transforming Established Institutions

The radicalization of youth activism that led Christian youth to participate in organizations like the Committee of Returned Volunteers (CRV) and make common cause with the leftist Liberation Support Movement (LSM) created awkwardness with existing institutions like ACOA, but it did not sever relations. Rather, the integration of more radical youth within these organizations and a willingness to collaborate across political and generational lines in pursuit of common causes helped transform established institutions. Youth organizations like the Southern Africa Committee (SAC) played important roles in shaping how major institutions confronted a changing international system and rethought traditional relationships with the Global South. This process has been underappreciated in 1960s literature, thanks to the lingering cliché of generational conflict and a tendency to highlight the loudest youth organizations that often eschewed broader collaborations. By contrast, the success of Lusophone solidarity depended heavily on the relationships that existed within and across major institutions. Multigenerational alliances provided avenues through which young activists accessed both expertise and funding while empowering reformist elements within established organizations that hoped to transform the political and moral calculations of institutions like ACOA and the National Council of Churches (NCC).

This process was directly aided by liberation leaders, whose practical needs and desire for broad political engagement encouraged inclusive visions of solidarity. FRELIMO's president Eduardo Mondlane—with his ties to church and liberal institutions—proved important in facilitating these shifts in the United States, but all the CONCP leadership highlighted the necessity of broad political fronts. FRELIMO's success in expanding U.S. support encouraged the PAIGC and, to a lesser extent, the MPLA to expend greater energy in North America, especially after Mondlane's assassination. The national crisis surrounding Vietnam facilitated this transformation by challenging sacred canards of anti-communism and U.S. superiority, but liberation leaders and activists went further by promoting the ambitious social agendas of the revolutionary movements that dovetailed with New Left priorities. Using Portugal's antiquated colonialism as a foil, the Lusophone revolutions offered opportunities to take aggressive positions on issues of empire, militarism, southern African liberation, and problematic Cold War alliances without having to directly associate with forces fighting U.S. soldiers in Vietnam. As a result, high-profile organizations such as ACOA and the NCC increasingly accepted ideas of militant liberation, the socialist parties of the CONCP, and their anti-imperial ideology. These institutional transformations began as a direct response to decolonization, but young activists facilitated this final step toward active, public support for revolutionary nationalists and their ambitious goals. Stalwart liberal institutions lurched to the left, empowering more assertive political agendas that challenged official and unofficial complicity in empire and white minority rule.

Changing the NCC

The institutional transformation of liberal organizations was part of an ongoing process in which decolonization challenged Western relationships with the Global South forged within and as a response to formal practices of colonialism. Especially within the religious community, reformers began rethinking the well-intentioned paternalism of Christian missions in ways that could preserve the concept of transnational community without reinforcing imperial structures. This involved greater attention to southern African perspectives, which explained Mondlane's ubiquitous involvement in church conferences, but it also involved empowering youth whose perspective on Christian mission increasingly centered on global visions of social and racial justice. This had been central to the Frontier Internship in Mission (FIM) idea, with the understanding that this new generation of Christian advocates would facilitate a transformation within larger church communities. While young activists regularly expressed frustration with the cautiousness of established institutions like the NCC and its denominational members, they understood they had allies within these organizations.

A commitment to institutional reform was central to the network that formed around the Zambia Group and the SAC. Their ties to early supporters of African freedom convinced these youth activists that ACOA and Protestant leaderships within the NCC were candidates for meaningful change. One of the SAC's foundational principles was to push the churches "to help make the many well-phrased resolutions [on Africa] be something more than words."[1] The Zambia Group's 1967 strategy document, which Margaret Flory circulated to NCC leaders, sought to establish a practical movement supporting southern African revolution led by youth but amplified by the resources of established groups.[2] Their stated goal to transform ACOA from "an elitist, single-strategy group to a catalytic membership organization" was part of this strategy. The Zambia Group urged individuals like ACOA employee and SAC member Janet Hooper (née MacLaughlin) to push Houser in that direction, and groups like the SAC to "work as closely as feasible with them" to shift the focus of the organization.[3] From the outset, youth activists understood that they needed to recruit established institutions—with their experience, resources, and connections—to complement grassroots efforts in order to build an effective national movement.

The churches became the logical starting point due to their power and existing ties with the SAC and Zambia Group network. Though many of the leaders in the NCC and its individual Protestant denominations trended toward a cautious liberalism, they had a unique ability to amplify and legitimize the message of the youth organizations. Their membership constituted some of the most influential lawmakers and business officials, as well as millions of stockholders and consumers. Churches were intimately connected to foundations, universities, and research groups, and the NCC communicated with top levels of the government and the State Department. The churches also had economic power. By the 1970s, the national institutions held roughly three billion dollars in various stocks, mostly tied to pensions.[4] Swaying the NCC leadership and key members to actively back the liberation movements not only held important ramifications for shifting official policy away from cooperation with Portugal and the minority regimes; it had the potential to pressure businesses as well. Most important, elements within the churches were clearly rethinking their relationships to the Global South and had been doing so even before the Vietnam War created new pressures on religious leaders. The conferences of the 1950s and Flory's FIM were just two examples of an evolving trend, so young activists felt optimistic that they could direct the churches toward more assertive positions.

Identifying a problem and responding to it were two different issues. While many of the NCC's constituent churches recognized the need for new directions in the Global South, church leaderships were generally cautious, and there was no new consensus. This contextualized the SAC's unsuccessful appeal to NCC members during the anti-apartheid bank campaign in 1965. The churches balked at the idea of divesting their funds for practical economic reasons and expressed unease with politicizing investments based on indirect corporate support for problematic policies. Yet only two years later the thinking at the top of the NCC looked much different. In 1967, the NCC expanded past efforts at building bridges to communist countries as part of an ecumenical humanism to openly questioning the moral foundations of the Cold War and the global mission of the United States. In a study entitled the "Imperatives of Peace and Responsibilities of Power," the council asserted, according to historian Jill K. Gill, that "justice must be the foundation for true national security and international peace in an increasingly interdependent world—not occupational military forces."[5] The NCC was beginning to articulate an anti-imperial critique of U.S. involvement in the Global South that extended to official support for countries like Portugal and South Africa.

The sudden change at the NCC was the result of the organization's reaction to events concentrated in the Global South. Though the NCC had long favored decolonization and opposed minority government, its direct and extended criticism of U.S. policies after 1967 was new. An overt patriotism gave way to a loyal opposition in response to the one-two punch in 1965 of expanded commitment to the Vietnam War and the Rhodesian Unilateral Declaration of Independence. Over the following two years, these two events necessitated a rethinking of core assumptions about foreign affairs. The NCC adopted more assertive programs that provided international complements to the domestic achievements of the civil rights era.[6] Actions on Vietnam earned the most attention during this initial phase, but the vision was global and demanded a rethinking of core tenets of U.S. policy. Specifically, the NCC leadership argued that justice had to trump the search for order and stability at all costs, recommending the protection of human rights, constraints on military adventurism, and support for the economic and cultural vitality of all peoples through the creation of Global South institutions free of U.S. control.[7] The new program focused on four areas that included global race relations, with a special emphasis on Vietnam and southern Africa, with the latter featuring a prominent space for Lusophone Africa.[8] The NCC worried that the U.S. government had embraced the status quo in southern Africa, raising the likelihood of expanded violence as the white governments refused to recognize the legitimate political and moral demands contained in calls for self-determination. Educational programs were needed to change the way that parishioners and the government viewed regional politics, lest the hint of communist intrigue turn yet another regional conflict into the next Cold War quagmire.

While youth activists would play a vital role developing these programs, their initial impetus came from an older generation with close ties to Luso-phone nationalists. The NCC's International Affairs Department looked to former missionaries to guide its new program. The fact that American Protestant missions had deep roots in southern Africa—the United Church of Christ operated in Angola for more than ninety years—promoted a sense of obligation alongside firsthand, usually sympathetic knowledge of the nationalist movements.[9] Clampdowns by the White Redoubt states after 1961 greatly reduced the number of missionaries in the region, but there remained strong connections to Christian-trained nationalists like FRELIMO's Eduardo Mondlane and the MPLA's Agostinho Neto, even as they adopted revolutionary tactics. Among their most vocal proponents was Bishop Ralph Dodge, an Iowa-born Methodist who began serving his mission to Angola in 1936 and helped facilitate Neto's studies in Portugal. After he was elected bishop by the Africa Central Conference in 1956, Portugal banned him due to his nationalist connections.[10] He continued to support the nationalist cause, trying to cultivate relations between ACOA and the MPLA in 1962.[11] As the NCC rethought its approach to the Global South, Dodge encouraged a search for a "new strategy" in southern Africa, which would ideally go beyond the traditional focus on apartheid to address what one church leader called the "real issues" associated with the active revolutions in "Mozambique, Angola, etc."[12] Dodge was joined in his efforts by Murray MacInnes, a Canadian missionary who served in Angola until 1964 and witnessed firsthand the violence the Portuguese used in crushing the 1961 rebellion.[13]

Because Dodge and MacInnes were not regularly around the NCC "God Box" headquarters, they benefited from the presence of youth activists who promoted and expanded their efforts. While much of the Zambia Group network left New York and founded new organizations to continue their activism, a handful remained and kept their religious connections. Among the SAC members involved in national church structures were Ken Carstens, beginning in 1966, Tim Smith soon after, and Gail Morlan intermittently by the end of the decade. They encouraged greater identification with the revolutionary movements, aided by this older generation with African ties. Dodge and MacInnes worked collaboratively with activists like Morlan and Carstens to help promote a southern African strategy that involved active identification with revolutionary parties challenging the White Redoubt and increasingly focused on the active struggles in the Portuguese colonies.[14] When MacInnes and others made recommendations on supporting the liberation movements, activists like Tim Smith championed their points in NCC deliberations.[15] This youth movement played a growing role within religious institutions' rethinking of their relationship with the Global South, especially in Africa.

The convergence of pro-nationalist missionaries and youth activists focused attention on the liberation parties, but the NCC's shift toward anti-imperialism initially sought to replicate elements of the civil rights movement by championing reforms through nonviolence. The idea of a military revolution remained anathema to top religious leaders, who hesitated to commit directly to the anti-imperial parties because they had taken up arms against Lisbon.[16] Even close allies like Dodge and MacInnes, who did not begrudge the nationalists the right to defend themselves, avoided overt advocacy for armed revolt. Adding to this general unease were the lingering Cold War concerns of some NCC officials, who retained a sufficient sense of anti-communist propriety to worry whether the guns used by FRELIMO, the PAIGC, and the MPLA came directly from the Eastern bloc.[17] These objections limited complete identification with the parties, much to the frustration of young activists. The youth did not celebrate violence; rather, they accepted the necessity of armed revolution as part of the larger political programs designed by the CONCP parties. It was hard to sell this idea to an older leadership, but they welcomed the internal debate as a step toward change. Among other realities, the question of whether to support militants made other, once radical ideas seem reasonable, even tame, by comparison. As a result, progressive denominations within the NCC changed their attitudes toward corporate investments in South Africa and the Portuguese colonies as a way of actively aligning with the liberation struggles, eventually inspiring a larger and more successful campaign against Gulf Oil that contrasted sharply with the failed Chase Bank efforts in 1965 (discussed in chapter 8).[18]

It was in this new context that FRELIMO's Mondlane provided the final ingredient for changing NCC policies. Given his prior reservations about military revolution, Mondlane was a perfect interlocutor in this generational debate. He appreciated the difficult decisions the churches faced, but his own conversion provided a model for adapting Christian internationalism to the needs of the tricontinental era. While justifying FRELIMO's struggle against Portugal, he emphasized the constructive aspects of the revolution that opened avenues for social support and formed the core of the CONCP strategy to win over Western officials. When he visited the NCC headquarters on Riverside Drive in early 1967, Mondlane explained the need for military struggle while stressing the moral duty church members had to support the national reconstruction of an independent Mozambique, with FRELIMO as the logical manifestation of this postcolonial government.[19] As the NCC considered new economic strategies for weakening Portugal and the wider White Redoubt, requests for medicines, textbooks, and similar nonmilitary support provided an opening for church leaders to engage with revolutionary parties and see them as something more than combatants.

Still, concerns about supporting revolution were slow to disappear among cautious church leaders. As the head of the Church World Services (CWS)—the NCC's international aid arm—explained to one of Mondlane's associates in Dar es Salaam, "We are not in the business to support political movements," especially when those movements were waging an armed struggle.[20] With encouragement from Bishop Dodge and his allies in the United States, Mondlane knew there was will for support, so he continued cultivating relations. After his 1967 visit, he sent Sharfudine Khan and the party's vice president to speak with church leaders in rapid succession.[21] FRELIMO consciously separated the medical program from military operations, reassuring church leaders that all donations could be directed toward civilian programs.[22] This mollified the NCC leadership, who approved assistance programs for FRELIMO by the end of 1967. While there were conditions placed on what supplies could be sent and to where, Bishop Dodge assured the leadership in New York that both Mondlane and the MPLA's Neto would "warmly welcome any assistance in meeting [humanitarian] needs in the occupied territories."[23] FRELIMO stressed that it preferred such assistance come from the West due to the high quality of its consumer and medical goods.[24] Church leaders had a way to respond to internal demands and support the anti-colonial cause without wholly backing armed revolution.

Mondlane hoped this social aid marked the first step in broader political support, but limited resources meant the FRELIMO president relied heavily on U.S. allies to promote this engagement, with youth activists playing a prominent role. While relatively junior within church leadership, they had unique knowledge and connections thanks to their overseas experience through the FIM and the Peace Corps, making them accessible resources as religious leaders and other institutions sought to understand the revolutionary parties. This was especially true in the case of Portuguese Africa. Senior figures like Bishop Dodge and Margaret Flory championed these young activists, with Flory finding positions for Zambia Group alumni and circulating the working paper that championed nation-building assistance to FRELIMO. After Bill and Ruth Minter returned from the Mozambique Institute in 1968, Flory arranged for them to work in New York, where Bill wrote a scathing critique of the Euro-American involvement in the liberation wars (published as *Portuguese Africa and the West*).[25] The NCC embraced these youthful perspectives as it advanced its Africa program, and Morlan, Carstens, Smith, and occasionally Minter encouraged the closer engagement with the revolutionary parties, while youth publications became required reading.[26] Smith, the field aide for African affairs for the United Church of Christ, who became particularly influential on investment issues, argued in an eight-page letter that made the rounds of the NCC leadership in 1969, "Revolution in Southern Africa is totally justifiable theologically, ethically, strategically, and politically. . . . The time is long past for us to sit and try to justify revolution theologically. It is time to try to interpret the African nationalist movements to the mass of an America fearful of any form of violence in the world, to press for a new American foreign policy (neither reactionary nor anti-revolutionary) which will insure that America will not intervene on behalf of the white status quo in Southern Africa, and to aid the liberation movements in as many ways as we possibly can."[27] For Smith and others, the rejection of armed revolution was a "hypocritical" remnant of the Eurocentric paternalism that many churches wanted to move past, so they needed to accept the liberation parties as the primary agents of change in southern Africa. As youth activists helped this thinking take hold, they joined with others in emphasizing the need to work most closely with the CONCP parties because—as Dodge explained—they were the ones "actually occupying territory in the southern block" and therefore had legitimate social needs that could be addressed by church assistance.[28]

These internal efforts gained powerful support from the one organization that claimed a broader membership than the NCC—the World Council of Churches. The WCC was the culmination of a liberal, activist strand of global ecumenism that broke away from the more conservative World Evangelical Alliance, whose members turned inward toward faith formation as liberal reformers sought global alliances to address social problems.[29] The 147 mostly Western, Protestant member churches that met at the first WCC meeting in 1948 focused on postwar issues related to poverty and refugees but quickly shifted to matters of war and peace as the superpower conflict solidified. During the 1950s, the WCC built connections with Eastern Orthodox churches and courted controversy by opening a dialogue with secular communists. A decade later, it embraced decolonization, welcoming new national members from Asia and Africa while providing moral support to solidarity efforts in the West. These attempts to position the ecumenical body between both East-West and North-South conflicts anticipated the political demands of the 1960s, which further encouraged WCC leadership to pursue this path. The fourth regular conference in the Swedish cathedral city of Uppsala in 1968 welcomed a membership much different from that of twenty years prior, with more than 2,400 delegates and staff from 240 organizations and 80 countries—many from the Global South. The conference theme of "worldwide revolution" self-consciously aligned the WCC with those fighting deep-seated global inequalities that separated richer Global North nations from the rest. Drawing on a biblical exegesis from Revelation that God "make[s] all things new," the delegates stressed "the positive character of mankind's revolutions—social, political, and economic—against old oppressions."[30] The deliberations promoted two elements that both reflected and encouraged Western solidarity activism: an increased attention to the demands of the Global South and expanded roles for young activists who embraced these ideas.

The result was direct WCC support for the liberation movements. The CONCP parties were familiar to many of the representatives at the conference. FRELIMO actively cultivated both religious and leftist allies across Europe in the mid-1960s, and the PAIGC was particularly popular in the Nordic countries. The July meeting was bracketed by the beginning of a major popular protest movement against Swedish corporate participation in the construction of Mozambique's Cahora Bassa Dam, which aimed to promote new Portuguese settlements in the colony.[31] With this campaign operating in the background, the Uppsala conference produced a series of reports that—in addition to taking positions on Christian practice and theology—promoted an activist stance on global economic and social developments. Notably, it broke with its historic summarization of members' missionary reports to produce a new, overarching statement of mission arguing that human rights, self-determination, and racial equality needed to become central components of religious life. The hope was that organized religious support could help "[divert the revolution] from destructive paths to constructive ways."[32]

It was notable that this statement revealed the growing attraction to positive ideas of revolution, which legitimized the idea of nation building in concert with militant struggles. As a result, the WCC embraced the CONCP parties, whose social programs in liberated territories aligned neatly with this conceptualization. Though the WCC worked with all of the Angolan parties, the PAIGC, the MPLA, and FRELIMO were the earliest and best-funded beneficiaries of the newly created Programme to Combat Racism, launched in 1969 to directly support movements redressing global inequalities.[33]

As the WCC view of the liberation parties intersected with that of U.S. proponents, the NCC agencies expanded their support for the liberation parties from 1968. Just months after church leaders sought assurances that FRELIMO would not use any aid for military purposes, the head of the Church World Services, Jan van Hoogstraten, dismissed these concerns, expressing an explicit desire for medicines to flow with FRELIMO over the border. "My sympathy is clearly with the Mozambique people and not with their foreign masters with whom we have through NATO an unholy alliance," Van Hoogstraten explained, confident that "our major denominational supporters have now complete sympathy with the cause."[34] Mondlane's assassination in early 1969 reinforced this shift, since it dramatized the pernicious violence arrayed against self-determination. Commemorations sprung up across the United States (and the world) with Theodore Tucker, the head of the NCC's Africa Department, providing the opening prayer for Mondlane's U.N. memorial service.[35] Religious celebrations of Mondlane, a man many knew personally, reinforced identification with his party. Just a few months later, the head of the NCC's international office offered his agreement with Gayraud Wilmore, director of the Presbyterian Commission on Religion and Race, that "assistance to FRELIMO [was] in this context assistance to social change in South Africa."[36]

Like their counterparts in the WCC, the NCC leadership recognized that the social programs created behind the lines were more than simply aid; they represented the creation of a new, legitimate nation replacing the colonies that failed African peoples. In the words of one internal NCC document from 1970, "Liberation movements are providing hope, change, [and] dignity in contrast to the 'order' and oppression of the minority regimes."[37] Religious leaders followed their youthful colleagues in viewing parties like FRELIMO as governments-in-waiting, which implied "accepting the military side of things" within church deliberations, since states had the power to resort to arms.[38] Crossing this intellectual Rubicon allowed most church

leadership—and by extension the NCC—to line up fully behind the nationalist causes and feel increasing comfort advocating for them domestically.
When asked at a congressional testimony whether he supported a "violent
revolutionist movement" in Angola, the head of the Presbyterian Southern
Africa Task Force responded clearly: "The pronouncements of the general
assembly of our church are generally consistent with and sympathetic to the
efforts of the people of Angola to achieve their independence, hopefully non-
violently, but as a last resort that they do have the right to seek by revolutionary means to overthrow the colonial government."[39]

The increased deference to Global South ideas reflected a more general
effort to move away from the top-down missionary model and embrace ideological diversity as part of the religious promotion of greater racial equality.
Internally, this included an expanded role for Black churchmen under the
leadership of the Presbyterian pastor Gayraud Wilmore, who alongside the
youth contingent was fast becoming—according to one internal memo—"a
new force in [the NCC's] involvement with Africa."[40] Wilmore explained in
1970 that the leftist critique offered by the tricontinental-influenced Black
Power movement led him to adjust his own thinking, because he now understood "racism as a permanent, institutionalized system related to American
expansion and intervention." He joined other African Americans within the
NCC in arguing that "blacks must free themselves. The role of the church is
to assist groups already engaged in liberation."[41] This reflected the New Left
emphasis on supporting authentic political movements, as much domestically as abroad.

The belief that the liberation parties best represented the ambitions of
their people, and the increased deference to African priorities this produced,
transformed institutional religious engagement with Lusophone liberation.
The NCC accepted not only FRELIMO but the broader CONCP alliance.
Humanitarian aid began flowing to the MPLA in the early 1970s.[42] And it
was the Angolan party that convinced the Quaker-backed American Friends
Service Committee to launch its Southern African Program, which served as
a milestone in the acceptance of the revolutionary parties, given the Quaker
commitment to pacifism.[43] As these associations grew, the churches adopted
policies that sought to transcend "'cold war' thinking."[44] They did so by consciously aligning with youth activists taking to the streets and lecture halls to
educate Americans about anti-imperial struggles. In 1969, the NCC asked in
internal discussions if a "campaign of military disengagement with Portugal
[could] be organized with support of anti-Vietnam forces[.]"[45] The answer

from members of the Zambia Group and the SAC—several of whom participated in these deliberations—was an enthusiastic yes. Rather than remaining passive until international crises made church actions ineffectual, as many felt had been the case in Vietnam, the denominations engaged in discussions of global inequality and revolution before they directly involved the United States. NCC denominations generally agreed with their Episcopal Church colleagues that "all too often the churches don't react until a crisis looms and then any action is usually too late to be really effective."[46] Support for the Lusophone struggle sought to change this.

The evolving southern Africa program incorporated core elements of New Left Internationalism into the major institutions of the NCC. While the most dramatic breaks came with the decision to support revolutions, this was one component of a broader reevaluation of international affairs that embraced radical visions of self-determination. This included a willingness to support a major reorganization of international political and economic structures. As one consultation between the NCC and WCC concluded, "[There can be] no justice in our world without a transfer of economic resources to undergird the redistribution of political power and to make cultural self-determination meaningful."[47] The churches were shifting from the paternalistic missionary activities of past generations to a new role of "empowerment." As a result, the NCC and many member churches sought to position their communities against what they increasingly understood to be a global system of racism, poverty, economic exploitation, and disenfranchisement sustained by colonialism and Cold War interventionism. "The problems of justice-liberation-development," one discussion among denominational representatives concluded in 1971, "are problems of peoples of other countries, of peoples of our own country, and of peoples in our own neighborhoods."[48] There was a transnational struggle for racial and economic justice, and support for the active revolutions in Africa provided a powerful force helping the church imagine, articulate, and pursue a new form of Christian mission.

ACOA and the Grassroots Revolution

A similar and closely related process played out in ACOA. Longtime secretary George Houser had been among the most assertive—even radical—civil rights activists in the 1950s, but the necessity of keeping ACOA funded and involved in Washington discussions constrained his willingness to embrace such broad criticisms of the international system. Houser was a pacifist, and he feared alienating liberal and church institutions as well as official allies, resulting in a careful adherence to a single-issue stance that was anti-colonial but avoided embracing the expansive anti-imperialism of the leftist liberation leaders. This frustrated youth activists, who appreciated ACOA's pioneering work but blanched at its preference for elite lobbying and unwillingness to break with outdated Cold War paradigms. Most glaringly, ACOA's history of support for Holden Roberto and his FNLA put the organization at odds with many youth activists, whose leftist politics placed them firmly in the camp of the CONCP and the MPLA. These associations and Houser's relationship with government officials led many to believe that the committee, as field-worker Prexy Nesbitt remarked, was "CIA . . . or somethin."[49] Zambia Group member Eileen Hanson recalled more simply that "they weren't radical enough."[50] Yet, as was the case with the churches, young activists continued to work with ACOA due to their commitment to the cause and the committee's unique resources, nudging it gently to the left. These two aspects of the solidarity movement—a willingness to collaborate across generational lines and the transformation of existing institutions—became a hallmark of the Lusophone African solidarity and its successors.

Both aspects of the movement depended on the influx of young activists into ACOA. SAC member Janet Hooper joined ACOA in the 1960s, becoming in the eyes of many activists a "deputy director" without the title.[51] She propped the door open for youth priorities, allowing knowledgeable activists like Bill Minter to consult on new informational programs.[52] ACOA's own web of connections drew in additional actors whose ideas expanded and often complemented the efforts of the radical-religious network. Among the more influential additions to ACOA's leadership was Robert Van Lierop, a young African American lawyer who represented the NAACP on the ACOA board. A native New Yorker deeply influenced by Malcolm X, Van Lierop's interest in Pan-African activism led him to develop strong ties to FRELIMO and active collaboration with ACOA.[53] While originating separately from the Christian-influenced Zambia Group's activism, Van Lierop's practical vision of Black Power shared the anti-imperial critique of a racialized system of global political and economic inequality and maintained space for interracial collaboration. Van Lierop championed Pan-African liberation, but his ideas of Black Power fit into the broader New Left idea that the struggles in southern Africa were establishing intellectual blueprints for liberation in the United States, Asia, and elsewhere. While Houser and others within ACOA

always understood the struggle for African independence as an extension of
the domestic civil rights movement, these new ideas attacked not just racism
within the United States but the practice of European and American hegemony writ large. While far from contradictory, the expansive visions of anti-
imperial activism pursued by the Zambia Group and Pan-Africanists like Van
Lierop challenged ACOA to move in more radical directions.

Houser understood these realities, and the influx of new ideas partially
reflected his efforts to position ACOA at the forefront of the growing solidarity movement. Plans included moving beyond its New York headquarters
and emphasis on U.N. work to strengthen its political lobbying while also
building connections to the grassroots. First, ACOA established its permanent Washington, D.C., office with church funding in hopes of strengthening
ties to U.S. government officials and sympathetic members of Congress. It
began operations with a single staffer in 1968, playing catch up to the successful lobbying efforts of the White Redoubt in the three years after Rhodesian UDI.[54] Second, the committee flirted with grassroots mobilization in
youth and African American communities. While ACOA included veteran
civil rights organizers, its small staff and prioritization of narrower forms of
anti-colonialism meant that its activities traditionally focused on collaboration with national and supranational organizations with clearer influence on
policy. This strategy contrasted sharply with the voluntarist ethic of the youth
generation, so the Zambia Group arranged a donation dedicated to promoting grassroots initiatives within ACOA.[55] The result was the creation of a
field-worker position in Chicago for Prexy Nesbitt, the satellite SAC member
who had recently returned from working with FRELIMO's propaganda office
in Dar es Salaam.[56] After Charles Hightower—a young African American recommended by Van Lierop—took over the Washington office in 1970, these
initiatives injected new ideas into ACOA that better aligned with the tricontinental vision of African independence promoted by the CONCP parties.[57]

The result was generational friction within ACOA that highlighted the
difference between the New Left's anti-imperial solidarity and Houser's anti-
colonial alliances forged amid the Cold War context of the 1950s. These debates
revolved around two main issues, the first being the appropriate partners for
liberation. The tricontinental influence meant that ideology was central to
solidarity, and parties won support by positioning their nationalist struggles
as leftist, global revolutions against capitalist imperialism operating in Latin
America, Africa, and Asia.[58] The PAIGC, FRELIMO, and the MPLA claimed
"authentic" status for their parties by positioning their CONCP alliance under

this ideological umbrella. The role such solidarity played in legitimizing parties was especially vital for the MPLA, whose armed struggle was the weakest
of the three and faced effective competition from the FNLA and Jonas Savimbi's UNITA. As FRELIMO and the PAIGC won new allies with their visions
of holistic revolution, they advocated for the MPLA as the only truly revolutionary party in Angola. "[The CONCP] acted as a group," UNITA member Jorge Valentim recalled. "They represented each other, and that had some
influence."[59] Beyond some Black nationalist support for UNITA (discussed in
chapter 8), young activists embraced the entirety of the CONCP alliance.

New Left support for the MPLA created difficulties within ACOA due
to its linkages with Holden Roberto. Even after Roberto's paranoia and iron-
fisted rule burned bridges in the mid-1960s, Houser refused to abandon
his old ally despite repeated MPLA overtures from at least 1963. Roberto
received the lion's share of ACOA and church assistance to Angola, which
Houser facilitated as Roberto's primary U.S. contact. Decades later, Houser
could not pinpoint the precise reasoning for this preference, but at the time
he claimed he was seeking to avoid nationalist politics. Officially, ACOA
deferred to the Organization of African Unity's (OAU) preferred list of liberation parties, but the committee was slow to reflect changing African opinion.
Despite the OAU's embrace of the MPLA and critical reports on Roberto
from ACOA allies, Houser refused to end the relationship, likely reflecting
a vestigial belief that anti-communists were more acceptable partners in the
Cold War context.[60] Board members questioned the decision, but it created
conflict with ACOA's younger elements. Chicago-area organizer Prexy Nesbitt spoke for many in saying that the MPLA was the most successful liberation group in Angola thanks to its ties to the wider Lusophone revolution and
support abroad.[61] This internal agitation helped break the impasse in 1969,
when ACOA assisted the medical services of the MPLA for the first time and
began a slow drift from Roberto.[62]

Once this initial hurdle was cleared, avenues for cooperation between
ACOA and the MPLA increased, at the expense of the FNLA.[63] As this transition occurred, Roberto lamented in 1970 that "the southern Africa movement
[in the United States] had gotten bogged down by internal political debates."[64]
But the reality was different: grassroots interest in African revolution was
expanding even as activists switched allegiance from the FNLA toward the
leftist CONCP parties. ACOA's shift coincided with the NCC's expanded support for the MPLA in 1969, with the NCC likely influencing Houser, given
the close collaboration between the two organizations. The acceptance of

leftist, Third World revolution undermined the FNLA's central appeal. This eventually forced the closure of Roberto's New York office once supported by ACOA, allowing CONCP representatives like Sharfudine Khan and Gil Fernandes to operate as the most visible representatives of Lusophone revolution, outside UNITA's very targeted appeals to the Black community. Young staffers remained frustrated that Houser retained personal connections to Roberto, but they welcomed the change to ACOA policies.

The party issue was a component of a second, larger divide separating Houser from his young staffers: their distinct ideological ambitions and strategic visions. Young anti-imperialists followed Amílcar Cabral and Mondlane in defining the African revolutions as part of a global attack on imperialism, which included Portugal's old-fashioned colonialism alongside new forms of economic neo-imperialism sustained by Western capitalism and Cold War defense networks. New Left activists linked the African liberation struggles with tricontinental conflicts waged by North Vietnam, Palestine, and even Cuba, along with domestic antiwar efforts. This contrasted sharply with ACOA's conscious decision to focus narrowly on African colonialism and postcolonial development, claiming an authoritative expertise that gave it access to powerful policymakers while limiting its exposure to contentious political issues outside its core interests. Many associated with the organization were involved in other causes, with Cora Weiss, for example, being active in Vietnam peace organizing while her husband Peter was president of the board. But members mostly undertook this work in their personal capacity, creating overlapping networks of activism without asking the committee to address all topics.[65] In addition, although ACOA was often critical of U.S. policy, Houser believed it was non-establishment rather than antiestablishment, meaning it worked independently with government and major national organizations to reach policy solutions rather than seeing them as central components of the imperial problem.[66]

This generational and ideological clash came to a head when ACOA's Washington representative Charles Hightower criticized Congressman Charles Diggs for not condemning Israel alongside Portugal and Rhodesia as imperial states.[67] For Hightower, Diggs's control of the House Foreign Affairs Subcommittee on Africa provided a platform for attacking broad conceptions of Western imperialism that Hightower wanted ACOA to champion. Houser worried that expanding beyond African issues of colonialism and minority rule would cause internal rifts, alienate supporters with firm views on Israel or communism, distract from ACOA's niche expertise on Africa, and ultimately dilute the committee's effectiveness. Hightower's attack on the committee's most important political ally touched all these bases. Houser joined the executive board in quashing attempts to formalize any linkages between Africa, the Middle East, and Latin America.[68]

For Houser, politicians like Diggs justified ACOA's continued collaboration with government officials despite years of frustration with the executive branch. Diggs was passionate about African issues, but his most important attribute was his ability to navigate Washington politics. One congressional profile described him as "a quiet, soft-spoken, some might say phlegmatic man" who was nonetheless defined by a "quiet aggressiveness, flashing out in occasional outbursts of temper and passion."[69] His investigations into southern African issues during his first year as chairman in 1969, along with an African study mission that included trips to Angola and Mozambique, demonstrated the rising congressional concern with Africa.[70] ACOA responded enthusiastically; Houser gave expert testimony sympathetic to the liberation movements at multiple hearings, and ACOA's first Washington director brainstormed ideas with congressional staffers. These discussions were directly reflected in Diggs's investigations into business operations in southern Africa in 1971, which publicly disclosed important information that informed later activism. ACOA even floated the idea of coordinating grassroots action against corporations operating in Portuguese Africa, though this idea took a few more years to come to fruition.[71] After years in the political wilderness, ACOA's allies finally had some institutional power, so Houser worried that youthful efforts to move too far, too fast might threaten this momentum and weaken their influence with politicians from the congressional Africa group.

ACOA and allies like Diggs wanted to inject new ideas into policy debates without transgressing Washington's political boundaries. While ACOA provided a list of expert witnesses that drew from academic, religious, civil rights, and youth activist circles—including members of the Zambia Group—Diggs opted at first for more establishment figures. Most testimony came from executive branch officials, corporate leaders, and professors, with the last trending toward revolutionary sympathizers like John Marcum. Beyond Houser, the primary movement testimony came from Robert Van Lierop—a lawyer with ties to the NAACP.[72] Nonetheless, archival material from the congressman's office shows that his staff utilized grassroots materials, notably a profile of FRELIMO from the Committee for Freedom in Mozambique and the Dutch Angola Comité's English-language rundown of revolutionary news, *Facts and Report*.[73] Collaboration with activist organizations provided

Diggs with direct access to liberation leaders, with ACOA helping to arrange for Amílcar Cabral to address the subcommittee in 1970.[74] Occurring just months after Mondlane's death when the liberation movements seemed to be on the defensive, Cabral's testimony explained the origins of the military struggle and discussed at length the management of the liberated territories. While he admitted under questioning that the PAIGC supported Cuba and the Vietcong, he contended: "Our ideology is nationalism, to get our independence ... [and] to cooperate with all other peoples in order to realize the development of our country."[75] The testimony gave Cabral a modicum of official recognition while amplifying his ideas through the publication of the twenty-page testimony. It also created a pathway through which Cabral could communicate directly with Diggs; just a few months later Cabral wrote to him about the use of Boeing aircraft for troop transport, which the congressman used to open an inquiry with the Department of State.[76] While Diggs's tactics were far from radical, they injected revolutionary perspectives into U.S. deliberations.

Still, such careful actions did little to assuage youth activists frustrated with what they saw as a hidebound liberal elite, leading directly to Hightower's outburst. ACOA made some concessions to New Left priorities—notably tying southern Africa to the Vietnam War in a 1968 election primer—but such linkages were carefully delimited.[77] The problem was that ACOA and collaborators like Diggs represented a generation of successful activists and politicians whose anti-colonial (and civil rights) bona fides were never in doubt but whose successes were measured against past restrictions and setbacks. Their attempts to target specific aspects of U.S. foreign policy that could produce incremental change led youth activists to conclude that they were either complicit with or intimidated by the Cold War and capitalist institutions that sustained Portuguese colonialism and apartheid. When news broke that the CIA funded liberal organizations as a way of undermining radical groups, many young activists assumed the worst of ACOA, especially in the Black community where—according to Prexy Nesbitt—young African Americans viewed ACOA's predominantly white staff with deep suspicion.[78] While age and race played a role, the core of the divide was ideological. Hightower captured this sentiment when he criticized Diggs's "ambiguous approach" to African affairs, which sought confrontation while relying on academic and business interests who advised gradualist approaches to Portugal and the minority regimes. "Diggs did not seem to know what he wanted," Hightower conveyed in sentiments that mirrored his internal criticism of ACOA, "a conference of specialists, or an educative meeting of grassroots Africanists, or some combination."[79] The principled, patient international activism of the 1950s ran afoul of the demands for deeper and quicker change present in the antiwar and Black Power movements.

These contrasting politics could have split the movement, and indeed this story of generational and ideological fracture is a common one among histories of 1960s politics. The opposite proved true for Lusophone solidarity, in part due to the intervention of African nationalists. FRELIMO urged sympathizers as early as 1964: "Channelize your support in order that your help can be concrete . . . in the sense that you can influence the attitudes of your government."[80] Mondlane worked assiduously to build a broad coalition before his death, and the PAIGC joined FRELIMO in expanding popular appeals to U.S. audiences after 1969.[81] Cabral embraced radical politics earlier than Mondlane but shared his diplomatic ambitions; he envisioned support committees and movements in the West that would include "effective people of all tendencies" and emphasized the value of winning over "people attached to the government or not marked as being extremist."[82] This approach earned official aid in 1969 from neutral Sweden, where popular activism coexisted with good relations with the left-of-center government. According to Trinike Weijdema, a prominent Dutch activist associated with the leftist Angola Comité, Frelimo's Marcelino dos Santos and Janet Mondlane used Sweden as an example when urging Western allies to adopt broad fronts: "If we wanted that, we'd have to move more to the center . . . so we changed."[83]

The practical vision of solidarity promoted by the CONCP parties demanded collaboration, cooperation, and compromise in pursuit of effective organizing. These ideas became central to the Rome Conference of 1970, which had the twofold goal of responding to Caetano's courtship of Western states and illustrating FRELIMO's vitality after Mondlane's assassination. The three CONCP parties gathered more than 177 solidarity organizations from sixty-four countries to strategize on how to promote the revolutions abroad, with delegates ranging from religious humanitarians to radical feminists and Eastern communists.[84] Liberation leaders even had an audience with Pope Paul VI. The diversity of attendees highlighted what FRELIMO called a singular "internationalist identity" that connected all people and militated against dogmatic divisions.[85] During a period of political division in the West, the CONCP leaders made personal appeals to their supporters at the conference to put aside minor differences to organize a "mass popular action" to weaken Portugal.[86] The Rome Conference offered a model that inspired Western

solidarity groups to hold annual "Easter" conferences with CONCP representatives to share and coordinate solidarity activities.[87]

ACOA was vital in promoting such action in the United States, since it
represented exactly the kind of politically acceptable organization that Cabral
desired, even if it did not fit easily at the forefront of a mass movement. Houser
was skeptical about the short-term prospects for independent grassroots organizing on behalf of southern Africa, likely believing that multiple groups could
not easily exist without fracturing the small coalition.[88] ACOA tried to central-
ize its place within the solidarity movement by creating new offices catering
to Washington and the grassroots, but the pushback it received from its own
staff militated against this role. What ACOA was good at doing was acting
as an informational clearinghouse, using its unique connections to Africa to
build interest in the liberation struggles. Like the churches, ACOA acted as a
gateway through which young radicals discovered Africa, winning sympathy
in the process. With the PAIGC and FRELIMO urging collaboration, there
were reasons to make this relationship work. Activists accepted ACOA's limitations, and Houser gradually adjusted his vision of the committee as occupying a key node in the expanding network of solidarity groups. He came to
see the committee as a "meeting ground for various forces" that could promote interest in southern Africa and coordinate between independent organizations.[89] Prominent institutions continued to trust ACOA under Houser's
careful stewardship, while the most ardent solidarity activists respected its
informational role. Like the NCC, ACOA acted as an access point through
which young radicals integrated their ideas into broader discussions of foreign
affairs, leaving their grassroots organizations to pursue the more antiestablishment positions demanded by their constituencies. ACOA could aid the expansion of solidarity organizing without controlling it—or being responsible for
its most radical ideas.

Activists across the spectrum recognized that individual organizations
had different roles to play. New Leftists never abandoned ACOA, but neither
could it represent their ambitious anti-imperialism; therefore, they worked to
convince Houser to accept a less central role. As board member Robert Van
Lierop explained:

> I do not think the ACOA can or should become a radical "move-
> ment" organization . . . [it] is and probably should remain one which
> is capable of pressuring churches, corporations, organs of govern-
> ment, etc. . . . The answer I think lies in the need for ACOA itself to

recognize its own limitations and to be willing to support field work and other projects without having itself necessarily identified as the sponsor of such activities . . . the ACOA may never see a return (such as increased membership or increased contributions) from supporting such efforts. But the fact remains that efforts such as these go a long way towards raising the political consciousness of many individuals within the United States.[90]

This conceptualization of ACOA's role fit the realities of the movement. With grassroots organizations seeking informational and financial assistance, the old community organizer changed his tactics. ACOA could act, in Houser's own words, as a "catalytic agent" in the creation and support of organizations that would better appeal to the diverse audiences needed to assemble an effective movement.[91] The CONCP parties envisioned a popular solidarity that incorporated diverse ideological and strategic tendencies that pushed beyond the limits of ACOA's comfort zone. As a result, the preeminent institution championing African interests in the United States needed to transition to a secondary role to help solidarity grow.

New Organizations, Common Goals

ACOA adjusted its strategy to support independent groups representing both grassroots and elite political interests, offering information and expertise that these groups could translate for specific constituencies. An early example involved the direct funding of the Chicago Committee for the Liberation of Angola, Mozambique, and Guinea (CCLAMG). This evolved from ACOA's earlier grassroots efforts, effectively replacing the Chicago field-worker position occupied by Prexy Nesbitt. His difficulty promoting ACOA within the youth and African American communities gave Robert Van Lierop and other executive board members enough evidence to convince Houser to adopt a still more localized approach.[92] ACOA needed an organization that could distribute information on the African revolutions free of institutional baggage, and the solution lay in the newly formed CCLAMG (pronounced "clam"). ACOA's relationship with the Chicago group set a new model for collaboration with local solidarity organizations.

CCLAMG emerged at the intersection of the two wings of the youth movement: religious and leftist internationalism. Eileen Hanson, the former

Frontier Intern and CRV member, founded the group with Nesbitt and fellow CRV alumnae Nancy Freehafer and Mimi Edmunds.[93] The group pledged support to tricontinental ideas and championed the CONCP parties as the most active southern African revolutionaries in 1971.[94] Politically leftist, CCLAMG's primary goals were education and organization, and members worked with whoever supported the mission. "We were a group of radicals, but we weren't burning down buildings," Hanson remembered. "We were just anti-imperialists."[95] The group was affiliated with the New World Resource Center (NWRC), a coalition with ties to the CRV that united other anti-imperial groups interested in Asia and Latin America. The collective's goal was to "awaken people in this country to the problems of injustice and oppression around the world, to deepen people's understanding of the fundamental causes of these problems, and to enable them to work actively for a world based on social and economic justice."[96] Though it would have been logical for a Vietnam-focused group to have led the NWRC, CCLAMG was its foremost member. The Portuguese colonies provided a global vision of Third World empowerment that went beyond simple antiwar messages to address matters of economic and racial justice that were vital to Chicago politics.[97] CCLAMG's ambitious anti-imperialism was exactly the kind of politics that gave Houser pause, but ACOA was the main donor supporting the establishment of the NWRC in 1971. Hanson joined with Van Lierop to convince Houser that radical grassroots organizations like CCLAMG and the NWRC were the best ways to expand the solidarity movement, with internal backing coming from the Zambia Group's Janet Hooper.[98] CCLAMG members debated whether the collective should accept money from ACOA, which Hanson remembered as a bit stodgy, but its willingness to cede initiative to youth activists proved sufficient.[99] ACOA kept both CCLAMG and the NWRC afloat during their early years.

CCLAMG became a regional hub in the growth of the grassroots solidarity movement. Its most important work involved informational campaigns and organizing in the local community. CCLAMG brought representatives such as FRELIMO's Sharfudine Khan and the PAIGC's Gil Fernandes to Chicago, supplementing regular talks by Nesbitt and others with personal knowledge of the revolutions.[100] Through the NWRC, it distributed a broad variety of literature throughout the upper Midwest, including publications from ACOA, FRELIMO, LSM, CRV, MACSA, and the Committee for a Free Mozambique (another product of the SAC-CRV nexus).[101] CCLAMG sponsored African dinners, visited schools, worked with churches, and boycotted local businesses

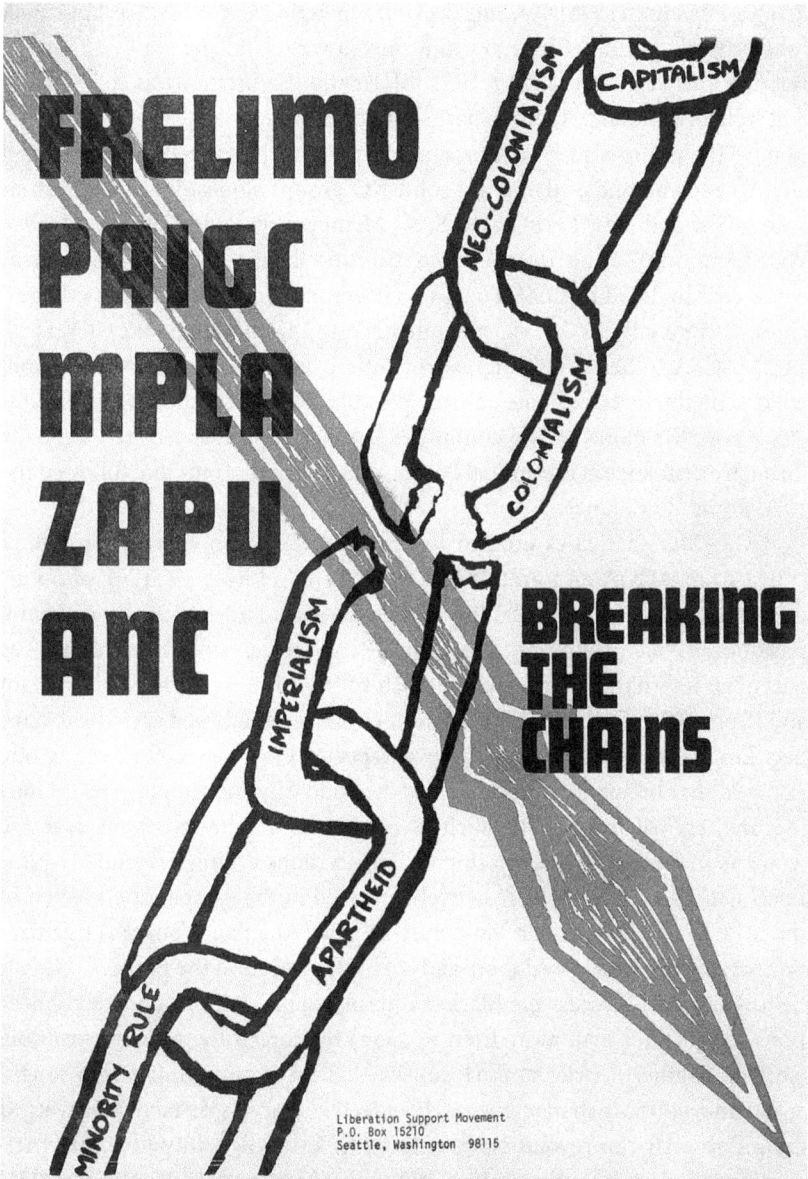

Figure 7. Liberation Support Movement poster, circa 1970. The poster highlights the "authentic" revolutionary parties that shared leftist politics and alliances, as well as the ideals they represented for many American organizers. Reproduced with permission. Lincoln Cushing/Docs Populi.

involved in southern Africa, such as Gulf Oil and GE.[102] When Nesbitt began his fieldwork in 1969, Chicago was a "media wasteland" on southern Africa. But just four years later CCLAMG's information saturation was so extensive that it helped broadcast a four-part series on southern Africa on local television.[103] The group also used Chicago's position as the United States' "second city" to become one of the major solidarity groups alongside the California-based LSM and New York–based SAC. Members spoke in Toronto, Ottawa, Washington, D.C., and Iowa City, substituting for the personal engagement conducted by FRELIMO's Khan, who concentrated his efforts on the largest cities.[104] Eventually, CCLAMG and other NWRC groups joined the CRV, LSM, and MACSA to help found the North American Anti-Imperialist Coalition, which sought to coordinate radical protests against reactionary U.S. policies across the globe.[105] The committee even had a presence internationally through attendance at the annual Easter solidarity gatherings that followed the 1970 Rome Conference.[106]

CCLAMG's activities crossed the political spectrum, using information culled from ACOA and groups like the LSM to address a variety of political persuasions. It took a leading role in the local anti-imperial movement, positioning Angola—the largest and most economically important colony—as part of an international triumvirate of Third World causes alongside Vietnam and (from 1973) Chile.[107] This tendency to link issues allowed activists to connect Lusophone revolutions with novel aspects of the New Left revolt. In one example that became common across the solidarity movement, the "founding mothers" of the NWRC such as Hanson and Edmunds won over the women's movement by promoting CONCP visions of greater gender equity. Local Chicago feminists were actively involved in the campaign on behalf of the MPLA's Organização da Mulher de Angola (Angolan Women's Organization, or OMA), which sold thousands of buttons to fund the group.[108] Nesbitt helped CCLAMG access the Black community, and Hanson's church connections (despite her drift away from religion) reinforced the NCC's expanding work on southern Africa at the local level. Diverse communities who sought social and political change but rarely agreed on targets or tactics converged around the African revolutions thanks to CCLAMG's ability to connect tricontinental ideas to local priorities. When Van Lierop worked with FRELIMO to produce a thirty-minute film on the liberation struggle in 1972, CCLAMG sponsored more than a hundred showings over the next year, divided evenly between Black groups, churches, and student organizations.[109] This inclusive support network reflected and anticipated intercommunal collaborations at the national level.

CCLAMG's activities in Chicago illustrate the broad appeal and ambition of the solidarity network, but they also demonstrate how ACOA's decision to quietly support grassroots organizing paid dividends. CCLAMG and the NWRC encouraged various constituencies in Chicago to continue their own research into the revolutions, and ACOA's carefully curated pamphlets were available alongside LSM's first-person accounts and polemical leftist literature. This helped legitimize the non-establishment ACOA as a reliable resource for leftists without forcing Houser to change its central identity. The relationship between ACOA and CCLAMG, alongside the interconnected radical and church origins of the activists in Chicago, illustrates a key tenet of the solidarity movement—and explains why its growth has long escaped the notice of historians. Rather than a single organization or group of activists, the Lusophone solidarity network relied on a web of loosely connected organizations and activists operating across local, regional, and national levels. This provided groups with an ideological flexibility that could sell the CONCP parties to diverse constituencies without losing focus on the need to identify with, support, and mobilize around Lusophone revolutions. While core organizers remained few, the Portuguese African revolutions spoke to intersecting racial, economic, peace, and gender issues, creating the opportunity to unite intersecting causes in an age of political fracture.

The power of this critique became increasingly influential as New Left ideas entered policy discussions, with new organizations arising to facilitate this exchange. The foundation of the Washington Office on Africa (WOA) in 1972 formalized the solidarity movement's growing ambitions by providing a permanent staff to lobby politicians in ways that reflected the emerging New Left Internationalism. And it required the support of the NCC and ACOA. Both organizations had increased their lobbying efforts in the 1960s, but African affairs was just a single issue for the NCC, and ACOA struggled to manage its D.C. outpost.[110] ACOA's Washington office was an extension of the New York headquarters, and disagreements over messaging combined with the small number of congressional allies to limit its effectiveness against White Redoubt lobbying. Notable stumbles included passage of the 1971 Byrd Amendment that allowed Rhodesian chrome imports and a new Azores base agreement one year later. What was needed was a formal lobbying organization that could coordinate with sympathetic legislators to frame issues while providing guidance to religious lobbyists and other allies on how to support new approaches and policies.[111] The NCC and ACOA agreed to combine their efforts with a few sympathetic trade unions to create WOA.

While WOA was imagined as another non-establishment organization, it aligned more closely with New Left visions of foreign affairs thanks to its leadership. Its director was the Rev. Edgar "Ted" Lockwood, an Episcopal priest, lawyer, and card-carrying socialist who became involved in civil rights while working in New England. He moved to Washington to work with the Institute for Policy Studies, a progressive think tank founded in 1963 that Lockwood described as "a kind of new left institution" dedicated to pursuing social justice through structural changes to the economy and state. His work involved researching the investment strategies of mainline Protestant denominations. He was surprised to find that few had ethical guidelines, and those that did were most concerned about old-fashioned temperance topics of tobacco and alcohol.[112] A proponent of the political transformation of the NCC in the late 1960s, Lockwood advocated for clear structures to direct church investments toward positive social change, adopting the problem of corporate investment in southern Africa shortly after it was highlighted by youth activists (discussed in chapter 8). This work put him in contact with Houser and Goler Butcher, a key staffer for Charles Diggs, who agreed to advise the Episcopal Church on new moral guidelines.[113] Lockwood was well placed to head WOA thanks to these existing contacts in Washington, his growing expertise on Africa, and good relations with religious leaderships. The churches largely funded the organization and provided office space at the United Methodist Building just blocks from the Capitol, where the NCC and many denominations had offices, and where other activist lobbying groups also found a home.[114]

Under Lockwood, WOA aligned with the politics of the liberation movements and their youthful New Left allies. The socialist pastor embraced a broad vision of justice that demanded systematic reform of the economic and political systems, both national and international. Houser's ACOA, Lockwood later reflected, was always "a bit uncertain as to whether it was really liberal or whether it was more left than that."[115] WOA was more decisive in its embrace of both New Left Internationalism and the decentralized grassroots solidarity movement, a stance made possible by the leftward drift of the church leadership that provided funding. Guiding the office in this direction was its eventual associate director (and WOA's only other employee) Christine "Chris" Root. She dropped out of Oberlin College, where she worked with future ACOA staffer Paul Irish, to focus on activism, joining WOA at its foundation with help from Tim Smith, now the assistant for African Affairs at the United Church of Christ's Council for Christian Social Action. Still in her teens when she arrived in Washington, Root was not as comfortable with senior political and church leaders as Lockwood, but she brought a desire to engage with grassroots activism that allowed WOA to fill a vital role. She explained:

> [Our] theory of change, or you could say our priorities, was that you try to organize constituents to affect their members of Congress . . . trying to influence legislation language. So, that was just always the case, that you're at the Capitol because partly to get to know people on the hill, to get to know the people who are your allies—which is incredibly important—and to try to figure out how to try to persuade other people. But most of your time, or a very significant chunk of your time, is looking the other direction. It's from standing there [in D.C.] and having the knowledge that comes from standing there, to reach out to people across the country who you hope will try to use their influence or organizing or political power to influence particular people in Congress. So, that's why you work with other groups that are trying to do that, because you each have different sets of constituencies. And, you know, there can be some overlap.[116]

The goal, then, was not only to lobby politicians and provide them with information but also to use knowledge of Washington politics to improve the quality and strategy of grassroots organizing.

In particular, the organization took advantage of the congressional response to the era's tumultuous politics. As students protested the war and ongoing social inequalities, they elected a generation of politicians interested in challenging the status quo. African self-determination offered a suitably anti-imperial issue that they could support without the baggage of Vietnam. Elections elevated longtime Africa watchers to the Senate, beginning with John Tunney in 1970, soon followed by Iowa Representative John Carver's lead staffer, Dick Clark, and eventually Carver himself. Progress on voting rights also introduced a strong cohort of young African Americans to the House, many of whom were interested in or had personal ties to Africa. Prominent among this latter group was the civil rights activist Andrew Young. "I had been keeping up with Angola since the early 50s. And I knew Eduardo Mondlane personally . . ." Young recalled later. "I knew they were all products of Christian missionary schools; I knew they'd all been educated essentially in the West; and I knew that they were fighting to free themselves from racism and not to be communist."[117] The influx of Black politicians led to a select committee of African American legislators, formalized as the Congressional Black Caucus in 1971. With Diggs as its first chair, self-determination and the revolutions in Africa became prominent components of its platform.[118] The influx of potential allies opened new avenues for the activist lobby. In one example, the joint testimonies of Robert Van Lierop and George Houser in the Senate against Nixon's 1972 Azores-base agreement inspired Ted Kennedy to send a scathing letter to President Nixon. The Massachusetts senator bucked the influence of his state's large Portuguese population in favor of aligning with his youthful and African American constituents.[119] While policies still favored the White Redoubt, liberation solidarity activists sensed a new momentum building.

WOA became a pivotal partner for the growing roster of politicians interested in Africa and foreign policy reform generally. It provided information for congressional offices while working to cultivate new allies. Professional staffs on the specialized foreign relations committees needed less education, since they featured individuals like Diggs's top assistant, Goler Butcher, who were deeply knowledgeable about and often trained in African affairs. WOA worked collaboratively with these staffs to craft congressional strategy and count votes, targeting legislators who might be receptive to changing—or developing—their positions on southern African affairs. Initially, the major issue was the problem of Rhodesian chrome imports after the 1971 passage of the Byrd Amendment, which mobilized the broadest array of legislators. Congressman Don Fraser and Senator Gale McGee became valuable WOA allies though their interest in human rights and international law, respectively.[120] WOA used these connections to expand support for legislation targeting Portugal or South Africa when opportunities arose. In these areas, it worked closely with Diggs and members of the nascent Congressional Black Caucus while cultivating relationships with the new generation of reformist politicians, notably Senator Dick Clark (D-IA).[121] WOA provided a consistent pathway through which activists, their publications, and their ideas could gain a hearing on Capitol Hill. As a result of this work, a new flow of information critical of Portugal and the minority regimes of southern Africa began to have greater and greater influence on congressional decision-making. In 1973, for instance, Congressman Charles Rangel (D-NY) introduced a bill to halt exports of chemical herbicides to Portugal while citing one of the LSM's interviews with an MPLA soldier.[122] The public discussion of issues like the renewal of the Azores lease reflected a growing attention to the problems of colonialism and minority rule even if WOA's allies could not yet block the treaty.

WOA used its position in D.C. to build a policy awareness that enhanced grassroots solidarity efforts. ACOA remained the primary point of contact with many liberation parties and maintained the largest informational program, but it relied on WOA to keep it abreast of policy issues. Lockwood and Root distributed information on pending legislation and debates to ACOA and grassroots organizations like CCLAMG, giving them quick access to material that took weeks to appear in official publications. This provided the movement with a dexterity that could help it frame issues for undecided legislators before they committed to specific policies. WOA also used this knowledge of legislators and their priorities to advise solidarity organizations on strategy as they launched regional and national campaigns. This helped grassroots groups tie local organizing to national policies and debates in ways that legitimized their movements and made their demands more legible for legislators.[123] WOA became a vital interlocuter between the various parts of the solidarity network because it embraced specialization and created complementary relationships with the churches, ACOA, and the grassroots organizations it sought to represent in Washington. It fulfilled Houser's unattained desire to link grassroots organizing with high politics while working toward the liberation movements' call to change official policies through the coordination of a mass movement.

WOA and CCLAMG demonstrate how Lusophone solidarity organizing, though a product of the revolutionary 1960s, owed a debt to the groundwork laid by liberal institutions in the first half of the decade and their willingness to evolve in support of militant African struggles for independence. An ideologically and strategically diverse set of organizations collaborated around the common goal of Lusophone liberation. The decentralized nature of the solidarity movement allowed individual components to retain their unique identities while promoting collaboration on specific projects. They were tied together through networks that began with the liberation movements but cohered around extensive personal relationships and overlapping group memberships. Though probably never numbering more than a few hundred active members at its core, few of whom were employed full time in activist work, the network survived the vicissitudes of life, movement, and employment changes based on shared values and the continuity provided by better funded allies associated with ACOA and the NCC. Local and regional organizations appeared and disappeared, but the dissolution of one group often meant the creation of another with access to new communities of potential supporters, all held together by this informal network. As CRVer Mimi Edmunds recalled, "You stayed connected to the African solidarity groups. We were like homing pigeons. That's where we felt we could do the most good."[124] This dedication to action preserved the core movement while slowly expanding the number of dedicated activists.

Continued collaboration owed much to the practical guidance of the CONCP parties. Mondlane, Cabral, and their representatives encouraged young, ideologically motivated activists to engage with established organizations without sacrificing their anti-imperial values, while nationalist sympathies convinced these institutions to adopt more radical positions. The centripetal force benefited the movement by promoting a specialization that mobilized the strengths of each group. SAC alumna Janet Hooper explained in the early 1970s how this worked for ACOA: "Monies come from the former constituents, mainly liberal whites who themselves have of course gone through many changes, but the main activities (with some exceptions) are sustained by the new [more radical youth and Black] groups or are picked up by them."[125] This "dichotomy" produced disconnects and frustrations, but it also revitalized southern African organizing by injecting anti-imperial ideas into national debates. Internal deliberations within the NCC and ACOA reflected these debates and hinted at an initial collaboration, with the elder generation guiding Washington efforts and humanitarian relief while youth activists drove boycotts and mass mobilization at the grassroots level. Support for organizations like CCLAMG and WOA better bridged these gaps by creating new structures to help manage and direct differing ideological and generational priorities. Maurice Isserman and Michael Kazin are therefore correct that the generational divide of the later 1960s arose as events "redirect[ed] the youthful spirit of idealistic commitment away from the official agendas of the 'liberal establishment,'" but many historians downplay how this new direction transformed these established institutions.[126] Where young activists retained connections with mainstream groups like ACOA and the Protestant churches, they reinforced Global South calls for a new approach to international affairs.

The collective embrace of militant tricontinental revolution reflected the legitimization of New Left Internationalist ideas. Vietnam and the domestic turmoil it caused shattered the Cold War consensus that defined the post–World War II era, merging with events in southern Africa and elsewhere to create space for once stalwart liberal institutions to explore new ideas of political and economic self-determination, especially as it pertained to the Global South and domestic minorities. Proponents sought to constrain U.S. interventionism in the Third World while seeking new programs for redressing the stubborn, often racialized inequalities created by a Eurocentric capitalist system. Africa acted as a meeting place for these ideas, but it envisioned a global reassessment of Western policy. As one church leader succinctly stated, this coalition of internationalists understood that Third World peoples wanted to "be truly free to pursue their own road to national development, unshackled by either rigged Western market exploitation or subversive [Great Power] political infiltration, communist or anti-communist."[127] New Left Internationalism enabled radicals to envision revolutionary challenges to the international system while convincing liberals to defer to the militant goals and strategies of Southern actors operating on the global frontiers.

CHAPTER 7

Forging Pan-African Solidarity

As the solidarity movement cohered, a missing component limited its political impact: mass African American participation. While Congressman Charles Diggs was the most influential political ally and activists like Robert Van Lierop and Prexy Nesbitt were prominent in solidarity work, there was an assumption that meaningful political action concerning Africa required highly visible African American participation and leadership. This reflected ethnic tendencies within U.S. politics as well as racialized presumptions about the shared identity of widely scattered Black populations. But there was also a distinct New Left logic to this expectation, as young white activists searching for political authenticity and cognizant of calls for Black Power hoped to align themselves with Pan-African movements that could personally articulate connections between African liberation and domestic revolution. Despite popular assumptions, transatlantic linkages were not innate, and many pragmatic African Americans felt that external issues were secondary to domestic priorities, visibly evidenced by the decisions of the American Negro Leadership Conference on Africa (ANLCA). But the rise of an internationally inclined Black Power movement and the Lusophone liberation parties' renewed emphasis on Western outreach provided the foundations for greater collaboration. African Americans disillusioned with the slow pace of civil rights in the mid-1960s and frustrated by growing domestic divisions found an assertive, radical, and unified model for political agitation in Portuguese Africa. This identification grew among prominent architects of Black Power in the 1960s, gaining wider support as the decade ended.

The dual processes of Pan-African identification and political organizing peaked with celebrations of African Liberation Day (ALD) in 1972 and 1973. The event acted as the international component of efforts in the 1970s to mobilize national, local, and grassroots efforts behind a single Black Agenda. Tens of thousands from across the nation united to demonstrate solidarity and demand new policies for the African continent. These efforts overlapped with the radical and religious organizing explored in previous chapters, but the history and goals of the Black movement were distinct. Whereas groups like the American Committee on Africa (ACOA) sought to transcend racial concerns in its support for Lusophone African independence, ALD organizing depended on the balancing of radical internationalism with Black-identity politics, which offered powerful anti-imperial critiques of U.S. society. Cold War hostility to radical Black internationalism and the CONCP parties' own ambivalence about politicizing race initially militated against the growth of a discrete Pan-African solidarity. But conditions within the United States compelled Black Americans to form what American studies scholar Melani McAlister calls an "alternative moral geography" through identification with revolutionaries abroad, which allowed the CONCP parties to make rapid headway in the Black community as they expanded their diplomatic efforts after 1970.[1]

As exchanges increased and knowledge of the parties expanded, the PAIGC and FRELIMO influenced the direction of Black radical politics and helped align it with their tricontinental visions of solidarity. They used race as a gateway for discussions of global exploitation, identifying it as a component of international imperialism that marginalized peoples of color for economic and sociohistorical reasons. Their socialist reading of global politics embraced the idea of common struggle uniting peoples from all the colonized regions and willing Western collaborators, but these linkages found their clearest articulation as part of a revolutionary Black diaspora that also drew on a sense of kinship and racial pride. The powerful vision of independent African states pursuing communal self-determination convinced many Black Power advocates that the socialist ideology at the heart of the Lusophone revolutions should be central to Pan-Africanism and domestic activism, even if it conflicted with popular racialized ideas of Black nationalism. These divisions eventually divided Black organizing, but the tricontinental influence opened pathways for multiracial collaboration with the decentralized solidarity movement explored in previous chapters.

The Radical Element Remains

Radical Black solidarity with Lusophone Africa existed at the margins of Black political life for much of the 1960s and set the stage for successful organizing as ideas of transnational Black Power overtook narratives that prioritized domestic civil rights.[2] Historian John Munro rightly notes that radical Pan-Africanism survived the 1950s era repression of W. E. B. DuBois's Council on African Affairs, using African revolutions to legitimize such ideas and preserve a modicum of optimism.[3] Lusophone Africa became prominent in this transatlantic imaginary after 1961, with the CONCP parties appealing to African Americans in two overlapping ways: in terms of racial solidarity and leftist anti-imperialism. Diplomatic priorities and the launching of revolutions limited direct connections with African Americans during this period, but there was sufficient exchange through reporting and interpersonal contacts to maintain attachments to Lusophone Africa after 1961.

The Liberation Committee for Africa (LCA) and its publication, the *Liberator*, captures both the angry vitality of nascent solidarity organizing and the tension between strands of radical and race-based identification. The New York City–based organization arose in response to the Sharpeville Massacre and the ongoing Congo crisis, led by architect-cum-activist Daniel Watts and white communist Lowell P. Beveridge Jr. The LCA adopted a leftist critique of the imperial system that centered on the capitalist exploitation of Africa and African peoples, continuing the legacy of the Council on African Affairs.[4] The LCA appears most prominently in histories as an instigator of the "riot" at the United Nations following the announcement of Patrice Lumumba's death, but the group actively supported the Portuguese revolutions, especially in Angola.[5] Alongside other Harlem organizations, the LCA provided a forum for revolutionaries to present their cases directly to the African American public, hosting live discussions with anti-colonial leaders where Blacks learned about anti-colonial ideologies and discovered ways to aid the movements. These appearances gave Americans unfettered access to Angola's Holden Roberto and Mozambique's Eduardo Mondlane, still at the United Nations in 1961 but soon to become president of FRELIMO.[6]

The LCA's newsletter, the *Liberator*, became a leading radical magazine of the era. Launched in March 1961, within weeks of the Angolan revolt, it used Pan-Africanism to promote revolutionary politics. Proclaiming itself "the voice of the Afro-American protest movement in the United States and the liberation movement of Africa," the magazine acted as a haven for internationally minded Black intellectuals and a megaphone for nationalists. Early issues featured letters from the Lusophone colonies and South Africa that highlighted anti-imperial justifications for armed insurrection.[7] The editorial tone was consciously aggressive, criticizing the U.S. government and mainstream

Black press for voicing little support for the liberation struggles despite their attacks on Portugal.[8] Rather than simply oppose colonialism, the magazine championed the political platforms of liberation parties when they remained largely anonymous to the average citizen. Importantly, it was among the first U.S. publications to feature the MPLA, presenting it as a revolutionary partner with Roberto's anti-communist FNLA.[9] While such articles coincided with a period of collaboration between the antagonistic groups, the failure to ideologically differentiate the parties revealed a shortcoming of this early solidarity: limited personal ties and information prevented strong identification with individual nationalist groups. While the *Liberator* tried to engage more closely with their ideas than the general calls for freedom present in contemporary religious organizing, the parties acted primarily as shibboleths for radical Pan-Africanism. The well-meaning but superficial understanding of the revolutions were inspirational but offered few concrete lessons to domestic organizers.

Still, the LCA was a prime example of the wider phenomenon in which African Americans frustrated with the limitations of civil rights discourse looked to Lusophone Africa to legitimize assertive alternatives. This took the form of direct interactions, especially in Harlem, where proximity to the United Nations and a history of radicalism encouraged deeper exploration of revolutionary ideas. In addition to the LCA, Roberto spoke with the Black nationalist Carlos Cook's Garvey-inspired African Nationalist Pioneer Movement.[10] More common, however, was the rhetorical use of the Portuguese African revolutions to give proof positive of an independent African personality that justified alternative directions in the domestic Black freedom struggle, usually involving direct confrontation with existing power structures or violence. It was no accident that Robert F. Williams, the head of the NAACP in Monroe, North Carolina, and an advocate of self-defense, labeled his home city "the Angola of the Americas" in a nationally published article where he justified violent responses to white resistance in the Southern United States.[11] African revolution could justify a variety of visions, since programs in Africa as well as domestic U.S. programs remained vague and tended to essentialize the other—problems common to solidarity organizing. The LCA and the *Liberator* expanded support for the revolutions, but that did not necessarily mean popular adoption of the leftist ideology it championed. Socialist internationalism involved an additional layer of identification beyond emotional ties of racial kinship that shaped the popular response to Angola in the early 1960s.[12] The Lusophone nationalists had supporters within the United States, encouraged by attention from publications like the *Liberator*, but there was not a singular movement.

Reinforcing this trend were the limited initiatives of the liberation parties themselves. After the Angolan revolution bogged down and Mondlane returned to Africa, opportunities for direct contact diminished. With limited time and resources, Mondlane prioritized contacts with organizations like ACOA, which had some access to powerbrokers. But the CONCP was also cautious in its appeals to the African American community, reflecting its special concern with race. Both the MPLA and the PAIGC had mixed-race leaderships; FRELIMO was multiracial and included a prominent role for Mondlane's white American wife, Janet. Their competitors used narrow definitions of Black African identity as a weapon, with Jonas Savimbi's UNITA being especially aggressive.[13] In response, the PAIGC and FRELIMO utilized a generalized, aspirational African cultural identity and the material promises of socialism to organize domestically, positioning their parties internationally as progressive, anti-racist responses to the divisive policies of colonialism. The parties hoped this strategy would win over foreign governments, but it meant that their early diplomacy soft-pedaled Black nationalist ideas and the Pan-Africanism implicit in Watts's writings.[14] Mondlane, for example, built strong relationships with African Americans through Black churches and civil rights organizations, but he stayed closer to his U.N. contacts in midtown when he visited New York, not Harlem's famed Hotel Teresa, as Mozambican critics pointed out.[15] Even Roberto, who was vocally hostile to the MPLA's mestiço leadership in Angolan propaganda, initially sought official support by positioning his party as an alternative to U.S. fears of racial conflict. As a result, nationalists were inconsistent in their courting of Black popular opinion specifically.

That is not to say that the liberation parties rejected this nascent solidarity movement, nor that Black Americans avoided the tricontinental ideas championed by CONCP parties. The LCA was notable for initially promoting a Marxist-influenced reading of the global system that aligned with Global South attempts to link domestic racial inequalities with imperialism.[16] This produced strident criticisms of the Kennedy administration's handling of Lisbon's imperial war in Angola, with the *Liberator* dismissing the famous 1961 U.N. vote as toothless posturing for "political capital."[17] African Americans needed to understand the realities of colonialism in Africa and to fight for the real isolation of Portugal—military and economic—if U.S. actions were to have an effect. These positions challenged mainstream civil rights leaders while earning praise from Mondlane. At the first ANLCA, in 1962, which Watts attended and criticized, the Mozambican explained that the "little-known group is about [the] only American Negro group who have managed to combine any active interest in the American Negro struggle for equality with an intense interest in African freedom."[18] Yet Mondlane's admonishing praise achieved little besides gratifying Watts. Civil rights leadership continued to prioritize domestic matters and sought changes to African policy only at the margins, avoiding serious discussion of the ongoing revolutionary wars in Africa and the role of U.S. support for Portugal. There is also no evidence that Mondlane's praise of the LCA produced greater collaboration.

Frustrations with the collective cautiousness of groups like the ANLCA pushed both the *Liberator* and the youth who gravitated toward it in more radical directions. A new generation of staffers embraced a racialized vision of Pan-Africanism, led by the former communist and critic of integration, Harold Cruse. Cruse incorporated Marxist rhetoric into his Pan-African thought in order to justify nationalist concepts of Black communal self-determination within the United States.[19] His movement worried about capital and exploitation of resources, but it concretely associated these ideas with global white power structures—mirroring the racialized essentialization of empire and anti-imperialism that troubled CONCP leaders.[20] Yet because few revolutionaries were present in the United States, and access to their writings was difficult, transnational resistance cohered most readily around race. Confrontational, Black nationalism targeted and alienated white communists like Beveridge, who left the *Liberator* in 1965.[21] This identarian form of Pan-Africanism won the day over a more inclusive leftist critique of empire, even as it incorporated some of its rhetoric.

Cruse's search for a new form of internationally influenced protest reflected the desires of a generation that Rolland Snellings (Askia M. Touré), a prominent member of the emerging Black Arts Movement and *Liberator* contributor, called "the Africanists." While participating in the civil rights movement, they grew disaffected by the slow pace of change and its ability to address the economic crises of the Black community. Calling for dramatic systemic reforms, they imagined themselves in closer alignment with the African revolutionaries demanding wholesale change at a rapid pace, and they set about looking for new models of political action.[22] Ghana's Kwame Nkrumah and Tanzania's Julius Nyerere offered some solutions with their visions of Pan-African nation building, but matters of state did not easily address the needs of a marginalized minority in the United States. Writings

from parties like FRELIMO and leaders like Cabral were not easily available, though Cabral's speech at the 1966 Havana Tricontinental Conference
cracked the gates in the second half of the decade. As a result, radical Black
youth lacked what one author called a "revolutionary ideology," leading to
unfocused manifestations of anger as occurred during the Watts Riots of
1965. This Africanist generation needed "a revolutionary group, with real
roots among the people, to explain to the people what they are fighting for
and to organize that fight."[23] This was the missing component, both in the
pursuit of domestic equality and in meaningful transnational solidarity with
the liberation struggles in Africa. Black resistance fueled conflict in the jun-
gles of Angola and the streets of Los Angeles, but there was no common
leadership or ideology to bridge the transatlantic gap.

CONCP nationalists could help guide Black African leaders, and for a
brief period they seemed to achieve results by influencing the Pan-African
organizing of Malcolm X. The charismatic speaker did not follow the path of
Snellings's Africanists but shared many of their conclusions, having openly
criticized the civil rights movement and its nonviolence for years. Rather,
Malcolm ascended the ranks of Elijah Muhammad's Nation of Islam, preach-
ing against cooperation with whites in power, urging self-defense, and using
sometimes violent rhetoric that sold papers and appealed to those unwilling
to abide by Gandhian tactics. Yet Malcolm X was thoughtful and curious, and
he clashed with Muhammad as he traveled the world and began incorporat-
ing leftist ideas of global revolution that moderated his views on race, inspired
greater attention to global structures of inequality, and led him to embrace
the core teachings of mainstream Islam. In a way, he was traveling the path
opposite to Watts and the *Liberator*. When he split with the Nation of Islam in
1964, Malcolm X offered an alternative nationalism based on a Pan-African
ideology that emphasized a leftist reading of the world situation, which he
formalized in the creation of the Organization of Afro-American Unity.[24] He
credited this transformation to his sojourn in Africa and the Middle East,
where he made connections with socialist African revolutionaries—specifically those from Angola, Mozambique, and Zimbabwe-Rhodesia—who
challenged Malcolm's thinking. They, along with Arab and independent West
African leaders, urged him to adopt a more nuanced, systematic approach to
global race issues. Influenced by these individuals and contact with Nkrumah, Malcolm embraced a new anti-imperial, anti-capitalist critique of the
international system.[25]

The results of this transformation in thinking were twofold. First, Malcolm wanted to instill a sense of national unity among Black Americans comparable to revolutionary fronts such as FRELIMO. He moderated his criticism of civil rights leaders like King and urged unity, from which the Black community could negotiate from a position of power. Second, he viewed the race problem through the lens of rights-based discourses that internationalized his ideas of rebellion. The situation of Blacks in the United States was more like that in "South Africa, Angola, Mozambique, Hungary, the Arab refugee problem . . . a world problem."[26] A comparison of these various pursuits of freedom illustrated to Malcolm that Black people in the United States and in Africa had a "common exploiter," which aligned closely but not completely with the color line.[27] Though Malcolm continued to refine his thinking, he was drifting toward the tricontinental conception of imperialism that used racism to paper over capitalist contradictions and demanded Global South leadership to challenge the extant system. This internationalist critique of the U.S. state and its role sustaining the global status quo increasingly tied together disparate ideologies into a single campaign. This could lay the foundation for a U.S. solidarity that merged leftist strategies for assessing global inequality with the powerful bonds of racial sympathy.

The realization of the global problem of inequality broke down the barriers of the Cold War consensus even as it challenged the equally constraining limitations of strict Black nationalism. The question Malcolm dealt with in the last months of his life was how to forge unity domestically and abroad. Having rejected religion, he was in search of what biographer Manning Marable has called a "secular basis for common ground."[28] Racial identification provided one obvious answer, but so then did anti-capitalist solidarity against exploitation, and the latter seemed to offer new prospects for meaningful action. In his final speeches, Malcolm offered both as foundations for a new ideology. The CONCP parties staked claim to an inclusive leftist internationalism that appealed to Malcolm during his time on the African continent, but he had not yet made the full commitment. His assassination prevented him from reconciling these two distinct pathways to solidarity, leaving a legacy of ambiguity that haunted relations with Africa even as his popularity exploded posthumously with this generation of "Africanists." Events in Angola and elsewhere inspired Watts, Malcolm X, and others to reassess their own beliefs, but they struggled to translate international trends to their domestic goals.

Black Power Internationalism

Efforts by Snellings's "Africanist" generation to translate ideas of continental African revolution to the U.S. context became a central element in the formation of the Black Power movement, which historian Peniel Joseph has described as "trumpeting a new militant race consciousness that placed Black identity as the soul of a new radicalism."[29] The movement popularized ideas explored by Watts, Cruse, and Malcolm X, and its adherents gravitated toward revolutionary parties after abandoning the pacifist resistance of the civil rights movement. Black Power was a broad project that incorporated varying ideas, from the territorial nationalism of the Republic of New Afrika groups to the increasingly Marxist-influenced revolution of the Black Panthers. Within these differing programs existed a common emphasis on the need for an independent, ambitious Black leadership. "Black people must develop power," Congressman Adam Clayton Powell (D-NY) explained after meeting with youth activists, "political, economic, and cultural power in Black communities before they seek any coalition with white people."[30] The growth of Black Power demanded the attention of the liberation movements, which reexamined their strategies for cultivating foreign allies amid their push for Western support. These expanded connections, and the better understanding of revolutionary ideology that came with them, helped transform Black political thought.

One of the keys to understanding this new solidarity was the deference to African leadership central to the Black Power movement. The LCA and Malcolm X actively sought to learn from Africa, in contrast to some civil rights leaders—and even Dubois for much of his life—who considered the educated African American elite as benefactors for the continent.[31] Common attitudes ranged from respectful paternalism to mild condescension, with the latter growing as domestic success in gaining political rights contrasted with difficulties in postcolonial Africa.[32] Stokely Carmichael, the radical head of the Student Nonviolent Coordinating Committee (SNCC) who popularized the term "Black Power," initially reflected such attitudes when he expressed skepticism of African leadership, reportedly dismissing Tanzanian leader Julius Nyerere as a "clown."[33] Yet as Carmichael chafed under the restrictive pacifism of the civil rights movement and limited economic reforms, he reassessed these views as he drifted toward the revolution envisioned by the "Africanist generation."

Central to this transformation was a fuller understanding of and direct contact with African liberation leaders, who became models for assertive

Black action. Carmichael respected revolutionaries in Vietnam and the Middle East who challenged U.S. power with force of arms, but this admiration did not automatically extend south of the Sahara—at least not until he visited Africa in 1967. In the Tanzanian capital, the civil rights organizer was hounded by rumors of his earlier comments, but he found an ally in Eduardo Mondlane. Seeing an opportunity, the FRELIMO president assured Carmichael, in the words of biographer Joseph, "of the political integrity of revolutionaries he had too casually dismissed."[34] This began a reassessment of continental African leadership for Carmichael, who counted among his mentors the Pan-Africanist socialist triumvirate in Conakry that included Sékou Touré of Guinea, the exiled Kwame Nkrumah, and PAIGC head Amílcar Cabral. Carmichael became their student, eventually changing his name to Kwame Ture in honor of the leaders who contributed to his evolving philosophy.

Carmichael's transformation reflected a trend in Black Power ideology, which followed Malcolm X in looking to Africa as it imagined assertive challenges to racism and inequality in the United States. As the most active sites of struggle, the Portuguese colonies were prominent sources of study and inspiration. In the wake of Carmichael's call for a Black revolutionary movement, several leaders declared their support and admiration for anti-imperialist campaigns. In 1967, SNCC Chairman Rap Brown argued that "the struggle against racism, colonialism, and apartheid [was] an indivisible struggle" and identified Mozambique and Angola as prominent fronts in this battle.[35] The *Black Panther* devoted regular attention to the various movements, reintroducing its one hundred thousand weekly readers to the revolutions that had been absent from mainstream papers since 1961.[36] Other groups also gravitated toward the revolutions, notably the Greensboro-based Pan-African collective known as the Students (later Youth) Organized for Black Unity (SOBU/YOBU). The collective's widely distributed newsletter included columns written by and with African nationalists, reclaiming the legacy of the *Liberator* but offering more extended engagement with revolutionary ideology as connections proliferated. Often, these articles highlighted U.S. cooperation with Portuguese imperialism, connecting two pieces of the anti-imperial movement in a concrete way.[37] In collapsing the geographical, linguistic, and political differences between Africa and the United States, radical activists legitimized their own movements through celebration of international achievements. Before the decade closed, Eldridge Cleaver of the Black Panthers articulated a common logic when he stated that the revolution against Portuguese colonialism "is a source of inspiration, and it has a direct influence on the determination of the people fighting the struggle [in the United States]."[38]

As groups like the Black Panthers and SOBU celebrated the Portuguese African revolutions, CONCP representatives responded. FRELIMO's Sharfudine Khan made a point of cultivating Black support after his arrival in the United States in 1967. His Muslim faith and service in Cairo strengthened his appeal to young Black radicals, linking FRELIMO's struggle to North African revolutions and the Muslim cultural renaissance in America.[39] Gil Fernandes, the PAIGC's roving ambassador, also bridged the cultural gap, having attended the historically Black Lincoln University during the Kennedy years before completing his degree at the University of New Hampshire.[40] Along with less frequent visits by Mondlane and Cabral, the parties responded to increased outreach from the Black community. As Black Power advocates adopted the cause of African liberation as their own, they became the logical constituency to lead the popular African American movement that the Portuguese had feared since the Kennedy era.

Yet commitment to the CONCP cause remained confined to a small cadre of activists and grassroots organizers. Mobilizing the democratic pressure envisioned by the CONCP parties required more than a few noteworthy advocates like Carmichael or the Panthers; it needed a mass movement. Publications like SOBU's recently renamed *African World* disseminated leftist internationalist ideas alongside its coverage of the revolutions, but it was a slow process. Prospects for mass support remained scarce, as evidenced by ACOA's setbacks working in Chicago's Black community in the early 1970s. Historian Martha Biondi has written that average people had trouble embracing Pan-Africanism in their daily lives. Cultural identification with Africa was on the upswing, but the plight of racial minorities in North America and colonized majorities overseas seemed distinct. YOBU member Mark Smith recalled that many could not force such solidarity to "connect up, either an explanatory framework or an action path, with the conditions that people felt in their lives."[41]

To help build a movement, the CONCP parties and their domestic supporters needed to clarify the relationship between foreign and domestic revolutions. Part of this program simply involved expanding knowledge of the revolutions, and it was here that CONCP work with established institutions and New Left groups paid dividends. While ACOA had trouble connecting with Black youth, the literature that it and organizations like the Madison Area Committee on Southern Africa (MACSA) distributed helped inspire new interest and initiatives in the Black community. Randall Robinson, who led a Gulf Oil boycott (discussed in the next chapter) and later founded Trans-Africa, remembered that it was "reams" of pamphlets and newsletters from ACOA that opened his eyes to the achievements of the liberation struggles and inspired "a thirst for other sources of information."[42] In 1971, ACOA's Washington lobbyist Charles Hightower noted there was a clear expansion of Black interest in African liberation, which he credited to "direct contacts with Africa, African students in our home, organizations such as [ACOA] publicizing the Africa issue."[43] Solidarity groups helped expand interest in African revolutions, but their predominantly white memberships did not speak to the racial and cultural ties central to the Black movement. The nationalists needed to work more directly with Black Power advocates and find ways to unite these Pan-African sympathies with a transnational ideology to produce popular action.

The parties turned to new domestic allies to help with this translation. One of the earliest was Robert Van Lierop, who straddled the line between multiracial and Black Power organizing. One of Snellings's "Africanists," the native New Yorker worked with the NAACP and civil rights organizations while understanding the appeal of revolutionary action.[44] His service on ACOA's board revealed an ever-present pragmatism, but he was deeply influenced by Malcolm X's later philosophical wanderings, though—like many of his generation—mostly after his assassination.[45] This epiphany guided Van Lierop to Africa after graduating in 1967 from law school, where he had begun collaborating with Mondlane and FRELIMO.[46] While serving on ACOA's board, Van Lierop formed the Pan-African Solidarity Committee (PASC) in 1969 to promote a celebration in New York honoring the slain FRELIMO leader and Malcolm X. ACOA lent support, but Van Lierop made a special point to keep this involvement in the background to maintain an African American leadership as a way of preserving PASC's Black Power ideals. Featuring Betty Shabazz and a speech by Khan, the event promoted "international black political consciousness" through the celebration of an African solidarity week.[47] Yet problems of participation and commitment scuttled ongoing activities after the first celebration, ending Van Lierop's attempts to build a Black movement from this initial event.[48] This was just one example of a wider phenomenon in which Black organizers interested in building a new, revolutionary Pan-Africanism faced challenges as they sought to scale up local displays of solidarity scattered widely across the country. African nationalists and their Black allies needed to promote a shared vision of struggle to create self-sustaining grassroots organizing.

People in the Streets: African Liberation Day

A movement developed because the work undertaken by Van Lierop and other nationalist allies intersected with a unique period in African American history. The momentum created by civil rights advances and the ideas of self-determination present in the Black Power movement inspired African American leaders to imagine a political front that could champion Black interests on the national stage. A series of meetings exploring this idea culminated in the National Black Political Convention held in Gary, Indiana, in March 1972, with an international component following a few months later with the first celebration of African Liberation Day in June. The Lusophone liberation struggles and the ideologies promoted by the PAIGC and FRELIMO were influential for both events, helping remake how African Americans understood the concrete connections between local, national, and international action. The celebration of ALD, and the African Liberation Support Committee (ALSC) that it produced, convinced many African Americans that their struggles against racism were linked to the African continent and that liberation movements provided lessons for domestic organizing. Though the nationalist-Marxist divide eventually hamstrung the movement, the ALD reflected the growth of solidarity and built support for the African liberation struggles at the grassroots level.

Central to these events in the early 1970s was the revolutionary dramatist, writer, and organizer Amiri Baraka. Formerly known as LeRoi Jones, the Newark, New Jersey, native gravitated toward Black Power and revolutionary politics in the 1960s, visiting Cuba, meeting collaborator Snellings at the 1961 U.N. protests over the Congo, and developing a relationship with Malcolm X.[49] He was instrumental in the foundation of the Black Arts Movement, which championed race pride and considered art a powerful didactic component of political revolution. After Malcolm X's death, he changed his name and gravitated toward Black nationalism, advocating for the cultural Pan-Africanism of Maulana Karenga, whose adaptation of African communitarian ideas developed a powerful influence on Black identity and the foundations for Kwanzaa. In 1970, Baraka's Committee for a Unified Newark became the guiding force within the Congress of African Peoples (CAP), a merger of local organizations hoping to engineer a political institution that could champion Black Power ideas at a national level. Baraka defined CAP's political evolution, emphasizing Black community investment and support for African American political candidates. Deeply critical of both racism and monopoly capitalism, Baraka drew from models of political organizing in the

Third World to establish a structure where grassroots activists collaborated with political elites to seize the levers of power. While Baraka increasingly identified with Maoism as he moved to the left, the cultural nationalists of CAP were initially interested in African revolutions, especially the concrete visions of Black nation building pursued by the PAIGC and FRELIMO.[50] Their practical ideas of revolution were important, since CAP's driving goal became the organization of a Black political party that could represent the minority community's interests on the national stage.

The attempt to unite disparate political ideologies and organizing traditions behind a single Black Agenda gave Lusophone solidarity organizing a powerful boost. While foreign affairs did not drive this effort, support for African self-determination provided a common ground between elected officials, civil rights activists, and Black Power radicals in the early 1970s. Several exploratory meetings between these groups led to the Gary Convention of March 1972. Roughly seven thousand delegates attended from all fifty states, with proceedings managed by a triumvirate representing national, local, and grassroots politics in the figures of Charles Diggs, Gary mayor Richard Hatcher, and Baraka.[51] Diggs had earned past criticism for his ambiguity toward activists and general cautiousness, which led the Congressional Black Caucus (CBC) to replace him as chair in 1972, but his aggressiveness on African affairs aligned him with the grassroots.[52] His resignation in protest from the U.S. delegation to the United Nations in 1971 along with work supporting the Gulf Oil boycott discussed in the next chapter won plaudits from activists. Baraka recalled that "Charlie Diggs finally came a long way in trying to be more sympathetic to the mass line" and filled a valuable role acting as intermediary between politicians and activists.[53] At the Gary Convention, the congressman kept the proceedings from bogging down in minutiae and later organized congressional representation for the ALD celebration. Still, there remained a distance between elected officials and strident Black Power interests, tied as the former were to the Democratic Party and its positions, which came under withering criticism at Gary. Debates about forming an independent Black political party and what issues to include in the national agenda turned contentious at times, but the meeting itself captured the continuing attraction of the assertive anti-imperialism that underlay Black Power while revealing a new interest in institutionalizing these ideas in meaningful ways. In effect, it created the grassroots linkages that Diggs and other politicians were increasingly interested in mobilizing, while lending credibility to programs pursued by activists like Baraka and CAP.[54]

The Gary Convention failed to advance an independent party, but the declaration it produced revealed the extent to which tricontinental ideas of "self-determination and true independence" were becoming central to Black politics. It attacked both major political parties for maintaining "the true 'American Way' of unbridled monopoly capitalism, combined with ruthless military imperialism," that marginalized not only Black Americans but "many of our brothers in Africa and the rest of the Third World." Dismissing liberalism as an insufficient response to global inequalities, the document positioned the African American community as "the vanguard in the struggle for a new society."[55] The radical core of this message sought a common ground on which new organizations like the CBC and the grassroots CAP could collaborate, but it also provided the foundations for transnational solidarity by echoing earlier critiques of the United States offered by the CONCP parties. Deep disagreements remained over the need for a Black political party and thorny issues like Israel, but collaboration gave Black Power advocates opportunities to change policies, with grassroots elements referencing Lusophone liberation strategies to legitimize the decision. As Baraka explained to his critics when justifying compromise with mainstream politicians like Diggs: "Amilcar Cabral says, the people are not fighting for ideas, but for material improvement to their lives. Let that sink in. They are fighting for goods and services. For institutions. Not abstractions, no matter how militant sounding!"[56] In this moment, radical activists like Baraka looked to multilevel collaboration as a way of translating Black Power ideas into concrete changes to domestic and international policies.

The ALD served as the international complement to the Gary Convention. Occurring just months later and drawing on the same political networks, it owed a greater debt to the personal diplomacy of the CONCP parties, specifically their influence on the ALD founder, Owusu Sadaukai (Howard Fuller). A prominent attendee of the Gary Convention, Sadaukai was the head of Malcolm X Liberation University in Greensboro, North Carolina, and was closely associated with YOBU. The university championed the education of Blacks in the skills necessary to reconstruct their communities into autonomous and assertive units. Sadaukai gained a reputation as an innovator and an expert on education within the new Black agenda. In the fall of 1971, he traveled to Tanzania to learn from the country's education system. What inspired him most in Dar es Salaam was not Julius Nyerere's African model of governance but the liberation project in Mozambique. When Robert Van Lierop arrived with SNCC photographer Bob Fletcher to make a film on FRELIMO's revolution

at the party's request, Sadaukai joined them in a trip to the liberated territories. Sadaukai spoke extensively with FRELIMO leaders about their model of
national reconstruction and how African Americans could support them.[57]
In these exchanges, the freedom fighters stressed the importance of explaining the revolution to Americans—especially African Americans. Knowledge
of the revolutions and the U.S. role sustaining Portugal would compel activists
to show "strong moral support" and "[their] concern through massive Black
protest and demonstration against U.S. involvement in Southern Africa."[58]

Sadaukai returned to the United States with a clear mission. Using the
broad network that he developed while founding Malcolm X Liberation University and recruiting many of the organizers behind the Gary Convention,
he assembled a coalition of Black supporters that crossed class and ideological
lines. Among the notables who agreed to assist in preparing the first ALD were
Baraka, Stokely Carmichael, Betty Shabazz, head of the Southern Christian
Leadership Council Ralph Abernathy, Black Panthers Huey P. Newton and
Angela Davis, *Black Scholar* editor Nathan Hare, Lucius Walker of the Interreligious Foundation for Community Organization, and four congressmen,
including Diggs. Baraka's nationwide CAP organization drummed up local
support for the event, while Diggs took the lead in Congress.[59] This ad hoc
organization, brought together by the appeal of Black liberation, achieved the
communal unity that Malcolm X desired. It also offered the political potential envisioned by the liberation parties, with a special focus on their needs.
Sadaukai explained before the event, "Portugal today is looked upon as one
of the most diabolical among all enemies of Africa," with Pretoria "running a
close second."[60] All that remained was to define the ideology that would guide
this movement.

In these early stages, however, ideology took a backseat to building sympathy with the foreign revolutions. Occurring as news of FRLEIMO and the
PAIGC were reentering the mainstream Black press, the rally needed to educate and politicize the African American population. Organizers wanted to
prove that the distant struggles for economic and political equality were inherently linked to domestic concerns. Physical protests at major governmental
and corporate backers of Portugal and South Africa helped Black Americans
connect forms of oppression at home and abroad.[61] ALD's goal was to create a shared identity around revolutionary struggle by fighting against the
"thinking patterns of the black community" that saw the world "only in terms
of the local and the immediate, and only in terms of pieces of the whole."[62]
Domestic advocacy helped FRELIMO and the PAIGC, but it also provided

the foundation for concerted action by African Americans that would be the first step in launching a domestic political revolution of undetermined means and tactics.[63] Timed to follow just two months after the Gary Convention, it was a show of political power by Black America unified around Pan-African ideas. "The strengthening of Africa," Baraka explained in the first public announcement of the ALD, "is the strengthening of ourselves."[64]

The steering committee planned rallies in iconic cities with large Black populations to increase the chances that sizable protests would draw official attention. Sites in 1972 included San Francisco, Toronto, and Antigua. The U.S. capital, however, served as the primary location for the ALD. As Baraka told readers of *Black News*, Washington represented the ideal location for organizing, since it contained "the government of our worst enemies, but paradoxically in a stronghold of Black life."[65] Marches and rallies in front of embassies and the State Department would physically represent demands for the United States to reconsider its policies supporting reactionary, oppressive foreign governments. At each location, speakers would educate the attendees about the individual crimes of Portugal, South Africa, Rhodesia, and the United States. Preparations and speeches included attention to all parts of the African continent still under minority rule, but organizers singled out Portugal as the weakest link. Activists praised the Lusophone revolutions as the vanguard of the "newest most effective stage in a line of historical resistance [to European rule]."[66] As the campaigns in Mozambique and Guinea-Bissau gained ground, African Americans hoped that their support might provide the final element needed to tip the scales in their favor. As one anonymous fan of the ALD suggested, perhaps "support[ing] the liberation struggles on our own homeland" might "thrust the Freedom Fighters [of the Portuguese territories] over that crucial hump after which total defeat of colonialism through armed peoples struggle will have to be admitted."[67]

Organizers expected a few thousand protesters on May 27, but the popularity of the liberation movements had grown in recent years to become a rallying point for Black organizers. The largest planned demonstration, in Washington, D.C., attracted African Americans from major cities up and down the eastern seaboard, the Midwest, and from as far away as Houston. Dozens of buses released thousands of activists of all ages and political persuasions onto the streets of the capital, demanding recognition for freedom fighters waging wars of independence in Africa. Marchers carried signs proclaiming solidarity with the liberation struggles and condemning the economic discrimination that kept Blacks subservient at home as well as abroad.

Figure 8. The march to the National Mall begins for the first African Liberation Day, May 27, 1972. The marchers are leaving Meridian Hill (Malcolm X) Park, with the next stop being the Portuguese embassy, followed by the Rhodesian Information Office, and the South African embassy. Reprinted with permission of the D.C. Public Library, Star Collection © *Washington Post*.

The parade made stops at the State Department and the embassies of South Africa and Portugal, where Congressman Diggs, Angela Davis, and community leaders urged listeners to adopt the African revolutions as their own and boycott corporate partners like Gulf Oil that fed the coffers of colonial rule. The demonstration culminated on the National Mall—renamed Lumumba Square for the festivities—where varying estimates claimed between fifteen thousand and twenty-five thousand people joined Owusu Sadaukai in chants of "We are an African People."[68] Organizers proclaimed it the "largest all-Black demonstration in Washington's history" and the largest nationally since Marcus Garvey.[69] Another seven thousand to ten thousand reportedly gathered in San Francisco, while smaller crowds of a few thousand attended rallies in Toronto and Antigua.[70] Historian Komozi Woodard describes the event as "one of the most important forces for African liberation in African American history."[71] It was likely the largest single demonstration for African freedom to take place in a Western country before the 1980s.

While these efforts were primarily aimed at mobilizing the Black community, there were political implications. The Nixon administration—acquainted with mass dissidence around Vietnam—downplayed the events, but the demonstrations proved disturbing to governments in southern Africa.[72] To these officials, the visible manifestation of Black discontent with U.S. policy represented a new and potentially problematic trend. The Portuguese ambassador claimed in the 1990s that the protests did not even disrupt the daily services of the embassy, but the rogue Black nationalists who attempted to bomb the Portuguese consulate in San Francisco just a few days after the marches challenged his bravado.[73] After the ALD, it appears Portuguese security agents paid closer attention to African American activists. Diplomats at the South African embassy also took note of events. They had been observing the preparations for the campaign with unreserved skepticism and expressed surprise at the turnout in Washington, with the ambassador noting the "special venom" that protesters reserved for Portugal. Despite the surprising size of the demonstration, South African officials still questioned the commitment of the Black community to sustaining this activism—especially given antecedents like the ANLCA—concluding, "There is not enough evidence at this stage that southern Africa is a high priority in the black community."[74] A sustained effort was necessary to expand popular participation in the ALD and convince onlookers that Black identification with Lusophone and other nationalists was a lasting phenomenon.

An Ideology of Black Revolution

ALD was a testament to rising domestic identification with the Lusophone revolutions, but the celebration itself and the events that surrounded it created new opportunities for the nationalists' cause. The barrage of propaganda and personal diplomacy paid dividends in the early 1970s. Beyond publications from activist organizations, the CONCP parties broke into the mainstream Black press. They attracted comment from a diverse array of Black leaders, who gravitated toward Cabral in particular, as they discussed ways to integrate the useful aspects of Black Power into practical politics.[75] Eduardo Mondlane's regular written salutation, "A luta continua" (the struggle continues), became a catchphrase to describe any ongoing campaign for equality. Even *Ebony* joined the fray when it featured a glossy spread on the war behind the lines in Mozambique.[76] African Americans finally discovered the Portuguese African revolutions, and the nationalists responded by placing new value on overt appeals to the community. The most iconic representations of Black Power may have been declining during this period, but the leftist Pan-African ethos it inspired laid the foundation for mass identification with the Portuguese African revolutions and the CONCP programs.

The ad hoc organizing committee behind ALD 1972 formalized into the ALSC with the goal of celebrating the event annually, but the year between the first two rallies produced a change in the nature of the program. The newfound enthusiasm for the revolutions in Portuguese Africa was not initially self-reflective, depending primarily on imagined ideas of racial kinship and a common enemy rather than any strong understanding of shared ideologies or even sociopolitical goals. But as familiarity with the PAIGC and FRELIMO increased, their tricontinental brand of imperialism challenged the centrality of racial identity held by cultural and territorial nationalists. Central to this shift were the personality and philosophy of Amílcar Cabral, who emerged as Africa's leading revolutionary theorist after his 1966 Havana speech and Mondlane's death.[77] Though the West African and Mondlane both applied a Marxist-inspired reading of the international system, neither demanded a single unifying theory. Rather, Cabral stressed the necessity of each movement defining strategies and philosophies that fit the unique national context and addressed the needs of local people. "Always bear in mind that the people are not fighting for ideas" but for material benefits, Cabral was widely quoted as saying.[78] Ideological correctness for both Cabral and FRELIMO was less essential than measurable improvements in education, health care, economic conditions, and a dozen other areas long ignored by the Portuguese. To best improve the lives of individuals in any revolution, leaders had to identify targets and strategies to achieve real change.

This practical vision of revolution won over activists like Baraka and became central to organizing after the first ALD. For the CONCP parties, communal unity and struggle against the imperial system were the most universal aspects of their model, with all specific policies emerging from those key goals.[79] This flexible leftist ideology and the texts that explained it, combined with similar writings on African socialism by Julius Nyerere, became the core of a new Black corpus that helped to define the later stages of Black Power. Both the Black Panthers and SOBU incorporated these readings of

the revolutionary world situation into their influential papers, quoting lib-
erally from Portuguese Africans and even hosting writings from solidarity organizations such as the Liberation Support Movement (LSM).[80] This
increased attention to existing work from nationalist collaborators like Basil
Davidson and encouraged leftist publishers to produce a growing number of
English translations of Cabral's writings, beginning in 1969.[81] These texts and
ideas became central to African American reading groups alongside those
of Nkrumah, Mao, and others, recreating in reverse the intellectual salons
that helped establish the CONCP—this time stretching beyond universities
to community centers, clubs, and even prisons.[82]

As interest grew, there were attempts to explain these ideologies specifically in the context of the Black American struggle, with one of the most
important examples being Robert Van Lierop's documentary *A Luta Continua* (The Struggle Continues), released in 1972. The lawyer-activist had long
felt that a film would offer the ideal translation of FRELIMO and CONCP
ideology for a Black American audience. Mondlane and Khan both discussed
the idea with him before 1969, and they successfully worked with European
activists on films that got some play in the United States. Yet the glosses of
white Europeans did not translate to the issues confronting the Black American community or the Pan-African bonds that motivated personal identification. Van Lierop set out to make a film that spoke to African American
concerns, assembling a Black film crew that journeyed into liberated Mozambique with FRELIMO to document the armed struggle and the social reconstruction occurring behind the lines.[83]

A Luta Continua teases out the universal implications of FRELIMO ideology and its relevance to the Black community in the United States. Brevity
and Van Lierop's sympathetic gloss minimize foibles, but all simplifications
reflect FRELIMO's self-styled image as a social-minded revolutionary organization that prioritized the construction of an egalitarian state. The film
emphasizes three CONCP narratives. First, it emphasizes the global nature
of the anti-imperial struggle, in which Mozambique was a victim both of
formal Portuguese imperialism and of the economic exploitation of Euro-
American multinational corporations. Second, it emphasizes the creation
of what Mondlane referred to as the "new and popular social order," which
established cooperative farms, schools, and health facilities in the liberated
territories.[84] In a film about a revolution, images of war constitute roughly an
eighth of the running time, and the military training camp is described as "an
educational institution, an agricultural institution, a health institution, and a

social services institution" rather than simply a place of war.[85] Finally, the film mirrors FRELIMO by defining real victory as the achievement of equality and social cohesion—regardless of race, class, or gender. The film details the party ideal of democratic participation in the struggle, which erased economic differences and assigned women and men equal positions of authority based on specific responsibilities. Juxtaposing this situation with urban schools in the United States, where teachers ended the day with trips to the suburbs, Van Lierop praises the revolutionary model where all are "part of the same mass movement, and the teachers live, work, and struggle in the bush with all of the people.[86] The film ends with FRELIMO's call to Mozambicans to cast off traditional tribal and gender identities to be reborn as a single, egalitarian nation. FRELIMO and Van Lierop believed that dramatizing the ongoing revolution (or an idealized version of it) could translate ideas of universal struggle and inspire their adaptation to U.S. circumstances. As one ALSC member remembered later, studying the nationalist movements helped explain the "way things are put together" in practice and not just in theory.[87]

Upon its release in 1972, the film became the key text explaining FRELIMO and CONCP ideology to U.S. audiences.[88] Activists and occasionally nationalists like Khan appeared at screenings, urging viewers of all races to participate in the revolution either by joining in activities or by donating directly to FRELIMO.[89] A discussion guide distributed with the film reveals the general tenor of such events. It urged viewers to boycott southern African goods, conduct their own educational campaigns, and launch "mass political actions against identifiable imperialist targets (e.g. corporations with investments in southern Africa, communications outlets that have failed to report on the wars of national liberation)."[90] A Luta Continua came to represent the entirety of the CONCP struggle for socialist liberation, headlining events supporting the MPLA in Angola and the PAIGC in Guinea-Bissau. Accordingly, the film symbolized the promise of all African liberation struggles for thousands of Blacks, challenging them to reconsider their own lives and the future of their communities in light of this model. Sylvia Hill, an educator who became a prominent anti-apartheid activist in the 1980s, saw the film, "for the first time having this sense that you can have a science of change because you have to think methodologically about what you're doing."[91] A Luta Continua established an adaptable model for struggle and unity that could inform this new stage of the Black freedom movement.

The film was shown widely to Black, youth, and religious audiences, and it joined with a proliferation of other media to accelerate the process through which African Americans engaged with CONCP ideologies. The *African World* newspaper and Baraka's *Unity and Struggle* reproduced texts from FRELIMO and the PAIGC. The resulting promotion of tricontinental anti-imperialism challenged some of the most conservative, racialized aspects of Pan-African identification. Nationalists reinforced this message, with Khan, Gil Fernandes, and others all urging not only ideological engagement with revolution but also multiracial alliances to expand the political power of Black solidarity. Yet it was Cabral whose words had the greatest impact. When he visited New York in late 1972, he met with 120 representatives from Black organizations and explained that effective Pan-African solidarity required more than racial affinity. "Naturally we like our brothers," Cabral responded to an audience member who addressed him as such, "but in our conception it is better to be a brother *and* a comrade . . . if we are brothers it is not our fault or our responsibility. But if we are comrades, it is a political engagement."[92] This dialogue was widely read as the centerpiece of *Return to the Source*, a collection of Cabral's speeches published by the Africa Information Service run by Van Lierop and Chicago Committee for the Liberation of Angola, Mozambique, and Guinea (CCLAMG) member Prexy Nesbitt. These texts worked in combination with other media like *A Luta Continua* to enhance the ideological foundations for Black American engagement with African revolutions.

The result was a drift toward tricontinental ideas, which received a boost from one final event. In January 1973, Amílcar Cabral was assassinated in Conakry by Guinean members of the PAIGC. The conspirators had run afoul of party leadership and complained bitterly about the Cabo Verdean dominance of the highest ranks. Portugal was widely blamed for the attack, and Black Americans saw it as another example of the violence used to suppress Black revolution. Cabral joined Malcolm X and Mondlane as transnational Black martyrs and symbols of progressive Pan-Africanism, with Cuba also enshrining him alongside Lumumba and Che Guevara in tricontinental propaganda.[93] Black Americans expressed their displeasure by picketing the Portuguese embassy in Washington and consulate in Boston.[94] The ALSC dedicated celebrations of African Liberation Day in 1973 to Cabral. The memorialization reinforced Cabral's rising position as a revolutionary theorist and focused attention on his writings. At the same time, reports that racial politics drove the Guinean assassins militated against strict identarian politics in favor of the kind of ideological solidarity Cabral championed in his speeches. As a result, the tricontinental reading of Pan-Africanism gained rapid ground within the ALSC over more racialized theories of Black nation-alism, with profound effects on the search for Black unity.

The leftward drift was reflected in the organization of ALD celebrations in 1973. Massive rallies in a few major cities gave way to a series of smaller demonstrations scattered across the country. These local demonstrations highlighted shared elements of imperial exploitation and its impact on individual lives, attempting to achieve Cabral's dictum of directly relating revolution to quotidian experiences. These local rallies allowed organizers to connect the immediate symbols of oppression with African liberation in a way that advocated for grassroots mobilizing. Organizers hoped these demonstrations would gently expand the base of their revolution beyond the strict limits of Black nationalism by targeting institutions that also angered the New Left. Adopting the long-winded theme "There is no peace with honor—the war continues in Africa and against Black People in this country," the ALSC sought to canalize popular radicalism focusing on Southeast Asia into the southern African cause. As Sadaukai explained in words reminiscent of radical white solidarity organizers at the time, "We feel very strongly that as the war 'winds down' in Vietnam it will be winding up in Africa."[95] The organizers' goal was to expanded audiences for their protests as they con-nected their Pan-African identities with general critiques of U.S. adventurism outside South Vietnam. Where government consulates or agencies were not available, organizers focused on companies that operated in southern Africa, with the main target being Gulf Oil's operations in Angola. By identifying local targets and articulating their relationship to inequalities in Africa, Afri-can Americans sought to define clear local actions that would allow people to act alongside the liberation struggles.

These changes produced a far different African Liberation Day. In May, roughly thirty cities across the United States, Canada, and the Caribbean held rallies (see figure 10). Attendance differed from one city to the next, but widespread participation demonstrated a depth of feeling among Afri-can Americans. New Haven produced well over a hundred participants; Raleigh, North Carolina, more than fifteen hundred; and the less than rad-ical city of Knoxville, Tennessee, saw four hundred marchers. In Portland, Oregon, over a thousand attended, including more than a few white leftists, while nearly two thousand filled the streets of Columbia, South Carolina. In Newark, New Jersey, Baraka's hometown and the center of a large Portuguese immigrant population, local efforts focused heavily on the Lusophone revo-lutions. Marchers designed a route that included "stops at many symbols of oppression against black people," which included the Portuguese consulate and the Portuguese airline TAP.[96] In Houston, a few hundred marched outside the Portuguese consulate and in front of the Gulf Oil building, before attending a rally of more than one thousand. Harlem, Oakland, and Washington all claimed gatherings of roughly five thousand people for their rallies. Earlier festivities in Los Angeles raised $17,000 from roughly three thousand attendees. A few cities, like Boston and Rochester, produced discouraging results, with activists blaming poor weather. Ultimately, the turnout for the piecemeal ALD proved far greater than many had expected, given its diffuse nature.[97] Local committees raised more than $41,000 in aid for the liberation groups.[98] Activist publications claimed that more than a hundred thousand people marched in the various cities, though the numbers are difficult to confirm.[99] Superficially, the celebrations looked smaller because no one event was as large as the showing in Washington in 1972, but there were likely more people involved in the planning and programs surrounding these events. As one activist remembered, for every one person who attended the rallies, there were likely three or four who participated at some level beforehand or after.[100] Each of these people found ways to engage with the liberation movements in their home regions.

The second ALD also pointed to a deeper incorporation of socialist ideology into African American solidarity organizing. Local groups, many of which were associated with Baraka's CAP, promoted interest in African parties in part by highlighting elements of their tricontinental ideology. Literature and films like *A Luta Continua* overwhelmingly emphasized CONCP positions because they focused so heavily on the successful revolutions waged by the PAIGC and FRELIMO, imbibing their specific ideas and strategies. The scholar-activist John Henrik Clarke recalled years later that the ALSC and its celebrations were "significant because they reached Black people who do not read Karl Marx, who do not read dogma, ordinary work-a-day porters, street sleepers, dishwashers. It was reaching grassroots."[101] Parties like FRELIMO and figures such as Cabral remained shibboleths for resistance, but there was now a rapidly expanding attempt to seriously engage with their specific ideologies as presented by liberation leaders and domestic allies like Van Lierop.

Reflecting these ideological influences and expanding awareness of southern African revolution, ALD celebrations in 1973 inched away from the niche of strictly racial interest. In locations such as Portland, where leftists cooperated across the color line, whites participated in ALD activities, though not without some consternation at the national level.[102] Major media outlets paid greater attention to the marches, devoting space to the demonstrations and the transnational ideology they articulated. An article on the front page of the *Washington Post*'s Metro section (above the fold no less) noted that the D.C. event was smaller than the prior year's but showed "correlations between the history and problems of both [Blacks here and Africans]."[103] The *New York Times* and smaller local papers provided similar coverage, noting how activists used the celebrations to direct new energy toward local issues. In Manhattan, borough president Percy Sutton declared the proposed Harlem site of an unpopular state office building African Liberation Square, effectively delineating it as a battleground that connected with the local theme "One struggle—many fronts."[104] In places where celebrations received no coverage outside the Black community, organizers charged racism. In Philadelphia, a group of young activists lambasted the city's major daily paper, the *Inquirer*, and other local media for their lack of attention. "A press that can uncover the Pentagon papers," they stated, tongue firmly in cheek, "cannot claim to have been unable to uncover information on African Liberation Day."[105] The ALD may have been a Black project, but organizers had aimed the protests at a much larger segment of society.

The ALD sought to build the political pressure desired by the liberation parties, bolstering the congressional representatives of the Black community who had strengthened their ties to the grassroots during this period. Charles Diggs organized a congressional delegation that traveled around Africa, discussing the growth of Black interest in the liberation struggles and urging coordinated pressure on the United States by independent governments as an international complement to grassroots organizing. ALD celebrations also spurred new congressional initiatives that worked—in the words of Diggs's committee staff—"to push, to pull, to tug, to embarrass, and to cajole the government into more considerate action."[106] Some State Department officials believed this burgeoning transnational coalition on Africa could have real consequences for U.S. policy toward the minority regimes, especially as the movement looked to harness the lingering energy of Vietnam War protests. The U.S. consul general in Luanda remarked, "[A] large number of critics of that war will be in search of a cause and may well adopt southern Africa ... [and] could put additional domestic pressure on [the] U.S."[107] FRELIMO agreed. Sharfudine Khan used the ALD celebrations and their enthusiastic reception in Africa to needle officials who continued to protect Portugal.[108] One State Department report openly wondered if a shift in policy might be inevitable if the Congressional Black Caucus and its grassroots allies could replicate the sustained activism in Europe that swayed the Nordic countries and the Netherlands to aid the liberation movements.[109]

This emerging grassroots-political alliance—given new weight by the continuation of ALD celebrations in 1973 and the community engagement it promoted—proved particularly concerning across the Atlantic. After trying to dismiss the prior year's event, the Portuguese government feared that its good relations with the Nixon administration could succumb to a potentially hostile U.S. legislature prodded by grassroots activists. Shortly after the first ALD in 1972, Diggs and the Congressional Black Caucus demanded an end to all aid to Portugal as a specific platform in its Black "Bill of Rights." Though unsuccessful, the move concerned Lisbon, leading the generally dismissive Portuguese ambassador to label it "the only initiative with a really onerous character" during a period of rapidly improving Luso-American relations.[110] As organizing expanded over the next year, the willingness of congressional representatives to talk openly of confronting the administration over its relationship with Portugal signaled that the tenor of U.S. politics was changing. Two months before the second ALD took place, when Assistant Secretary of State David Newsom commented that the U.S. government had to acknowledge "growing domestic manifestations against Portuguese policy," Lisbon's exasperated foreign minister complained that "10,000 people marching on African Liberation Day should not form U.S policy."[111] The ALD signaled that a Pan-African identification with the struggles in southern Africa had taken hold within the Black community, adding a powerful new component to the solidarity campaign with Lusophone Africa.

By 1973, there was a new level of international awareness and involvement in the Black community. This sentiment had never fully disappeared, but it was now mobilized and visible. Both leftists and race-first nationalists pledged solidarity to the successful parties of southern Africa. The PAIGC and FRELIMO became symbols of assertive political and economic self-determination, which appealed to African Americans demanding full equality in their own communities. Internationalists such as Daniel Watts of the LCA, Amiri Baraka, and Owusu Sadaukai linked the liberation cause with domestic frustrations in a continuous Pan-African critique of the Cold War United States. As historian Brenda Gayle Plummer argues, these "African vistas . . . provided an alternative to white nationalism and its political agenda," as well as an alternative to the constrained vision of protest accepted by many civil rights leaders in the 1960s.[112] The Black Power movement and the new attention of the African nationalist parties helped activists collapse the distance not only between Africa and the United States but between foreign and domestic policy as well. This transnational perspective helped activists break free from the confines of Cold War liberalism and imagine grand programs for global liberation.

Organizing in the early 1970s created a new momentum for U.S. support of African liberation, albeit one that had to overcome ongoing conflicts concerning authentic ideology. Over a decade, a loosely connected network of activists and organizers forged a solidarity with the struggles in southern Africa. This supports historian John Munro's argument that a radical, Black internationalist tradition survived the 1950s, and it points to the structures, activists, and causes that helped adapt and promote these ideas for the post–civil rights era.[113] Distance, language, and culture separated African Americans from their co-racialists abroad, but the construction of solidarity with African liberation struggles reinvigorated radical internationalism as the core ideas of Lusophone revolution offered new ways to conceptualize Black Power. In supporting the positive cause of liberation advanced by the most successful parties of the socialist CONCP, African Americans expanded what scholar Komozi Woodard has referred to as a "fictive kinship" that erased physical and linguistic distance from the African continent.[114]

Helping this process were the practical, flexible ideologies of the Portuguese African movements, whose tricontinental vision provided useful foundations for defining this affinity while promoting a socialist iteration of Pan-Africanism that appealed to Black Power advocates, civil rights organizers, and mainstream politicians. The pursuit of common goals led to the Gary Convention but found sustained engagement on the most obvious area for common ground: African freedom. This provided an ideological framework to unite a broad spectrum of Black politics behind this new program and opened pathways for new coalitions with additional elements of society that shared similar goals. This reinforced the role that the Lusophone struggles played in transforming the politics of the era, as the CONCP parties' inclusive appeals laid the groundwork for issue-based collaborations that united the diverse racial and ideological communities that aligned behind New Left Internationalism.

CHAPTER 8

The Interracial Coalition Politics
of the Gulf Boycott

The growth of grassroots African American interest in Portuguese African liberation completed the U.S. solidarity coalition. From the streets of Houston and the campuses of California to the halls of power in New York and Washington, D.C., a rising anti-imperial sentiment championed self-determination in Africa and sought to challenge the national policies and practices that underwrote the continuation of colonialism and racial inequality in the southern third of the continent. Supporters had different origins and embraced varying intellectual traditions of humanism, radicalism, and Pan-Africanism, but they found common cause in the revolutions of the Conference of Nationalist Organizations of the Portuguese Colonies (CONCP) and their visions for postcolonial socialist nations. Ideologically and demographically distinct forces, ranging from the most progressive elements of the National Council of Churches (NCC) to the increasingly leftist leadership of the African Liberation Support Committee (ALSC), converged under the broad umbrella of New Left Internationalism. Given the diversity of collaborators and their differing priorities, this was less formal ideology than common worldview, which understood the world in terms of domestic and global inequalities that operated along racial, economic, and political lines. New Left Internationalism established both a set of problems and shared responses that informed individual action as well as an emerging vision for U.S. foreign affairs. This worldview incorporated elements of tricontinentalism—critiques of capitalism and empire, concern with the North-South divide, and a willingness to accept revolution—while focusing on how people living in North America (and the Global North generally) should support processes of political, economic, and social decolonization.

Though groups cohered around common campaigns and goals, specifically Lusophone liberation, the multipolar nature of this coalition prevented the formation of a singular organization that might attract historians or political scientists. Instead, the overlapping membership of these organizations converged around specific issues with wide appeal.

In the early 1970s, the Gulf Oil boycott campaign offered a powerful example of this collaboration, linking African liberation with U.S. domestic economic and racial issues to mobilize all corners of the anti-imperial coalition. Gulf Oil's operations off the coast of Angola represented the largest U.S. corporate investment in the Portuguese economy, and the selection of this cause, its framing, and the collaboration that took place around it reveal the workings of the solidarity network. While nominally about removing Gulf dollars from Portuguese coffers, the true goal of the campaign was to integrate Global South anti-imperialism into domestic debates on good governance and corporate responsibility, challenging the indifference that allowed Portugal to develop new alliances to offset the costs of its extended wars. The boycott mobilized grassroots efforts, a priority for both young radicals and Black activists, but it is worth noting that its initial impetus grew from institutional religious efforts with support from the American Committee on Africa (ACOA). The interaction between these constituencies and the ways they collaborated to move from boardroom debate to street-level protests reveal the vitality and complexity of the solidarity movement. Though not always coordinated, the actions undertaken by groups representing youth, religious, and African American priorities generally complemented each other.

The Gulf boycott also highlighted the ideological fissures that existed within the movement. Generally, decentralization allowed for accommodation of differences as groups managed their participation in accordance with their priorities and identities. Personal connections further blunted the hard edges of ideological conflict as young radicals accepted the limitations of religious denominations or the Congressional Black Caucus, taking help where it was offered. These ideological differences proved more difficult to accommodate within the project for a national African American agenda, especially when the Gulf boycott highlighted the lingering question of which nationalist party and ideology to support in Angola. Ideological contests split the African Liberation Support Committee and the broader Black political movement. While this has often been depicted in the historical literature as a signal of decline, the role that Black activists played in the Gulf boycott reveals that it might be more accurately called a realignment, in which components of the Black Power movement sought power through pragmatic cooperation under the umbrella of New Left politics. This reshuffling of political constituencies around a New Left Internationalism—with visions of Lusophone revolution as a vital component—set the stage for a new era of solidarity organizing when the Portuguese dictatorship finally collapsed under the weight of its colonial wars.

The Beginning of the Gulf Oil Boycott

Activists long viewed economic demonstrations as a way of building support for African revolutions. Beginning with attempts to boycott South African goods in the 1950s, American protests of businesses operating in the white minority states sought to shift successful civil rights tactics to international issues. The CONCP championed an economic boycott of Portugal as a way of bringing the war to Europe.[1] Economic activism also had the ability to internationalize domestic critiques of corporate capitalism present in both youth and Black radicalism. These two issues motivated the short-lived Chase Manhattan Bank campaign in 1965, organized by the Students for a Democratic Society (SDS) and the Southern Africa Committee (SAC). The effort won support from ACOA, which saw it as an early attempt to create grassroots support for southern African freedom, but it failed for two key reasons. First, most of the powerful institutions likely to advance the effort—notably denominational leaderships affiliated with the National Council of Churches (NCC)—were not ready to embrace either the African liberation movements or that level of economic activism in 1965. The proposal occurred almost simultaneously with Lyndon Johnson's escalation of the Vietnam War, and the major Protestant denominations had yet to be jostled out of their old ways. Stocks were economic tools rather than political levers, and the indirect role that private loans played in propping up South Africa or Portugal were viewed separately from local boycotts of segregated stores. Indeed, of all the major denominations, the only moral calculus used to consistently guide large-scale investments related to temperance-era concerns about tobacco and alcohol among Baptists and Methodists.[2] This mindset changed as the Vietnam War forced a reckoning with institutional policy, increasing the power of New Left advocates like SAC alumnus Tim Smith in the United Church of Christ (UCC) and future Washington Office on Africa head Ted Lockwood within the Methodist leadership.[3] By 1968, Protestant denominations began discussing the use of investments to shape corporate policy, with Smith's UCC becoming the first to actively encourage "corporate social responsibility" around issues of racial and economic justice, peace, Third World development, environmental protection, and gender equality.[4] These attitudes gradually spread across the membership of the NCC but too late to support the Chase Manhattan Bank campaign.

In the years it took the churches to rethink corporate responsibility, the Chase campaign faltered for a second reason: the difficulty of mobilizing support for anti-apartheid work without an active revolution. Apartheid was widely reviled, but South Africa cracked down on activities of the African National Congress (ANC) in the early 1960s and overwhelmed the party's foreign relations efforts for much of the decade. As active wars in Vietnam and the Lusophone colonies demanded attention, the anti-apartheid revival sputtered. The coalition behind the Chase campaign drifted in different directions; it was effectively dead when South Africa chose not to renew the loan in 1969 as economic conditions improved. Southern Africa groups claimed some credit for the withdrawal, citing Princeton University and a few other institutions that stated they would not do business with banks involved with the South African government, but where to go next was unclear.[5] For many interested in southern Africa, the Portuguese colonies offered a better opportunity. There were three active revolutions, and all the CONCP parties criticized Western investments that sustained Portugal's settlement schemes and costly wars.[6] Lisbon's NATO connections also tied any campaign to the antiwar effort that was diverting attention from southern Africa. The missing component was a well-known corporation that could dramatize these issues and was sufficiently ubiquitous to serve as a locus for activism across the country. As one ACOA staffer explained in 1969, activists needed to find "ways of 'Chase Manhattanizing' the economic and military institutions through which we work with Portugal."[7]

Gulf Oil provided the solution. During the 1960s, Portugal's most promising foreign investments came from oil companies eager to tap the "sleeping giant" of Africa.[8] Firms proposed exploration involving all three of Portugal's mainland colonies, but Pittsburgh-based Gulf Oil was among the first to begin operating in Angola in the 1950s, later showing interest in Mozambique. In 1964, FRELIMO criticized Gulf for providing the expertise and capital to exploit African resources in a situation "where the mother-country has no economic possibilities of its own."[9] African nationalist frustration mounted after Gulf discovered oil off the Angolan exclave of Cabinda and began exporting crude in 1968. Production of crude tripled by 1969, increasing

annual payments for Portugal.[10] The money indirectly funded military ven-
tures, since almost half of Portugal's annual budget went to maintaining the
three war fronts in the 1970s. Gulf quibbled about how much the funds contributed, but Portugal benefited. Gulf's reported $11 million in payments in
1969 equaled roughly 45 percent of the Angolan defense budget.[11] By 1972,
the $61 million paid by Gulf to the state amounted to almost 60 percent of
Portugal's military expenditures in Angola, or just under a third of those in
Mozambique.[12] For a country as poor as Portugal, these Gulf revenues were
a windfall that offset the rising costs of war.[13] According to the nationalists,
such investment also made their countries indirect colonies of the United
States, with Portugal maintaining the conditions necessary for corporate
exploitation of their mineral wealth.[14]

As Gulf's investments and nationalist criticism grew apace, the solidarity
network responded to African calls for action. Discussions about a Gulf boycott began in 1969. ACOA hesitated, concerned that the necessity of fuel in
car-dependent America and the complexity of corporate payments to Portugal would hamper growth, so it floated the idea of instead targeting Angola's
primary export, coffee.[15] But radical grassroots organizations believed Gulf
was a perfect encapsulation of the anti-imperial ideology promoted by FRE-
LIMO and the PAIGC. For New Left activists seeking to define economic
neo-imperialism, Gulf's direct involvement in Angola offered a clearer illustration of expanding U.S. power than would purchases of colonial coffee on
the open market. The Committee of Returned Volunteers (CRV) established
the outline of this argument in their widely read study of Mozambique, beginning a multiyear process of building information on Gulf's activities.[16] A few
months later, SAC alumnus Bill Minter worked with ACOA's Jennifer Davis
to publish a carefully researched investigation of U.S. involvement in the
Portuguese colonies for *Africa Today* that included strong criticism of new
oil investments.[17] Finally, in 1971 the CRV New York branch that included
FRELIMO associate and future founder of the Chicago Committee for the
Liberation of Angola, Mozambique, and Guinea (CCLAMG), Nancy Freehafer, produced a detailed attack on Gulf's operations in Angola. The pamphlet
made a tricontinental appeal by arguing the company "literally engulfed the
globe" with a "long (oily) history" supporting reactionary regimes in South
Africa, Bolivia, Iran, the Philippines, and Taiwan. Puns aside, the CRV provided detailed support to African claims that Gulf payments aided Lisbon's
wars.[18] These facts, along with the firm's close ties to the U.S. military, made it
a powerful symbol to rally New Left opposition.

As the New York CRV finalized its research, it appealed to the solidarity network to launch a grassroots campaign. Joining with the SAC, it convinced ACOA and—most surprisingly—members of the NCC to stage a protest at the 1970 Gulf stockholders' meeting in Pittsburgh. Tim Smith, the Africa specialist on the UCC's Council for Christian Social Action, spearheaded efforts to win over Protestant leaders, who by this point had committed to supporting the nationalist cause.[19] ACOA also put aside its strategic reservations to embrace the Gulf campaign in light of the grassroots energy; George Houser still questioned whether the country would respond, but he was sufficiently frustrated by the years of "dialogue too often followed by inaction" that he aligned the committee with its young allies.[20] The New York–based organizations reached out to the Gulf Action Committee, a group of Pittsburgh radicals opposing the corporation's collaboration with problematic regimes abroad and hostility to unions at home.[21]

This coalition launched the Gulf campaign by disrupting the corporate shareholders' meeting in April 1970. More than three dozen protesters arrived holding proxy tickets for major investors or having bought a single share that would allow them entrance to Pittsburgh's Carnegie Music Hall. Four hundred more protesters marched in front of the entrance waving flags emblazoned with "Gulf Kills," chanting constantly for the corporation to abandon its alliance with Lisbon's blatant colonialism. Youth protesters chanted slogans, only quieting down when activists lined up at floor microphones to make statements on the wrongs of Gulf Oil. Some impassioned speakers went on for so long that Gulf Chairman E. D. Brockett had them forcibly removed.[22] Their list of demands was simple: end exploitation of resources in the developing world, stop feeding the military sectors of the United States and Portugal, and replace the board with representatives democratically elected from the communities in which Gulf operated.[23] One by one, protesters nominated their own candidates for the board, drawn mostly from liberation movements abroad and the radical fringes of U.S. society. Among other names proffered were PAIGC head Amílcar Cabral, David Dellinger of "Chicago Seven" fame, and Black Panther Angela Davis. In a nod to his changing allegiances, Houser nominated Agostinho Neto of the MPLA in a lengthy speech before pro-management attendees shouted him down as he attempted to read excerpts from Neto's poetry. Regular chants of "throw him out" proved almost as disruptive as the demonstration itself, reminding Gail Hovey of the Passion play cries of "Crucify him!" she knew from church.[24] The disruptions led to several arrests, mostly of youth activists who refused to abandon the microphones.[25]

The action illustrated the potential of this coalition even as it highlighted the ideological and strategic gaps between members. Even allies chuckled at one communist's demands to do away with the money system, while one senior church leader was visibly uncomfortable in the increasingly raucous context. John Coventry Smith, the secretary-general of the United Presbyterian Church in the United States of America, was present to voice his denomination's dismay at Gulf's operation in Angola but declined to speak when given the chance, explaining he had communicated his objections to Chairman Brockett in a written statement.[26] Such disagreements were less apparent from the outside. Brockett and Gulf President B. R. Dorsey spent much of the two and a half hours defending their record overseas and at home. Amid the commotion, no one had a chance to nominate the management's slate to the board of directors or elect outside accountants. Brockett announced both before he had a chance to pick up ballots for shareholders voting in person, confirming the corporation's undemocratic nature in activist eyes. Lacking the votes to pass their amendments, the protesters exited the auditorium to march through the city and link up with other local protests. During the period of quiet, Brockett announced that earnings had fallen 15 percent in the first quarter despite an increase in production volume.[27] He did not speculate about the relationship between the drop in profits and the protesters. While the stockholder protest that day did not succeed, it demonstrated the vitality of the solidarity coalition and its attempts to promote its New Left Internationalism, which sought to inject new moral calculations into foreign affairs by demanding that corporations recognize and redress the North-South divide.[28]

In the months following the board meeting, the Gulf campaign expanded through a combination of visible protests and shareholder activism that revealed the special advantages of coalition organizing. SAC, CRV, the Madison Area Committee on Southern Africa (MACSA), and the Liberation Support Movement (LSM) promoted a grassroots boycott, targeting local Gulf stations while highlighting the company's global operations to win over antiwar activists.[29] ACOA joined the churches in focusing less on the boycott than on stockholder activism and the threat of divestment, a more elite project but one that proved highly visible. It also kept an eye to the grassroots by looking to universities, distributing a list of major collegiate investors in Gulf and working with students to mount peaceful protests to sway administrative policies.[30] The NCC continued to engage with local Pittsburghers but encouraged its denominations to use their large holdings of company stock to mount an internal insurrection that aligned better with the professional

expertise of the religious leadership. The NCC hoped to force internal, institutional change. Individual Protestant churches began publicly criticizing
Gulf, claiming their rights as investors to speak on company policy. Most
prominent among these was Tim Smith's UCC, which had missionary ties
to Angola dating back to the 1880s and felt a sense of obligation to the colony.[31] While tactically distinct from the boycott idea, this elite-level activism
became a catalyst for growing grassroots interest in the related campaigns.

The UCC challenge to Gulf became a flashpoint in the movement because
its size and legitimacy demanded a response from the company. In 1970, the
UCC's regional conference in Ohio approved a resolution criticizing Gulf for
its cooperation with Portugal. It urged church members to return Gulf credit
cards and cease using company products "until Gulf Oil discontinues the use
of its African operations in ways that cause human suppression and suffering." The conference also urged stockholders to retain their shares to maintain voting power and challenge company policies from within, but pairing
the strategy with a boycott took the conference beyond other churches.[32] Gulf
management criticized inaccuracies within the UCC's initial statement and
used some creative accounting to minimize the payments Gulf made to the
Portuguese government. More important, Gulf trotted out a familiar Cold
War argument: "Angola, as other areas with which we deal, is a vital source
of oil needed by the free world. That's why we're there." Claiming to adopt
neutrality vis-à-vis the domestic politics of host nations, Gulf awkwardly
attempted to win over its religious critics by claiming, "[We] must do business in many countries because oil is where God put it." With a final attempt
to hide behind Nixon's policy of engagement in southern Africa, Gulf concluded that its presence in Cabinda was justified.[33] The problem was that
churches like the UCC, galvanized by their own rethinking of their global
mission, no longer shared this perspective. The UCC and allies such as the
ACOA-associated scholar John Marcum criticized Gulf for using "dated Cold
War jargon" to justify its operations.[34] Rather than thinking in terms of free
and unfree worlds, the church urged Gulf to think of the new binary of "the
developed Western and Eastern nations and the developing Third World."[35]
This new paradigm, focused on assuaging inequalities between North and
South, became the base criterion for judging morality, rather than the struggle
between democratic capitalism and Soviet communism.

The church's actions touched a nerve on both sides of the debate. The
Ohio UCC's point-by-point rebuttal of the company's defense established
a critique of capitalism that linked New Left priorities with mainstream

moralism, reinforcing the drift in liberal religious politics toward a focus on North-South issues. Demonstrating a poor understanding of the tenor of the times, a defensive Gulf implied possible legal action, inviting national media attention on the Angolan issue. Reporters had a field day with the story of corporate greed attacking religious do-gooding. The press hoped court proceedings would reveal the inner workings of the country's tenth-largest company—and one of its most internationally active—while one acerbic journalist envisioned a Gulf victory sending bailiffs into "sanctuaries to seize the silver crosses . . . to be melted down and recast in the shape of little oil derricks."[36] Gulf backtracked, but the exchange opened a national debate on the need to change business practices in response to decolonization.[37] UCC members and their colleagues in the NCC were simultaneously angry and encouraged by Gulf's response. It steeled their resolve to engage in a broader corporate responsibility campaign, with southern Africa as its centerpiece.

Gulf's ham-handed dealings with the UCC galvanized the campaign and helped activate the solidarity network. With support from the UCC and the Episcopal leadership, the United Presbyterian Church introduced four resolutions to the 1971 Gulf proxy statement urging the company to study the Angola situation, increase the size of the board to improve democratic control of the corporation, and end its activities in all colonial areas. The church contacted six hundred university stockholders, ten banks, and several mutual funds with requests to support the proxy statement.[38] Legislators with established interests in Africa responded to initiatives proposed by major religious institutions and requests for official assistance from both the NCC and ACOA. In April 1971, Representative Jonathan Bingham (D-NY) invited his colleagues to add their signatures to a letter supporting the church resolutions for Gulf, joining with New York Republican colleague and fellow Africa watcher Ogden Reid to promote bipartisan criticism of the oil giant.[39] One month later, the Gulf issue emerged as a prominent component in Charles Diggs's House Foreign Affairs Subcommittee on Africa hearing on business in southern Africa, pitting corporate spokesmen against the nascent Gulf coalition.

The hearings reflected the movement's success, but it also fed new information into it. Testifying before the subcommittee, Josiah Beeman, the head of the Presbyterian Southern Africa Task Force, endured a withering assault from Pittsburgh Republican James Fulton—who defended imperial Portugal as "a geographically separated country"—but the subcommittee also published new details of Gulf's operations provided by its vice president Paul

Sheldon.[40] Sheldon claimed that Gulf remained "politically nonpartisan abroad" and that it worked only with "those foreign nations whose governments [were] recognized by the United States," defending his company by asserting that its payments to Portugal paled in comparison to its investment in the local economy. He claimed that most jobs went to Black Angolans, but questioning revealed these were mostly low-level laboring or service positions and that higher-level positions paid directly by Gulf were held predominantly by white Portuguese. These statistics were reproduced by various elements of the Gulf campaign.[41] Diggs noted how unusual it was for Gulf (along with Polaroid, which faced its own internal protests over operations in South Africa) to send representatives to testify, since most corporations did not cooperate with subcommittee investigations. But this was its own testament to the power of the movement. ACOA's Charles Hightower argued in his testimony immediately following Sheldon's that attempts by Gulf and Polaroid to defend themselves in the official record was a logical response to "a growing interest on the problem [of southern African investments]."[42]

This high-level sparring energized grassroots organizing, most clearly illustrated in the formation of the Ohio-based Gulf Boycott Coalition (GBC). It emerged from the Congregation of Reconciliation in Dayton, an experimental nondenominational community associated with the UCC whose unifying identity came from an active commitment to social justice activism. Under the leadership of Presbyterian pastor Richard Righter, the congregation developed a strong interest in local corporate-responsibility issues related to civil rights and poverty. It supported the Ohio UCC conference's actions on Gulf and adopted the cause as its own after the company threatened legal action.[43] In March 1971, Righter and congregant Patricia "Pat" Roach formed the Gulf-Angola Committee to expand the campaign nationwide. Though fearful of retribution from Gulf, the community justified its action with scripture and the right to self-determination advanced by the United Nations. The result was a project that the Congregation hoped would appeal to both religious and secular activists.[44] The fledgling organization hosted a conference in July to coordinate efforts that included representatives from ACOA, the UCC, and unspecified participants from New York, Chicago, San Francisco, and Philadelphia (likely the SAC, CRV, and LSM).[45] Having accepted its role as catalyzing agent, ACOA supported the project, providing material to the educational efforts of the newly rechristened GBC and lending staff member Paul Irish to act as spokesman for the gathering. The event closed with a Fourth of July procession through Dayton that ended at Kelly's Gulf Station, where Pat Roach raised a massive "Boycott Gulf" balloon amid American flags and pennants demanding Angolan independence, much to the consternation of poor Mr. Kelly, who probably needed help finding Angola on a map.[46]

The balloon that angered the Dayton storeowner signaled a new era in the campaign. The UCC, and even the activists at the Pittsburgh meeting, focused on higher-level appeals and disruptions aimed at the leadership of the company. This earned attention from media, but it engaged a small number of actual actors, most of whom were already committed to African liberation. Local boycotts never went beyond the planning stages. The GBC's decisions to emphasize grassroots organizing pioneered new directions while offering what it called "practical action for 'little' people who want to effect freedom in Angola"—and by extension the rest of southern Africa.[47] This not only promoted a greater investment in the Lusophone solidarity movement, it connected to the participatory ethos central to New Left thinking. Utilizing the extant solidarity network, the GBC assembled a list of partners that encompassed ten cities within just a few weeks, most in the near Midwest and Northeast.[48]

The campaign grew by seeking small victories to sustain the Gulf boycott's momentum and translate popular appeals into actual policy. The model for such action was the GBC's efforts to convince Dayton's local government to end its contract with Gulf when the agreement expired at the end of the year. Though the contract was worth more than $50,000, losing would not seriously impact the oil giant, but it would dramatize the power of civic action on international issues. Months of protests, campaigning, and education followed, culminating in December 1971 when Dayton rejected Gulf's low bid for gasoline in favor of Standard Oil, citing Angola as the reason for the decision. The GBC hailed the moment as its "first real victory."[49] For its part, Gulf dismissed the growing activism as the result of an overzealous Christian elite who, in the words of B.R. Dorsey, "tend to sit in parish headquarters and worry about world problems."[50] Yet the corporation's casual dismissal ignored the rapid growth of the Gulf boycott and the diversity of its burgeoning list of collaborators.

With the GBC, the churches, and ACOA as central nodes, the boycott expanded rapidly by tapping into a reality of New Left organizing—its diffuse, issue-based nature. The coalition utilized the overlapping religious and activist networks, but it won new converts by placing the relationship between Angolan freedom and U.S. institutions at the center of its activities. The implications

were broad, touching on multiple concerns that emerged from the 1960s. The
GBC and its allies recognized this reality and integrated the Lusophone liberation struggles into new streams of advocacy, with Gulf providing an immediate
symbol. With headlines like "Southern Africa will not be the next Vietnam; it
already is Vietnam," the GBC joined African liberation to the antiwar movement, blurring the lines between conflicts by highlighting Gulf's Southeast
Asian operations and the Western weapons that defended the company's Angolan holdings.[51] It also opened avenues of support by using the unique problems
of oil to connect with the popular environmental movement, linking Gulf's
undemocratic Portuguese-backed operations off the Angolan coast with galvanizing events like the 1969 Santa Barbara oil spill.[52] Emphasis on unequal work
conditions and Portugal's history of forced labor won over progressive union
leaders, who adopted the Gulf issue as a relatively innocuous way to appeal to
youth and minorities distrustful of the rally-around-the-flag complacency of
the American Federation of Labor.[53] These constituencies embraced the Gulf
boycott for different reasons, but the political boost their support gave to the
campaign and the larger Lusophone solidarity effort was real.

   Like radical solidarity organizations before it, the GBC built broad fronts
while emphasizing New Left goals. Early on, Righter convinced close friends
at Americans for Democratic Action to provide a mailing list, and he contacted dozens of influential liberals, who lent their names to the movement.[54]
Such name recognition provided the small organization with legitimacy and
a bit of notoriety, but it was the small actions of individual protest that were
the most celebrated. A United Farm Workers member sent receipts for gasoline bought at competing stations to Gulf headquarters, while eighth-grade
students In Philadelphia wrote term papers on the company's involvement in
Angola.[55] In 1973, the War Resisters League and the Vietnam Peace Parade
Committee in New York City joined together to protest the Portuguese consulate partially as a result of the boycott.[56] The GBC newsletter listed such
actions while offering strategies that individuals and local groups could adopt
to take part in the movement without formally joining an organization. By
1974, Pat Roach boasted that the coalition had active associates in more than
fifty metropolitan areas in the United States made up of local GBC chapters,
unions, student organizations, and others, with myriad shows of individual
support trickling in.[57] It was not the goal to build a centralized movement;
instead, a diverse coalition of like-minded activists demanded new national
approaches to the cause of Southern self-determination.

Solidarity at the Pumps

The GBC's efforts spearheading left and religious organizing had its complement in the African American community. As Black activists sought concrete
transatlantic ties, the idea of an exploitative multinational corporation intersected with the economic grievances that drove Black Power thought. ACOA's
Hightower stated during his appearance before Congress that concern with
business in southern Africa "goes to the heart of the American profit motif. It
includes the disdain or apathy concerning the rights and humanity of black,
beige, brown, red, and yellow peoples."[58] While African Americans like Hightower and Diggs played central roles in the Gulf campaign, the decentralized
nature of this movement and the emphasis Black Power placed on independent leadership augured for a Black equivalent of the GBC, which took shape
in Boston's Pan-African Liberation Committee (PALC). Inspired by some of
the same sources as the Dayton group, its campaign highlighted Black priorities and worked with the organizers of African Liberation Day (ALD).
The influence of CONCP ideology also promoted collaboration across racial
lines, creating the foundations for a larger and more successful Gulf boycott.

The relationship between Black Power organizing and the broader Gulf
movement was present from the beginning. The churches failed in their
attempts to recruit universities to the Gulf proxy movement in 1971, but their
efforts inspired action by the recent Harvard Law School graduate Randall
Robinson, best known as a prominent anti-apartheid activist in the 1980s.
Robinson's interest in African liberation began with ACOA literature, and
he worked with his then wife, Brenda Randolph, South African exile Chris
Nteta, and other members of the Boston and Harvard communities to begin
education initiatives in the late 1960s. He journeyed to Dar es Salaam after
graduation, where he met personally with FRELIMO leaders, then returned
to Boston to cofound the PALC with the goal of moving beyond political
education to direct advocacy. Inspired by the church's proxy fights, the PALC
requested that Harvard divest its stocks from Gulf Oil, receiving early support from Congressman Diggs. After months of discussions in which the
PALC encouraged Harvard to rethink the ethical foundations of its investment policies, the university's president rejected their request. The PALC
joined with African American undergraduates to launch a public-pressure
campaign, announcing the effort at a joint conference alongside Diggs when
the Congressional Black Caucus visited campus in April 1972. When Harvard
again demurred, the PALC and its student allies occupied the university's

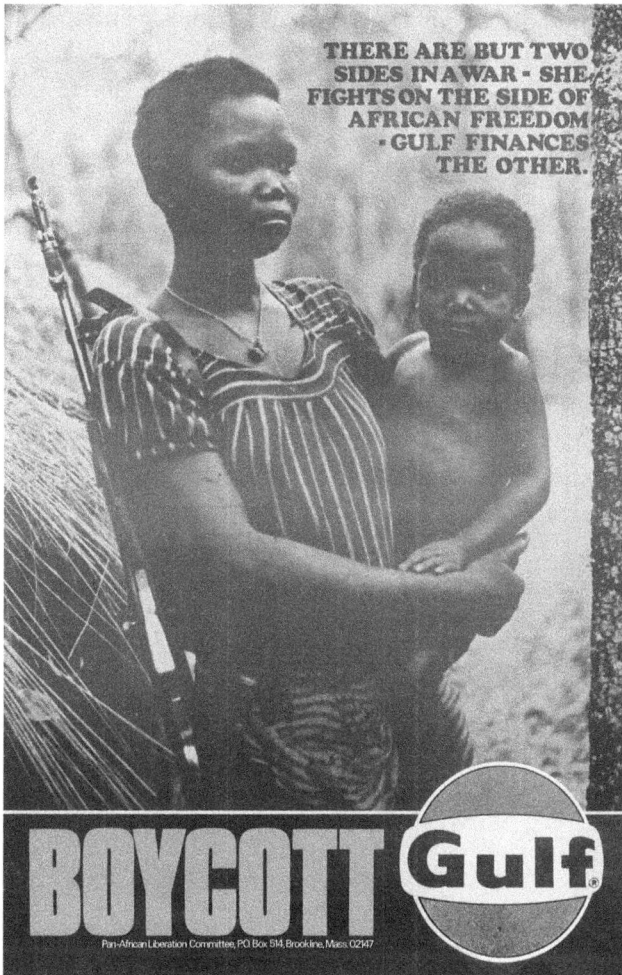

Figure 9. Pan-African Liberation Committee poster, circa 1972. The widely used Gulf boycott poster presented an image that became ubiquitous within the African solidarity movement of the female revolutionary with child and gun. Originally drawn by artist Emory Douglas for the *Black Panther*, it was adapted as a poster by Cuban artist Lázaro Abreu Padrón in 1968 for international distribution by *Tricontinental* magazine. Multiple Lusophone groups composed photos to recreate this imagery, encouraging its widespread adoption among Western activists. Reprinted with permission of Brenda Randolph, Michigan State University Libraries Special Collections.

main administration building for nearly a week, earning national attention.[59] One *New York Times* columnist cited the PALC's strident demand for university divestment as an important new front in the corporate responsibility movement.[60]

ALD organizers embraced the Gulf campaign because it provided a concrete issue to articulate Pan-African interests. Already working on liberation day activities in Boston, Robinson and PALC colleague Jim Winston pushed for the inclusion of the Gulf matter as a central issue in the celebrations.[61] During Owusu Sadaukai's rousing speech at the culminating rally on the National Mall in Washington in May 1972, he singled out Gulf as a target for Black activism and urged local boycotts.[62] The next month, Students Organized for Black Unity concluded that the Gulf boycott was the best "positive action for the Black community that can give concrete substance to our support" for African liberation.[63] The PALC led organizing efforts in the wake of the first ALD, working with the newly formalized African Liberation Support Committee (ALSC) to mobilize Black public opinion against Gulf in more than a dozen states, including seven of the most lucrative markets for the oil giant.[64] While the campaign was part of the larger attempt to organize Black political power, the immediate goal was to connect ALSC organizing with existing efforts by the GBC and others to put real pressure on Gulf. As Robinson explained to Congressman Diggs, "If in the key states we can win overwhelming Black support in addition to marginal support from whites, Gulf's profit margin can be substantially reduced." By August, the ALSC adopted the plan in preparation for ALD celebrations in 1973.[65] Utilizing the company's poor record in hiring minorities, the PALC gave Black activists a local symbol of collective racial oppression that allowed them to identify and directly engage with foreign struggles.[66] This approach mirrored efforts by the GBC but spoke more directly to the Black community by highlighting Pan-African connections in ways the predominantly white organization simply could not. In essence, the PALC carved out a visible leadership role for Black activists within the solidarity movement. It accomplished this with an eye toward national impact as it called "on all Black people and others who believe in freedom to boycott the products of the Gulf Oil Company."[67]

The results of the campaign were impressive. Utilizing networks attached to the ALSC and Amiri Baraka's Congress of African People (CAP), the PALC coordinated an informational campaign across twenty states in the run-up to the second ALD celebrations, in May 1973. In April, a "flood" of bumper stickers, posters, and foldouts appeared from Miami to Seattle.[68] The Gulf boycott coordinator in Florida reported distributing two thousand posters in two weeks across the state, noting special success in the university city of Gainesville. Churches and community organizations opened their doors to anti-Gulf speeches, and local radio and TV stations allowed for a weekly news spot devoted to Gulf campaigning. In New York, the PALC representative covered subways with twenty-five hundred posters and handed out informational booklets at local ALD celebrations. Through Diggs, the PALC also assembled dozens of Black celebrities and officials to support the campaign.[69] Their names appeared on full-page advertisements in *Jet* and *Ebony* saying the Portuguese African struggle "is also our war," eliciting a frantic response from Gulf in the Black media.[70] This made anti-Gulf activities prominent components of local ALD celebrations, inspiring a coordinated national picket in more than twenty-five cities in September 1973.[71]

The PALC was a self-consciously Black movement, but this did not preclude it from cooperating with like-minded organizations when opportunities arose. Specifically, the PALC worked with ACOA and the GBC as they sought to mobilize and distribute information.[72] Robinson argued, "We can learn a lot from [the GBC's] experience," and he encouraged local activists to collaborate.[73] In cities where interracial activist relationships existed, such as St. Louis, New York, and Atlanta, informational exchanges turned into cooperation as the PALC and the GBC united in attacking Gulf.[74] Still, Robinson believed that the Gulf boycott needed to be a "Black community thrust." The PALC barred white membership to maintain a focus on African American priorities and messaging.[75] When white Boston activists showed interest in joining early efforts, Robinson advised them to organize their own group to support the Black movement.[76] This model of organizing—guided by a radical Pan-Africanism but willing to work with a spectrum of allies by appealing to an inclusive anti-imperialism—helped push the ALSC away from strict nationalism while paralleling the evolution of other Black Power organizations that embraced tricontinentalism.[77] This model directly informed Robinson's later work with the Black lobbying organization TransAfrica during the height of the anti-apartheid movement.

While Black and predominantly white activism remained distinct, an ability to work toward similar goals benefited the CONCP parties. FRELIMO's Khan and the PAIGC's Fernandes supported the movement, speaking at events and connecting domestic actions to the revolutions. But the Gulf campaign's focus on Angola provided the MPLA with new opportunities, and it responded enthusiastically to the boycott. When a Philadelphia journalist

CANADA

UNITED STATES

MEXICO

Pacific Ocean

Gulf of Mexico

Atlantic Ocean

City with notable activist organization(s)
City with African Liberation Day celebration(s) in 1972
City with African Liberation Day celebration(s) in 1973
City with notable organization(s) and African Liberation Day celebrations in both 1972 and 1973

Richmond
Seattle
Portland
San Francisco
Oakland
Los Angeles
Denver
Winnipeg
St. Paul
Madison
Chicago
East Lansing
Detroit
Indianapolis
Dayton
Nashville
Knoxville
Atlanta
Columbia
Columbus
Durham
Greensboro
Raleigh
Gainesville
New Orleans
Houston
Toronto
Montréal
Rochester
Buffalo
Newark
Cambridge
Boston
New Haven
New York City
Philadelphia
Wilmington
Washington, D.C.

BLACKMER MAPS

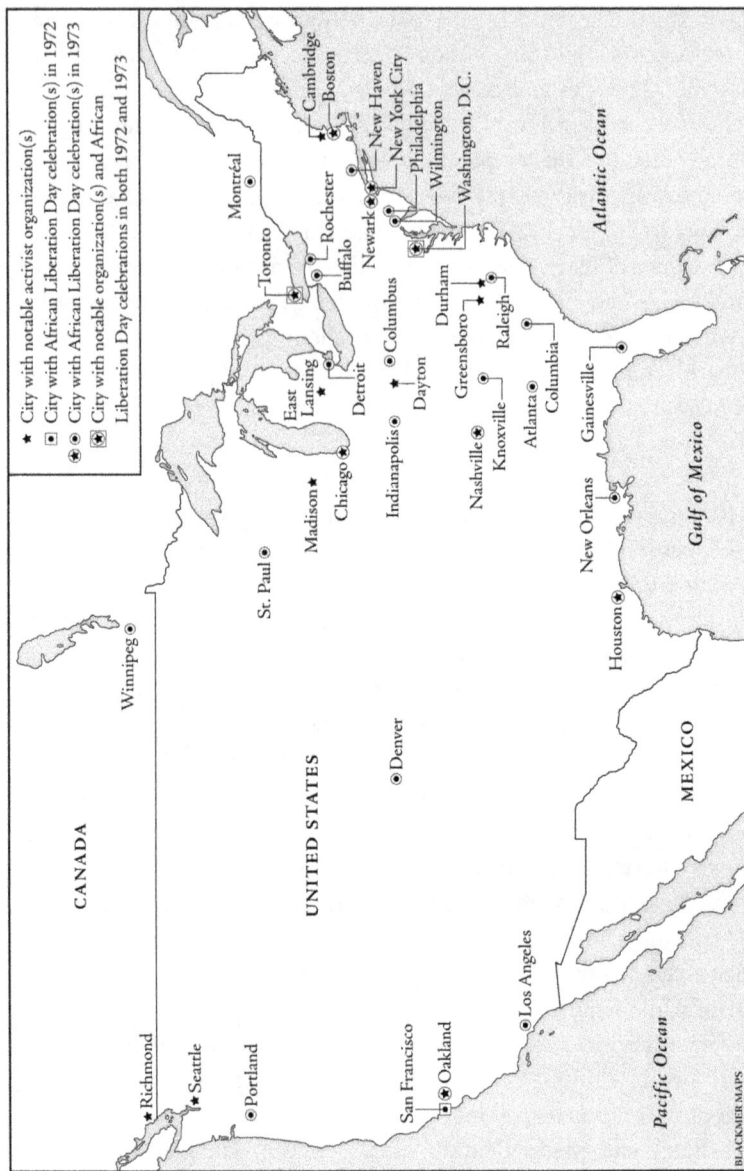

Figure 10. Map of Lusophone African advocacy in North America, 1967–1974. African Liberation Day celebrations in 1973 that took place beyond North America included those in Antigua, St. Vincent, and Dar es Salaam, Tanzania.

asked the MPLA's information director Paulo Jorge what Americans could do to support his movement, he responded emphatically: "Expose and demonstrate against Gulf Oil's investments in Angola."[78] The party still struggled to send representatives overseas, but the coalition provided human faces as popular interest grew. The life histories published by the Liberation Support Movement (LSM) in California introduced Jorge and military commander Daniel Chipenda to U.S. audiences and published one of the first English-language collections of speeches by Agostinho Neto.[79] Abel Guimaraes, a student in Brooklyn and a member of the National Union of Angolan Students loosely associated with the MPLA, traveled widely and provided a first-person rebuttal to Gulf's claims that its investment helped local peoples.[80] ACOA even invited MPLA president Neto on a multicity speaking tour that would coincide with Gulf Oil activities, though he was unable to make the trip.[81] These information campaigns humanized the parties, while weekly and daily acts of protest allowed Americans to feel like active participants in the revolutions.

There were also signs that the combined campaigns, especially the one coming from the Black community, worried Gulf. While its private deliberations remain inaccessible, publicity efforts sought to mitigate the campaigns' effects. From mid-1973, Gulf took out full-page advertisements in major Black publications that positively highlighted its role in the community while touting increased investments in minority training programs.[82] U.S. officials noted that Gulf even floated the creation of "betterment programs" in Angola as a direct response to domestic protests, which it cited in response to inquiries by institutions like Harvard.[83] Gulf was clearly aware of its tarnished image, but the reality was that gasoline was a necessity—and political considerations became a harder sell as the oil crisis began in 1973—so the company seemed content with these targeted responses. The Portuguese government was confident that Gulf would not leave Angola, but growing support for African liberation parties worried Lisbon's U.S. ambassador, who warned his colleagues in mid-1972 not to "underestimate what the campaign can do."[84]

The warning was prescient because the goals of the Gulf campaigns were bigger than just to elicit a response from the company itself. Rather, success was measured by the expansion of solidarity through concrete action in ways that, in the words of one ACOA staffer in 1969, "makes the Portuguese worry, costs them time, money, and diplomatic manpower, and puts them for once on the defensive."[85] At their most ambitious, the divestment and boycott strategies sought to change the cost-benefit analysis for new companies by raising the specter of domestic opposition, further isolating Portugal, as the liberation movements had long requested. As Tim Smith explained the strategy in late 1972, "We must begin to mount pressure and raise American consciousness on Gulf's support for the Portuguese. At the least this will cause other companies to assess investment or expansion in the colonies."[86] This latter point had been a specific concern for the nationalists, with Cabral publicly worrying about Esso's interest in Guinea-Bissau's Bijagós Archipelago.[87] As the domestic campaigns gained ground in 1973, there seemed to be some effect. That year, Exxon abandoned proposed investments in Angola after ACOA, the Unitarian Church, and African American activists threatened to expand the boycott.[88] There were even signs that Gulf itself was making new calculations. It promised not to invest in either Mozambique or South Africa on economic grounds, but activists saw a connection between this logic and their actions over the previous years.[89] Gulf remained in Angola, but similar investments faced new obstacles—to the chagrin of Lisbon and its white minority allies.

Expanded support for Lusophone liberation also encouraged more aggressive official policies, especially in Congress. A growing roster of sympathetic legislators tried to erect new barriers to cooperation with Portugal. Elected officials like Diggs were actively expanding their work with activists to raise pressure on companies, while new investigations provided information to the movement.[90] Joining this coalition were new classes of legislators elected or emboldened by the mix of antiwar and social justice campaigning, which included House members like Andrew Young and senators like Dick Clark in 1973. While they faced headwinds in passing legislation, there was an increasing willingness to act. Among the most ambitious was the 1973 amendment to the Foreign Assistance Act that would enshrine the arms embargo against Portugal as law. A year prior, a congressional workshop agreed this should be the top priority for pro-liberation legislators, and growing support hinted the measure might find success.[91] In the House, it was the first amendment that Congressman Young offered after his election.[92] The Senate bill was sponsored by Ted Kennedy of Massachusetts and John V. Tunney of California—two pro-African senators emboldened by the grassroots energy and their collaboration with the recently established Washington Office on Africa.[93] ALD celebrations and the Gulf campaign helped drown out Portugal's defense of its wars on national security grounds by demonstrating that key constituencies for Northern Democrats and moderate Republicans—namely, religious, liberal, and Black voters—actively cared about Lusophone African independence.[94] As Young explained shortly after his election, "Backing up the power of progressive electoral politics is the equally important power of people's movements."[95]

By the end of the year, the legislation passed both houses despite strenuous objections from the Nixon administration.[96]

The grassroots-congressional opposition limited executive freedom of movement, as Secretary of State Henry Kissinger learned when he tried to renegotiate Luso-American relations in October 1973. After Portugal granted the United States refueling rights in the Azores as it scrambled to aid Israel during the Yom Kippur War, the lone European nation to do so, Lisbon sought to parley this good will into better access to U.S. arms for its African wars. Kissinger was "prepared to explore with [Portugal] the possibility of providing weapons without any publicity," but he found domestic and congressional opposition a major obstacle.[97] Cold warriors on Capitol Hill praised Portugal, but pro-liberation legislators anticipated such efforts and erected new barriers—highlighted by the Kennedy-Tunney bill. While the administration prepared to send a handful of naval missile systems to Portugal, getting congressional approval for anything that could be used for its land wars proved difficult—even unarmed C-130 transport planes recalled earlier criticism of the sale of Boeing troop carriers. Hesitant to even broach the topic given a likely defeat in Congress, Kissinger asked third parties such as Israel to satisfy Lisbon's demands.[98] The administration was more willing to aid Portugal than at any point since Eisenhower held office, but a popular-congressional agitation for independence finally constrained executive action.

Multiracial Solidarity and the Collapse of the ALSC

The Gulf campaign, and its encouragement of pro-liberation organizing structures, attested to the success of the transactional but ultimately collaborative nature of the decentralized solidarity movement. But it also could accentuate political divides, most visibly in the African American community. The simmering tensions between Black nationalists and leftists undermined the big-tent politics of the of the early 1970s as tricontinental ideas and multiracial collaboration became more prominent in the Gulf boycott movement and preparations for ALD 1973, marginalizing race-first visions of Pan-African solidarity. The result was a year of sometimes violent infighting in 1973 that split the ALSC as the wider pro-liberation movement it supported reached new heights.

At the center of this divide was the increased prominence of leftist political thought within the leadership of the ALSC and its most vital affiliates, which

were influenced by increased engagement with the philosophies of the PAIGC
and FRELIMO. Tricontinental tendencies had long been present within Black
solidarity organizing, as evidenced by Robert Van Lierop's gloss in his documentary *A Luta Continua* and Owusu Sadaukai's rhetoric at the first ALD.
But Amiri Baraka's conscious embrace of a Third World Marxism accelerated
a leftward drift, thanks to the influence of his nationwide CAP organization.
Baraka's shift emerged at the intersection of global and local politics. As he
and others increased their engagement with CONCP ideas, Baraka grew disillusioned by his partnership with Newark's first Black mayor, Kenneth Gibson.
While positioning Gibson's election in 1970 as an opportunity to "nationalize
the city's institutions, as if it were liberated territory in Zimbabwe or Angola,"
Baraka felt betrayed when the mayor courted businesses threatening to flee the
New Jersey city.[99] The increasingly acrimonious relationship forced Baraka to
confront the limits of racial solidarity, and leftist tricontinental ideas provided
a new philosophical home. Over the next decade, CAP moved toward what
it eventually called "Marxism-Leninism-Mao Tsetung Thought," but Cabral
featured prominently in the initial transition.[100] The Guinean revolutionary
acted as a bridge figure between Black nationalism and tricontinental left-
ism, providing the structural explanation for global racial inequality and the
defection of "bourgeois" actors like Mayor Gibson, who pursued what Baraka
considered a form of economic neocolonialism.[101] While Baraka's experience
was deeply personal, the transformation of CAP reflected a broader reality
in the Black movement. Members of groups like Youth Organized for Black
Unity (YOBU) and many within the leadership of the ALSC reached similar
conclusions as they confronted the messy realities of political organizing while
reading nationalist texts more closely.

The rise of tricontinental thought had important ramifications for how
many Black activists understood solidarity organizing, moving beyond Pan-
Africanism to situate the domestic push for racial equality as part of a Third
World anti-imperial struggle. As Baraka explained, his adoption of leftist
philosophies meant that his struggle was no longer "against white people" or
simply "to liberate Black people"; it was to liberate "also all oppressed people."
In this definition of Black empowerment, he said, "we ought to ally ourselves
with any people who are serious about struggling to smash the degenerate
system."[102] For most activists, this meant allying with Latino, Asian, and other
Global South peoples—both internationally and domestically—but it also
implied collaboration with predominantly white or multiracial groups on
the model pursued by Robinson's PALC. Tricontinental ideas inspired local

ALSC chapters to request that other nonwhite peoples such as Latinos and Asian Americans be allowed to participate in marches for ALD 1973. Strict Black nationalists objected, but roughly two-thirds of ALSC leadership voted to allow other minority ethnicities to join local celebrations, though it barred them from holding positions of authority.[103] This decision promoted cooperation with diverse groups while maintaining a core Black leadership. It also signaled the beginning of a new confrontation over the direction of Black organizing.

Symbolic of this emerging competition was the increasingly tense debate over which liberation party to support in Angola—an issue exacerbated by the Gulf campaign. That such an important issue remained unresolved reflected a specific reality of how the tripartite Lusophone struggles were framed in the United States. While the CONCP parties represented a united front abroad, each of the three major revolutions came to represent something unique in the U.S. conceptualization of African liberation. Cabral became the figurehead, the philosopher, whose books were most widely read and whose ideas laid the intellectual foundation for understanding the CONCP parties. FRELIMO was the model party, the prime example of a government-in-waiting. This had its origins in early efforts to fund the Mozambique Institute in Tanzania, but it cohered after Mondlane's death as the party championed its nation-building efforts alongside its military revolution in literature and films like *A Luta Continua*. Angola was the country of reference, the economic and strategic center of Portugal's African empire that had forced Lusophone Africa into the international imagination in 1961. As the Gulf campaign illustrated, Angola connected the empire and its opponents to matters of global importance, even as its complex domestic politics and the MPLA's hamstrung diplomacy militated against automatic identification with a single party. While the PAIGC and FRELIMO championed the MPLA and won it support from various groups in the early 1970s, the tendency to refer to Angola broadly allowed individual constituencies to support alternate parties—like George Houser's reticence to abandon Holden Roberto—without completely scuttling the movement.

The Gulf campaign's attempts to promote the MPLA challenged this tendency and caused problems within the ALSC, where many favored the rival UNITA under Jonas Savimbi. A nonpartisan approach to Angola was the norm in the Black community for much of the 1960s, but UNITA made special appeals to Black nationalists, partially to offset its difficulties waging armed struggle in Angola and winning allies in Europe.[104] After breaking from Roberto's FNLA, Savimbi built support among the Ovimbundu majority

in eastern provinces near the Zambian border, but UNITA struggled to sustain a meaningful guerrilla war. Backed by China as part of the Sino-Soviet
conflict with Moscow, UNITA embraced aspects of Maoism but was fluid in
how it presented itself to international audiences. Expanding an approach he
began with Roberto, Savimbi embraced a race-first Black nationalism when
addressing U.S. audiences. Leading the charge was Jorge Sangumba, who
attended Lincoln University in the early 1960s and served as UNITA's minister of foreign affairs.[105] While Sangumba's leftist critique of the international
system differed little from that of CONCP leaders like Agostinho Neto, he
attacked the MPLA for its domination by overeducated mestiços and foreign
interests, denigrating its dependence on Western allies like Basil Davidson
(and probably the LSM) as "white gurus [speaking] on black peoples struggles."[106] A canny diplomat, Savimbi self-consciously limited his travel in favor
of sending agents like Sangumba, arguing he preferred to operate "where the
fight is," in a direct, and not always accurate, contrast to the exiled, itinerant
leadership of Roberto, Neto, and even Amílcar Cabral.[107]

The appeals won adherents among Black organizers. While activists like
Robert Van Lierop, Prexy Nesbitt, and Randall Robinson leaned toward the
MPLA for ideological reasons and personal ties to liberation leadership,
UNITA gained powerful supporters within the ALSC, primarily through their
claims to an overtly Black identity. After the first ALD backed all liberation
parties, Baraka's CAP threw its support behind UNITA because it was "the
only Black Nationalist Liberation Group in Angola (Others are supported by
white leftists)."[108] Florence Tate, the prominent Tennessee-born civil rights
activist who managed communication for the ALD organizing committee in
1972 and later worked closely with UNITA, remembered the reasoning for
aligning with Savimbi's party explicitly: "They represented the 'Black' Black
people—those in the southern part of Angola who were more rural, agrarian
folks—not the sons and daughters of the Portuguese."[109] UNITA's Maoist tendencies proved acceptable enough for these nascent stages of the leftist shift,
meaning its appeals to a transnational Black identity won it adherents within
the movement.

UNITA seized the opportunity to court the ALSC, sending two representatives to promote the party within the Black community. Joining Sangumba
was former representative to Sweden Stella Makunga, another Maoist, who
provided UNITA's own claim to a popular CONCP topic: the dual liberation of
the nation and women through revolution.[110] This was part of a broader effort
in which UNITA replicated many of the CONCP parties' successful strategies

for selling their revolutions while accentuating its Black African identity. Notably, Savimbi arranged for Leon Dash, a Black writer for the *Washington Post*, to spend ten weeks in Angola, where he penned a series of sympathetic articles on Savimbi, party ideology (noting difficulties with mestiços), and efforts to build schools and clinics along the eastern border.[111] Coinciding with the renewed interest in Angola spurred by the Gulf campaign, UNITA's efforts offered an immediate link with a Black revolution for many young African Americans, while the MPLA relied heavily on its CONCP partners, groups like the LSM, and students already in the United States, such as Abel Guimarães, to promote it.[112] When proceeds from ALD 1973 forced the ALSC to finally choose sides in Angola, a contentious vote resolved that UNITA was most actively advancing the struggle in Angola and deserved aid alongside the PAIGC and FRELIMO.[113] ALSC leadership even sponsored a fourteen-city tour of the United States for Sangumba.[114]

While UNITA initially benefited from increased attention to Angola, it gradually produced a schism as engagement with the CONCP agenda promoted alignment with the MPLA. In direct contrast to UNITA, the MPLA reasserted that its struggle targeted "tribalist trends and racist prejudices fostered by the colonialists."[115] As Black activists embraced tricontinental ideas—and flirted with multiracial New Left alliances—the MPLA proved a better ideological fit with expansive ideas of anti-imperialism while aligning with the tripartite vision of Lusophone revolution promoted by the PAIGC and FRELIMO. Leading the charge for the MPLA in the Black community was a familiar set of activists. The African Information Service—according to co-organizer Prexy Nesbitt—"helped kick-start the process of rejecting Savimbi" by using critical information from a network of contacts in the United States and Europe.[116] As YOBU and other Black radical groups joined the African Information Service and LSM in championing the MPLA, general calls for Angolan liberation clarified into open partisanship. Though the MPLA found the most support from leftists and fellow travelers, party identification did not cleave neatly along the Left-Nationalist divide. CAP's Maoist drift, for instance, aligned it with leftists while arguing that support for UNITA was a way of rejecting Soviet imperialism. So the contest over Angola often became deeply personal. As historian Manning Marable summarizes the situation, "Old friends turned against one another; marriages were broken over which African liberation organization one chose to support."[117]

Fueling this vitriol was a new assertiveness from the leftist wing of Black organizing, which pushed the ALSC in more doctrinaire directions at the summer 1973 meeting in Frogmore, South Carolina. An expanded national committee voted to accept the individual participation of progressive white activists as participants in future activities, though it remained wary of direct cooperation with majority white groups.[118] It also elected one of the leading socialists on the national committee, Dawolu Gene Locke, to replace Sadaukai as national chair. A native of Houston who helped organize a regional precursor to the ALD, Locke was supported in his leadership bid by YOBU head Nelson Johnson and influential Chicago sociologist Abdul Alkalimat. Together, this group developed a statement of Marxist-inspired principles that laid out what Alkalimat and Johnson called the "theory of class struggle with a correct analysis of racial oppression."[119] The new, Marxist-inspired organizational goals emphasized resistance to a capital-driven imperialism and the role of class in shaping Black politics, promoting greater cooperation with whites who opposed political and economic exploitation. The leftists argued that these tenets and the empowerment of a multiracial working class were prerequisites for true Black unity and the advancement of the cause. The ALSC would act as the center of a united front, which, in Alkalimat and Johnson's words, would enhance the African American "ability to carry the fight against racism and imperialism to different groups of people around different issues, yet maintain our course."[120] These goals incorporated Pan-African identities, tricontinental language, and New Left strategies in an attempt to move the ALSC beyond its racial core, positioning it as the Black-led vanguard of a movement for social justice that could build powerful political alliances around specific causes.

Black nationalists—what Alkalimat and Johnson dismissively termed proponents of "pure race theory"—were disturbed by the document and the rapid transformation of the ALSC. Stokely Carmichael considered Sadaukai and his closest advisers political neophytes, and he became the unofficial leader of the anti-left opposition. For years, Carmichael discussed the importance of understanding the "scientific socialism" taught by Malcolm X, but his iteration of the ideology was critical of capitalism for deeply cultural reasons. More than its monopolies of power, capitalism ran counter to traditions of African "communalism." Under this ideology, racism evolved not from capitalist attempts to divide the working class but from the natural clashing of races and European attempts to subdue darker peoples. In this view of the world system, Carmichael proclaimed: "Pan-Africanism is the highest form of Black Power."[121] This was an exclusive vision of solidarity, which made room only for darker peoples who understood the specific experience of racial exploitation. It was a form of anti-imperialism, but one devoid of serious Marxist influence and deeply suspicious of people who were not Black. It fitted neatly with UNITA's propaganda that denigrated the MPLA for its dependence on European ideologies and white allies. Supporters of Carmichael such as the poet and ALSC member Haki Madhubuti said that Blacks could not benefit from following the "white boy" theories of the increasingly Marxist ALSC leadership. In an especially stark attack, Madhubuti dismissed iconic tricontinental advocates Fidel Castro and Che Guevara as "another set of white boys that are just as racist as Thomas Jefferson, George Washington, Abraham Lincoln, John Kennedy, etc., each using their special system of control both steeped in and based on white supremacy."[122] Other nationalists may have hesitated to lump Kennedy with Guevara, but many agreed that most socialists outside Africa were nothing more than what one former ALSC member referred to as "red fascists."[123] Aligning with Savimbi while taking theorists like Cabral at their word that they were not communist, nationalists contended that Marxists could not understand the needs of Black people, so adoption of their tactics threatened to undermine the movement toward racial self-determination.

Over the next year, the socialist-nationalist divide tore apart the ALSC. By the fall of 1973, rivalries at the top of the organization filtered to the local levels, with disastrous results. In local meetings, nationalists and leftists confronted one another, even descending into violence. Prexy Nesbitt remembers hearing tales of gunfights breaking out over the question of support for the MPLA versus UNITA.[124] In less polarized communities, local chapters sided with one element or the other of the national leadership. Leftists backed the national structure, while nationalist chapters threatened to secede and host independent ALD celebrations.[125] These divisions proved intractable, and the Howard University Conference held shortly before ALD 1974 split the ALSC along ideological lines. With the support of Baraka and CAP, YOBU leaders advocated for uniting Black workers against imperialism and capitalism in collaboration with multiracial alliances of like-minded allies that included whites. This was the last straw for Carmichael and other Black nationalists. In the final, acrimonious debate that followed, one observer noted that Cabral stood alone as the "major theoretical author ... popular with all tendencies in the black movement for their own reasons."[126] While Cabral's anti-racism, support for the MPLA, and ideological affinities were clear, his mistranslation was a natural byproduct of the difficulties managing a decentralized solidarity movement and articulating an independent revolutionary worldview within the closely policed ideological borders of the Cold War. Cabral's writings fueled competing definitions of Black anti-imperial struggle, which activists refined by aligning the PAIGC and FRELIMO with their preferred revolutionary partners in Angola to create transnational justifications for their local efforts.

The ideological incongruence permanently split the ALSC but did not negate its impact on the wider solidarity movement. The organization continued, but there were competing ALDs in 1975 as nationalists mounted a challenge to the increasingly leftist organization.[127] There were even divisions among the leftists, with CAP's support for Maoism and UNITA pitting Baraka against socialist MPLA supporters like Alkalimat.[128] The divided ALSC and the collapse of Black unity envisioned by the one-two punch of the Gary Convention and the ALD is illustrative of declension narratives in literatures of Black Power and sixties radicalism more broadly, but situating it in relationship to the Gulf campaign and the broader solidarity network hints at a more complex reality. The collapse of Black unity emerged partially as a response to deepening engagement with African revolutions and like-minded constituencies operating beyond narrow racial and ideological contexts. Disagreements arose as concrete efforts were made to deepen collaboration with both, which successfully drove Gulf organizing while highlighting unresolved tensions within the Black agenda. The agenda divided the leaders of the ALSC, but they did not undermine the impact of events like ALD, which reawakened and expanded identification with Africa and its political goals at a grassroots level, where ideological distinctions were less strongly felt. At the same time, successful campaigns like the one against Gulf highlighted a new generation of activists, who gained the ability to shape political conversations. Noteworthy among these was Randall Robinson, who parleyed his Gulf efforts into a staff job with Charles Diggs that positioned him to revisit key elements of his PALC strategies as the founding director of TransAfrica—the Black lobbying organization central to national anti-apartheid work in the 1980s. A core tenet of the organization was transactional collaboration with groups like WOA and ACOA without dilution of the Black leadership that focused on community messaging and issues. Such issue-based alliances faced their own difficulties handling matters that lacked clean narratives or a modicum of consensus, but major issues like apartheid revisited and expanded the success of New Left Internationalist coalitions first hinted at by the Gulf campaign.

Epilogue: The End of the Portuguese Empire

As solidarity organizers balanced the success of the multiracial Gulf campaign with the collapse of ALD organizing, they were given an unexpected boost. On April 25, 1974, a group of young military officers toppled Portugal's Caetano regime in a bloodless coup. Exhausted by years of fighting and struggling under the weight of a weakened economy, the country welcomed the Carnation Revolution, named for the flowers Lisbon residents showered onto the rebel tanks. The sources of this revolution were centered in Africa, where the PAIGC and FRELIMO had stretched the Portuguese military to the breaking point while exhausting the treasury that Salazar had worked so assiduously to build. International pressure on Portugal reinforced this sense of crisis and contributed to the alacrity with which the population accepted the change of government. The combination of Western arms limitations and Eastern bloc aid to revolutionary parties like the PAIGC and FRELIMO meant Portugal fought with inconsistent, sometimes antiquated weaponry against an increasingly sophisticated response, damaging already precarious military morale. Domestically, the country suffered an economic downturn under the weight of mass mobilization; industrialists were frustrated by the wars' impeding of foreign investment and role in creating foreign hostility to Portugal's entrance into the European Economic Community.[129] This mixture of colonial, domestic, and international pressure finally ended Europe's oldest dictatorship with barely a shot fired in Portugal itself.

U.S. activists reacted to the events with a mixture of surprise, elation, and determination. With activities like the Gulf campaign peaking in 1974, many were engaged in solidarity work when the news broke. SAC member Stephanie Urdang heard it over the radio while visiting PAIGC cadres in Guinea-Bissau. Euphoria gave way to skeptical disbelief, with the revolutionaries patiently waiting to see what plans the still-forming Lisbon government had for the colonies.[130] An ocean away, Prexy Nesbitt was hosting South African activist Ruth First at Northwestern University when he heard the news. He passed a note to the speaker, and "without skipping a beat" the anti-apartheid advocate began explaining what the events could mean for the wider struggle in southern Africa and the future of the continent.[131] Revolutionaries and activists understood that the coup was momentous, but it did not resolve the problems central to their work. Independence for the colonies was not guaranteed, nor was the transfer of power to the CONCP parties.

At the forefront of everyone's mind were the interrelated questions of who would lead the new Portuguese state and what role the United States and its Western allies would have in that decision. The coup ended the dictatorship, but there was no clear successor government in place. Charles Diggs openly worried about this reality and peppered the State Department with questions, asking about the likelihood of support for decolonization and openly wondering about the possibility of Rhodesia-like unilateral declarations of independence by white governments in Angola and Mozambique.[132] General António de Spínola, a former general in Guinea turned critic of the war, stepped into this vacuum and became president as the most prominent member of the Armed Forces Movement (Movimento das Forças Armadas, or MFA). Deeply conservative, his ambiguity on decolonization and flirtation with a Lisbon-led commonwealth earned criticism from African nationalists, their U.S. allies, and leftist factions within the MFA, leading to his ouster after only a few months. The radicals who replaced Spínola set off alarm bells in Washington, leading Secretary of State Henry Kissinger to spend months working behind the scenes to promote a more moderate government.[133] While Portugal's democratic future would not be assured until after the failure of a communist coup attempt in November 1975, the leftists in charge of the MFA during that first year set the stage for decolonization in all of Portugal's colonies except Macao. The government recognized the PAIGC's already declared control of independent Guinea-Bissau in September 1974 and made plans to transfer power in other colonies across the next year. The recipients of these transfers were predominantly CONCP members, including the PAIGC in Cabo Verde, FRELIMO in Mozambique, and the exiled Movement for the Liberation of São Tomé and Príncipe.

Unsurprisingly, Angola proved more complicated. The three major parties—the MPLA, FNLA, and UNITA—made peace with the Portuguese government but turned their weapons on each other with the goal of controlling the national capital, Luanda. While fighting continued, party leaders agreed to conduct negotiations with Lisbon as a bloc, and a series of meetings culminated in the Alvor Agreement in January 1975. The agreement set a November date for the transfer of power after elections were held for a national assembly the month prior. These elections never took place. The fighting resumed between the three parties as Portugal, whose small military force was outnumbered by the nationalist factions, did little to enforce the accords in advance of the planned withdrawal date. The leftist Portuguese government and its high commissioner in Angola favored the MPLA, permitting both colonial and outside arms to reach the party while allowing it to consolidate its base in Luanda and surrounding provinces.[134] Kissinger and other Western leaders were most concerned about events in Portugal, but the possibility of an MPLA government demanded greater attention as the year progressed.

As these events occurred, activists in the United States claimed a measure of victory even as they faced the question of how to redirect solidarity organizing. Many organizers felt that the collapse of the Portuguese government vindicated their support for other southern African struggles. As activists looked to the next stage of organizing on behalf of Zimbabwean independence and against South African apartheid, the Portuguese phrase *a luta continua* remained in regular use, earning a new aura of victory.[135] The popularity of the Lusophone struggle also meant that organizing continued during the complex negotiations, because the transfers of power remained unsettled and domestic inequality pernicious. In one example, Philadelphia activists continued to protest Gulf Oil well after the Carnation Revolution.[136] Some actions, however, fit uneasily with the new reality as Gulf, the MPLA, and the other Angolan parties entered discussions about the relationship that the oil giant would have with the postindependence government. This newly adopted wait-and-see attitude hinted at the changing interests of the nationalist parties as they prepared to govern. This first step in nationalist self-determination complicated relationships with U.S. activists, whose opposition to companies like Gulf had everything to do with how they operated and not just with whom they collaborated.

This period reflected a moment of transition for African nationalists. The transfers of power and transition to independent statehoods demanded a reorientation of colonial structures, new formulations of national unity, and—in the case of Angola—negotiation between three hostile parties. The CONCP parties hoped the transnational networks they built could assist in postcolonial development, but it was not clear what roles they might play or how traditions of stateless diplomacy would coexist with new international opportunities presented to nationalist governments. The one area of agreement was on the underlying fear of reactionary responses from white settlers and Portugal's Western allies. Anticipating and addressing this probability was central to CONCP solidarity organizing, with Cabral asserting before his death that the parties needed to maintain, as he put it, "vigilance not to allow a new form of colonialism to be established among us, not to allow any form of imperialism among us, not to allow neocolonialism."[137] After Diggs met with liberation leaders in 1974, he left with the task of investigating what

CIA activities might be occurring in southern Africa, lest they undermine or condition these transfers of power. The U.S. solidarity movement and its congressional allies would, according to Diggs, act as "watchdogs on U.S. policy."[138] "Afro-Americans must be ever vigilant," Diggs told the ALD crowd in 1974, "if they are to really make a difference in the cause of African Liberation."[139] From the early years of religious organizing to the broadsides of the Gulf campaign, this goal of preventing "the next Vietnam" in the Lusophone countries had been a powerful appeal to New Left organizers; now it was the primary task of the solidarity movement and their congressional allies.

PART III

Institutionalizing New
Left Internationalism

CHAPTER 9

A Precedent Against Intervention

More than two hundred people stood in subfreezing temperatures on the steps of the Capitol in Washington. It was January 19, 1976, and they were gathered to protest President Gerald Ford's intervention in the former Portuguese colony of Angola. "Welcome back," veteran activist David Dellinger spoke into the microphone. Many of those in attendance knew one another well. Most partook in the Portuguese African solidarity movement at one point or another over the previous decade. Many had overlapped in other movements as well—antiwar, civil rights, and anti-imperial. White, Black, man, and woman, they cheered as presenters spoke scathingly of Ford's attempt to undermine the Soviet-backed government of the MPLA, which had already consolidated power in the capital, Luanda. Among the speakers besides Dellinger were the peace advocate and ACOA collaborator Cora Weiss, Representative Bella Abzug, Howard University professor and member of the African Liberation Support Committee (ALSC) Ronald Walters, and the Reverend W. Sterling Carey, former head of the National Council of Churches (NCC). Under signs reading "Hands off Angola," the attendees demanded an end to the war developing in the African state, comparing it to the quagmire in Vietnam that the United States had escaped only a few years before. At the beginning of a year that would see the president, the House, and much of the Senate seeking reelection, Dellinger stated in no uncertain terms that the assembly taking place that cold January day in front of the Capitol was "a warning."[1] Within a few weeks, this warning would be heeded by the House of Representatives when it approved a bill that denied covert funding for Angola and removed the amount already spent there from the defense budget. After fifteen years of organizing, the transnational solidarity coalition was defending socialist claims to self-determination and changing national policy.

Figure 11. Howard University professor Ronald Walters addresses the Hands Off Angola rally, January 19, 1976. Besides the main organizers, other groups represented at the rally included the Anti-Apartheid Movement, U.S.A.; Campaign for a Democratic Foreign Policy; Clergy and Laity Concerned; D.C.-Chile Solidarity Committee; Friends of the Filipino People; Office of Social Ministries, Jesuit Conference; Women's Strike for Peace, and the United Auto Workers. Reprinted with permission of Chris Root, African Activist Archive.

Yet this outcome was far from certain as events unfolded. Historian Robert David Johnson has pointed out in his overview of congressional activity during the Cold War that the liberal internationalism that helped force an end to the Vietnam War in 1973 was already on the decline by the time Angola gained independence two years later.[2] What scholars at the time referred to as a legislative "revolution" expanded the oversight abilities of Congress and its power to influence foreign affairs but never fully overturned the entrenched Cold War values of containment and anti-communism.[3] Indeed, Angola seemed to offer a perfect test for post-Vietnam Cold War policy: Cuban and Soviet support for the leftist-nationalist government in Luanda offered an almost unprecedented projection of communist power, while Ford's material support of local forces offered a measured response. There was little sense that Congress would respond negatively. Movement allies in Congress like

Charles Diggs, Andrew Young, John Tunney, Ted Kennedy, Dick Clark, and a host of other legislative reformers sought to transform U.S. foreign policy along New Left Internationalist lines, but they struggled to constrain military spending and aid for anti-communist regimes after the high-water mark of 1973. Many would be gone after only one term on Capitol Hill. By 1979, Congress, led by a Democratic president who entered the Oval Office advocating human rights, approved the supply of arms to Afghan rebels resisting a Soviet invasion in a region where the United States had few direct interests. The following decade witnessed the rise of the Reagan Doctrine, which empowered anti-communists to attack sitting leftist governments and fed the coffers of reactionary regimes across the Global South.

The victory over Angolan intervention therefore demands explanation, and it can be found in the lively collaboration of these legislators with the activists who gathered in Washington on that cold January day. The lingering effects of Vietnam, the contested independence of Angola, and the quadrennial debate on national priorities created by a presidential election all converged in 1976 to create a moment of fluidity in U.S. politics, where Cold War priorities were discussed, debated, and perhaps altered. It is in such moments of punctuated equilibrium that sociologists Margaret Keck and Kathryn Sikkink identify advocacy networks' greatest chances of policy success, so long as organizations exist with sufficient expertise, membership, and access to official institutions to shape the emerging political agenda.[4] The protection of independent, socialist Angola became the first moment when the popular-congressional linkages forged over the previous years could have a serious policy impact, well before an expanded version of this coalition forced South African sanctions on a reluctant Ronald Reagan in the 1980s.[5] The constituent components of the Portuguese African solidarity movement maintained its links to legislators and activist networks, applying the strategic lessons learned during the anti-colonial struggle. As the CONCP parties prepared for the long-delayed transfers of power, U.S. sympathizers rallied to aid them. Protecting an MPLA-ruled Angola would be the measure of their accomplishments. After years of warning that Western intervention in Africa was inevitable, the solidarity network was proven correct.

Both legislators and activists now worked to safeguard Portuguese African self-determination against the meddling of their own government in Washington. By uncovering the existence of covert executive branch assistance to Holden Roberto and Jonas Savimbi, and then mobilizing public opposition to it, the network of activists and lobbyists reframed discussions of Angola around the heuristic of Vietnam and the North-South divide. Congressional internationalists seeking to challenge the Cold War narrative offered by the administration incorporated these ideas into legislative checks on the administration, utilizing the grassroots-legislative connections forged over the prior decade. Popular criticism and activist defenses of leftist African nationalists helped rally undecided congressional opinion against the covert intervention before President Ford could even present his case. While the administration pledged not to send advisers or troops to Africa as the government had done a decade earlier in Southeast Asia, the activist comparison of the two conflicts won over Congress and large segments of the public. The network connecting grassroots organizing, lobbying, and legislative politics emerged during the Vietnam War era but faced its first proactive test in Angola. Its success established the model for constraining reactionary executive policies for the remainder of the Cold War.

New Left Internationalist Ideas in Congress

One cannot understand the congressional reaction to Angola without understanding the way that Vietnam and other movements in the late 1960s and early 1970s, including the Lusophone solidarity movement, reshaped U.S. politics. While the Southeast Asian war illustrated the limitations of U.S. power, the collapse of the consensus around anti-communist containment demanded a wholesale reassessment of foreign policy. Jeremi Suri has drawn direct lines between the rise of domestic activism and the executive policy of détente, in which President Richard Nixon and National Security Adviser Henry Kissinger addressed the relative weakening of U.S. power by reducing tensions with the Soviet Union, launching arms limitation talks, and relying more on regional allies like Iran and South Africa.[6] This trend was reinforced by the more proactive Congress that reflected popular frustration with the Vietnam War. Many legislators came to oppose the war if only to keep their jobs in the face of increasingly vocal challenges from their constituents, but a few saw doing so as a chance to reassert Congress's role in managing foreign affairs and limiting what they saw as an imperial presidency.[7] Many of these legislators also supported new initiatives in Africa. While Nixon's withdrawal of troops from Vietnam in 1973 calmed the loudest attacks on military spending, demands for structural reforms were buoyed by revelations about the CIA's "dirty tricks" and the slow-burning Watergate scandal that led to Nixon's resignation in August 1974. Calls for congressional oversight came both from sitting members like Charles Diggs, who gained the platforms and support to voice louder critiques of existing policy, and from the election of assertive new members like Andrew Young in the House and freshman Iowa senator Dick Clark. These individuals and their closest colleagues sought to use Congress to articulate a new vision of foreign affairs that they believed better captured the national mood, with Angola becoming a prime test case for their cause.

In the realm of international affairs, these reformers converged around policy programs that aligned them with the New Left Internationalism championed by the Portuguese African solidarity network. At the core of their beliefs was opposition to anti-communist adventurism and rejection of the great-power politics personified by Kissinger. Members of this loose coalition defined themselves by different political labels, from socialist (a few) to liberal (many) with a handful of moderates thrown in, but they cohered around a set of shared priorities: the reprogramming of military funds toward domestic programs on a Great Society model, a more internationally engaged foreign policy centered on peaceful trade relationships and cooperative aid, greater engagement with the United Nations, and international leadership through moral means. The internationalist contingent also believed that these policies had to better address the needs of the developing world. Many came to support the U.N.-approved target of 0.7 percent of gross national product to be devoted to development assistance. Importantly, such policies were not simply humanitarian but relied upon a calculation of U.S. interests starkly different from the Eurocentric ideas of Kissinger. Part of the critique implied shifting heavy spending from military to aid programs, to alleviate global problems before they became so dire as to produce conflict. The longtime Africa watcher and former Marine captain John Culver (D-IA) explained the logic in prophetic terms: "The third-world problem [food, development, trade, potential instability] in the year 2000 will be every bit as great a threat to our security as the U.S.-Soviet balance."[8] Getting on the right side of the North-South divide was just as important to many of these legislators as managing Cold War tensions, and for some far more important.

Attempts by a sizable minority in Congress to grapple with North-South relations reveal the broader rethinking of foreign affairs during this transitional period in U.S. policy. Barbara Keys rightly contends that Congress played an outsized role in defining divergent paths toward restoring ideas of "American virtue" abroad, but her focus on contemporary formulations of human rights downplays the radical global economic and structural reformism that held sway during this period.[9] The Congressional Black Caucus, for example, emphasized the need for "parity between nations in decisions about their relationships," emphasizing that U.S. economic assistance should prioritize the developmental priorities of Global South states to achieve "genuine interdependence and mutual respect."[10] Specific policy proposals urged support for initiatives favored by many African and Asian states, including expanding multilateral institutions, trade reform, the destruction of nuclear stockpiles, and a respect for sovereign borders. A key staffer to Andrew Young pithily summarized the position: "[The U.S. government] should structurally reorient its approach toward participation rather than continue a posture of economic and imperial hegemony."[11] At the pragmatic level, brewing North-South conflicts threatened U.S. well-being, as evidenced by the Arab oil embargo of 1973, so crafting collaborative foreign policies offered prospects for guaranteeing access to vital raw materials overwhelmingly concentrated in the Global South. Yet more broadly, these ideas sought to recapture the promise of U.S. global leadership by reorienting it to address the deep inequalities that separated North from South. As Dick Clark explained to one critical constituent, "As the wealthiest nation in the world, we do have some obligation to help others that barely have enough food to survive."[12] For Clark and his collaborators, addressing the North-South divide was not only practical, it was a matter of economic and moral justice that could restore the sense of national mission.[13]

One of the key conclusions shaped by this New Left Internationalist thinking was that intervention occurred in the wrong ways and in the wrong places. The United States needed to use its economic and political leadership to address this clear global divide. That was the way to expand U.S. prestige and restore the proper goals of the U.S. mission. As historian Robert David Johnson explains, the reformist legislators shared a "vision of demilitarized foreign policy that stressed economic cooperation, cultural exchange, and ideological issues such as human rights and support for democracy."[14] It also included greater respect for self-determination. Too often Cold War concerns led the United States to respond negatively to local leaders whose attempts to address economic and political inequalities either smacked of communism or pushed them into alliances with the anti-imperial states of the Eastern bloc. Such logic motivated the military intervention in Vietnam and justified the 1973 coup against Chile's Salvador Allende, and many African leaders feared similar responses might happen in Angola or Mozambique. Mindful of this poor track record, legislators advocated for a new set of policies that, in the words of John Tunney (D-CA), would "emphasize social and economic initiatives, not military reaction."[15] Since this line of thinking was slow to take hold in the executive branch, motivated legislators positioned Congress to be an equal partner in the construction of foreign policies. They sought support from key institutions that shared their attitudes, connecting with major organizations like the NCC and smaller ones like ACOA.[16] The goal, according to Andrew Young, was to establish both legislative precedent and new avenues for information gathering and assessment to turn back the tendency in which "Congress increasingly finds itself reacting rather than acting."[17]

Recentering international affairs around the North-South axis meant moving away from rigid Cold War orthodoxy. While many of these legislators were not fans of communism, they recognized that revolutionary ideas espoused by Global South actors, despite their Marxist elements, were best understood as ideologies of self-determination and national improvement for their people. "Communists don't have to come to tell them they're hungry," Young jibed in 1973, "unless we are sensitive to the needs of reform in those countries in the world, we're going to find ourselves relating to them in a military fashion because we wait too long too late to do anything politically and socially and economically."[18] While more centrist reformers like Senator Tunney continued to use Cold War rhetoric—especially during election years—the common attitude was that East-West conflicts should take a backseat to the problems of the insurgent Global South and constructive diplomacy with the regions.[19] These new attitudes made room for acceptance and even support for groups like the MPLA, hoping a less rigid application of Cold War policies might negate the need for Southern radicalization. "Perhaps," Senator Clark's office wrote to a like-minded constituent, "it is finally time for the United States to truly assume a positive role in world affairs—and to use our power for humanitarian ends, not [to] be the 'world's policeman,'" a term Clark considered synonymous with Cold War containment.[20] While these ideas were not as radical as either youth or Black Power movements desired, they aligned with the broad New Left Internationalism that united radicals, religious institutions, and Pan-Africanists in coalition behind Lusophone liberation.

Leading this charge in its earliest phases was the Congressional Black Caucus (CBC), whose attempts to assert Black political interests in the 1970s made it a vocal proponent of Global South concerns. Diggs achieved early prominence, but the expansion of its ranks in the elections of the 1970s gave it powerful new voices, including Representatives Cardiss Collins (D-IL) and Ron Dellums (D-CA). Included in this group was Andrew Young (D-GA),

whose name recognition positioned him as a prominent advocate of this
new approach to international affairs. At the heart of the CBC's efforts were
attempts to inject new perspectives into U.S. decision-making that broke with
old patterns of U.S. chauvinism and hegemony. Young saw the diversification of governmental positions as addressing more than just the domestic
"race problem": "You see it's a solution to the peace problem too . . . [because
whites raised in segregation] would not react comfortably to a mass movement amongst colored people. So their tendency is to send for the Marines
whenever there's trouble."[21] The prioritization of Euro-American priorities
was one of the primary Global South frustrations. Tanzanian president Julius
Nyerere explained that the problem with the United States was always that
it "listen[ed] to Western Europe much more than to Africa about African
matters."[22] Thanks to the work done in prior years connecting Pan-African
struggles and building pathways for exchange with African leaders like Nyerere, the CBC believed it was uniquely positioned to inject Global South concerns into U.S. deliberation. Its membership consisted of people marginalized
within their own country, engaged in the local component of a larger tricontinental struggle for equal rights and development. As Young summarized,
"Nobody understands a problem any better than the folk who suffer from
it."[23] And because Africa played an outsized role in the conceptualization of
Black identity in the United States, the extra attention it received made it the
proving ground for this new vision of global affairs.

While the CBC represented the most coherent bloc championing these
ideas, its members were joined in their efforts by the wider coalition of legislators that cohered over the previous decade. This began in the House first,
where the localized nature of elections allowed for more idiosyncratic politics
than the state-level contests of the Senate. Prominent reformers drew heavily
from the lists of attendees at the legislative Africa conferences, including Jonathan Bingham (D-NY) and Don Fraser from Minnesota, whose championing of human rights incorporated economic-justice issues. As post-Vietnam
and post-Watergate House classes entered, they found longtime reformers like
Diggs and Fraser already holding committee positions that allowed them to
promote legislation. The staider Senate was slower to reflect these new attitudes due to the power of seniority, but Vietnam changed minds. The most
influential of these men, like Stuart Symington (D-MO), underwent a transformation from anti-communists to Cold War critics, spurred largely by
what they considered overreach in Southeast Asia and a military-industrial
complex run amok. They made common cause with a young generation of

politicians who gained their seats by opposing Vietnam and pushing for greater oversight after Watergate. These new Senate classes included liberals like Dick Clark, John Culver, Joe Biden (D-DE), and Floyd Haskell (D-CO—a former Republican). They led the charge against Cold War politics as usual, opposing Vietnam, questioning major defense projects like the B-1 bomber, and famously investigating the covert operations of the CIA with a committee led by the increasingly reluctant Frank Church (D-ID).[24] These elections were essentially "products of the student movement of the 60s," according to Andrew Young, and the new legislators wanted to establish "a new kind of consensus" after Vietnam.[25] Angola offered them an opportunity.

Responding to IA Feature

Angola reentered the world stage just over a year after the Portuguese revolution toppled the imperial government. Guinea-Bissau, Cabo Verde, and Mozambique gained independence under the leadership of CONCP parties, the PAIGC and FRELIMO, respectively. Solidarity activists welcomed the events in the Northern summer of 1975, sending expert volunteers from Europe, Canada, and the United States to help establish the new nations.[26] But the deep divisions between the three nationalist parties in Angola prevented a smooth transition to peace. The MPLA confronted a combined front made up of the erstwhile enemies the FNLA and UNITA. Though Holden Roberto and Jonas Savimbi had been antagonistic since the Ovimbundu leader abandoned the FNLA in the mid-1960s, they entered an uneasy truce in opposition to the MPLA. As its leaders had for a decade, the new FNLA-UNITA coalition looked abroad for aid, and they found partners in Portugal's Western allies. This new set of alliances forced the Cold War back into the lives of Angolans and gave the U.S. solidarity movement a goal for organizing. In the months leading up to independence, both sides withdrew to their regional strongholds in preparation for the fighting that would take place after the transfer of power. The MPLA looked to Cuba and the Soviet Union for assistance, while Roberto and Savimbi established alliances with Zaire (formerly the Congo) and South Africa, respectively. The final piece in this puzzle was the small but vital aid provided by the United States to the nominally anti-communist forces, a program known as IA Feature.

IA Feature had its origins in the early months of 1975. Kissinger remained as dismissive as ever of the world beyond Europe.[27] Vietnam and the Middle

Figure 12. Angola's competing nationalist leaders, June 1975. As independence loomed in Angola, Kenyan president Jomo Kenyatta futilely attempted to mediate a cease-fire between the feuding Angolan parties. From left to right are Holden Roberto (FNLA), Jomo Kenyatta, Agostinho Neto (MPLA), and Jonas Savimbi (UNITA). Keystone Pictures USA/ZUMAPRESS.

East crisis did little to shake this bias, especially as it pertained to Africa. In 1974, Kissinger and the State Department were distracted by events in Portugal, which the Ford administration feared could produce a communist government in Western Europe. Only after Lisbon moderated its leftward drift and independence for the colonies neared did the administration turn its attention to Angola, which Kissinger believed was in the "backwaters of foreign policy."[28] Mobutu Sese Seko brought the matter to Washington's attention. The Zairean strongman won few popularity contests, but Kissinger wanted to maintain the precarious peace that Mobutu had established in the former Congo and appreciated his role as a dependable anti-communist on the African continent. Mobutu worried that events in Angola were working against Roberto and that the defeat of the FNLA at the hands of the Moscow-backed Luanda government could promote unrest along the borders of his massive state.[29] He urged Kissinger to respond to the competition brewing in Angola.

Kissinger was loath to waste time on Africa for much of the tumultuous year of 1974, but he reacted quickly and assertively after he learned that the MPLA might take control with Soviet aid. He pushed the administration to expand its support for the FNLA and, to a lesser extent, UNITA. The "loss" of Angola could combine with the North Vietnamese invasion of Saigon in April 1975 to put the United States on the defensive, at least in the realm of public and international opinion. Given Ford's upcoming presidential campaign and the challenge the inheritor of détente was receiving from the right of his own party, such a perception of weakness was unacceptable to the president, who lent his support to his embattled secretary of state.[30] It was the domino effect all over again. With Ford's backing, Kissinger told a group of high-ranking officials in June, "We can't let the communists win there." The secretary was deeply concerned about what U.S. inaction would mean for regional politics and African relations with the United States. An MPLA victory could alienate Zaire and upset the tenuous balance of power.[31] It could also lead to a deeper global crisis of confidence in Washington's leadership against the Soviets and threaten the administration's continued tenure in the face of the rising conservative challenge in an election year.

By June, Kissinger and Ford had made the decision to send their new allies millions of dollars in financial support and, indirectly and later directly, weapons. Mobutu provided arms to the anti-MPLA forces, with the United States resupplying the Zairean military. New M-16s flowed into Kinshasa, while older weapons were redirected into Angola. The United States provided artillery and anti-tank weaponry and backed the recruitment of non-American mercenaries to train the FNLA-UNITA troops.[32] Eventually, Zambia also provided arms to UNITA, as did Israel through purchases by South Africa. Portuguese officers provided additional training in Zaire.[33] The goal of this massive influx of arms was not necessarily outright victory for U.S. allies but to "balance off" the Soviet and eventually Cuban aid that strengthened the MPLA.[34] The Ford administration hoped to maintain a status quo in Angola that would force the parties to share power, or at least resolve their disputes without direct Soviet participation. Conscious of the deep divisions that remained within the United States after Vietnam and the pockets of strong feelings about Portuguese Africa, the White House felt that it was pursuing a constrained policy that avoided most political pitfalls and remained aligned with détente. No American troops were committed to Angola (beyond a few CIA advisers and trainers secretly in Zaire), and expenditures were relatively modest. When CIA director William Colby expressed concern that the Angola issue might cause a scandal with Congress or the public if revealed, Ford responded dismissively: "We can't sit here and worry about six Committees [in Congress] if we do what's right."[35] The bleed over between passive support to colonial Portugal and active support for African anti-communists that the solidarity movement had anticipated since the 1960s finally came to pass.

The administration, however, had not accounted for the anti-interventionist zeal of the internationalist minority on the Hill. The House was traditionally the most active chamber on African affairs under the influence of Diggs and the CBC, but a reorganization of foreign affairs subcommittees in mid-1975 limited activity.[36] These legislators had like-minded colleagues in the Senate who appreciated their efforts and were positioned to take action.[37] The lack of seniority limited the influence of these senators, but Africa's minor strategic importance placed Angola under the purview of one of the most committed and capable of the internationalist minority, first-term Democratic senator Dick Clark of Iowa. Clark was neither an expert on Africa nor an activist. He was a history and political science professor before entering politics as an aide to Congressman John Culver, helping guide a Democratic resurgence in the socially conservative farming state. After walking 1,312 miles across Iowa during his 1972 campaign, the personable Clark entered Washington firmly committed to liberal, antiwar causes.[38] He quickly joined the reformers pushing the congressional revolution in foreign policy. Deeply interested in foreign affairs, articulate, and hardworking—described by one observer as "a spirited and determined academic type, with a puritanical streak"—Clark became one of the leading voices of the group.[39] Given their natural affinities, the Washington Office on Africa (WOA) identified him immediately as an ally and made contact with his staff.[40] Outspoken as he may have been, his opinions did not carry weight during his first two years in the Senate, as he had little clout in policymaking circles. This changed slightly at the beginning of the Ninety-fourth Congress (1975) when he received the chairmanship of the Subcommittee on Africa, the least desirable chair on the Foreign Relations Committee, given to the least senior member (Clark ranked above only the equally green Joe Biden). Rejecting Biden's joking request to cede the chair, Clark took his role seriously and began educating himself about the continent.[41]

Central to this education was a series of hearings Clark held on southern Africa in the summer of 1975, taking advantage of one of the revolutionary changes that occurred in Congress over the previous five years. Vietnam demonstrated that the executive branch had a virtual monopoly on information; Congress struggled to verify facts produced by the executive and therefore lacked an informed independent perspective. As the dangers of this conundrum became more apparent in Southeast Asia, there emerged a simple solution that opened doors to popular advocates and the New Left Internationalism of the 1970s. New laws provided the authorization and funds to nearly double personal congressional staffs, who now had the ability to pursue independent investigations into foreign policy issues.[42] Yet these congressmen and staffs still faced the daunting challenge of mastering a world of complicated foreign politics, so they relied on existing experts to shape their research. When it came to Africa, there were few more knowledgeable or convincing than the members of the solidarity network that formed around the Lusophone revolutions. From June through July, Clark held a series of hearings to learn from some of the few experts on southern Africa outside the executive branch—the academics, activists, and church members who had forged alliances with the socialist nationalist movements of FRELIMO, the PAIGC, and the MPLA over the prior decade.[43]

While it is unclear how Clark assembled the list of nearly thirty witnesses, it is likely that either ACOA or WOA had a hand in the matter. In addition to WOA's early identification of the senator as an ally in 1973, the office worked closely with his predecessor, Gale McGee, when he chaired the committee during the Nixon years. Clark remembered later that he "had a lot of close contact with [the two groups]." One of his key staffers, Marianne Spiegel, earned a master's degree in African studies and was probably familiar with ACOA and its publications.[44] The leaders of both groups were well represented at the hearings. WOA director Ted Lockwood testified, as did ACOA deputy director Jennifer Davis, with ACOA's George Houser providing the closing commentary of the two-month process. An academic at heart, Clark gave preference to professors over the grassroots organizers that Diggs increasingly invited to Washington, but most witnesses had ties to ACOA, local groups like the Madison Area Committee on Southern Africa (MACSA), and personal contact with the CONCP parties.[45]

The hearings covered events in all the countries of southern Africa, but Angola and South African apartheid stood as the most pressing issues. As Kissinger and Ford were secretly deciding on the levels of involvement in the colony in the summer of 1975, Clark's experts warned of the dangers of U.S. intervention. In one of the earliest testimonies, University of Minnesota professor, MACSA member, and close FRELIMO associate Allen Isaacman explained the long history of American support for the Portuguese wars. The professor hinted that the Ford administration might be providing aid to anti-communist groups in the region, but he could not provide details.[46] Angola experts Douglas Wheeler and Gerald Bender were more forceful than Isaacman. They made no claims to secret knowledge but sounded the alarm about potential action.[47] Bender was especially direct in his challenge: Congress should use its oversight powers "to insure that neither the CIA, DIA [Defense Intelligence Agency], nor any other intelligence agency or private corporation is currently providing covert assistance to any of the Angolan parties."[48] Here for congressional consumption was the warning of a new Vietnam that activists had been sounding for nearly five years.

Arguably the most important individual who shaped Clark's thinking was John Marcum. Marcum had worked with ACOA while living on the East Coast in the 1960s, had consulted with the NCC, and was generally acknowledged to be the authority on contemporary Angolan nationalism.[49] An erstwhile friend of FNLA head Holden Roberto, he rejected the Bakongo leader's ethnocentrism and suitability as a leader of a free Angola. In his testimony, he defended the MPLA against allegations that it was dangerous to U.S. interests in the region. Marcum expressed concern about the governing potential of the alternative parties. He also told Clark that the vague reports of U.S. aid to Roberto and Savimbi circulating around the country rang true, since the FNLA's ties to the U.S. government stretched back to 1960. It had, after all, been Marcum who worked with the Kennedy administration to administer the Lincoln University exchange program during the same period. Marcum mirrored ACOA in shifting his Angolan alliances over the preceding years, but he suspected that Washington continued to see Roberto as a capable and dependable anti-communist. Kissinger's recent warnings about spreading Marxist ideologies hinted at an official suspicion of the MPLA. Marcum told Clark, "Washington should, above all, avoid the trap of overreacting to hostile rhetoric and socialist advocacy and of identifying potential 'enemies.'"[50] His advice effectively recovered the anti-colonial movement's warnings of U.S. meddling in the region and attached it firmly to the bellwether state of Angola.

Marcum's testimony influenced Clark and the way he understood the potential for disastrous intervention in Angola. As he opened his hearing featuring administration representatives, the senator quoted directly from Marcum's testimony: "The most important thing the American government can do in Angola is to refrain from projecting parochial or ideological intolerance into its perception of the situation there."[51] This statement set the tone for subsequent questioning, when both Clark and Biden peppered the witnesses with questions about arms dealings and the potential for anti-communist aid to specific Angolan parties. At all points the State Department representatives denied favoritism or major assistance of any kind, explaining that the White House backed Portuguese efforts to form an Angolan government of national unity through diplomatic channels.[52] Clark harbored suspicions, but the government roundly denied U.S. involvement in the tense standoff between the nationalist parties. The activist and academic communities continued to push the issue, though. On the final day of the hearings, when asked by Clark for his recommendations concerning future policy, ACOA's George Houser urged the senator to conduct an "immediate investigation" into allegations that Zaire was providing heavy military material to the FNLA on behalf of the U.S. government.[53] Activists had long ago accepted the likelihood of Cold War intervention in southern Africa, and they urged the internationalist wing of Congress to step in and act as the arbiter of unchecked executive power in international relations.

This convinced Clark to conduct a thorough investigation of the Angola situation. He arranged a trip to Africa for the August break with the explicit goal of contacting FRELIMO in Mozambique and "the interim government in Angola," hoping to establish good relations with parties that had limited connections with U.S. officials.[54] He also requested to be briefed on CIA operations. As a member of the Foreign Affairs Committee, he had the right to receive information on covert activities thanks to the Hughes-Ryan Act, passed the year before with the goal of increasing congressional oversight of executive operations abroad. The CIA had, in fact, consulted with the Hill but left Clark out of the closed-door sessions. Kissinger later claimed that IA Feature was never "all that covert," due to forty congressional briefings conducted by various departments. At the time, however, Kissinger admitted that many of the legislative consultations did not "amount to much more than [CIA Director] Colby talking to [Senate Foreign Relations chair John] Sparkman and [ranking minority member Clifford] Case."[55] Both senators accepted the limited goals of the covert program and voiced no objections. Kissinger was upset, in fact, when he discovered that the senior legislators had shared information with the hostile senator from Iowa.[56] Shortly before his departure, Colby finally briefed Clark in person. According to CIA operative John Stockwell, the spymaster was disingenuous, explaining that the United States was only restocking weapons that Mobutu provided to the combined FNLA and UNITA in their attempts to forestall an MPLA takeover before the elections. The administration had no specific program of aiding either the FNLA or UNITA. For his part, Clark felt that Colby spoke in platitudes, and he could not recall anything significant being discussed in the meeting.[57] Nonetheless, it represented the first time that the internationalist element in Congress was directly told of any operation in Angola. It would be the first step in a six-month campaign that brought covert activities to an end.

In mid-August, Clark left for Africa accompanied by Biden, aide Mary Ann Spiegel, and Foreign Relations staffer Dick Moose. The trip confirmed the expert testimony from the summer and steeled his resolve to act. He arranged to visit a handful of countries, where he consulted with the competing Angolan nationalists, Mobutu, Kenneth Kaunda of Zambia, Julius Nyerere in Tanzania, and Samora Machel in Mozambique.[58] The administration attempted to conceal its activities, with the CIA coaching Roberto and Savimbi on what to discuss with the congressional delegation.[59] But Clark's extensive travel made this deception hard to maintain. Vague responses and fudged numbers could not conceal what the critical observer saw and heard in the chaotic pre-independence atmosphere. Upon landing in Angola to meet Savimbi, the Americans discovered a South African plane waiting on the tarmac, which aroused Clark's suspicions of the connections between UNITA and the apartheid state. In Luanda, Clark was positively impressed in his meetings with MPLA leaders, which included Neto and Foreign Minister José Eduardo dos Santos.[60] His impressions were reinforced by the U.S. consul general and a CIA agent, who advised him that "putting money into Roberto and Savimbi was a hell of a bad idea and wouldn't work."[61] Clark returned to the United States even more skeptical of the venture and determined to stop it.

Clark did not, however, know what the most effective form of action would be or how he would find sufficient support for his plans. Beyond a few key allies like Culver and WOA collaborators Tunney and Kennedy, Clark found few willing to help him. He remembered later, "No other senator showed much interest" in Angola or the problem of the covert operations.[62] Some were actively hostile to the junior senator's cause. While Clark flew to the continent, South Africa tapped into its political network to lobby the Senate. Targeting conservative Republicans and Southern Democrats, the Afrikaner government utilized relationships with some of the most powerful men in the upper chamber, including Senate Foreign Relations chairman John Sparkman (D-AL) and Appropriations Committee head John McClellan (D-AR). Throughout the fall, more than twenty senators agreed to approach the administration in support of Pretoria's interests, including its strong opposition to the MPLA.[63] This bloc of anti-communist (and often segregationist) politicians were a hurdle for Clark because their influential committee positions gave them power over many indifferent and undecided legislators seeking their largesse for personal projects. Clark believed that much of the U.S. public would support an amendment and help nullify such calculations, but the Senate's rules constrained him from disclosing the facts. Fortunately, a deeply divided executive branch, the U.S. press, and popular activism helped solve his conundrum.

Press reports soon revealed details of the U.S.-backed coalition in Angola, allowing activists to begin a public campaign. In late September, *New York Times* correspondent and former Pentagon staffer Leslie Gelb wrote a front-page piece about foreign intervention in Portugal and Angola, highlighting the role of Mobutu and providing background on Roberto's relationship to the United States.[64] Gelb's article—focused more on Portugal than on Angola—did not inspire popular outrage, but it provided an excuse for internationalists on the Hill and their activist allies to begin making noise about the Ford intervention. It was especially timely given that Roberto used his advantage in U.S.-supplied heavy weapons to push back MPLA forces in the north of the country, threatening to overtake Luanda shortly before Gelb's article appeared in print. The MPLA held off Roberto's forces, but the FNLA leader vowed to take the city so he could accept the Portuguese transfer of power in November. The arrival of Cuban instructors and Eastern bloc weapons alleviated the MPLA's relative military disadvantage against UNITA in the south, but it was unclear whether September's events would tip the scales in any one party's favor.[65] As this information trickled through the media to the outside world, U.S. activists focused less on the fighting and more on the reactionary intent of executive branch aid to Roberto through the Zairean regime. Over the seven weeks preceding the independence ceremony on November 11, ACOA and WOA publicized Gelb's revelations and inspired additional articles.[66] This reignited activist attention on Angola slowly filtered into the mainstream.

When the Portuguese flag was finally lowered in Angola, the MPLA remained in control of Luanda, but the fighting continued unabated, with foreign aid pouring in on all sides. Shortly thereafter, Clark submitted a rider to the foreign-aid bill that banned additional involvement in the newly independent country without congressional approval. In addition to challenges from pro-South African politicians, the Iowan was opposed by elder liberals concerned about the Cold War stakes. Among these latter critics were former vice president Hubert Humphrey (D-MN), who was afraid of appearing soft on communism and urged moderation. Even more critical was Gale McGee, the former Africa subcommittee chair, whose opposition to Rhodesia coexisted with a continued adherence to Cold War containment.[67] The mainstream press also provided a surprisingly muted response. A handful of Black newspapers aligned with former African Liberation Day activists offered scathing commentary that utilized WOA information, but most, like the influential *Chicago Defender*, said little. The Black newspapers rallied around the freedom struggles, but they adopted neutral positions when it came to domestic matters of African states. When reporters criticized Kissinger, they generally did so for the covert nature of U.S. operations rather than rote assistance to anti-communists or indirect support for South Africa.[68] With few outside Clark's circle willing to speak out against a president responding to direct Soviet intervention in far-off Africa, the senator faced an uphill battle.

Clark's struggles reveal that Vietnam loomed over the Angola debate, but not always in the way historians usually suggest. From a contemporary perspective, it seems logical that an activist Congress forged amid the Southeast Asian war would overwhelmingly condemn foreign adventurism and militarism. Yet for much of 1975 Clark and his colleagues sympathetic to New Left Internationalism struggled to advance their ideals. In the Senate Defense Committee, Stuart Symington and John Culver scored few victories. Final votes on their bills to rein in the Cold War military-industrial complex failed by an average of nearly two dozen. Congress approved the expansion of military operations on the Indian Ocean base of Diego Garcia and refused to end arms shipments to Turkey despite liberal protests over the country's activities in the disputed territory of Cyprus. Even the ardor against covert operations, so strong after the Chilean coup of 1973, waned. An attempt by one House critic to publicize the CIA budget was defeated by 120 votes that summer.[69] In the midst of his subcommittee hearings in June, Clark worried that the more constructive foreign policy he and his allies championed was in danger, especially after the fall of Saigon in April. They believed that the lessons of Vietnam repudiated the use of force and heavy-handed tactics in the Global South, but the senator saw his opponents drawing on another lesson: "The administration, and . . . the majority in Congress, have somehow become so embarrassed or falsely humiliated by the experience of Southeast Asia, that they may in fact react the other way [toward the fetishization of force and an 'abrasive' foreign policy]."[70]

The revisionists in Congress struggled to make headway on Angola exactly because the lessons of Vietnam remained opaque to many policymakers.

Politicians like Hubert Humphrey were not cold warriors, but neither did they wish to appear weak in the face of Soviet expansion.[71] The revelation in November that Cuban troops were arriving in Angola, at the apparent behest of Moscow, offered an unprecedented projection of communist power absent even from Vietnam. Many legislators did not know how to react. Even the CBC and Diggs were slow to take a public stance, since the Angola issue still divided the Black community. The Detroit congressman explained to one Black newsman that the caucus had not yet made plans to take any action as late as December, though members expressed interest in Angola and Diggs was investigating the situation at WOA's request.[72] Vietnam imparted not just a single lesson but many. One supported by Clark, legislative reformers, and New Left Internationalists viewed the war as a repudiation of U.S. interventionism, which opened the door for a constructive, multilateral internationalism based on human rights and ideological flexibility. Another, more conservative camp believed that Vietnam had been mishandled. U.S. troops should not have been on the ground in such a remote part of the world, but confronting Soviet expansion remained necessary. The latter conclusion fueled a new emphasis on aid—both covert and overt—to anti-communist forces. Many in Congress sat undecided between these two poles, worried about which direction their constituents might lean. Angola presented the perfect opportunity for these two contrasting lessons of Vietnam to battle for the heart of the legislature. Clark needed popular and congressional outrage to match his own perspective if he was going to disrupt the administration's plan.

The Iowan found some help from the same groups who had first pointed him toward Angola. The activist network that emerged from earlier solidarity organizing rallied behind the congressional internationalists. ACOA and WOA took the lead shaping legislative discussions in these early stages. Both groups invested heavily in the Vietnam analogy during the anti-colonial struggle, which presented covert assistance to reactionary regimes in Africa as the first step in the creation of a new anti-communist quagmire. The propaganda had created broad support for the CONCP parties just the year before in the form of a mass boycott of Gulf's operations in Angola, and they believed it would be able to sway the Congress now. Letters flowed to constituencies beginning in October, and WOA arranged meetings for congressmen to speak with MPLA representatives during a brief visit to Washington that same month.[73] The activist groups hoped normalizing the MPLA might prepare U.S. politicians to take a more proactive stance when independence ushered in the seemingly inevitable competition for power in Angola.

By far the most important event of the Northern autumn was the meeting convened by ACOA, WOA, and various grassroots organizations in Madison, Wisconsin. MACSA hosted what it billed as a "work session" to coordinate solidarity activities in the United States and Canada regarding Angola. The conference gathered forty solidarity organizations that represented practically a who's who of 1970s organizing—religious, radical, and African American. Attendees included a handful of chapters from Amiri Baraka's Congress of African People (CAP), the leftist branches of the ALSC from Atlanta and elsewhere, the Chicago Committee for the Liberation of Angola, Mozambique, and Guinea (CCLAMG), the American Friends Service Committee (AFSC), the Freedom Information Service from Mississippi, various church groups, and a few smaller organizations. Panels focused on bringing everyone up to speed on the latest developments in U.S. policy toward southern Africa and providing a forum in which local organizations could discuss potential campaigns with representatives of the liberation groups. An entire day of workshops was dedicated to discussing organizing tactics, with the hope of "exchang[ing] ideas for strengthening [local action]."[74]

At the conference, the assembled minds made decisions that guided the movement against Angolan intervention while establishing a formal framework for cooperation on future African issues. First, they agreed to focus their energies on resisting any U.S. attempts to intervene in Angola and other newly freed states rather than on the topic of foreign intervention generally, since the Lusophone movements had relied on socialist aid before independence and would continue to do so. This aligned the conference attendees more closely with the MPLA and CONCP alliance, who viewed Soviet and Cuban support as a necessary response to the permanent threats from white minority governments. Second, they agreed on a list of action priorities that included the establishment of a "national campaign to stop U.S intervention in Angola, a 'Hot-Line' telephone news network," and continued action against the Union Carbide company that imported Rhodesian steel. Finally, the working groups selected individual organizations to help coordinate activities on these topics. They tapped WOA to lead the lobbying for legislative opposition to Angola and ACOA to be the central distributor of news on solidarity activity.[75]

These conclusions were not arrived at easily or unanimously due to deep ideological divides that continued to hamper complete unity, but they offered a starting point. The CAP chapters, for instance, refused to sign the final statement because of a disagreement over the exclusion of armed struggle as a necessity for liberation, while proposals to link southern African demands for equality with domestic class issues were narrowly defeated, to the frustration of the more radical MACSA and CCLAMG. Yet all parties agreed that cooperation would be necessary to achieve maximum victory for the African revolutions, and most committed themselves to working together even if a little less than half joined the official framework.[76] The Madison conference effectively began the process of recognizing and formalizing the decentralized network of pro-liberation solidarity activists, who began to build a structure to coordinate local activities in order to achieve national results. This all came into existence nearly a month before the official independence of Angola, positioning the activists to shape the congressional agenda well before most legislators began paying serious attention to the issue.

Tasked with national coordination of local activism at the Wisconsin confab, ACOA and WOA reached out to former and current allies in hopes of drumming up support for the Clark amendment. More than forty organizations responded, representing an array of religious and ideological viewpoints.[77] Church organizations sent communiqués to their congregations urging them to write to their legislators, as did local radical committees working on southern Africa. These groups reproduced or drew on information sent from the national organizations, including WOA's eight reasons for opposing the intervention. The first of these widely reproduced arguments claimed that "Angola may prove as tragic and costly as in Indochina," while others targeted the CIA and defended the MPLA against charges of it becoming a "Soviet puppet."[78] WOA also appealed to its allies with clout in Washington. It had some success with unions, using comparisons with Vietnam and the recent revelations of covert actions in South America to cajole them toward support for, or at least acquiescence to, the Clark amendment.[79] Concerned activists also made direct contact with congressmen. Ted Lockwood made this point most dramatically in his November testimony to Diggs's new committee shortly before Angola's independence in November. Expressing concern at growing evidence of anti-MPLA activities and the muted response of leading foreign policy critics, the WOA director counseled: "U.S. intervention in Angola has already become as costly and as dangerous as its involvement in Chile only a few years ago. Surely the tragic lessons of Chile should teach us to oppose immediately and vehemently every sign of covert or overt intervention in the troubled political affairs of another country. We call on the United States government to end its intervention in Angola. We urge Congress to take every action in its power toward this end."[80] The activists hoped this early lobbying and constituent mail would sway Hill politicians against Ford's Angola policy before the administration could make its case.

Throughout November and December, WOA lobbying emphasized the damage such a poorly planned intervention could have on the wider region, a point aided by news that South Africa had sent troops into Angola weeks before independence. The influx of communist instructors and Eastern bloc weapons allowed the MPLA to reassert control of Luanda in the weeks before the Portuguese transfer of power, unnerving South African officials who had been providing arms to both the FNLA and UNITA since August. In mid-October, it sent troops over the border to fight with Angolan forces.[81] Fearing a rout of UNITA in the south, it did so without consulting the United States.[82] The MPLA military forces fell back in the face of the invasion but held onto Luanda and were reinforced in November by Cuban troops. Soon there were more than thirteen hundred foreign soldiers in Angola, who helped turn the tide against the South Africans. Pretoria had kept its role in the fighting secret, but as the MPLA took the offensive on the battlefield and in the international media, it became harder to deny the participation of white troops from below the border. South Africa denied the allegations for the first weeks of December, but the capture of two soldiers by the Cubans on December 13 ended all speculation.[83] The activists had the weapon they needed to link U.S. policy with the reactionary white regimes. As revelations of the incursion became public in the first weeks of December, a National Security Council (NSC) memo worried: "[The revelations will] increase significantly the political price we will have to pay in Africa, the Third World, and with segments of the American public and Congress."[84]

The NSC was right to be concerned: the mobilized activist network pounced on the issue. George Houser penned the unofficial manifesto of this coalition in an op-ed for the *New York Times* in December that detailed the Vietnam analogy. Entitled "Communism and the War in Angola," it cast the administration's reading of the situation as simplistic, asking why the United States had rallied to the cause of self-determination only when a foreign government was aiding a socialist liberation group. There had been no such intervention—political or otherwise—during the decade of anti-colonial struggle. Houser also highlighted the role of South Africa and its use of Angola as a smokescreen for reaffirming control of neighboring Namibia. As in Southeast Asia, regional competition between socialists and their enemies was pulling the United States into a predicament that had minimal relation to wider geopolitics. "It would be a tragedy for the United States to repeat the errors of Vietnam," Houser concluded, "because it looks upon the Angolan conflict as an occasion for another anti-communist crusade."[85] MPLA officials reinforced these readings by claiming a neutrality that contextualized their alliance with the Soviet Union and Cuba alongside their decade of Western solidarity campaigning. Elísio de Figueiredo, the party's U.N. ambassador, explained: "It is imperative for the American people to know here that throughout the 14 years of our armed struggle against the Portuguese, we appealed to Western nations to give us help, but no country really would give us a grenade to fight against the Portuguese at that time. The socialist countries, and also including Sweden, Denmark, Norway, and various progressive groups around the Western world, helped us."[86] The defense spoke directly to New Left Internationalist frustrations with U.S. policy and fed into legislators' indirect defense of the MPLA. "None of these liberation groups are going to exchange 15 years of fighting against the Portuguese," Clark commented, "only to be taken over as a satellite of the Soviets."[87]

As Clark and the activists raised the heat on the administration, ham-fisted handling of Congress further damaged the prospects for covert operations. Nearly a month after Angola's independence, Ford and Kissinger continued to publicly deny the accusations.[88] A few senators were briefed on the matter, but like Clark, they were told by CIA and State Department officials that no American arms were entering Angola. Clark suspected that the Congress still did not know the whole story. He arranged for secret hearings to ascertain details of the program and allow the administration to present its case. In early December, the Foreign Relations Committee invited CIA Deputy Director Bill Nelson and Deputy Assistant Secretary of State for African Affairs Ed Mulcahy to testify. Arriving after Nelson had spoken, Mulcahy confidently stated that the United States was not supplying arms to any Angolan factions, not realizing that the CIA deputy had revealed the truth to the committee just minutes before. Confronted by the politicians, Mulcahy reversed course, but the damage had been done.[89] Furious with administration attempts to conceal its activities from Congress, the Foreign Relations Committee recommended termination of future funds for Angolan activities and sent the bill to the floor.

A secret Senate session began on December 17 to deliberate on the bill. Seeking to strengthen Clark's push against IA Feature, John Tunney of California upped the ante when he submitted an amendment to the defense bill that prohibited further aid to Angola and reduced the total allocation by $33 million, roughly what Congress believed was spent in Angola. The move was designed to shock; no amendment to a defense bill had left the

Senate unaltered since the start of World War II. Tunney, however, felt the
bill would work.[90] The son of famed pugilist Gene Tunney, the Californian
had championed non-intervention in Angola since 1973, when he attempted
to block aid to imperial Portugal.[91] An old ally of WOA, he felt that congressional outrage and effective lobbying would win the day.[92] "We must reassert
the Constitutional principle that war-making power resides with Congress,"
Tunney told constituents, "Congress is a partner with the President in shaping American foreign policy."[93] In this instance, Tunney sought to use that
power to roll back the military methods that presidents used in the Global
South for decades.

Ford and his congressional allies scrambled to mount a workable defense
but, after months of using secrecy as their primary strategy, were caught flat-
footed. Several administration-inspired amendments flowed into the chamber, aiming to derail the vote or at least give the administration time to work
out a public defense over the Christmas break.[94] None succeeded. The White
House next turned to a group of Republicans, who filibustered the bill on
the 19th. The filibuster aimed to put pressure on the reformers to accept the
compromise offered by Appropriations Committee Chairman John McClellan (D-AR), who offered an additional $9 million to the administration in
exchange for Congressional consultations before additional funding.[95] Tunney, Clark, and their compatriots refused the offer, even as they struggled to
find the 60 votes to force cloture.[96] Seeing the likelihood of eventual defeat,
the White House backed away from stalling tactics, allowing the vote to happen. The maneuver sought to place the full onus of Soviet gains in Angola on
the Senate, which Ford hoped might give undecided voters—and by extension the House—pause. The tactic did not work, and the chamber passed
the Tunney Amendment by what two academics referred to as the "star-
tlingly decisive result" of 54 to 22.[97] With no time for debate in the House, the
defense bill would have to wait until next session.[98] Clark's bill lingered until
after the recess as well, overtaken by Tunney's more sensational defense rider.

The Senate vote was a major victory for the youthful contingent in Congress. Through effective use of the hearing system and assistance from the
activist network, they swayed their colleagues to oppose Ford's intervention.
Reporter Leslie Gelb commented that its passage was not so much a surprise as was the overwhelming number that supported it.[99] While Vietnam
conditioned this vote, Clark and his colleagues sold a framing of events
that reflected the solidarity network's public warnings—and won support
across the political spectrum. Shortly before the vote, Senator Lowell Weicker

(R-CT) lambasted Angola as "a mirror of our entry into Vietnam. . . we are being sucked into a growing involvement through old Cold War rationales . . . [while] ignoring the history of Africa."[100] Even Humphrey rallied around the internationalist flag as the vote forced him to take sides. After nearly a month of seeking to give the White House some leeway, the Minnesota senator fell into the ranks of the skeptics when confronted by the press. "This is exactly what happened in the Vietnam situation," he exclaimed, "involved a little bit at a time . . . without any oversight." Faced with a White House operating behind the backs of both Congress and the American people, he had no option but to vote with the internationalist reformers.[101] While frustration with Kissinger and the executive branch accounted for much Senate support, the policy reflected more ambitious attempts to reshape U.S. approaches toward self-determination and diplomacy in the Global South. Clark cryptically explained after the vote that "many of us have an opposition [to the intervention] on two levels," even if the Tunney and Clark amendments were constructed "not to prejudge whether we ought to be in Angola."[102] This gamesmanship used popular opposition to constrain the executive branch while winning support from moderates in the legislature.

The vote did not signal the end of the legislative battle as the House needed to adopt the Tunney Amendment and the entire Congress had yet to consider Clark's motion. Still, there was clear momentum against the Angolan intervention. The anti-communist alliance remained active but was increasingly on the defensive. In an interview on national television, UNITA's U.S. representative Jeremias Chitunda assured viewers that the party would fight on and still needed U.S. aid. He also denied reporting that South Africa supported his party, but by that point the activists and congressmen opposed to intervention had established a narrative that linked UNITA to the apartheid state, effectively undermining Chitunda's lie before it was stated.[103] With a handful of exceptions in the African American community where support died hard, most who continued to back UNITA would do so while expressing open sympathy for the white minority regimes. This created an easy division to mobilize public opinion against Kissinger's intervention while also reinforcing the emergence of two distinct visions of U.S. foreign policy.

The vote on Angolan interventions has generally appeared in histories as a reaction to the Vietnam War, but this is not the whole story. The lessons of Southeast Asia were far from settled, so aligning the Congress against a relatively minor intervention in Western Africa demanded action. After a decade of organizing, the CONCP-aligned solidarity network was well-positioned to respond. It did so by utilizing alliances it built in the Congress, where a minority of elected officials aligned with key aspects of New Left Internationalism. These legislators did not all rate Angola or the rest of Lusophone Africa as central priorities, but they accepted the necessity of moving past a myopic focus on East–West conflict to redress the economic and political imbalances that drove conflict between Global North and South. This made them especially receptive to the urgings of solidarity activists and their academic allies in the summer of 1975. The result was a congressional campaign to restrain the executive branch, led by the Senate but fed information by the professional lobbying groups and vocally supported by a loose network of grassroots activism. The rapidity of this victory, and the overwhelming support in its favor, was a testament to the decade of organizing that preceded it, honing political messages and the organizations needed to gather information from African liberation groups, direct it to politicians, and mobilize popular pressure. Exactly because the debate over the lessons of Vietnam continued, this victory was far from assured, and in the same way that New Left Internationalist activists campaigned for their preferred foreign policies, so too did their opponents scramble to maintain and expand their visions of containment. As organizers pressed for final passage of the Tunney and Clark Amendments in the first months of 1976, Angola presented its own opportunity to help revive and transform the anti-communist crusade to better fit the era of decolonization.

CHAPTER 10

Cold War Crucible

T he Senate vote on the Tunney Amendment was a political earthquake. It represented the first time the legislature moved to proactively block a Cold War intervention. But its final passage was far from assured because there was no consensus on foreign policy. The reformers sympathetic to New Left Internationalism in the Senate successfully framed the issue with the help of their allies, but they did so by proactively seizing on an issue, weaponizing unique knowledge on the topic, and crafting the powerful Vietnam analogy to convince undecided colleagues to back their play. As proponents of containment and anti-communism recognized the trend, they rallied. This response failed to block the passage of either the Tunney or the Clark Amendments, which both sailed through Congress in the first months of the year. Instead, it laid the groundwork for an extended challenge to the reprioritization of the Cold War and championship of Global South causes that Clark, Diggs, and their allies in and out of government hoped to promote.

Angola galvanized two rival camps that spent the next decade competing over the proper direction of foreign policy. Opposing supporters of New Left Internationalism was an alliance of cold warriors, led by a conservative revival that assembled its own coalition of ideologues, frustrated Democrats, and Cold War moderates. They remained deeply concerned about Soviet aggression, aligning with an anti-communist worldview that saw retreat from Angola as an overreaction to the problems of Vietnam. This coalition cohered around a mission of steeling national resolve against the Soviet Union and the more assertive Global South that challenged the centrality of Western values, expectations, and interests. The result was a powerful backlash against both anti-interventionists in Congress and subsequent attempts by the Ford administration to adopt a more proactive role in southern Africa that might assuage critics on the left. As these two visions for U.S. foreign policy clashed, they mirrored earlier competitions over southern Africa by adopting similar organizing strategies as they sought to politically outflank their opponents, linking Washington decision-makers with political theorists, lobbyists, and grassroots activists who saw Angola as a decisive moment in the global American mission. This competition helped institutionalize forms and networks of political protest developed over the previous decade, especially on the left, as Angola led New Left Internationalists to believe they could achieve their goals, forcing the nascent conservative revival to mobilize against what it believed was a national retreat from America's global mission.

Battling for the Soul of Foreign Policy

In the interim between the Senate and House votes, a different reading of the Angola situation took hold amid conservatives that viewed the lessons of Vietnam much differently from the way New Left Internationalism did. For the conservative wing of the Republican Party, the presence of Soviet arms and Cuban troops in Angola looked nothing like the strategic miscalculation that led to the Southeast Asian quagmire; rather, it was the natural outgrowth of the policy of détente. Hardline anti-communists like the influential columnist William Buckley Jr. had never warmed to Kissinger's grand strategy.[1] They argued that a blind dedication to cooperation allowed the Soviet Union to quietly expand its nuclear arsenal and consolidate power in Eastern Europe. For Americans who viewed communism as an existential threat, reducing the Cold War to diplomatic haggling smacked of appeasement. Now Cold Warriors had evidence of escalating Soviet ambition. The decision to arm the MPLA and—by all accounts—deploy Cuban proxies proved that the USSR had entered into what historian and political commentator Theodore Draper termed at the time "an imperial, expansionist phase" with the ominous goal of establishing "a 'new relationship of forces.'"[2] The novel Cuban presence was among the most difficult issues for critics to dismiss, evidenced on national television in December when the MPLA's U.N. Ambassador Elísio de Figueiredo awkwardly downplayed the subject before admitting that there were troops present alongside Angolan fighters.[3] The Soviet role in transporting these soldiers across the Atlantic reinforced rumors of Soviet ambitions for an African naval base—despite MPLA objections—hinting that Angola represented an escalation of Soviet adventurism that surpassed Vietnam.[4] With the covert operation trending toward failure, conservatives wondered why Kissinger remained reluctant to tie the African conflict to arms limitation talks or other Soviet agreements. Angola therefore offered a visible, highly provocative proof of the decline of U.S. power, which could not even dissuade the Soviets from interfering in a strategic backwater. "The grand results of Kissinger's foreign policy seem to be this," opined the conservative weekly *Human Events* in an analysis of Angola, "the harder the U.S. pursues détente, the tougher the Soviets seem to become."[5]

Here, then, was a Vietnam lesson different from the one adopted by New Left Internationalism. Conservatives lamented strategic blunders that included fighting a limited war in Southeast Asia and pursuing détente, neither of which directly addressed the central problem of Soviet expansion. A small minority of pundits made this argument for years, but the intersection of Angola with the election year of 1976 encouraged the conservative anti-communist wing of the Republican Party to mount an insurrection. The banner was taken up by Ronald Reagan, the charismatic former governor of California. The onetime actor turned corporate spokesperson was even more hostile to communism than he was to taxes, and he aligned with both social conservatives and marginalized Cold Warriors in his search for national office. Citing Angola as proof that Ford was a weak leader, Reagan hammered the president. In January, he launched his bid for the Republican nomination for president with a rousing condemnation of Ford's foreign policy. Echoing conservative tastemakers, Reagan took special aim at détente, arguing that the reduction in tensions only benefited one side, proved the decline of U.S. power, and allowed the Kremlin "to further its aim for world conquest."[6] Angola was prime evidence of U.S. weakness even as it represented a clear opportunity to arrest this slide. "It's time to straighten up and eyeball it with Russia," Reagan said, "and the time to start is in Angola."[7]

Reagan's tough rhetoric touched a chord with a segment of the U.S. public concerned about the decline of U.S. power. Up to this point in the debate on Angola, the right had been unable to defend Ford's aid package from internationalist critics. It had been caught flat-footed by events and struggled to articulate a clear counternarrative. The California governor finally offered an attractive alternative. Asked how he would respond to the Soviet Union, Reagan recommended an "intervention . . . to counter the Russian thrust."[8] Most of the press criticized his vagueness, but conservatives applauded what they believed was Reagan's call for a more assertive policy. Buckley captured the general sentiment when he praised the upstart contender for championing "a simple commitment to preserve a rough equilibrium in this world rather than to let it dribble off piecemeal to the aggressors."[9] This conceptualization of Angola affirmed in many ways the New Left critique of anti-communists, who knew little of Angola beyond its role in regional and (more often) global geopolitics, and who showed minimal interest in learning. For those on the right, such concerns were beside the point. Angolan politics mattered less than the perception that by intervening unopposed the Soviet Union was expanding its reach and proving détente's failure. Primary voters agreed, and Reagan made surprising gains in the polls. From the first primary on January 19—just days before the House vote on Angola—Reagan polled well against the incumbent. As his campaign continued, Reagan used Angola as a symbol for declining American power.[10]

The sense of crisis strengthened conservative resolve and inspired a belief that the Angolan legislation could be halted. The Congress's lower chamber had served as an obstacle to the internationalist agenda of Senate reformers in recent years, and it seemed in January 1976 that it might play spoiler again. When Director of Central Intelligence William Colby discussed the possibility of reprogramming funds toward Angola with the Appropriations Defense Subcommittee in December, he was pleasantly surprised at the mild reactions of its members.[11] As Reagan made Angola a political issue, the administration and its allies used the winter recess to coordinate a positive argument for intervention. Ford quickly made a statement condemning the action in the upper house. Striking directly at the Vietnam comparison, the president protested: "Angola is not, never has been, and never will be" a question of deploying U.S. troops. Instead, it was an attempt to oppose intervention by communist powers that sent soldiers thousands of miles away to support a leftist government. By failing to recognize the severity of the situation and the important role the United States had to play, Ford and Kissinger claimed that the Senate undermined the administration's attempt to maintain the balance of power and the foundations of détente. "This abdication of responsibility," Ford cautioned Congress, "will have the gravest consequences for the long-term position of the United States and for international order in general."[12] Throughout January, Ford attacked Congress and its interference with his foreign policy prerogative. While few representatives were fans of IA Feature, conservatives heard the noise Reagan was making on the campaign trail, and many undecideds feared binding the president's hands.[13] Hill members openly wondered, in the words of moderate Republican senator Jacob Javits of New York, whether the House would be "in any mood to do anything about Angola."[14] Senate Foreign Relations

Chair John Sparkman (D-AL) agreed with Javits, assuring his constituents that the House would strike down the Tunney Amendment.[15]

There was now competition over the meaning of Angola, but the solidarity coalition remained better mobilized and clearer in their messaging. After deferring to Clark and the Senate in the fall, Diggs—with support of Congressional Black Caucus (CBC) members—led the fight in the House. In January, he attended the Organization of African Unity (OAU) meeting in Addis Ababa, Ethiopia, to canvass the continent's leaders. He found only minor support for the U.S. position. A plurality of African states backed the MPLA, with others remaining neutral or undecided. Only seven openly championed the FNLA/UNITA, with four more expressing concern about the role of the Soviet Union's support for the MPLA.[16] Once more Diggs sought to prioritize Global South voices over Cold War concerns. For the congressman, the Angolan intervention boiled down to the inability of Washington officials to "adjust to political and economic realities of the seventies" and Kissinger's "proclivity toward viewing conflicts in terms of exercises in east–west one-upmanship."[17] As Ford and Reagan attempted to reduce the conflict to a simplistic Cold War lens, opponents in Congress pushed back. Tunney sent aide Mark Moran to meet with the high-ranking MPLA officials, reporting that the party desired improved relations with the West and blamed increased bellicosity firmly on the United States. Armed with a secret memo leaked to the MPLA that showed Kissinger's hostility to the party, Tunney accused the United States of escalating the Angolan competition into a superpower conflict.[18] Rather than a sign of Soviet adventurism, opponents argued, the United States was blundering into a regional rivalry in ways that few African states appreciated. Andrew Young openly wondered why administration officials offered barely a word about the troublesome meddling of the South African military within their strident criticism of the Soviet Union and Cuba.[19] The Georgia congressman acidly concluded: "Kissinger doesn't know very much about what goes on below the equator."[20]

Mobilization in the House echoed Clark's framing around the executive-legislative rivalry, but with Diggs and Young adding an additional emphasis on the North-South divide that served as subtext in the Senate. Returning from Addis Ababa with new vigor, Diggs described the U.S. policy on Angola as "the biggest blunder in the history of [American] relations with Africa" and implied that Kissinger should resign over the matter.[21] He distilled his eleven-page report on African attitudes toward the conflict into a "Dear Colleague" letter that urged support for the MPLA even as it prioritized a message of self-determination by calling for a withdrawal of all foreign forces from Angola.[22] More so than the Senate, whose members had larger staffs, House members relied upon activist allies to help make their case. When Congress reconvened in late January, Young welcomed fellow congressmen with an information session featuring ACOA's George Houser, Washington Office on Africa (WOA) director Ted Lockwood, Madison Area Committee on Southern Africa (MACSA) founder Dave Wiley, Ron Walters of the African Liberation Support Committee (ALSC), and Courtland Cox representing the anti-CIA Center for National Security Studies.[23] After a decade of organizing, the members of the activist network had forged the necessary political bonds to give them access to power when it mattered most.

House deliberations coincided with the rallying of popular opinion, which produced an especially strong reaction in the Black community. The inevitability of U.S. intervention after the collapse of the Caetano government in Portugal was a common refrain within Black solidarity organizing over the previous decade and the theme of the second African Liberation Day (ALD). Activists were ready to respond, and they received additional motivation after South Africa intervened in Angola, which created new unity after years of division over the territory. Accepting assistance from the apartheid state made it difficult for UNITA to claim the mantle of Black nationalism, while the MPLA gained credibility for opposing the United States–South Africa alliance. In the words of the *Baltimore Afro-American*, recent events in Angola took Black people "a shade closer to seeing events in Africa for what they are . . . communism unwittingly has been [Africans'] greatest ally rather than our enemy."[24] With apartheid propping up its competition, many African Americans pledged support to the MPLA and demanded an end to U.S. meddling. The sudden surge in Black opinion attracted the attention of Walter Cronkite's national television newscast, which profiled the communal view of Angola in December 1976.[25] Protests targeted the South African embassy and the White House around the New Year's Day holiday. The South African ambassador dismissed the dozens of protesters as a paltry number compared to the displays that accompanied ALD, but they represented a return to the confrontational style of activism that had gone on hiatus after the Carnation Revolution.[26] One group in Harlem even proposed the creation of a "volunteer Lumumba Freedom Fighter Brigade" to help defend the MPLA government from South Africa and the CIA.[27]

An overarching anti-interventionist refrain united the Black community, even if the Angolan divide did not fully disappear. Elísio de Figueiredo's presence as its ambassador at the United Nations finally gave the MPLA a permanent presence in the United States, though it still compared poorly with UNITA's multiple representatives, including its future vice president Jeremias Chitunda. UNITA also retained its share of supporters among the Black community, who blamed news reports for smearing the party by associating it with South Africa. Notable among these supporters was Amiri Baraka's Congress of African People (CAP), whose Maoist leanings added an extra justification for maintaining its alliance, since China backed UNITA in the face of Soviet intervention.[28] These ideological differences prevented CAP from fully aligning with the MPLA-aligned conclusions of the Madison Conference in late 1975, but it still opposed both U.S. and Soviet involvement. This stance allowed it to support a general anti-interventionist message, which both activists and congressional advocates would sometimes present in hopes of winning support from political moderates as wary of Soviet expansion as they were of U.S. adventurism. The few organizations and individuals that openly championed UNITA leader Jonas Savimbi faced a backlash, with withering criticism directed at the Congress of Racial Equality's Roy Innis after he tried to recruit Black veterans to join UNITA.[29] "Due to my activities in support of UNITA, I was labeled a spy for both [the CIA and South Africa]" former ALD organizer Florence Tate recalled. "I became a persona non grata and was denounced, shunned, and blackballed."[30] This hostility led Savimbi to redirect his party's diplomacy toward conservative anti-communists, allowing the Black community to unite behind the anti-interventionist trend that even groups like CAP found appealing.

The vocal African American response was one part of increasingly visible grassroots organizing after the Senate vote. ACOA again led the way. The committee sponsored advertisements in major papers, warning readers: "We are now at the crucial Gulf of Tonkin stage." It urged concerned citizens to organize, demonstrate, and, most important, write to Congress demanding it end military assistance.[31] ACOA also provided a valuable source of information as the press and public, still unfamiliar with Angola, looked to activist organizations for answers. Alongside ACOA's national work, leftist grassroots groups sponsored local informational campaigns that more overtly advocated for the MPLA. In the Midwest, for example, the Chicago Committee for the Liberation of Angola, Mozambique, and Guinea spent the first third of the year speaking, publishing news articles, holding fundraising events for the party, and screening A Luta Continua more than fifty times across 1976 as a way of dramatizing the constructive ideologies of the parties from the Conference of Nationalist Organizations of the Portuguese Colonies (CONCP).[32] Similar activities occurred in the Bay Area, New York, and Boston thanks to the web of solidarity organizers, which brought other groups into the fray. The African Studies Association, the premier academic conference on Africa in North America, voted overwhelmingly for unilateral U.S. withdrawal from Angola, with MACSA's Dave Wiley leading discussion.[33] Adding to these efforts was the immediacy of the Vietnam comparison, which acted as a magnet for groups that supported aspects of Lusophone African solidarity, like the Gulf Oil campaign, and understood them as part of a larger reassessment of U.S. foreign policy. Widely recognized anti-war organizations such as Clergy and Laity Concerned, Americans for Democratic Action, and Women's Strike for Peace conjured memories of the 1960s as they joined the lobbying effort. WOA and allied lobbyists channeled these objections into letter-writing campaigns, and they publicized opinion polls critical of U.S. policy.[34] The result was a flood of constituent mail to Congress that trended strongly against intervention. By the time the House prepared for its vote in late January, polls showed more than 70 percent of Americans opposed involving the nation in internal wars like the one in Angola.[35]

There was also a return to active protests that dramatized popular opposition. Activists began organizing in December, with small demonstrations opening the new year.[36] Local coalitions of religious, civil rights, and anti-war groups drew on old alliances. In one such rally at the end of December, the Fellowship of Reconciliation united with the American Friends Service Committee, representatives of the Catholic Worker movement, the Episcopal Peace Fellowship, and the War Resisters League to picket the U.S. and Soviet missions to the United Nations.[37] Rallies spread across the nation in January, broadcasting popular discontent with the intervention and the surprisingly widespread acceptance of the MPLA. Large solidarity gatherings took place in Chicago, Boston, Philadelphia, and Norfolk, while smaller pickets and marches occurred nationwide—including the WOA-organized rally in Washington that opened the section.[38] In one of the largest demonstrations, more than a thousand people marched through the streets of downtown New York in protest of the government's policy. Activists designed their efforts to simultaneously educate local populations on the issue and demonstrate to legislators how seriously their constituents opposed foreign intervention.[39] The vocal condemnations did not escape the attention of Washington officials. Stunned South African diplomats noted the unprecedented pressure placed on the Ford administration not just by Congress but by "the media, religious organizations and radical activist groups."[40] Conservative advocates for Angola sought to steel anti-communist resolve, but they faced a multilayered, multiracial network of left-leaning activists built by a decade of work in support of the CONCP struggles.

The New Right Coalesces

Popular pressure combined with ongoing lobbying to swing the House firmly behind the Tunney and Clark Amendments by the time Congress reconvened at the end of January.[41] The floor debate represented the last chance for the White House to salvage its policy. Ford warned: passage of the Tunney Amendment "will send a message of irresolution . . . to United States allies and friends throughout the world." He appealed directly to Speaker Carl Albert (D-OK) to oppose the vote and possibly delay it. Nothing worked. Only a handful of conservative Republicans spoke in favor of the intervention.[42] These rare statements paled in comparison to the strong sentiment against Angolan aid. In a last-ditch effort, the FNLA sent two party representatives to Washington to lobby for congressional support, but they made little headway.[43] Critics set the tone and content of the arguments, as almost all statements revolved around the comparisons between southern Africa and Vietnam. The two sides haggled over the accuracy of various aspects of the analogy, but its centrality to the debate demonstrated the victory of the solidarity network's framing of the issue.

Less debatable was where the most vocal constituents stood just months away from going to the polls, at least based on the data available. Legislators returned again and again to the deep unpopularity of the White House's actions, quoting from WOA-produced documents on national opinion.[44] This made supporting administration policy difficult even for those with minimal interest in African affairs or new foreign policies. As Democrat John Burton of California stated, anyone willing to vote fifty million dollars for the Angola adventure "should get ready to draw retirement."[45] Appropriations Committee Chair George Mahon (D-TX) and other cold warriors maintained their opposition to the bill, but they recognized that passage was inevitable. "It is perfectly clear," Mahon said resignedly, "that the sentiment in Congress and in the country is opposed to heavy involvement of the United States in Angola."[46] The U.S. commitment may have been small, but that was beside the point. The twin pressures of the Vietnam framing and the mobilized domestic outrage pushed legislators to overwhelmingly condemn the Ford-Kissinger policy in southern Africa. By a three-to-one majority, the House backed Tunney and forbade the administration's granting of any additional aid to the competing Angolan nationalists. Both chambers passed the Clark Amendment a few days later.

After passage of the Clark Amendment, the administration faced a difficult decision. It would have to request direct assistance to continue its operations. In the weeks following the Senate defeat, this hope had kept the anti-communist coalition in Angola together.[47] Ford's dilemma had few solutions, none of which seemed likely to succeed after the overwhelming vote in the lower house. The president retained the power to veto the legislation and force it back to Congress, request additional military aid for Zaire, or seek public approval of the funds he had promised Mobutu. While the veto seemed an attractive option in a White House that wielded the weapon with aplomb, the move would win few friends among those legislators already angry at the secrecy of the whole project. It was also unlikely to go over well with a hostile public—a dangerous prospect in an election year. The second option, providing additional military aid to Zaire with the implicit understanding it would be sent to Angola, raised legal questions. The administration ultimately concluded that overt assistance would be possible only through new authorizing legislation or an amendment to the Foreign Assistance Act. The most promising proposal included a bill that tied new assistance to the pursuit of a negotiated settlement and a prohibition against the deployment of U.S. personnel. A National Security Council memo predicted it would be a difficult road but believed putting the "hard choice" directly to Congress "[may] bring us unexpected support, especially in the House."[48]

Cold Warriors, especially from the Republican Party's conservative wing, encouraged Ford to take the stand. Some legislators quietly supported the program, believing that Angola demanded a larger U.S. commitment while avoiding the limelight for fear of a public backlash. Others abstained or otherwise avoided taking a firm stand. There existed a possibility that Ford could find support in these corners if he publicly committed himself to opposing the Soviet-Cuban presence.[49] Senator Barry Goldwater (R-AZ) felt this way. He told Ford that the votes existed to pass the funding if only he would submit the request directly to the Senate on its own merits. The problem, according to Goldwater, was not popular opinion or congressional sentiment but that a bunch of "sob sisters on Vietnam" had railroaded the legislation through the Senate before pro-intervention members were able to gather their forces.

Goldwater assured the president in private, "If you veto it . . . I think we could support it . . . we got a lotta votes."[50] Ford had already discarded the veto idea, but Goldwater's encouragement hinted at the possibility of an overt funding package finding a positive reception. Some press outlets estimated that a presidential request for Angolan funds stood at least a fifty-fifty chance.[51]

These assurances rarely factored in the success of the popular effort mobilizing against the intervention. Despite Reagan's insurrection from the right, Ford seemed most worried about popular opposition to further tussling with Congress. Protests continued, with the majority calling for official recognition of the MPLA. In Philadelphia, Black activists who previously supported the Gulf boycott now marched to demand that the oil giant make accommodations with the leftist government in Angola.[52] In California, the former head of the Congress of Racial Equality and Elaine Brown formed the Black Coalition Against U.S. Intervention in Angola, which criticized African Americans working on behalf of UNITA and others opposing MPLA interests.[53] Letters of protest continued to pour into Washington. Many that made it into the White House files came from religious organizations with connections to the anti-imperial and anti-war movements. In one example, the national board president of the YWCA wrote to Ford offering her advice. The letter, which reached National Security Adviser Brent Scowcroft's desk, cautioned the president against "increasing the potential for destruction" through further aid to warring parties, recommending instead a sole focus on diplomatic initiatives.[54] Ford could complain about the decision of Congress, but he realized that the votes represented the most vocal elements of the country. Ignoring these constituents could prove disastrous for his chances of returning to the Oval Office.

By February, the decision to accept Congress's decision was essentially made. The administration doubted that Angola would be worth a second black eye from Congress. Kissinger had been among the first to face facts, pondering defeat during the winter break. "Maybe we should let Angola go," the embattled secretary told Scowcroft. "Maybe we should just not have started that operation." Scowcroft scoffed, "We should not have done what is right[?]" Kissinger answered with seeming resignation, "The defeat [that Clark and Congress] are inflicting on us is worse."[55] Deeply frustrated with Congress and flirting with resignation, Kissinger continued to agitate for Angola only because Ford offered his full support to his secretary of state.[56] Ford insisted on the rightness of the policy, but the January vote forced the president to recognize that the intervention was over. His most forceful reaction was to lash out at Congress for having "lost its guts," effectively turning Angola into an election issue.[57] Observing closely from the sidelines, South Africa's permanent representative at the United Nations articulated what many Americans had already realized: "The administration is powerless to act . . . and the Russians and the Cubans, at least for the foreseeable future, have nothing stronger than words to worry about."[58] In the battle between two views of what was the "right" course of action in Angola, the administration lost to a determined congressional cadre and a vocal popular minority. Ford continued to see Angola as a Cold War crisis and threatened action, but he admitted behind closed doors that he would not submit a bill. The defeat in Washington sapped the will of the Angolan anti-communists, who were already on the defensive. By the end of March, South Africa withdrew its final troops. The MPLA consolidated its power across much of Angola, though UNITA continued its guerrilla struggle in the south.

Ford's acceptance of his defeat only steeled the resolve of conservatives who saw Angola as a worthy anti-communist cause. The problem for advocates of a more aggressive foreign policy toward the Soviet Union was not necessarily that Vietnam had sapped the U.S. will to act forcefully abroad. Rather, politicians were either unwilling or unable to confront the internationalists that had overtaken Congress and popular opinion. What was needed was a determined and charismatic politician who could rally those fearful of U.S. decline and convince others that this phenomenon was real. In 1976, Ronald Reagan offered the solution. As Buckley observed in yet another rumination on Angola, "If the President and his secretary of state cannot bring the people to understand why it is necessary to exert ourselves in order to survive, then Reagan must labor to do so."[59] Reagan's national campaign during this first serious Cold War defeat after Vietnam allowed him to become the figurehead of a new pro-defense movement that galvanized around Angola. Secretary of Defense Donald Rumsfeld predicted that there would be a catharsis after the effects of the Clark Amendment were understood, releasing the Vietnam guilt and inspiring a new concern about Soviet expansion: "You'll see the mood in this country shift; you'll see people become concerned about defense."[60]

And shift it did. As Reagan attacked Ford and Kissinger for making "preemptive concessions" to Russian concerns, several pundits and politicians weighed in on the future of U.S. power.[61] Buckley revisited familiar ground when he begged the question that if the United States could not even provide arms and moral support to those fighting the MPLA, would the U.S. response be any different when Soviet aggression involved "Formosa? Yugoslavia?

Turkey? Israel?"[62] The rhetorical question captured a renewed commitment to containment that focused on drawing a line in the sand protecting the West's extended outposts, rather than dithering about the postcolonial ambitions of the Global South. Such attitudes were becoming popular on the right, but the implications of the vote were equally worrying to many political moderates, the ones who had to be convinced by their colleagues and activists to end the intervention. Lee Hamilton (D-IN), a member of the House Foreign Relations Committee, worried that Angola might enter history as the latest in a series of "well-meaning congressional initiatives" that had unintended consequences for U.S. interests.[63] Emboldened defense advocates began pushing a more active agenda, winning a surprising victory in March. After five years of slashing budgets, the House Armed Services Committee abruptly reversed course and recommended that spending be raised above White House requests. The press concluded that the new attitude on the Hill was a response to campaign rhetoric and the fact that "Angola lent credence to Pentagon arguments that the Kremlin was indeed in an aggressive, troublemaking phase."[64] Angola revived a popular anti-communism even as it handed the internationalists what was arguably their greatest victory after Vietnam.

These dissonant trends placed the administration in a difficult position, particularly in Africa, as it tried to recover from the Angolan debacle. Speaking to New Left Internationalist priorities, Diggs argued that the "blunder of the U.S. posture in Angola dramatizes the need for a total reassessment of U.S. policy toward Africa."[65] Surprisingly, the administration agreed, as events showed the costly side effects of continued collaboration with the white minority regimes. To burnish its tarnished image, the Ford administration adopted a new approach to southern Africa, beginning with a slight relaxation of its opposition to the MPLA. The secretary allowed the sale of a Boeing 737 to the government and did not protest when Gulf Oil made plans to resume its operations with payments going to Luanda. Still, the White House refused to normalize relations and opposed MPLA requests to join certain international agencies.[66] More dramatically, the fiasco convinced Kissinger to abandon the U.S. tradition of quietly backing the minority regimes in favor of more direct involvement in negotiations favoring majority rule. Beginning in February, the secretary expressed interest in Rhodesia/Zimbabwe and eventually applied his famous shuttle diplomacy to the problem of self-determination in the minority state. The sudden about-face in policy united the administration with many of its most vocal critics, including the activist network, Clark, Tunney, and the CBC.[67] The legislators

Figure 13. Senator Dick Clark (center) and staff meet with Prime Minister Lopo do Nascimento of the MPLA in Angola, November 1976. Clark continued to push for active engagement with southern African issues after blocking President Ford's intervention. Dick Clark Papers, University of Iowa Special Collections.

retained a healthy skepticism of Kissinger's intentions, but they believed the politics that necessitated the shift signaled—according to Andrew Young—"a new era of at least minimal recognition of the importance of the Third World in U.S. policy."[68] These strange bedfellows would have been nearly impossible to imagine just a few months before, but Angola pushed the United States to rethink matters of self-determination and human rights in its dealings with southern Africa.

In doing so, the policy shift encouraged new attacks by its conservative and Cold War critics. Driving this wave of animosity was the serious overlap between those who favored Angolan intervention and those who had mobilized over the previous decade in support of the White Redoubt. Reagan tapped into this well of support; he expanded his defense of the Angolan intervention to encompass both Rhodesia and South Africa, citing the minority governments as valuable anti-communist allies in an increasingly hostile region. Lumping Angolan anti-communists—nominally UNITA—with the minority regimes softened the racial edge of the appeal while still satisfying those who supported the countries' defense of white rule. Reagan's conservative program was undoubtedly at the heart of his national appeal, but the unusually prominent role of Africa in his campaign rhetoric was noteworthy, especially in the American South. When Reagan won an overwhelming victory in the Texas primaries over Ford, the media partially credited his positions on Rhodesia and South Africa.[69] This was the first in a series of primary victories that saw Reagan mount a strong if ultimately unsuccessful challenge to the sitting president. The former governor tapped into a deep anxiety that existed on the right about the direction not only of the country but also of its foreign policy. As the *Wall Street Journal* opined, "[Ford] has seemed to give ground without a fight, to Congress, to the Soviets, to the Third World, when a firmer hand could have meant the holding of ground without a fight. Mr. Reagan has identified those weak points and is striking a responsive chord with voters."[70] Such arguments fit neatly with historian Sean Byrnes's assertion that resistance to the assertiveness of the Global South, and their allies in the United States, helped shape the "New Right."[71] Frustration with détente and what conservatives perceived as anti-American trends within the Global South drove the more assertive vision of foreign policy that Reagan personified after Vietnam, and they intersected powerfully in the struggle over intervention in Angola.

Adding to the momentum of the New Right were the first inklings of a major reorientation of political coalitions: the transformation of onetime liberals into neoconservatives. Journalists and historians have captured the central role the Cold War played in convincing these internationally minded intellectuals to rethink their party allegiances and policy positions, but there has been less appreciation that changing approaches to the Global South accelerated this transition.[72] While many of these former liberals accepted the necessity of decolonization in the 1960s, they did so with the understanding that the United States would attempt to preserve its influence and guarantee the transfer of power to governments acceptable to the West. This had motivated Kennedy-era policy, much to the frustration of nationalists and their U.S. allies. Indeed, the New Left Internationalist emphasis on self-determination hoped to weaken the all-important second part of that liberal anti-communist formulation of decolonization. As a result, many stalwart liberals saw southern African policy in 1976 as a testament to a post-Vietnam meekness that heralded a national crisis of leadership, what Ernest Lefever termed "an American confusion." A one-time Christian pacifist who consulted with Hubert Humphrey and the National Council of Churches (NCC) on foreign affairs, Lefever balked at the drift from policies of containment, arguing inaction in Angola was the result of "a creeping policy paralysis induced by breast-beating on Capitol Hill and in the media."[73] The budding neoconservative editor of *Commentary* magazine, Norman Podhoretz, went one step further in accusing the internationalist segment of Congress who had opposed Vietnam, investigated the CIA, and blocked Angola of being "new isolationists" dismissive of American liberty.[74] This seeming abandonment of traditional approaches to international affairs, and the Global South in particular, aligned this alienated segment of political establishment with the assertive foreign policy advocated by Reagan.

Reinforcing this shift were allies who clung tenaciously to traditional ways of viewing the global Cold War. Unsurprisingly, South Africa expressed discomfort with the new drift in U.S. foreign affairs, blaming the domestic reaction around Angola to an "almost total American ignorance about South Africa." The government-aligned media urged an aggressive push to reframe debates in the United States around the same issues that had justified relations since 1961: avoiding "racial conflagration in Africa," blocking communist expansion, and safeguarding strategic resources and trade routes.[75] The problem was that too many in the United States had lost sight of the real threat to global peace after years of détente. South African observers criticized legislators like Dick Clark for their tendency to see regional events "as a North-South conflict" rather than part of the Cold War.[76] While such attitudes were unsurprising from South Africa, U.S. allies in Europe and Asia also expressed concerns about what one termed a "constitutional crisis" that threatened to weaken the Western ability to respond to potential threats.[77] In the speech that earned her the sobriquet "the Iron Lady," British opposition leader Margaret Thatcher echoed U.S. conservatives in decrying the "dangers of falling for an illusory détente" that had not "dissuaded [the Soviets] from brazen intervention in Angola."[78] Allies from across the globe warned of falling dominoes and the damage this could do to American and Western interests, recalling a constant—and seemingly inaccurate—fear regularly cited by U.S. officials during the Vietnam era that manifested anew around Angola.

The challenge to traditional Cold War thinking presented by New Left Internationalism and its adherents seemed like a dangerous overcorrection for those who still understood communism as the greatest threat to the international system. Former Kennedy-era officials like Dean Rusk were among those who expressed support for the Angola intervention.[79] While Vietnam offered lessons about the problem of deploying troops and even making commitments to unpopular regimes, the measured attempt by the Ford administration to contain—or at least raise the costs—of Soviet involvement in Africa seemed worthwhile. Rusk joined other moderate Democratic politicians like Lee Hamilton and Gale McGee in pushing back on the attempts to decentralize Cold War concerns. This effort led directly to the formation of the Committee for the Present Danger in late 1976, which hinted at the new coalition developing behind anti-communist foreign policies. It featured a collection of prominent policymakers and public intellectuals associated with both major parties who called for the reaffirmation and expansion of U.S. leadership in the face of Moscow's expanded influence in the Global South. Among its members were former Kennedy officials like Rusk, Eugene Rostow, and George C. McGhee, neoconservative foreign policy analysts like Lefever, Podhoretz, and Jeane J. Kirkpatrick, and Nixon cabinet members William J. Casey and George Shultz. Democratic signatories like Rusk and Kirkpatrick had voiced support for African liberation in the past, but they did so for preemptive anti-communism reasons that hoped to avoid the radicalization and revolution embodied by the MPLA. Now that elected Democrats were leading the charge to recognize such a government, they joined their political opponents in defense of containment as they wrung their hands about the end of the Cold War consensus.[80] Referencing the threatening direction of events in the Middle East and Africa, the committee in its first broadside expressed the need to "restore our will, our strength and our self-confidence" in order to "find resources and friends enough to counter that threat."[81]

Though the Committee on the Present Danger only implicitly referred to Angola in its short statement, the country's influence was clear. It was the most glaring example of a self-inflicted post-Vietnam defeat but also provided cold warriors with the ability to reorient U.S. rhetoric around Southern interventions toward more laudable goals. Barbara Keys has noted that anti-communists integrated human rights ideas into their rhetoric as a way of reclaiming American virtue, but cold warriors also co-opted the language of anti-imperialism as they reasserted U.S. power.[82] By attacking communist imperialism, with Angola as the poster child thanks to the involvement of Cuban troops, conservatives claimed the mantle of protecting both human rights and self-determination. This also allowed a conglomeration of political supporters of decolonization including liberals, Black nationalists, and even some leftists to drift toward the foreign policy of the New Right as part of this reorientation of political coalitions. Among the most stunning converts was the

THE WORLD OF KEITH WAITE

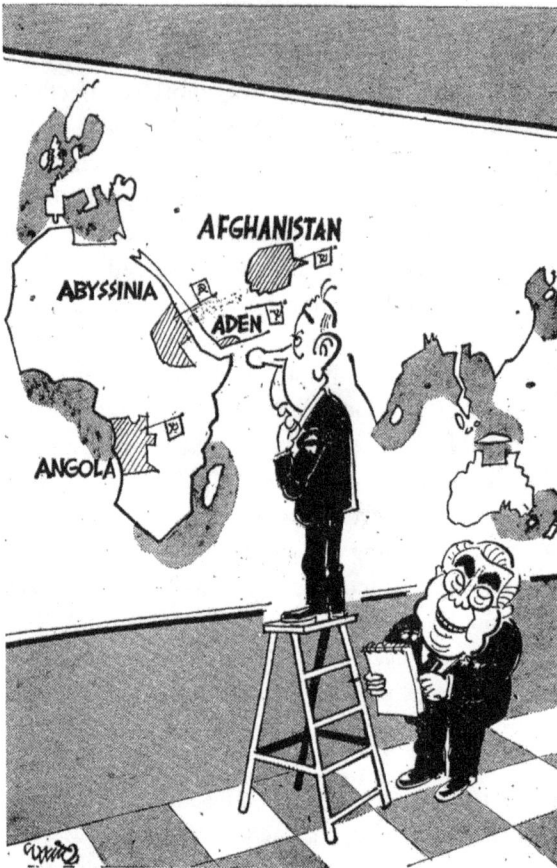

"Any more A's before we start on the B's?"

Figure 14. Keith Waite, "Any more A's before we start on the B's?" *Daily Mirror*, January 21, 1980. Angola signaled a new stage in the Cold War in which Cuba and the Soviet Union actively deployed military units in the Global South, notably in Ethiopia (Abyssinia) and Afghanistan. Conservatives in both Europe and North America worried about this new ability to project communist power and looked to local movements like UNITA to raise the costs of perceived expansion. Reprinted with permission of Waite family, British Cartoon Archive, University of Kent.

socialist civil rights leader Bayard Rustin, who argued in 1977 that the Angola situation was comparable to the Munich Compromise of 1938. He believed that the MPLA victory showed the "impotence of the democratic world" in the face of "the new imperialist threat in Africa."[83] Attacking the thesis that leftist liberation groups like the MPLA were authentic representatives of national majorities, Rustin argued that Soviet rule was worse than colonialism, and leftist revolution more threatening than apartheid. He urged the U.S. government to recognize the "warning signal" provided by Angola.[84] In this formulation of policy, insurgent groups like UNITA represented a new generation of freedom fighters resisting Soviet domination, and they deserved aid.

In addition to borrowing rhetoric from solidarity campaigners, the New Right echoed the decentralized, issue-oriented grassroots organizing, building on concepts explored during lobbying for Rhodesia in the 1960s. Conservative-oriented think tanks and lobbying groups arose in the years immediately preceding Angola to counter both the proliferation of New Left groups and the drift of mainstream institutions, such as ACOA and the NCC. These included the Americans for Freedom (1969), the Heritage Foundation (1973), and Lefever's Ethics and Foreign Policy Center (1976). Lefever, a longtime Africa watcher disillusioned with Western policy, proved especially aggressive. His publications through the Ethics and Public Policy Center sought to create a distinct counter-morality to the left-leaning ethos that aligned with Southern revolution, expanding early criticisms of the United Nations into an extended attack on World Council of Churches activities in the Third World.[85] A distinctly anti-communist worldview justified a critical reading of global rights that positioned the Soviet Union and communist system as the primary violators of human dignity.[86] This logic opened up critics of the Cold War to attacks as either naive or Soviet tools for undermining the West, reinforcing political divides and creating opposing infrastructures of foreign affairs analysis. When one Senate subcommittee invited the NCC to testify in support of the New International Economic Order favoring the Global South, it elicited a blistering protest from conservative senator John Sparkman, whose partisan reading of the body's history left no doubt it was deeply influenced by communists.[87] While such attacks were not new, the polarized views of organizations like the NCC illustrated an increasingly stark divergence in the informational structures that informed New Left and New Right activities in Congress. By 1978, Lefever was advising senators visiting South Africa on whom to contact to gain an accurate picture of Cold War conditions in the region, which he felt was underrepresented by official contacts after the shift in U.S. policy.[88] Both sides sought to increase congressional independence from executive foreign policy, but they did so by tapping into distinct transnational networks that reinforced divergent worldviews, especially regarding the Global South.

Nowhere was this reality more apparent than in Angola. With New Left legislators rallying behind the MPLA, rival UNITA found a new source of support as an anti-Soviet alternative. Within months of the Clark Amendment's passage, New Right organizations targeted the law as they urged a more aggressive foreign policy through support of nominally anti-communist leaders like Savimbi.[89] The Angolan guerrilla leader recognized the opportunity and needled the United States in ways that drew conservative admiration. "In the face of the total abdication of the United States to resist the expansionist onslaughts of Russia, as a consequence of the defeat that America suffered in Vietnam," Savimbi lamented in 1978, "Western countries prefer to go along with Russo-Cuban imperialism against our people."[90] Cold Warriors relied on existing grassroots networks—whose influence expanded as politicians like Reagan moved to the forefront of the conservative movement—to voice their concerns about the direction of policy. Before the end of 1976, membership groups like the American Legion called for more aggressive, anti-communist policies in Angola that implied closer alignment with groups like UNITA.[91] Pundits and publications that supported the White Redoubt for primarily Cold War reasons now found in Savimbi a way to champion a Black revolutionary in opposition to communist ideals, all while remaining aligned with South Africa. By 1978, the Heritage Foundation, an influential think tank on the right, identified Angola as "a singular opportunity" because the popularity of the party in UNITA-held territory allowed Westerners "to support a 'people's liberation army' against a repressive regime."[92] The Angolan intervention failed in 1976, but it revitalized the old commitment to Cold War containment while updating the rhetoric and self-conception of anti-communism for a postcolonial era.

Institutionalizing New Left Internationalism

This backlash meant that there would be no new foreign policy consensus as Andrew Young and others on the left had hoped for. Rather, there would be competing visions of how the United States should operate in the world that jockeyed for power and influence over the next decade. For while it did not become dominant, New Left Internationalism had made gains, as evidenced by the decisive congressional intervention in the Angolan crisis of 1976. It proved that a popular internationalism could confront the heretofore dominant Cold War tendencies of the government—and win. This was not just a reaction to imperial hubris in Vietnam or an objection to the successful coup in Chile but a proactive political opposition to Third World intervention writ large. It was possible for activists to challenge the politics of superpower competition, even if these activists and their policymaking allies could not

decisively prioritize addressing the North-South divide. With new governments like the MPLA making claims to legitimacy across the strict divisions
of the Cold War, supporters in the United States worked to organize and formalize linkages to influence policy in a sustained way, even in the face of
brewing opposition.

The outline of this network was apparent in efforts to recognize the MPLA.
In February 1976, the party arranged for a support meeting in Havana, where
it gathered nineteen organizations sympathetic to its cause from the United
States, including ACOA, WOA, the Chicago Committee for the Liberation of
Angola, Mozambique, and Guinea (CCLAMG), the American Friends Service Committee, the Coalition for a New Foreign Policy, the National Council
of Churches, and the National Conference of Black Lawyers.[93] These groups
represented the pinnacle of the solidarity movement assembled over the prior
decade, drawing from youth-activist, religious, and African American constituencies. For five days, three MPLA representatives fielded questions from
the groups and laid out the goals of their newly established government in
the familiar CONCP areas of agriculture, health, and education. The government would pursue a nonaligned policy, which provided room for American cooperation even as it depended on Cuban and Soviet assistance and
began installing a communist domestic system.[94] The party understood that
it would continue to face resistance within the United States and some other
Western nations, so it urged its allies to champion its cause as it focused on
the development of the nation. The MPLA specifically requested assistance
with promoting its image in America, nation-building support in the form
of medical aid programs, the arrangement of functionary visits to the United
States, and—most important of all—political lobbying for official recognition
of the MPLA government.[95] Upon their return, these solidarity organizations
became the popular voice for the MPLA and pushed for legislation acknowl-
edging the party's legitimacy.[96]

Working closely with these groups were valuable allies on Capitol Hill.
While no elected representatives attended the Cuba meeting, for obvious
political reasons, the same individuals who had stopped the intervention
became the MPLA's champions within the U.S. government. Clark, Diggs, and
Young took the lead, with Clark arguing that "the only real option in Angola"
was dialogue with the MPLA, since it was the "strongest faction" and shared—
according to the senator—the goals of a peaceful and nonaligned Angola.[97]
The three deferred to prominent African leaders who largely accepted the
continued Cuban presence as insurance against South Africa (and the United

States), urging recognition as a first step in reducing tensions.[98] And when they advocated for specific policies regarding Angola and wider regional issues, they did so in direct collaboration with activist groups like ACOA and WOA.[99] Young lamented that the events of 1976 were "so haunting to our national psyche" that they prevented recognition—thanks in part to the conservative backlash—but this minority of activist legislators continuously pressed for a reevaluation of priorities in Africa.[100]

Politically, the defeat of IA Feature encouraged the emerging internationalist coalition that questioned the traditional tenets of the Cold War. In their statement on U.S. policy drafted in April, the Black Caucus revealed the impact of the popular-congressional struggle over the former colony:

> The U.S. debacle in Angola exposed the bankruptcy of U.S. policy toward Africa—a policy permeated with racism and conceived as a by-product of U.S. relations with its European allies and as a minor addendum to U.S. Soviet policy. . . . The African momentum toward liberation in southern Africa from minority rule and full liberation in Black Africa from the shackles of neo-colonialism leaves the United States no choice [but to adjust U.S. policy]. Past and present policy for supporting white rule in Africa has placed the United States in an untenable position. Internationally, the United States can only lose if it fails to get on the side of freedom in Africa. Domestically, such a policy cannot be sustained.[101]

Southern Africa became in 1976 *the* cause for the new internationalism supported by legislators, liberals, and grassroots activists. Renewed congressional attention to the region, including efforts to overturn the pro-Rhodesian Byrd Amendment and to confront apartheid, drew on the same core of activists, lobbyists, and legislators that opposed Angola, along with the broader coalitions they helped mobilize.[102] "Many persons who worked hard during the Vietnam era are now seeing Southern Africa as the, or at least, one of the, major areas of concern . . . for challenge to growing American militarism, economic dominance, support of illegitimate, minority, racist governments," one CCLAMG member explained to the American Friends Service Committee. "There are issues of self-determination, human rights, arms sales, New International Economic Order, etc. all wrapped in one."[103] There was hope this popular and political attention to southern Africa could begin the process of addressing the lingering inequalities hindering North-South relationships.[104]

The timing of these initiatives is vital for understanding the impact of the Portuguese African solidarity movement. Historians looking at American policy in southern Africa have long seen the Soweto uprisings that began in mid-June 1976 as a pivotal moment that helped inspire widespread resistance to apartheid, but Angola galvanized existing networks and heralded the emergence of a new, more critical voice on U.S. involvement in Africa and the wider developing world. During a moment of political reorientation, it provided momentum for a segment of American society to push policies respecting sincere self-determination, based less on style of governance than perceived popular will. As one WOA staff member noted at the time with reference to U.S. policy, "After Angola, the [liberation of South Africa] entered a new phase w[ith] new possibilities."[105] At the grassroots level, organizations refocused their work on the minority regimes and expanded their campaigns on behalf of liberation movements. As the American Friends Service Committee reflected days before Soweto, activists had to seize the opportunity to reach new audiences after Angola forced southern Africa "into a spotlight for American attention" and revealed the extent to which "church, academic, black, and peace activists" were already organizing.[106] As a result, Americans were primed to adopt the anti-apartheid cause with new vigor when popular protests in South Africa elicited a violent state response.

Of equal importance is that this U.S. activist movement involved widespread support for liberation parties, not simply opposition to apartheid or minority rule. Indeed, the fact that so many organizations gathered in the capital of communist Cuba to directly collaborate with the MPLA—albeit now a sitting government—represented a sea change in attitudes from just a few years before. Even pacifist groups like the Quaker American Friends Service Committee accepted the necessity and legitimacy of armed liberation struggles and the parties that sponsored them, though direct aid continued to focus on the nation-building aspects of their programs.[107] And this support was not limited to activists, as politicians made their New Left Internationalist sympathies clear. Tunney, who continued to rely on Cold War rhetoric in the election year of 1976, nonetheless concluded: "The vote of Congress signals . . . to Africa that we understand and empathize with their drive for freedom and independence and will not automatically interpose ourselves in the way of African liberation."[108] This widespread acceptance of the legitimacy of liberation struggles was a direct outgrowth of the work done by the CONCP parties, which activists and politicians extended to other southern African movements. When politicians like Diggs and Clark traveled to Africa, they sought meetings with activist Steve Biko and the imprisoned Nelson Mandela alongside consultations with government officials in South Africa.[109] While conservative proponents of Rhodesia likened Prime Minister Ian Smith to George Washington, Clark and others argued that it was the Zimbabwean nationalists who were fighting a "struggle for freedom and independence, just as we did 200 years ago."[110] Such sentiments stirred controversy at home and abroad, but they spoke to the extent to which U.S. politicians joined activists in embracing the cause of African liberation.

What helped politicians move in these new directions was the support they received from grassroots and nongovernmental organizations, which aided and encouraged their policy initiatives. Lobbying organizations like WOA and ACOA generated information that not only helped motivated politicians understand issues outside the sanitized perspective offered by foreign governments but also helped frame issues in ways that could sway undecided officials and legislators. At the same time, grassroots demonstrations convinced political fence-sitters that voters cared about distant problems. "An effective Africa policy . . . requires a broad political base of support at home," Clark told a student audience in 1978. "Members of Congress and the President must face the public in elections. It takes more than courage. We need support. Only with an informed public and an informed Congress can we get that support."[111] The solidarity organizing that sustained and normalized the liberation struggles now influenced policy and integrated elements of their revolutionary agendas into national debates. Diggs hinted at the power of the grassroots-congressional nexus in a strident speech at the 1976 African American political convention, asserting: "We cannot guarantee domestic tranquility should the administration decide to aid directly or indirectly, overtly or covertly any of the incumbent minority regimes in Southern Rhodesia or South Africa."[112] Diggs essentially articulated what the proceeding years had shown: that there existed a constituency attentive to issues of African freedom that legislators could mobilize as they sought to challenge executive policy.

That this movement was diverse, decentralized, and at times chaotic became an accepted part of the post-Vietnam reality in U.S. foreign affairs, though there were attempts to expand networks, coordinate work, and formalize connections. Organizations like the Ad-Hoc Coalition for a New Foreign Policy (CNFP, after the Ad-Hoc was dropped) grew from Vietnam activism but rallied against IA Feature, redirecting some of the energy from the anti-war movement. The CNFP evolved from the Coalition to Stop Funding the War, pivoting to broader foreign policy issues after 1973. It shared

WOA's vision of multilevel Washington activism, with director Brewster Rhoads describing it as an interlocutor that could help "rationalize and focus the grassroots for lobbying work . . . in a way that has an impact on policy."[113] Located next door to WOA's office in the Washington Methodist Building, the CNFP also used church donations (and facilities) to operate, becoming enmeshed in the professional and social networks that supported New Left Internationalism, of which WOA was a core component. As a result, it adopted southern Africa as a central organizing priority and later became active resisting Cold War interventions in Latin America.[114]

Another noteworthy institutionalization of ad hoc political structures was TransAfrica. A descendant of the Black Convention Movement, the lobbying group gained traction after OAU meetings regarding Angola led Diggs to propose that the CBC and Black community leadership "form the nucleus of a lobby of Blacks and their supporters for Africa" with the goal of making Africa "a factor in U.S. domestic politics."[115] Given the strong interest in the continent that remained from the ALD and other initiatives, such an organization would encourage better African policies and act as a test case for organizing behind other issues important to the Black community.[116] While cognizant that African Americans had limited routes to shape policy directly, the organizers were confident because the new organization would draw on existing linkages to "grass roots organizations and institutions that ha[d] extensive communication networks."[117] As TransAfrica formed in 1977, the group tapped Diggs staffer Randall Robinson as its first director, taking advantage of his legal training, wide-ranging connections, and experience in the Gulf boycott. Though it would work regularly with ACOA, WOA, and other organizations on issues ranging from MPLA recognition to apartheid protests, it maintained a Black leadership that could champion Black priorities and speak directly to African American audiences.[118] Drawing on lessons from earlier solidarity campaigns, TransAfrica's strength came in its ability to voice the concerns of a specific community while existing within a collaborative network that championed overlapping goals. As conservatives and traditional cold warriors established their own set of ideals and organizations, advocates of New Left Internationalism formalized once ad hoc efforts to press their collective vision of U.S. foreign affairs.

Angola was a pivotal moment in the history of U.S. foreign affairs toward the developing world. It helped institutionalize and disseminate a New Left Internationalist critique of U.S. interventionism. In contrast to the case with Vietnam and Chile, an assertive activist network had helped Congress proactively constrain executive power. It articulated how Angola offered a clear analogy to Indochina that militated against covert operations and embraced a more cooperative approach to Global South matters. At the same time, it bred a sincere distress among Americans still dedicated to fighting the Cold War, fellow citizens who felt that the Southeast Asian hangover had to be ended in the bush around Luanda. "The Angola debate suggests there is no consensus on foreign policy," the *Boston Globe*'s Crocker Snow Jr. lamented, "and very little trust."[119] The observation captured the reality of U.S. policy disputes in the wake of the collapse of the once dominant Cold War paradigm in the face of successful challenges by a revolutionary Global South. Rather than signaling a new consensus, Angola helped institutionalize competing transnational worldviews that adopted similar, multilevel political organizing as a direct response to the grassroots challenges to dominant paradigms created by the 1960s.

If there was anything resembling a consensus, it was the extent to which a more popular democracy now shaped foreign affairs, even in areas of marginal national interest like Africa. This directly reflected the effects of decolonization's challenge to traditions of Western superiority and the related rejection of status quo politics by radical youth in the 1960s. As historian Van Gosse argues, Vietnam created a political earthquake opposed to the basic tenets of the Cold War and launched a new era of grassroots engagement with the government. The multitiered activism that emerged not only around Indochina but also around the revolutions in Portuguese Africa did not disappear—not after the fall of Saigon nor that of the Lisbon regime; "rather," in Gosse's words, "it melded into the fabric of our political institutions and habits, and by doing so, changed them profoundly."[120] The institutionalization of this decentralized movement relied on the efforts of activists, lobbyists, and legislators working together to address ongoing problems of American policy, notably in the region of southern Africa.

The leftist-centrist coalition that formed around Lusophone liberation and concrete activities such as the Gulf boycott demonstrated its longevity with Angola in 1976, while also spurring the creation of a similarly powerful grassroots Cold War reaction. This latter movement was led by conservative cold warriors like Ronald Reagan, but it adapted and extended the logic of great-power competition in the Global South that motivated administrations from Kennedy to Nixon. While Julian Zelizer is correct that Angola "fueled conservative demands for tougher anticommunist policies," it was more than an unanticipated legacy of the Vietnam War amidst the rise of the

New Right.[121] Rather, it established the rules and coalitions in a competition between this resurgent right and the institutionalized elements of a New Left for influence, even control of foreign policy. This domestic conflict over ideas, values, and the proper form of international affairs reflected the intersection of the East–West conflict over competing ideologies of modernization and the North–South struggle to achieve equality for states long colonized by these same Euro-American empires. Given their distinct meanings within these competing worldviews, the former Portuguese colonies of Angola and Mozambique remained at the heart of this transnational ideological debate until the end of the superpower conflict.

Conclusion

The contested U.S. response to Angolan independence ushered in a new era of competition between right and left over issues of foreign policy, but the long history of solidarity organizing reveals that the events of 1975 were more than an example of the Vietnam syndrome amid the rise of the New Right.[1] A New Left Internationalist ethos cohered behind specific issues like Global South self-determination, mobilizing a coalition of interrelated groups and politicians behind new policies. This provided the foundations for the "anti-colonial, pro-human rights environment of American politics" that hamstrung Ford, in historian Thomas Borstelmann's words, even if it did not achieve a new status quo.[2] These facts challenge a historiography of the 1970s focused on the conservative revival without discounting that major trend.[3] Rather, the construction of competing ideological camps reflect what Daniel Rodgers describes as an "age of fracture" beginning in the 1970s, in which the search for a common American identity and singular normative society broke down as faith in common institutions like government and mainline religion faltered, and citizens embraced individual, sometimes conflicting identities.[4] Rodgers's astute reading of late twentieth-century history captures the decline of consensus politics, but, like Petra Goedde, he downplays the extent to which the diversification—even decolonization—of the U.S. experience demanded new coalitions that united distinct political communities behind common goals.[5] Myriad studies on the New Right explain how a conservative coalition formed around a small government ethos at home and a muscular confrontation with the Soviet Union abroad, but there has been less appreciation of similar dynamics on the left. Solidarity with the parties of the Conference of Nationalist Organizations of the Portuguese Colonies (CONCP) represented a small but important corner of such organizing. It hints at the nature, achievements, and challenges of the

New Left Internationalist ideas that emerged from this period, while defining a major theater in which contrasting visions of U.S. foreign policy competed.

Defining New Left Internationalism

The history of Lusophone solidarity attests to the existence of a movement for a new U.S. foreign policy meant to replace the reaction, interventionism, and Eurocentrism common to the post-1945 period. Both at the time and since, it has been difficult to classify this movement thanks to its coalitional nature and diverse ideological membership, but the New Left Internationalist umbrella helps explain its core ideas. Early efforts to formalize this intellectual shift occurred within church leadership structures and at the political margins in the formation of organizations like the Institute for Policy Studies, a kind of Brookings Institution for reimagining foreign policy along "radical liberal" lines, which once employed Washington Office on Africa director Ted Lockwood.[6] Such ideas were at the core of New Left Internationalism, but the movement went beyond simply calling for progressive foreign policy outcomes, demanding a reformulation of the very process through which policies themselves were created.

Specifically, New Left Internationalism emphasized participatory democracy, in which actors beyond the executive branch could and should shape decisions in collaboration with Southern populations affected by U.S. actions. Activists built transnational connections that allowed them to develop independent visions of the world and used methods ranging from peaceful public protests and grassroots education to divestment and lobbying to promote their views. At the same time, sympathetic legislators recognized activist networks as useful partners in conceptualizing and promoting policies that broke with the executive branch and the Cold War mindset entrenched in Washington. The result was an ambitious, multilevel concept of foreign policymaking that emphasized multilateral diplomacy, social justice, universal rights, and a sensitivity to Southern priorities. Popular anti-Vietnam protests encompassed many of these ideas and added momentum to African liberation organizing, but African issues earned sustained attention and plumbed deeper ideological depths. While scholars have seen international legacies of 1960s political organizing in later decades, they have had trouble concretely connecting the institutional and intellectual strands because they have looked past movements like the one that formed around southern Africa, which internalized

New Left ideas while building popular support for them.[7] The myriad organizations that championed Lusophone liberation pioneered a lasting, patient,
though admittedly precarious model of organizing that reflected the fractured landscape of post-1960s politics and addressed an increasingly complex
global environment.

This maturation of New Left Internationalism owed a debt to the uniquely
appealing struggles waged by the CONCP parties. While fighting against
archetypal colonialism, they championed a tricontinental anti-imperialism that
encompassed critiques of existing racial, geographic, economic, and even gender relations. These ambitious visions of self-determination stretched beyond
their borders to inspire subjugated populations and marginalized communities
to dream of new futures, whether as independent nations or within countries
like the United States. Marxists in North Vietnam, China, and Cuba popularized similarly radical visions of economic and political reform, especially among
frustrated Western youth, but Cold War politics made identifying with such
states difficult for many Americans. The more palatable *anti-colonial* struggles
occurring in Lusophone Africa created a safer space to explore tricontinental ideas that stretched beyond radical and African American constituencies
to encompass groups across the political spectrum. *Dream the Size of Freedom*
therefore echoes Frank Gerits's call to recognize African visions of modernity
as viable alternatives to U.S. and Soviet models that are worthy of study, but
it goes further by offering a concrete demonstration that such programs had
universal applicability and directly influenced Western politics.[8]

The scholarly tendency to overlook the mobility of Global South ideas
has obscured the power of post-1945 rejections of empire, especially within
the United States. Popular movements embracing Southern ideas did not
automatically replicate what Ian Tyrell and Jay Sexton call "the intellectual
and social traditions of anti-imperialism" familiar to U.S. historiography.
Rather, Americans drew on distinct traditions of anti-colonialism from the
Global South that most clearly articulated their challenges to diverse practices
of empire in smaller movements that operated alongside the better-studied
debate over military involvement in Vietnam.[9] As a result, anti-war organizing gave way to interrelated grassroots agitations against apartheid, U.S.
interventions around the Caribbean, Cold War support for repressive dictatorships in Asia and Latin America, and exploitative multinational companies. The anti-imperialism that motivated these movements went beyond
the limited political understanding of decolonization championed in the
1960s by U.S. officials—steeped as it was in domestic traditions of free-trade

capitalism, developmentalism, and assumptions about spheres of influence—
to target an expansive, deterritorialized Western dominion centered on the
United States. This was a multinational vision of empire—encompassing both
formal colonialism and hegemonic neocolonialism—that Southern nationalists understood intimately and rejected with militant calls for true political,
social, and economic self-determination.[10]

As decolonization forced a wholesale reassessment of global relations,
pro-liberation and anti-imperial organizing around Lusophone Africa not
only inspired a generation of young activists but also influenced centrist
organizations. They connected leftist anti-imperialism and liberal humanism, a reality made possible by the careful grassroots diplomacy of CONCP
leaders. Widespread support for decolonization among liberals, religious
leadership, and non-establishment organizations like the American Committee on Africa (ACOA) enabled the socialist CONCP leadership to encourage
the transformation of traditional conduits for interreacting with the Global
South. They helped reorient missionary, technocratic, and even pan-African
connections, deemphasizing Western expertise and guidance in favor of
greater deference to continental African programs and movements. Collaboration with reformers and youth advocates institutionalized these ideas and
forms of interaction, transforming the tenor of Western politics.

A key tenet of New Left Internationalism, and perhaps the main reason
its progressive vision for U.S. foreign affairs has escaped the attention of many
historians, is its self-consciously decentralized structure. Distinct ideological
and ethnic identities emerged from the search for authenticity and embrace
of communal self-determination, spawning many groups. They organized
around differing personalities and agendas but shared similar worldviews
shaped by concerns about common problems. They were also united by overlapping personal networks. ACOA had long-standing ties to religious institutions, which were intertwined with youth activists like the Zambia Group, who
built relationships with activists pursing a Black Agenda in the 1970s, which
ultimately won adherents from the leftist wing of the Black Power movement.
The CONCP parties facilitated cooperation among these organizations, offering mutual goals and promoting broad-front politics that encouraged issue-
based alliances. The result, ACOA's George Houser argued, was the "basis
of unity" for "bring[ing] together liberal and militant, black and white on a
minimum program supporting the liberation struggle in Africa."[11] Individual
activists maintained their sense of independence and commitment to specific
ideals while actively working toward practical outcomes that included changes

to institutional and governmental policies. Assertive elements sometimes strained unity, as demonstrated by the split within the African Liberation Support Committee (ALSC) and strategic disagreements among leftists, but this decentralized model strengthened commitment to organizing by making identification with issues like African liberation deeply personal.

Global South leaders reinforced such identifications by making themselves accessible icons for change. Algeria looked to world opinion while waging its revolution and African nationalists like Tom Mboya interacted with political figures such as John Kennedy, but the Lusophone solidarity movement helped perfect a form of transnational advocacy in which stateless parties cultivated popular support via direct appeals and consistent representation. This grass-roots diplomacy allowed CONCP leaders to directly influence U.S. political thought, filling roles necessitated by the New Left search for authenticity and Global South leadership. Domestic organizers translated these movements for local contexts, but they did so with the understanding that they were playing supporting roles in a global revolution, acting almost as quasi-ambassadors to the future governments of independent states. The Lusophone model of solidarity established the groundwork that later made South African figures like Nelson Mandela and Archbishop Desmond Tutu household names across the globe. It bridged the high-level, impersonal "diplomatic revolution" pioneered by the Algerian National Liberation Front and the deeply personal conception of transnational struggle that stirred anti-apartheid divestment campaigns and turned college campuses into mock shantytowns in the 1980s. Direct knowledge of and close identification with African nationalists and their programs replaced a generalized, even caricatured belief in decolonization. This process of translation could create divergent interpretations of nationalist ideology and strategy—and pressure to line up behind specific political parties based on limited knowledge—but it also produced personal, lasting, and ideologically influential identification with Southern causes.

The public demonstrations of solidarity with the socialist MPLA in Angola from 1975 to 1976 provide a case study for the political impact of this personal identification with liberation programs. In prior years, opponents of U.S. policy in Vietnam and Chile suffered from an insufficiently critical and organized public, but this was not the case after nearly a decade of organizing on behalf of the CONCP parties in Portuguese Africa. Transnational activists refined their ability to frame foreign issues and mobilize popular-political support to constrain an executive branch that continued to lean toward intervention in situations where pro-Western stability seemed imperiled. Angola offered the first demonstration that such an approach could be successful outside the unique circumstances of the late stages of the Vietnam War, and it established guidelines for action that informed domestic debates on countries throughout the Global South: Mozambique, South Africa, El Salvador, Nicaragua, and others. While Angola also produced a backlash that informed new conservative coalitions, it provided proof positive that New Left Internationalist ideas could change official positions. Collaboration around such unifying, issue-based campaigns challenged reactionary policies aimed at corralling Southern governments that transgressed Cold War boundaries. This success offered an important check on the rising New Right, which looked to champion its own anti-communist forces in the Global South as part of its Cold War revival.

These transnational advocacy networks competed most aggressively in Congress because the executive branch consistently deferred to European interests and Cold War calculations. Beginning in the late 1960s, a new generation of reforming legislators battled cold warriors for control of foreign affairs, especially on issues related to the Global South. Victory for one side or the other depended on the ability of grassroots political-advocacy networks to build coalitions, with Portugal and its White Redoubt partners making effective anti-communist appeals throughout the 1960s. Anti-Vietnam dissent opened a space for criticism of militarism and intervention, but it required political work to extend these critiques beyond Southeast Asia. The Lusophone solidarity network achieved this feat in ways that allowed it to preempt the Angolan intervention in 1975. This created a model in which grassroots political coalitions worked collaboratively with Southern actors to organize against foreign adventurism by framing policy options and providing alternative information, gaining real power without needing to mobilize hundreds of thousands for mass protests.

Dramatic public demonstrations popular in the 1960s and early 1970s gave way to more patient organizing and lobbying, supplemented by conspicuous displays of civic engagement at pivotal moments. This shift institutionalized negative appraisals of Euro-American foreign policies while simultaneously expanding beyond Portuguese Africa to encompass regional and global perspectives. This transition happened fluidly because Lusophone solidarity recruited anti-war and anti-apartheid activists through appeals to a broad anti-imperialism. Thus, a more general opposition to minority rule in southern Africa and Western hegemony abroad seemed natural after the collapse of the Lisbon regime. In addition to groups like ACOA, WOA, and the Liberation Support Movement—who always operated regionally—groups emphasizing Lusophone solidarity used Western attention to Africa in 1976 to expand their advocacy against Rhodesia and South Africa. A notable example is the transition of CCLAMG to the Chicago Committee for African Libera- tion. In Oakland, African Liberation Day celebrations emphasized Zimbabwe and South Africa but did so under the banner "A Luta Continua" and priori- tized recognition of the MPLA.[12] By refocusing their efforts after 1976, activist groups provided an experienced and well-connected leadership ready to sup- port the liberation struggles of Zimbabweans, Namibians, and South Africans while outlining a framework that would be applied to other regions.

Competing for African Policy

The continued popular interest in southern African affairs directly influenced policy debates during the presidential administration of Jimmy Carter. Like Kennedy, Carter was more ideologically flexible and less cynical in his view of the Global South than his immediate predecessors, but he still fought the Cold War. His emphasis on diplomacy and human rights was as much a way of com- bating the Soviet Union on moral terms as it was pursued for its own justness.[13] This internal tension seeped into political debates in Washington, much as it had done for Kennedy sixteen years prior. In Carter's White House, National Security Adviser Zbigniew Brzezinski championed an anti-communist world- view that clashed with that of Secretary of State Cyrus Vance, a diplomat who adopted a more internationalist, human-rights-centered approach to interna- tional affairs. One of the areas where these two perspectives conflicted most consistently was in southern Africa, particularly Angola, where the United States had yet to normalize diplomatic relations. Brzezinski saw an upstart communist state inviting Soviet and Cuban presences into the heart of Africa, but Vance and movement alumnus Andrew Young, now U.N. ambassador, worried that an obsession with communist influence in the region would dis- tract the Carter administration from achieving a just resolution to the nagging problems of self-determination that better served long-term stability.[14] As it had under Kennedy, Brzezinski's support for a greater interventionism slowly won out as the pugilistic national security adviser outlasted both Young and Vance. Tensions between the United States and Soviet Union that first broke into the open around Angola gradually worsened, convincing Carter to adopt more hawkish policies that historian Aaron Donaghy argues launched a Sec- ond Cold War.[15] The shift enabled Brzezinski to delay the recognition of the

Angolan government while laying the groundwork for future aid to Jonas Savimbi's guerrilla war against the MPLA.

In contrast to Kennedy, the debate in the Carter White House occurred under *sustained* pressure from outside forces. Angola was a Cold War flashpoint filled with Soviet weapons and Cuban advisers, but in the new context of the late 1970s there was no clear mandate for U.S. action. Vance and Young had an extensive list of allies who supported a more positive engagement with the (now openly) communist government of Angola and liberation parties in Rhodesia/Zimbabwe. Beyond the vague spirit of human rights increasingly present in U.S. discourse or the diffuse "Vietnam syndrome" much discussed by historians, a concrete coalition of internationalist activists and reformist politicians continuously urged Carter to recognize the MPLA and engage sincerely with questions of African self-determination. This coalition was led on the Hill by the Congressional Black Caucus (CBC), but it also included organizations such as ACOA, WOA, and—after 1977—the African American lobbying group TransAfrica under the leadership of Randall Robinson.[16] Influenced and encouraged by these and other grassroots groups, a small core of congressman regularly counseled the president, in the words of Paul Tsongas (D-MA), to downplay Cold War considerations in favor of a policy defined by "our own values and the aspirations of black Africans."[17] The Cuban presence and increased Soviet attention to Africa emboldened hawkish politicians as the 1970s progressed, but congressional opinion and its defense of the Clark Amendment constrained Brzezinski's ambitions to fund UNITA and reignite the Cold War in Africa.[18] At the same time, popular and congressional support for new forms of engagement aided Vance and Young as they pushed successfully for negotiations over Rhodesia/Zimbabwe. Victories for the New Left approach included the repeal of the Byrd Amendment that enabled the import of Rhodesian chrome and Carter's active participation in transfer-of-power talks, which led to the independence of Zimbabwe in 1980. The U.S. role in addressing the penultimate white minority state owed much to the network of internationalists dedicated to challenging traditions of U.S. policy in the Global South.

Even as Carter focused on the Rhodesian problem, Lusophone Africa—and its symbolic center in Angola—remained a contested piece in this puzzle. As the administration considered the possibility of normalizing relations with Angola when Cuban troops still patrolled the country, it faced a situation where domestic constituencies were likely to condemn it for any action. Either the president would suffer the wrath of the left and its vocal elements in Congress for "injecting the cold war into Africa," or he would be "rake[ed] over the coals" by anti-communist organizations such as the AFL-CIO and their Washington allies "for 'betraying' a pro-Western African leader [Savimbi]."[19] The nation and Congress were deeply divided between a coalition of hawk-ish cold warriors and the newly empowered network dedicated to New Left Internationalism.[20] Both sides gained and lost advocates based on the vicissi-tudes of national politics, with conservatives racking up victories as the decade progressed. Many driving personalities lost election bids, particularly in the Senate, notably John Tunney (1976), Dick Clark (1978), Don Fraser (1978), and John Culver (1980). Tunney and Clark's opponents directly criticized their African policies, with rumors circulating that South Africa helped fund the Republican challenger in Iowa.[21] Andrew Young resigned from his position as U.N. ambassador in 1979 after meeting with representatives of the Palestinian Liberation Organization, and Charles Diggs left office in 1980 after being con-victed of taking kickbacks from employees. The Clark Amendment remained law until 1985, limiting options for aiding UNITA, but it became the favorite punching bag for conservatives eager to take the fight to the Soviet Union. The loss of these proponents of more measured approaches to the Global South paved the way for a revival of Cold War interventionism and the explosion of covert support for anti-communists in Nicaragua and elsewhere under Ron-ald Reagan, which proved just as contentious as Angola in 1975.[22]

At the same time, grassroots solidarity experienced its own challenges. Identifying so closely with individual parties created difficulties when they failed to live up to the ideological and practical expectations that they pro-moted—and that were imagined for them by supporters. CONCP nationalists outlined ambitious dreams for their postcolonial states during their liberation struggles and dismissed shortcomings as the product of ongoing wars, but they faced rough transitions to ruling parties. All three of the CONCP parties leaned toward authoritarianism as they sought to unify their countries. The hard-pressed MPLA used violent crackdowns to fend off internal and exter-nal challenges. Racial tensions divided the PAIGC and contributed to the 1980 coup in Guinea-Bissau that deposed Amílcar Cabral's half-brother Luís, ending the binational project with the separation of the mainland state from Cabo Verde. Solidarity activists in the United States struggled to respond to these events. They were skeptical of negative reports after years of dismissing Portuguese propaganda and closely identifying with the new ruling parties. Activist information networks accustomed to championing liberation per-spectives now replicated official propaganda that downplayed PAIGC ten-sions, arrests in Mozambique, and the thousands of secretive executions that followed the failed 1977 coup in Angola.[23] As knowledge of these events circulated, and both FRELIMO and the MPLA adopted more doctrinaire forms of Soviet communism, it became difficult for many Americans to celebrate the parties with the same fervor as before.

The reality was that clear black-and-white issues, like colonialism versus liberation, proved better at motivating grassroots activism and congressional advocacy than did the messy, complex, and sometimes deeply compromised realities of postcolonial governance. The CONCP parties won allies by selling idealized visions of their social revolutions, but reality often fell short of these lofty expectations. The reasons were numerous: active hostility from neighboring white minority countries and Western states, economic challenges, shortcomings of party leadership, and the inherent difficulties transitioning from military discipline to postwar governance in diverse, multiethnic states. Key organizations like WOA, ACOA, and TransAfrica agitated against official support for Savimbi's UNITA and the Resistência Nacional Moçambicana (Mozambican National Resistance, or RENAMO), in line with popular criticism of Cold War interventionism, but committed activists found it more difficult to mobilize grassroots support for the parties themselves.

American organizers also faced less receptive partners abroad as liberation parties adjusted to the demands of leading postcolonial states. These governments-in-waiting always prioritized their future control of the nation-state and understood transnational advocacy as a strategy to achieve this goal. Having gained official status, parties could negotiate directly with states, businesses, and major NGOs, calling into question the necessity of grassroots diplomacy even as their ambitious calls for global structural change concerning economics and other issues could have benefited from popular Western support. Transnational advocacy became just one option in the diplomatic toolbox of independent governments that was utilized less regularly as power dynamics changed and the parties embraced the privileges reserved for sovereign states.[24] FRELIMO continued to cultivate Western allies to build Mozambican infrastructure and anti-UNITA lobbying always had value, but postcolonial needs and ambitions often diverged from the expectations of mobilized civil societies in the West.[25] Because successful organizing within decentralized New Left Internationalist structures required a modicum of unanimity in goals and benefited from active collaboration with Southern actors, building successful movements around the complex desires of FRELIMO or the MPLA became harder.

Frayed relationships and the need to rally support around clear issues help explain the rise of a human rights politics focused on individuals in the 1970s, rather than the more ambitious campaigns for global social justice that animated the Lusophone movement. It was easier to earn widespread backing for protections of basic rights to life, political expression, worship, and free travel for individuals rather than calls for the wholesale redefinition of global economic and social structures.[26] Barbara Keys has noted that activists and politicians on the left and right converged on the common language of human rights with distinct emphases, the left criticizing authoritarian U.S. allies while the right emphasized violations in the Soviet Union and its client states.[27] Moderate politicians and citizens could easily attach themselves to either reading, even both in separate situations, creating a ready-made language to win support for causes and policies. For supporters of New Left Internationalism, emphasizing individualistic human rights not only won support from moderates, it offered a pathway to maintain solidarity with the *people* of countries like Angola and Mozambique without automatically aligning with the parties that frustrated some activists. But this narrower rights-based discourse downplayed the stridency, anti-interventionism, economic justice, and deference to Southern priorities that were central to New Left organizing. The individualistic conception of human rights that gained ground during the Reagan era was therefore always a compromise that sought to achieve a measure of consensus between two competing visions of foreign affairs.

Anticipating Anti-Apartheid Organizing

The strategic use of human rights discourses in the 1980s to pursue a common ground has obscured the extent to which broader New Left Internationalist worldviews continued to motivate activism, with the most successful example being the anti-apartheid movement. It drew directly on legacies of Lusophone solidarity organizing as it entered the national zeitgeist. There was not an unbroken line between the Portuguese African struggles and later activism, with everything from the cycle of university enrollment to ANC setbacks causing disruption. But there existed continuities that demonstrate how attention to Lusophone liberation anticipated and structured anti-apartheid efforts. Groups organized in the late 1970s and early 1980s drew on a generation of activists who first engaged with Africa through these active struggles. In one illustrative example, the Boston Coalition for the Liberation of Southern Africa—which promoted the first successful statewide anti-apartheid divestment bill—emerged from the decision of former Gulf Boycott Coalition members to refocus their efforts on South Africa after the Soweto uprisings.[28] While histories often point to events like Soweto as a catalyst for reviving attention to southern Africa, the reality is that many Americans—from street-level activists to religious institutions to legislators—were already deeply invested in the region when reports of the severe South African police response grabbed global headlines in June 1976.

Even where breaks occurred, organizers in the late 1970s and 1980s looked back on the earlier success of the Lusophone movement to legitimize and encourage action. When university students began demanding institutional divestment from South Africa in places such as Harvard, they consciously drew linkages to the earlier Gulf boycott.[29] Moreover, key aspects of the larger New Left Internationalist ethos were highlighted by the form these protests took, focused as they were on economic boycotts, institutional divestment, the limitation of arms sales, solidarity with the imprisoned Nelson Mandela and the ANC, and black empowerment. While moderate politicians used the language of human rights to justify support for the anti-apartheid cause and related legislation, the grassroots movement more often focused on collective social justice and support for a sometimes-violent liberation party seeking self-determination against white minority rule. It is this final point where Portuguese African solidarity probably made its greatest contribution by offering proof that change was possible in southern Africa and that Westerners could play an active role by supporting revolutionary organizations. Portugal's collapse after more than a decade of determined local and transnational resistance renewed the momentum of decolonization and self-determination after it ground to a halt in the mid-1960s.

Dream the Size of Freedom demonstrates that the seemingly unique global anti-apartheid movement was in many ways an extension, expansion, and perfection of older trends of anti-colonialism and anti-imperialism that took root around Lusophone Africa during the 1960s and 1970s. Arguments by Sifiso Mxolisi Ndlovu and others that the ANC built support for regional allies such as FRELIMO and the MPLA may well be true for the 1980s, when identification with the Lusophone parties flagged, but for more than a decade the process operated in reverse.[30] During the period when the exiled ANC struggled to mobilize global populations behind its vision of a free South Africa, the environment that allowed later activism to flourish took shape.[31] CONCP depictions of egalitarian social revolutions justified Western support for militant leftist parties as extensions of domestic struggles for racial equality, economic reform, youth revolts, and a general challenge to the orthodoxy of the Cold War. Networks of activists and policymakers formed around southern Africa, while the inclusive internationalism of the CONCP parties inspired Americans to imagine their own domestic liberation in terms comparable to African struggles happening an ocean away. Victory first over Portugal and then over U.S. intervention convinced activists that change could happen. When anti-apartheid activists went looking for people to join protests and divestment campaigns in later years, they found, according to organizer Joseph Jordan, "a receptive audience among people whose consciousness had been raised during the campaigns of the 1970s."[32]

Activists also found existing pathways for bringing popular concerns about Western foreign policy to legislators, who they now knew could challenge policies that favored the White Redoubt. While leading legislators of the 1970s fell victim to the resurgent right, the institutionalization of New Left Internationalist ideas in lobbying groups and congressional organizations like the CBC filled the vacuum left by Diggs, Clark, and others. Congressmen like Ron Dellums (D-CA) and Senator Ted Kennedy continued to champion productive relationships with the Global South, and they were joined by newly elected legislators like Mickey Leland (D-TX) and Howard Wolpe (D-MI). Both entered the House in 1979 and quickly became experts and proponents of African issues, with Leland leading the CBC during the pivotal period from 1985 to 1987 and Wolpe chairing the Africa subcommittee for much of the 1980s. Activist organizing continued to support legislative efforts. All these congressmen cooperated with WOA or TransAfrica and often made grassroots connections. Former ALSC president Gene Locke served as administrative aide and legal counsel for the Houston-based Leland, while Wolpe developed good relations with the Madison Area Committee on Southern Africa's Dave Wiley, whose job at Michigan State University placed him in the congressman's district.[33] Grassroots-congressional networks advocated for Global South causes while helping existing allies and newly elected legislators to frame issues in ways that resisted and modified Cold War narratives. These legislators spent years keeping apartheid alive in national conversations, then helped advance legislation when Cold War openings and the expansion of grassroots energy in the mid-1980s compelled persuadable colleagues to reassess their views of South Africa.

Sustaining Anti-Imperialism

Beyond its legacies for anti-apartheid organizing, the Lusophone solidarity network both reflected and helped established the structures and strategies that sustained the broader goals of New Left Internationalism. This movement encompassed intersecting campaigns that included peace organizing, antinuclear advocacy, general disarmament, the environment, global women's rights, skepticism of U.S.-led economic globalization, and much more. While the priorities of these individual campaigns diverged, and their success waxed and waned at different moments, they drew from similar worldviews and personal networks. The Lusophone and southern African movements occupied unique positions under this umbrella due to their operation at the intersection of global debates about race, empire, economics, Cold War conflict, and religious mission in a decolonizing world. These campaigns pioneered strategies to promote specific issues and, at their moments of peak vitality, were able to unite distant corners of these overlapping coalitions because they touched on many pressing matters. As a result, the themes explored in *Dream the Size of Freedom* provide a foundation for understanding the vitality of New Left Internationalist organizing into the 1980s and beyond.

One key insight is the important role played by establishment institutions, which transformed to support the energy, ideas, and activism of the sixties generation. The role of religious institutions is especially noteworthy here, since they influenced the moral foundations of many activists and provided start-up funds for these same organizers as they moved away from formal church structures. This underappreciated history recovers the legacy of religious progressivism that went temporally and spatially beyond the high tide of the civil rights movement. Ironically, this success reveals one reason for the subsequent decline of mainline Protestant churches associated with the NCC after the 1960s: many youths found civic action a substitute for religious observation, while other parishioners bristled at the leftward drift of church leaders and sought refuge in rapidly growing evangelical denominations associated with the New Right. Yet because of the strong foundations created by the 1980s, New Left organizations grew even as they came to rely on support from better endowed foundations intertwined with activist networks, such as the Stewart R. Mott Foundation and the Samuel Rubin Foundation, the latter's leadership including ACOA associate Cora Weiss.

The interconnectedness of New Left Internationalism, and the importance of southern African organizing to it, are especially apparent in the growth of

Latin American solidarity, with a prominent example being the Washington Office on Latin America (WOLA). WOLA became a leading critic of Reagan-era interventions in the 1980s and continues to work on human rights issues, acting as a conduit through which policymakers can learn from Latin Americans and their U.S. advocates. From its foundation in 1974, WOLA modeled itself directly on WOA, which demonstrated, according to founder John Sinclair, "that such an office could be effective."[34] WOLA initially relied on church funding and pulled from religious activists, and it occupied offices in the United Methodist Building alongside WOA. Longtime WOLA director Joseph Eldridge remembers personally observing WOA's balancing of relations between Southern actors, politicians, non-establishment organizations, and a disparate collection of grassroots activist groups.[35] This admiration for WOA, which only predated its Latin American counterpart by a year, reveals how pioneering the African solidarity movement was and the power its proof of concept had for broader applications of New Left Internationalism.

The relationship between these and other D.C.-based groups also hints at the ways that informal, almost invisible collaboration overcame some limitations of decentralized activist structures. These offices existed separately to pursue distinct agendas and mobilize specific constituencies, but they were part of the community pioneered in the early 1970s. As Eldridge recalled, "We were all part of the progressive foreign policy movement, trying to influence official policy."[36] Outwardly discrete issue-specific networks interacted in local spaces where activists pursued common goals applied to different topics, and where professional and personal relationships overlapped. The tendency for offices to cluster created opportunities for collaboration that rarely entered the archival record. The Stewart R. Mott Foundation that hosted the Coalition for a New Foreign and Military Policy (CNFMP) and the United Methodist Building that housed interreligious offices, WOA, and WOLA were the primary residents of a small triangular block on Maryland Avenue near the Capitol. Brewster Rhoads of the CNFMP recalls pizza-fueled envelope-stuffing parties that assembled anyone available from across like-minded offices, with the understanding that you would return the favor for the next big campaign. Groups shared mailing lists, and individuals attended one another's rallies.[37]

There were myriad products of these exchanges, not least of which was an ability to connect campaigns across regional divides when opportunities arose, tapping into the overlapping networks of activism that once fueled the growth of Lusophone solidarity. In the 1980s, for instance, WOA strengthened

Campaign for Political Rights

Peter Weiss
Center for Constitutional Rights

Lynn Jennings
Women's International League
for Peace and Freedom

Covert Action Information Bulletin

Ed Killackey
Maryknoll Fathers and Brothers

Ray Nathan
American Ethical Union

Bob Alpern
Unitarian Universalist Association

Washington Interreligious
Staff Conference
Foreign Policy Task Force

Chris Root
Washington Office on Africa

Joe Eldridge
Washington Office on
Latin America

Coalition for a New Foreign
and Military Policy

Harry Scoble
Human Rights Internet

Center for International
Policy

Friends of the
Filipino People

Friends of the
Korean People

Allan Adler
Center for National
Security Studies (CNSS)

Mort Halperin
CNSS

Laurie Dulcer
Common Cause

Trin Yarborough
Institute for
Policy Studies (IPS)

Bob Borosage
IPS

Charles Briody
Chile Legislative Center

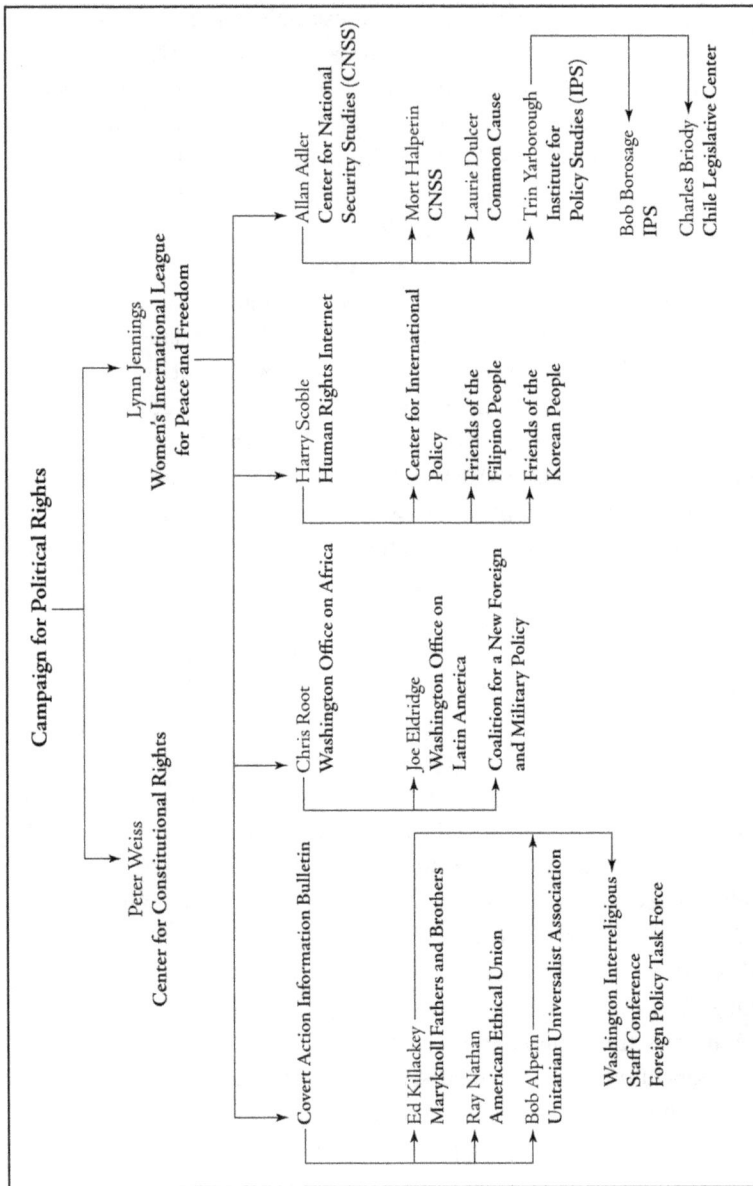

Figure 15. Covert Operations Task Force phone tree, circa 1980. Reproduced from a document in the WOA Papers, Yale Divinity Archives.

its condemnation of official support to UNITA by linking to similar programs on Latin America.[38] These ad hoc connections produced such collaborations as the Covert Operations Task Force, a phone-tree formalization of existing relationships that allowed discrete groups to efficiently communicate and mobilize diverse constituencies against Cold War interventions. WOA and former ACOA president Peter Weiss filled key nodes alongside WOLA, CNFMP, the Unitarian Universalist Association, the Institute for Policy Studies, and many groups that cosponsored the "Hands off Angola" rally a few years earlier (figure 15).[39] These relationships bled over into Congress, where legislators carved out specializations but worked collaboratively to pursue New Left Internationalist priorities. Longtime Africa watcher and human rights advocate Don Fraser became a vital congressional ally of WOLA in its early years.[40] Houston congressman Mickey Leland, who gained prominence for his work on African issues, spearheaded criticism of Reagan's policy in El Salvador in 1981, linking it with official ambivalence on apartheid to condemn the administration's approach to the Global South.[41] Perhaps most famously, congressional efforts to use riders to limit U.S. aid to Nicaraguan Contras in the early 1980s drew on the tactics of the Tunney and (less successfully) the Clark Amendments, producing the compromise Boland Amendments and deeply entwining the two Global South regions in Washington debates.[42] Individual offices and campaigns adopted issue- or geographic-specific foci to promote clear narratives for public consumption, but their efforts were understood as contributing to common goals.

The D.C. example is unique for the paper trail it left, but it hints at the ways that New Left Internationalism operated at the grassroots level as well. Major campaigns around Nicaragua and El Salvador had many parallels with the Lusophone movement. They had origins in the intersection of progressive religious networks and leftist organizing, embraced decentralized campaigns to create broad fronts of diverse political groups, amplified Latin American voices to identify Global South problems, and used local organizing to inspire personal identification. These efforts successfully reframed issues locally in ways that supported national efforts spearheaded by WOLA and other groups, turning grassroots energy into policy by collaborating with motivated legislators who won over moderate colleagues to pass laws constraining executive power.[43] These parallels owed much to the legacies of overlapping advocacy networks that cohered under the umbrella of New Left Internationalist politics, from liberal church leadership to the anti-imperial organizers that emerged from multiregional collectives like Chicago's New World Resource

Center. Sociologist Christian Smith discovered in his study of Central American peace advocacy that most leading activists had worked around other New Left causes, ranging from antinuclear and anti-war demonstrations to women's rights, with roughly a quarter of the members of the prominent Sanctuary movement being involved in southern African work.[44] These early affiliations often radicalized organizers, even as many retained ties to religious and other established organizations that added institutional weight to campaigns through the 1980s. At the same time, the Central American peace movement experienced internal tensions similar to those of Lusophone solidarity, including differing strategic goals and protest styles among the overlapping groups, illustrating a common challenge for New Left Internationalist coalitions.[45]

As with Lusophone solidarity, different foci and flavors of ideology compelled strategic compromises and collaborations and carefully crafted appeals for general support, but the wider ambitions of New Left Internationalism remained consistent. The Vietnam syndrome and human rights discourses offered welcome, inclusive rhetoric that rallied different parts of the movement and helped Latin American peace campaigns win institutional assistance while claiming a certain bipartisan appeal.[46] Yet, at the grassroots level in particular, popular enthusiasm was greatest when articulating deeper, anti-imperial critiques of U.S. policy. In 1985, the year before the passage of the Comprehensive Anti-Apartheid Act over President Reagan's veto, national protests took place in major cities across the country, with activists embracing four broad demands: disarmament, an end to interventions in the Global South, an end to apartheid, and reduced military spending. The commitment to these broad ideas was so strong that organizers felt increasing pressure to publicly recognize the cross-issue connections that had always operated behind the scenes. In 1987, popular expectations compelled the veteran anti-war group the New Mobe to expand its anti-Contra campaign to include apartheid and covert assistance to groups like UNITA, resulting in the National Mobilization for Justice and Peace in Central America and Southern Africa.[47]

These underappreciated collaborations between parallel activist networks preserved common strategies and vocabularies that questioned U.S. power and Western superiority, which emerged in the 1960s and cohered around southern Africa organizing in the 1970s. This New Left Internationalism articulated a measured, humble, and ultimately anti-imperial vision of foreign policy that contrasted sharply with Cold War traditions, challenging Reagan-era diplomacy and intersecting with popular objections to the neoliberal globalization that the country pursued in the triumphalist 1990s.[48] This ambitious and inclusive brand of anti-imperialism was promoted by the grassroots diplomacy of Southern actors like those in the CONCP parties, who exploited the ideological openings created by decolonization and the political reorientations of the 1960s to inject new ideas into Western debates. The movement that they inspired in the United States helped pioneer a participatory, collaborative approach to foreign affairs that shaped U.S. political debates long after the collapse of Portugal's empire.

NOTES

Introduction

Epigraph: The Committee for a Free Mozambique, "Our Dream has the Size of Freedom: The Struggle for Liberation in Mozambique" (New York: 1971), 1.

1. Africa Fund, "Voices of Liberation #1: Message to the Nation on his Investiture as President of the People's Republic of Mozambique," n.d. [c. fall 1975], African Activist Archive. For descriptions of the independence ceremony, see Gloria Negri, "Flag Raising Ceremony Heralds Free Mozambique," *Boston Globe*, 26 June 1975.

2. Gloria Negri, "Flag-Raising Ceremony Heralds a Free Mozambique," *Boston Globe*, 26 June 1975; letter, Janet Hooper to Joaquim Chissano, 17 August 1975, Box 79, American Committee on Africa Papers, Amistad Research Center (New Orleans, LA).

3. Dial Torgerson, "500 Years of Portuguese Rule Ends in Mozambique," *Los Angeles Times*, 25 June 1975.

4. Odd Arne Westad, *The Global Cold War: Third World Interventions and the Making of Our Times* (New York: Cambridge University Press, 2005).

5. See, for example, Lise Namikas, *Battleground Africa: Cold War in the Congo, 1960–1965* (Stanford: Stanford University Press, 2013); Sergey Mazon, *A Distant Front in the Cold War: The USSR in West Africa and the Congo, 1956–1964* (Stanford: Stanford University Press, 2010); Salim Yaqub, *Containing Arab Nationalism: The Eisenhower Doctrine and the Middle East* (Chapel Hill: University of North Carolina Press, 2006).

6. Westad, chapters 6–7; Fernando Andresen Guimarães, *The Origins of the Angolan Civil War: Foreign Intervention and Domestic Political Conflict* (New York: Macmillan Press, 1998); Piero Gleijeses, *Conflicting Missions: Havana, Washington, and Africa, 1959–1976* (Chapel Hill: University of North Carolina Press, 2002); Witney Schneidman, *Engaging Africa: Washington and the Fall of Portugal's Colonial Empire* (Lanham, MD: University Press of America, 2004); Tiago Moreira de Sá, *Os Estados Unidos e a Descolonização de Angola* (Lisbon: Dom Quixote, 2011).

7. Natalia Telepneva, *Cold War Liberation: The Soviet Union and the Collapse of the Portuguese Empire in Africa, 1961–1975* (Chapel Hill: University of North Carolina Press, 2022).

8. See, for example, Jeffrey S. Ahlman, *Living with Nkrumahism: Nation, State, and Pan-Africanism in Ghana* (Athens: Ohio University Press, 2017); Renata Keller, *Mexico's Cold War: Cuba, the United States, and the Legacy of the Mexican Revolution* (New York: Cambridge University Press, 2015).

9. Matthew Connelly, *A Diplomatic Revolution: Algeria's Fight for Independence and the Origins of the Post-Cold War Era* (New York: Oxford University Press, 2002), 4–5.

10. Ryan M. Irwin, *Gordian Knot: Apartheid and the Unmaking of the Liberal World Order* (New York: Oxford University Press, 2012); Christopher R. W. Dietrich, *Oil Revolution:*

Anticolonial Elites, Sovereign Rights, and the Economic Culture of Decolonization (New York: Cambridge University Press, 2017).

11. R. Joseph Parrott, "Tricontinentalism and the Anti-Imperial Project," in *The Triconti-nental Revolution: Third World Radicalism and the Cold War*, ed. R. Joseph Parrott and Mark Atwood Lawrence (New York: Cambridge University Press, 2022), 1-40; see also Anne Garland Mahler, *From the Tricontinental to the Global South: Race, Radicalism, and Transnational Solidarity* (Durham: Duke University Press, 2018), introduction.

12. Young defines Cabral as a central element of the tricontinental canon, extending some of the ideas of Fanon. Robert J. C. Young, *Postcolonialism: An Historical Introduction* (Malden, MA: Wiley-Blackwell, 2001), chapter 20. See also Peter Karibe Mendy, *Amílcar Cabral: Nationalist and Pan-Africanist Revolutionary* (Athens: Ohio University Press, 2019), 202; Jock McCulloch, *In the Twilight of Revolution: The Political Theory of Amilcar Cabral* (London: Routledge and Kegan Paul, 1983); Manji Firoze and Bill Fletcher Jr., eds., *Claim No Easy Victories: The Legacy of Amilcar Cabral* (Dakar: CODESRIA, 2013); Carlos Lopes, ed., *Africa's Contemporary Challenges: The Legacy of Amilcar Cabral* (New York: Routledge, 2010); R. Joseph Parrott, "Brother and a Comrade: Amílcar Cabral as Global Revolutionary," in Parrott and Lawrence, 245-75.

13. Campbell Craig and Fredrik Logevall, *America's Cold War: The Politics of Insecurity* (Cambridge, MA: Harvard University Press, 2012).

14. See for the former, Laura Pulido, *Black, Brown, Yellow, and Left: Radical Activism in Los Angeles* (Berkeley: University of California Press, 2006); Brenda Gayle Plummer, *Rising Wind: Black Americans and U.S. Foreign Policy* (Chapel Hill: University of North Carolina Press, 1996); Pamela E. Pennock, *The Rise of the Arab American Left: Activists, Allies, and Their Fight Against Imperialism and Racism, 1960s-1980s* (Chapel Hill: University of North Carolina Press, 2017); James H. Meriwether, *Proudly We Can Be Africans: Black Americans and Africa, 1935-1961* (Chapel Hill: University of North Carolina Press, 2002); Carol Anderson, *Bourgeois Radicals: The NAACP and the Struggle for Colonial Liberation, 1941-1960* (New York: Cambridge University Press, 2014). For the latter, Van Gosse, *Where the Boys Are: Cuba, the Cold War, and the Making of the New Left* (London: Verso, 1993); Max Elbaum, *Revolution in the Air: Sixties Radicals Turn to Lenin, Mao, and Che* (London: Verso: 2002).

15. Quinn Slobodian, *Foreign Front: Third World Politics in Sixties West Germany* (Raleigh: Duke University Press, 2012); Christoph Kalter, *The Discovery of the Third World: Decolonization and the Rise of the New Left in France, c. 1950-1976* (New York: Cambridge University Press, 2016); Giuliano Garavini, *After Empires: European Integration, Decolonization, and the Challenge from the Global South 1957-1986* (New York: Oxford University Press, 2012). There has also been attention given in recent years to the reaction against it, see Quinn Slobodian, *Globalists: The End of Empire and the Birth of Neoliberalism* (Cambridge, MA: Harvard University Press, 2018).

16. This was an extension and expansion of the process begun within empires themselves. See Dalila Cabrita Mateus, *A Luta Pela Independência: A Formação das Elites Fundadoras da FREIMO, MPLA, e PAIGC* (Mem Martin: Inquérito, 1999); Michael Goebel, *Anti-Imperial Metropolis: Interwar Paris and the Seeds of Third World Nationalism* (New York: Cambridge University Press, 2015).

17. See Doug Rossinow, *The Politics of Authenticity* (New York: Columbia University Press, 1998).

18. For the domestic influence of tricontinentalism, see Mahler; Pulido; Cynthia Young, *Soul Power: Culture, Radicalism, and the Making of a U.S. Third World Left* (Durham: Duke University Press, 2006); Joshua Bloom and Waldo E. Martin Jr., *Black Against Empire: The History and Politics of the Black Panther Party* (Berkeley: University of California Press, 2016).

19. Judy Tzu-Chun Wu, *Radicals on the Road: Internationalism, Orientalism, and Feminism During the Vietnam Era* (Ithaca: Cornell University Press, 2013).

20. This form of public diplomacy or anticipatory nation branding from governments-in-waiting is present in histories of both decolonization and the anti-apartheid movement. See for the former, David Stenner, *Globalizing Morocco: Transnational Activism and the Postcolonial State* (Palo Alto: Stanford University Press, 2019); for the latter, Rob Skinner, *The Foundations of Anti-Apartheid: Liberal Humanitarians and Transnational Activists in Britain and the United States, c. 1919–64* (New York: Palgrave Macmillan, 2010); Robert Kinloch Massie, *Loosing the Bonds: The United States and South Africa in the Apartheid Years* (New York: Doubleday, 1997).

21. For the anti-war movement, see Charles DeBenedetti with Charles Chatfield, *An American Ordeal: The Antiwar Movement of the Vietnam Era* (Syracuse: Syracuse University Press, 1990); Terry H. Anderson, *The Movement and the Sixties* (New York: Oxford, 1995); Melvin Small, *Antiwarriors* (New York: Rowman and Littlefield, 2002); David Farber, *The Age of Great Dreams* (New York: Hill and Wang, 1994); Elbaum. For Black Power, see Manning Marable, *Race, Reform, and Rebellion: The Second Reconstruction and Beyond in Black America, 1945–2006* (Oxford: University of Mississippi Press, 2007), chapter 6; Bloom and Martin, chapters 15–16. Todd Gitlin, *The Sixties: Year of Hope, Days of Rage* (New York: Bantam, 1993), chapter 17.

22. Petra Goedde, *The Politics of Peace: A Global Cold War History* (New York: Oxford University Press, 2019).

23. Doug Rossinow, *Visions of Progress* (Philadelphia: University of Pennsylvania Press, 2008), chapter 6; Michael Kazin, *American Dreamers: How the Left Changed a Nation* (New York: Vintage, 2011), 248–264; Jeffrey O. G. Ogbar, *Black Power: Radical Politics and African American Identity* (Baltimore: Johns Hopkins University Press, 2019), 191–198.

24. The tendency to measure successful foreign policy initiatives solely through the executive branch—and speak vaguely of presidential responses to popular organizing—has obscured how grassroots organizers directly influenced policy while downplaying the impact of alternative foreign policy formulations like pan-African internationalism. See Jeremi Suri, *Power and Protest: Global Revolution and the Rise of Détente* (Cambridge, MA: Harvard University Press, 2003); Fredrik Logevall, *Choosing War: The Lost Chance for Peace and the Escalation of the Vietnam War* (Berkeley: University of California Press, 2001); Richard D. Mahoney, *JFK: Ordeal in Africa* (New York: Oxford University Press, 1983). For examples of pan-African internationalism, see Penny Von Eschen, *Race Against Empire: Black Americans and Anti-Colonialism, 1937–1957* (Ithaca: Cornell University Press, 1997); Meriwether.

25. Barbara J. Keys, *Reclaiming American Virtue: The Human Rights Revolution of the 1970s* (Cambridge, MA: Harvard University Press, 2014); Sarah B. Snyder, *Human Rights Activism and the End of the Cold War: A Transnational History of the Helsinki Network* (New York: Cambridge University Press, 2013); Brenda Gayle Plummer, *In Search of Power: African Americans in the Era of Decolonization, 1956–1974* (New York: Cambridge University Press, 2013); Benjamin Talton, *In This Land of Plenty: Mickey Leland and Africa in American Politics* (Philadelphia: University of Pennsylvania Press, 2021).

26. Cynthia Arnson, *Crossroads: Congress, the President, and Central America, 1976–1992* (State College: Penn State University Press, 1993); Coletta A. Youngers, *The Washington Office on Latin America: Thirty Years of Advocacy for Human Rights, Democracy, and Social Justice* (Washington, DC: Washington Office on Latin America, 2006); Roger Peace, *A Call to Conscience: The Anti-Contra War Campaign* (Amherst: University of Massachusetts Press, 2012)

27. Margaret E. Keck and Kathryn Sikkink, *Activists Beyond Borders* (Ithaca: Cornell University Press, 1998), 2.

28. Jeffrey W. Knopf, *Domestic Society and International Cooperation: The Impact of Protest on US Arms Control Policy* (New York: Cambridge University Press, 1998), 50, 251. On the role of media, see William A. Gamson, "Bystanders, Public Opinion, and Media," in *The Blackwell Companion to Social Movements*, ed. David A. Snow et al. (Hoboken: Wiley, 2008).

29. See Robert David Johnson, *Congress and the Cold War* (New York: Cambridge University Press, 2005), and Julian Zelizer, *Arsenal of Democracy: The Politics of National Security— From World War II to the War on Terrorism* (New York: Basic Books, 2012).

30. Håkan Thörn, *Anti-Apartheid and the Emergence of a Global Civil Society* (London: Palgrave Macmillan, 2009); Jackie Smith and Dawn Wiest, "The Uneven Geography of Global Civil Society: National and Global Influences on Transnational Association," *Social Forces* 84, no. 2 (December 2005): 637–639.

31. Thomas Bender, "Historians, the Nation, and the Plenitude of Narratives," in *Rethinking American History in a Global Age*, ed. Thomas Bender (Berkeley: University of California Press, 2002), 6–9. See Dietrich, 14.

32. A brief note on terminology: Global North and Global South differentiate the regions of the world defined by modern, multi-continental Euro-American imperialism with connotations of cultural and racial supremacy on the one hand, versus the local peoples of Asia, Africa, and Latin American that existed on the other end of the spectrum of conquest and domination. East and West align with the familiar Cold War division between the communist, generally authoritarian Soviet Union and its European allies and the predominantly democratic, capitalist countries in the North Atlantic Treaty Organization. Both counted among the relatively wealthy countries of the Global North. Tricontinentalism defined a revolutionary, anti-imperial, nationalist internationalism that was leftist and worked with Eastern bloc countries without fully aligning with any one Cold War camp. Tricontinentalism was a particularly revolutionary brand of Third Worldism, and the latter term will be used occasionally to refer to this broader independent impulse in world affairs. Finally, the solidarity that developed between Southern revolutionaries and U.S. sympathizers borrows from geographer David Featherstone, defining it as a relation between two nominally distinct groups based on shared perception of and participation in a common struggle, often against a perceived repression or other wrong. The process of imagining this bond is inventive and often transnational, emphasizing local identities and concerns to create an empathy that transcends barriers by highlighting racial, ideological, class, and/or political commonalities. David Featherstone, *Solidarity: Hidden Histories and Geographies of Internationalism* (New York: Zed, 2012), 5–6.

Chapter 1

1. "Honouring Henry the Navigator," *Guardian*, 8 August 1960; "16 Nations Honor Henry, Navigator," *Washington Post*, 8 August 1960.

2. Odd Arne Westad, *The Global Cold War: Third World Interventions and the Making of Our Times* (Cambridge: Cambridge University Press, 2005), chapter 3.

3. Filipe de Ribeiro de Meneses, *Salazar: A Political Biography* (New York: Enigma Books, 2009), chapters 1–2.

4. See Werner Baer and António P. N. Leite, "The Peripheral Economy, Its Performance in Isolation and with Integration: The Case of Portugal," *Luso-Brazilian Review* 29, no. 2 (Winter 1992): 2 and 23.

5. Basil Davidson, *In the Eye of the Storm* (New York: Doubleday, 1972), 121.

6. In Guinea-Bissau there were fewer than a thousand settlers, eighteen thousand in Mozambique, and just over twenty thousand in Angola. In no colony did settlers approach 1 percent of

the total population. See Chabal, 20; Malyn Newitt, *A History of Mozambique* (Johannesburg: Wits University Press, 1995), 442; and Gerald J. Bender, *Angola Under the Portuguese: The Myth and the Reality* (Berkeley: University of California Press, 1978), 20.

7. See Newitt, *Mozambique*, 454–456. See also Malyn Newitt, "Angola in Historical Context," in *Angola: The Weight of History*, ed. Patrick Chabal and Nuno Vidal (New York: Columbia University Press, 2007), 58; Bender, 147.

8. Bender, xx.

9. Margarida Calafate Ribeiro, "Empire, Colonial Wars and Post-Colonialism in the Portuguese Contemporary Imagination," *Portuguese Studies* 18 (2002): 134.

10. Newitt, "Angola in Historical Context," 60–65.

11. Newitt, *Mozambique*, 478–481; David Birmingham, *Frontline Nationalism in Angola and Mozambique* (Trenton: Africa World Press, 1992), 20–24.

12. Patrick Chabal, *Amilcar Cabral: Revolutionary Leader and People's War* (New York: Cambridge University Press, 1983), chapter 1.

13. Luís Nuno Rodrigues, *Salazar-Kennedy: A Crise de uma Aliança* (Lisbon: Notícias, 2002), 27–29.

14. U.N. General Assembly Resolution 1542 (XV), "Transmission of Information Under Article 73e of the Charter," 15 December 1960, Fifteenth Session, Reports Adopted under the reports of the fourth committee, 30.

15. Telegram, Purves to Selwyn Lloyd, 16 August 1957, FO 403/480 [Archives Direct], National Archives of the United Kingdom (Kew, England). Hereafter, UKNA.

16. See H. W. Brands, *The Specter of Neutralism: The United States and the Emergence of the Third World, 1947–1960* (New York: Columbia University Press, 1989).

17. See Lise Namikas, *Battleground Africa: Cold War in the Congo, 1960–1965* (Palo Alto: Stanford University Press, 2013), chapters 2–6.

18. Apontamento de Conversa, entre Eisenhower e Salazar, Palacio de Queluz, 19 May 1960, Pasta 2, AOS/COE-2, Arquivo Nacional da Torre do Tombo (Lisbon, Portugal). Hereafter TT-PT.

19. John Marcum, *The Angolan Revolution* (Cambridge, MA: MIT Press, 1969) 1:60–65. See also, Holden Roberto, "Biographical Statement," in Ronald H. Chilcote, *Emerging Nationalism in Portuguese Africa* (Stanford: Hoover Institution Press, 1972), 62–64.

20. Letter, Houser to Necaca, 14 May 1956, Box 79, American Committee on Africa Papers, Amistad Research Center, Tulane University (New Orleans, LA). Hereafter, ACOA. Also see George Houser, *No One Can Stop the Rain* (New York: Pilgrim Press, 1989), 42.

21. Draft Statement of Purpose, n.d. [c. 1953], ACOA, Proquest History Vault.

22. Memo, Houser to Executive Board, 25 April 1958, ACOA, Proquest History Vault; David Hostetter, *Movement Matters: American Anti-Apartheid Activism and the Rise of Multicultural Politics* (New York: Routledge, 2009), 17–23.

23. "Annual Report: American Committee on Africa June 1, 1960–May 31, 1961," *Africa Today* 8, no. 6 (June 1961).

24. Form Letter, "The worst thing about Portuguese Africa . . .," n.d. [1958], Internal Memos, Reel I, Records of the American Committee on Africa, Part I: ACOA Executive Committee minutes and National Office memoranda, 1952–1975 (Bethesda, MD: University Publications of America, 1992). The AASF supported the "Kennedy airlift" proposed by Kenyan Tom Mboya in 1959.

25. Letter, Houser to Ncaca, January 25, 1958, Box 79, ACOA.

26. Houser, *Rain*, 79.

27. David Macey, *Frantz Fanon* (New York: Picador, 2000), 370; Marcum, *Angolan Revolution*, 1:65; José Freire Antunes, *Kennedy e Salazar: O Leão e a Raposa* (Lisbon: Dom Quixote, 2013), 92.

28. UPA, "O Comunismo e a Africa," "La Voix de la Nation Angolaise," 30 September 1960, 7, Armstrong Papers, New York Public Library (New York, NY). Hereafter, NYPL.

29. Letter, Homer Jack to Winifred Armstrong (Office of John Kennedy), 6 January 1960, Box 1, Winifred Armstrong Papers, JFK Library; Letter, Lloyd Garrison to Emanuel R. Freedman, 5 January 1962, Box 37, New York Times Foreign Desk Records, NYPL.

30. Theodore Tucker of the NCC commended Roberto to one diplomat as a moderate anti-communist nationalist. Memcon, Theodore Tucker, 8 January 1961, Box 1821, CDF 60–63, RG 59, National Archives and Records Administration (College Park, MD). Hereafter, NARA.

31. See "Revolt in Angola Is Reported Here," *New York Times*, 8 March 1960.

32. "Aims and Purposes of the American Committee on Africa," n.d. [c. 1953], Folder: ACOA—Statement of Purpose (Drafts), Box 29, ACOA.

33. See Memo, Houser to Executive Committee, "Trip to Washington," 2 February 1959, Internal Memos, Reel I, Microfilm Records of the American Committee on Africa, Part I: ACOA Executive Committee minutes and National Office memoranda, 1952–1975. Gerald Horne criticizes ACOA's liberalism in the 1950s and 1960s, comparing it negatively with the Council on African Affairs. See Gerald Horne, *Mau Mau in Harlem?* (New York: Palgrave Macmillan, 2009), 164, 171–172.

34. Houser, *Rain*, 91–92. Memo, Gilbert Jonas to Don Harrington, 9 October 1958, Interoffice Memoranda 1/4, ACOA Series I, ACOA; Letter, William X. Scheinman to Roberto, 22 March 1961, Folder 13, Box 10, William X. Scheinman Papers, Hoover Institution (Stanford, CA).

35. See Frederick Cooper, *Decolonization and African Society: The Labor Question in French and British Africa* (New York: Cambridge University Press, 1996), part IV.

36. The MPLA claimed credit for the Luanda uprising and postdated its revolution to the event; no sustained revolt emerged. See Marcum, *Angolan Revolution*, 1:123–130; Guimarães, 42–45; Jean-Michel Mabeko Tali, *Dissidêdencias e Poder de Estado: O MPLA perante si próprio (1962-1977),* (Luanda: Nzila, 2001), 1:68–76.

37. See Associated Press, "Whites Slain in Angola; Airlift of Refugees Is On," *New York Times*, 18 March 1961.

38. "Interview with an Angolan Nationalist," n.d. [likely early 1961 or late 1960], Armstrong Papers, NYPL.

39. Mahoney, 14–33; Philip E. Muehlenbeck, *Betting on the Africans: John F. Kennedy's Courting of African Nationalist Leaders* (New York: Oxford University Press, 2014), 34–41.

40. ACOA, Annual Report, 1960, Folder 2/14, Executive Committee Minutes Jan–May, 1961, ACOA, Proquest History Vault.

41. ACOA, Annual Report, 1960, Folder 2/14, Executive Committee Minutes Jan–May, 1961, ACOA, Proquest History Vault.

42. Houser interview; Houser, *Rain*, 268–269.

43. Mahoney, 14–33.

44. Memcon, Rusk with Luis Esteves Fernandes, 10 March 1961, Box 1821, CDF 60–63, RG 59, NARA.

45. Telegram, SecState to AmEmbassy Paris, 7 March 1961, Box 1821, CDM 1960–63, RG 59, NARA.

46. Untitled document (Ministério dos Negócios Estraingeiros), Visita do Snr. Harrman ao Conselho, 3 March 1961, PAA 287, Pasta 922, AHD; Memo, George C. McGhee to McGeorge Bundy, 25 May 1961, Box 154, National Security File, John F. Kennedy Presidential Library (Boston, MA). Hereafter, NSF, JFKL.

47. Telegram, Elbrick to SecState, 4 March 1961, Box 154, NSF, JFKL.

48. Schneidman, 15–16.

49. Telegram, Elbrick to SecState, 29 March 1961, Box 154, NSF, JFKL; "Conversa teloficina com Overseas minister 25/3/61," Pasta 9, AOS/CO/UL-30D, TT-PT.

50. The young diplomat Franco Nogueira became foreign minister, the reform-minded Adriano Moreira overseas minister, and Salazar confidant Theotonio Pereira ambassador to Washington. Salazar assumed the defense portfolio after an unsuccessful coup by Botelho Moniz, which some historians have attributed to U.S. involvement. De Meneses, 472–482. U.S. officials knew of Botelho Moniz's complaints and may have considered supporting a coup, but there is little evidence of direct participation. See Antunes, 239–266—most of Antunes's evidence comes from interviews with individuals close to Salazar, who believed the coup to be a U.S. plot. Rodrigues believes the United States distanced itself at the last minute. Rodrigues, 65–66.

51. Holden Roberto, "Statement of Mr. Holden Roberto, President of the Union of Populations of Angola," 15 March 1961, ACOA, Armstrong Papers, NYPL. "Interview with an Angolan Nationalist," n.d. [likely early 1961 or late 1960], Armstrong Papers, NYPL.

52. "U.S. Praised by Angolan," Sun (Baltimore), 25 March 1961; Holden Roberto, "Statement of Mr. Holden Roberto, President of the Union of Populations of Angola," 15 March 1961, ACOA, Armstrong Papers, NYPL. "Interview with an Angolan Nationalist," n.d. [likely early 1961 or late 1960], Armstrong Papers, NYPL.

53. "U.S. Praised by Angolan," Sun (Baltimore), 25 March 1961.

54. Telegram, Plimpton to SecState, 16 March 1961, Box 1821, CDF 60–63, RG 59, NARA.

55. "Holden Roberto Title?," n.d. [likely 1960 or early 1961], 5, Armstrong Papers, NYPL.

56. Holden Roberto, "Statement of Mr. Holden Roberto, President of the Union of Populations of Angola," 15 March 1961, ACOA, Armstrong Papers, NYPL. "Interview with an Angolan Nationalist," n.d. [likely early 1961 or late 1960], Armstrong Papers, NYPL.

57. The NBC documentary aired domestically and on the BBC. Quoted in Len Addicott, Cry Angola! (Amsterdam: SCM Press, 1962), 28. See also "Angolan Leader a Moderate Man," Guardian, 27 June 1961.

58. Telegram, Rusk to Leopoldville, 21 March 1961, Box 1821, CDF 60–63, RG 59, NARA; Memos, Hilsman to Bundy, 23 May 1961; Rusk to Johnson, 18 June 1961; and Johnson to Hilsman, 17 July 1961, FRUS Africa, 543–547.

59. See Memo, Nunley to Kohler, 17 January 1961, 5, Box 1815, CDF 60–63, RG 59, NARA.

60. Telegram, State to Lisbon, 10 March 1961, Box 1813, CDM 1960–63, RG 59, NARA.

61. See PIDE Informational. 242/61-GU, 2 March 1961, Pasta 20, AOS/UL-32C, TT-PT; PIDE Informational, 242/61-GU, 2 March 1961, Pasta 20, AOS/UL-32C, TT-PT.

62. Telegram, Lisbon to SecState, 7 March 1961, 2, Box 1813, CDF 60–63, RG 59, NARA.

63. See Gilberto Freyre, The Portuguese and the Tropics, trans Helen M. D'O Matthew and F. De Mello Moser (Lisbon: 1961), 5–27. Portuguese proponents were less excited about the idea of racial miscegenation, which they believed unnecessary for cultural synthesis.

64. "Comments by the Portuguese Delegation on the General Assembly Debate on the 'Situation in Angola," n.d. [likely 1962], Armstrong Papers, NYPL.

65. See Armando Cortesão, "African Realities and Delusions," Agéncia do Ultrumar, 1962, Northwestern University Library.

66. See Mário de Oliveira, "Essential Problems of Urbanization in the Overseas Provinces" (Lisbon: Agency General for Overseas, 1962); "Portugal Today" (Lisbon, 1973), Northwestern University Library.

67. Bender, 3–12. See also Antonio Julio de Castro Fernandes, "Unity in Nation," in Chilcote, 8.

68. Telegram, Lisbon to SecState, 7 March 1961, Box 1813, CDM 1960–63, RG 59, NARA.

69. Telegram, Lisbon to Secstate, 29 March 1961, Box 154, National Security File, JFKL.

70. Telegram, Paris to SecState, 8 March 1961, 1–2, Box 1813, CDM 1960–63, RG 59, NARA.

71. Frédéric Bozo, "France, 'Gaullism,' and the Cold War," in *The Cambridge History of the Cold War*, vol. 2, ed. Melvyn P. Leffler and Odd Arne Westad (New York: Cambridge University Press, 2012), 159–168.

72. Conversa, O ministro de negócios extranjeiros com secretário-geral do Ministério das Relações Exteriores da França, 23 August 1958, Pasta 4, AOS/COE-2, TT-PT.

73. Daniel da Silva Costa Marcos, *Salazar e de Gaulle: A França e a Questão Colonial Portuguesa, 1958–1968* (Lisbon: Ministério dos Negócios Estrangeiros, 2007), 68.

74. "Portuguese Overseas Territories Talking Points," n.d. [likely May 1961], DO 195/181, UKNA.

75. Glynn Stone, "Britain and the Angolan Revolt of 1961," *Journal of Imperial and Commonwealth History* 27 no. 1 (1999): 117–121. See Foreign Office to Lisbon, 20 April 1961, FO 371/155438 JP 1018, UKNA.

76. "Tripartite Talks in Oslo: Portuguese Africa," n.d. [c. 4 May 1961], FO 371/155445, UKNA.

77. Entretien du Général De Gaulle avec le Président des États-Unis à l'Elysée, 1 June 1961, Document 265:III, Ministère des Affaires Étrangères, *Documents Diplomatiques Français 1961*, vol. 1 (Paris: Imprimerie nationale, 1997), 684.

78. Memo, George C. McGhee to McGeorge Bundy, 25 May 1961, Box 154, NSF, JFKL.

79. Literal translation: "in the fridge" ["'no frigoríco"]. Conversa com Sr. John H. Ferguson, 15 May 1961, PAA 287, Pasta 922, AHD.

80. "Address by Kwame Nkrumah on Tragedy in Angola to the National Assembly," May 30, 1961, in "The Angola Story: Grim Struggle for Liberation," *Bulletin on African Affairs*, 2, no. 113 (August 1962), Armstrong Papers, NYPL.

Chapter 2

1. Connelly, 281.

2. In 1961, the African colonies had roughly thirteen million people but sent only two thousand university students (both black and white) to metropolitan universities. Memcon, Rusk with Luis Esteves Fernandes, 10 March 1961, Box 1821, CDF 60–63, RG59, NARA.

3. Dalila Cabrita Mateus, *A Luta Pela Independência: A Formação das Elites Fundadoras da FREIMO, MPLA, e PAIGC* (Portugal: Inquérito, 1999), 66–75.

4. Quoted in Mário de Andrade, "Amilcar Cabral e a re-africanização dos espíritos," *Nô Pintcha* 2, no. 225 (12 September 1976), Arquivo de Mário de Andrade, Projecto Casa Comum, Fundaçao Mário Soares. Hereafter CC. See also Mario de Andrade, *Amílcar Cabral* (Paris: François Maspero, 1980), 32.

5. *Amílcar Cabral, The Revolution in Guinea (New York: Monthly Review Press, 1969)*, 77. Chabal, *Cabral*, 29–35.

6. *Amílcar Cabral, Return to the Source: Selected Speeches of Amilcar Cabral*, ed. African Information Service (New York: Monthly Review Press, 1973), 63.

7. Basil Davidson, *In the Eye of the Storm* (New York: Doubleday, 1972), 154.

8. Marcum, 1:27–31; Chabal, 52.

9. Julião Soares Sousa, *Amílcar Cabral: Vida e Morte de um Revolucionário Africano* (Lisbon: Vega, 2012), 184–191.

10. Allen Isaacman and Barbara Isaacman, *Mozambique: From Colonialism to Revolution, 1900–1982* (Boulder: Westview Press, 1983), 79–80.

11. Estatutos do PAI, 1956, Folder 04999.001, Cabral Archive; Cabral, *Revolution*, 67. See also Cabral, "Une lumière feconde éclaire le chemin de la lute," 1970, 11, Folder 04602.118, Cabral Archive.

12. See R. Joseph Parrott, "Brother and a Comrade: Amílcar Cabral as Global Revolutionary," in *Parrott and Lawerence*, 245–75.

13. The CONCP was preceded by the Frente Revolucionária Africana para a Independência Nacional das colónias portuguesa (FRAIN), which evolved from the Movimento AntiColonialista (MAC) launched by Amílcar Cabral in 1958. De Andrade, Neto, and Dos Santos were also involved in these earlier groups. Mateus, 88–92.

14. MPLA, "Exploitation Esclavagiste Resistance Nationale," 42, Folder: Angola, Box 6, Winifred Armstrong Papers, NYPL.

15. CONCP, Statuts, 1961, Pasta 04604.023.015, CONCP, Movimentos Anti-Coloniais, Documentos Amílcar Cabral, Projecto CC. Hereafter, DAC, CC.

16. Mario de Andrade, "Mario Andrade Speaks," *Spearhead*, January 1963, 23, Folder: Angola, Box 6, Armstrong Papers.

17. Marcum, 1:135, 140.

18. Fenner Brockway, *The Colonial Revolution* (London: Hart-Davis, MacGibbon, 1973), 400.

19. Letter, Lara to António Nogueira Santos, 25 January 1960, in Lúcio Lara, *UM Amplo Movimento ... Itinerário do MPLA atraves de documentos de Lúcio Lara*, vol. 2 (1961–1962) (Luanda: Ficha Técnica, 2006), 22.

20. Amílcar Cabral, *Unity and Struggle* (New York: Monthly Review Press, 1979), 19; Marcelino dos Santos, "Organização do trabalho do Secretariado da CONCP," Pasta 04604.023.003, CONCP, Movimentos Anti-Coloniais, DAC, CC.

21. Conferência dos Líderes Nacionalistas das Colónias Portuguesas, "Communicado à Imprensa [Press Release]," 6 December 1960, in Lúcio Lara, *Documentos e Comentários para a História do MPLA: Até Fev. 1961* (Lisbon: Publicações Dom Quixote, 1999), 569.

22. Mario de Andrade, "Angolan Nationalism," reprinted in *Chilcote, 190–191*.

23. While Houser offered to assist the MPLA at the United Nations in 1962, there is no sign that any relationship developed. Letter, Houser to Neto, 2 October 1962, Folder 79, Box 5, ACOA.

24. Marcum, 1:40–43.

25. MPLA, Communicado de Imprensa, 24 May 1961, in Lara, *Amplo Moviment*, 2:89.

26. Telegram, Lisbon to SecState, 24 May 1961, Box 154, NSF, JFKL.

27. "Status Report on Portuguese Africa," attachment memo, McGhee to Bundy, 25 May 1961, Box 154, NSF, JFKL.

28. ACOA, "Annual Report, June 1, 1960–May 31, 1961," n.d. [June 1961]; see Homer Jack, "Angola: Repression and Revolt in Portuguese Africa" (ACOA, 1960), African Activist Archive (Michigan State University): http://africanactivist.msu.edu/. Hereafter, AAA.

29. Marvin Harris, "Portugal's African 'Ward'" (ACOA, 1960), AAA.

30. Program, Africa Freedom Day, 17 April 1961, AAA.

31. "Meany Exhorts Europe: Radio Carries His Call for Freedom to Red Lands," *New York Times*, 2 May 1961, 31.

32. See letter, unknown [Nova Lisboa] to Theodore Tucker, 26 July 1961, and George W. Carpenter, "Visit to Kimpangu and Kimpese—July 5–6, 1961," 8 August 1961, Box 11, RG8, National Council of Churches Papers, Presbyterian Historical Society (Philadelphia, PA). Hereafter NCC, PHS.

33. Draft Letter, National Council of Churches, 19 May 1961, Box 11, RG8, NCC, PHS.

34. Letter, Martin Camacho to Pedro Pereira, 7 December 1961, Box 11, RG8, NCC, PHS; Eugene L. Smith, Report to the Council of Bishops and the Board of Missions, 9 March 1962, Box 11, RG8, NCC, PHS.

35. Malcolm McVeigh, "The Present Situation in Angola," July 1961, attachment to Houser letter, 12 July 1961, AAA.

36. "Record of Special Meeting on Angola," 20 June 1961, Box 11, RG8, NCC, PHS.

37. Examples included the National Student Association and the Transport Workers Union later in the year. M. Stanton Evans, *Revolt on Campus* (Chicago: H. Regnery, 1961), 155; Malcolm Nash, "Rebel Leader Says Portugal Uses NATO Arms in Angola," *New York Amsterdam News*, 2 December 1961; Letter, Douglas C. Cook to National Christian Student Federation members, 3 November 1961, Box 11, RG8, NCC, PHS.

38. "NATO Ouster Threat over Angola Urged," *New York Times*, 23 June 1961.

39. Letter, Cabral to Marcelino dos Santos, 8 June 1961, Pasta 04604.023.009, CONCP, Movimentos Anti-Coloniais, DAC, CC.

40. Brockway, 400. See AAG, CFPC "Cause for Alarm," September 1962, Folder 49, KZA Papers, IISH.

41. "During the last three months," Brockway told a crowd in Trafalgar Square, "more Africans have been killed in Angola than in the Union of South Africa in the last century." "'Portuguese spies at Angola rally,'" *Observer*, 9 July 1961.

42. MPLA, "Exploitation Esclavagiste Resistance Nationale," 42, Folder: Angola, Box 6, Armstrong Papers.

43. "Angola Protest by Missionaries," *Guardian*, 19 June 1961.

44. World Council of Churches, Press Release, 22 June 1961, Box 11, RG8, NCC, PHS.

45. "Baptist Minsters' Angola Protest," *Guardian*, 26 June 1961; "Churches' Nation-wide Support for Angola Petition," *Guardian*, 28 June 1961.

46. "Church Protest on Angola Growing," *Guardian*, 24 June 1961.

47. "Church Leaders' Request to See Lord Home About Angola," *Guardian*, 21 June 1961.

48. War on Want first donated two thousand medical books for MPLA personnel. Letter, Marcelino dos Santos to Franck Mercourt-Munning, 23 July 1961, Pasta 04604.023.024, CONCP, Movimentos Anti-Coloniais, DAC, CC.

49. Len Addicott, *Cry Angola!* (Amsterdam: SCM Press, 1962), 71.

50. See "'Flimsy Excuses' over Portugal," *Guardian*, 6 July 1961; "On Record," *Guardian*, 25 June 1961.

51. Stone, 125–127.

52. Norman Shrapnel, "Tory Back-bencher Rebukes Premier on Angola," *Guardian*, 23 June 1961.

53. "Comunicados sobre os acontecimentos de Luanda, o caso do Santa Maria, as prisões na Guiné, etc.," c. 1961, DAC, CC. .

54. G. Mennen Williams, "Report of the Chairman of the Task Force on Portuguese Territories in Africa," 2 July 1961, Box 1816, CDM 1960–63, RG59, NARA.

55. Memo, Samuel Belk to Bundy, 29 June 1961, Box 154, NSF, JFKL.

56. Memo, J. Wayne Fredericks to SecState, 13 July 1961, Box 1816, CDM, 1960–63, RG59, NARA

57. Memo, Bundy to SecState, 18 July 1961, *Foreign Relations of the United States, 1961–1963, Volume XIII: Western Europe and Canada* (Washington, DC: USGPO, 1994), 902.

58. Quoted from Memo, Blue to Tyler, 27 September 1961, Box 1815, CDM 1960–63, RG 59, NARA; Telegram, Geneva to SecState, 10 July 1961, Box 5A, NSF, JFKL. Report to the President, "Sub-Saharan African Students Seeking Higher Education in the United States," State Department, September 1961, Box 2, NSF, JFKL. John Marcum, phone interview with author, 24 September 2012.

59. Telegram, Lisbon to Secstate, 21 June 1961, Box 154, NSF, JFKL.

60. See Frank Kowalksi statement, 8 August 1961, Congressional Record—House, 14962.

61. See pages 8–10 and 13 of Williams, "Report of the Chairman," 2 July 1961.

62. Telegram, Lisbon to SecState, 16 August 1961, Box 154, NSF, JFKL.

63. Telegram, Lisbon to SecState, 16 August 1961, Box 154, NSF, JFKL; Memo, Rostow to President, 14 September 1961, Box 154, NSF, JFKL.

64. Memo for SecState and Secretary of Defense, 20 August 1961, Box 154, NSF, JFKL. Officials only investigated complaints about exceptional items—notably NATO F-86 Sabers stationed in Guinea. Less noise was made about the diversion of older planes.

65. Charles P. Howard Sr., "Report NATO Bombs Used to Kill Angolan Civilians," *Afro-American*, 2 December 1961.

66. U.S. naval craft became central to Portugal's riverine warfare. Aniceto Afonso and Carlos de Matos Gomes, eds., *Guerra Colonial*, 4th edition (Cruz Quebrada: Noticias, 2005), 104–106, 162–163, 176–177; John P. Cann, *Brown Waters of Africa: Portuguese Riverine Warfare, 1961–1974* (St. Petersburg, FL: Hailer, 2008), 61–63.

67. Rui de Azavedo Teixeira, *A Guerra de Angola, 1961–1974* (Lisbon: Quidnovi, 2010), 71.

68. Telegram, Lisbon to SecState, 8 December 1961, Box 155, NSF, JFKL.

69. "Text of Questions Put to Salazar and His Replies," *New York Times*, 31 May 1961.

70. Marcum, 1:190.

71. Senate Foreign Relations Committee, "Activities of Nondiplomatic Representatives of Foreign Principles in the United States" (Washington, DC: U.S. Government Printing Office, 1963), 849–850. In Britain, Portugal employed the conservative British public relations consultant E. D. O'Brien.

72. The regime-backed Overseas Companies of Portugal hired Selvage and Lee for more than a million dollars, with half of the funds being spent in the first year. See Daniel M. Friedenberg, "The Public Relations of Colonialism: Salazar's Mouthpiece in the U.S." *Africa Today* 9, no. 3 (April 1962): 4–6, 15–16. O'Brien had previously consulted for various British colonial interests. Philip Murphy, *Party Politics and Decolonization: The Conservative Party and British Colonial Policy in Tropical Africa, 1951–1964* (New York: Oxford University Press, 1999), 108.

73. Portuguese-American Committee on Foreign Affairs, "A Story of Depravity" (Boston, n.d. [1961?]), Box 25, International League for the Rights of Man Records, Central Branch, NYPL.

74. Quote: "On the Morning of March 15th" (Boston: Portuguese-American Committee on Foreign Affairs, [1961?]). See also Adriano Moreira, "In the Name of the Victims," speech delivered to the Angola Legislative Council, 2 May 1961 (Lisbon, 1961).

75. See Thomas Noer, "Segregationists and the World: The Foreign Policy of the White Resistance," in *Window on Freedom: Race, Civil Rights, and Foreign Affairs, 1945-1988*, ed. Brenda Gayle Plummer, 141–162 (Chapel Hill: University of North Carolina Press, 2003); and Jeff Woods, *Black Struggle, Red Scare: Segregation and Anti-communism in the South, 1948-1968* (Baton Rouge: Louisiana State University Press, 2004).

76. Armando Cortesão, *African Realities' and Delusions* (Lisbon: Agénica Geral do Ultramar, 1962), 50.

77. António Alberto de Andrade, *Many Races, One Nation* (Lisbon: Agénica Geral do Ultramar, 1961); Bender, 200–204, 212–217.

78. George S. Schuyler, "The Portuguese Way: Racial Integration and Intermarriage," *Pittsburgh Courier*, 1 July 1961; De Meneses, 358–359.

79. Howley testified at the United Nations, and his piece appeared alongside an article by the Communist turned conservative Max Yergan in *Behind the Terror in Africa/Angola: The Strange American Policy* (Pleasantville, NY: Reader's Digest, 1961).

80. George S. Schuyler, "Views and Reviews," *Pittsburgh Courier*, 30 December 1961.

81. See "Letters to the Times," *New York Times*, 20 October 1961.

82. Marcum, 1:186, 344–345.

83. Letter, Houser to National Committee and Executive Board, 30 November 1961, ACOA Microfilm, Reel I.

84. Letter, Kenneth T. Downs to Paul Wagner, 12 October 1961, cited in Senate Foreign Relations Committee, "Activities of Nondiplomatic Representatives of Foreign Principles in the United States," 849.

85. *New York World Telegram*, 23 March 1961; quote in Marcum, 1:182.

86. Memo, Samuel Belk to Bundy, 24 August 1961, Box 154, NSF, JFKL.

87. Letter, Camacho to Roger N. Baldwin, 20 December 1961, and statement, folder: General Correspondence Portugal (1), Box 25, International League for the Rights of Man Records, Central Branch, NYPL; Letter, Leonard M. Perryman and George M. Daniels to Friend, 7 March 1962, and attachment, Box 11, RG 8, NCC, PHS.

88. Letter, José Alves Rodrigues to Barry Goldwater, 30 November 1961, PAA M288, AHD.

89. Memo, Samuel Belk to Bundy, 24 August 1961, Box 154, NSF, JFKL.

90. See Memo, HHS to Robert Komer, 31 January 1962, Box 155, NSF, JFKL.

91. "Presidential Task Force on Portuguese Territories in Africa," 12 July 1961, Box 1816, CDF 1960–63, RG59, NARA.

92. Memorandum of Conversation, 27 November 1961, FRUS Europe, 907.

93. Memo, Bundy to Kennedy, 31 August 1961, FRUS Africa, 548.

94. Lisbon to SecState, 7 March 1961, 2 (corrected), Box 1813, CDM 1960–63, RG59, NARA.

95. Memcon, President and Elbrick, 27 November 1961, Box 154, NSF, JFKL.

96. Senate Foreign Relations Committee, "Activities of Nondiplomatic Representatives of Foreign Principles in the United States," 851.

97. R. Joseph Parrott, "The Year After Africa: How the UN Response to Angola and Goa Militarized Decolonization," in Rui Lopes and Natalia Telepneva, *Globalizing Independence Struggles of Lusophone Africa Anticolonial and Postcolonial Politics* (London: Zed, 2024), 83–102.

98. See Sandrine Bègue, *La Fin de Goa et de l'Estado da India*, vol. 2 (Lisbon: Colecção Biblioteca Diplomática do MNE, 2007), 1058–1070, 1093–1143.

99. Telegram, Harold Macmillan to Prime Ministers of Canada, Australia, and New Zealand, 27 December 1961, PREM 11/3782; Memo, Robert J. Johnson to Kaysen, 12 December 1961, Box 155, NSF, JFKL.

100. "Portugal May Quit U.N., Salazar Says," *Washington Post*, 4 January 1962.

101. Telegram, Washington to Jamieson, 27 February 1962, FO371/163794, UKNA.

102. Parrott, "Year After Africa,"

103. Roger Fieldhouse, *Anti-Apartheid: History of a Movement in Britain* (London: Merlin Press, 2005), 42, 69.

104. See statement of Hastings Keith, 29 January 1962, Congressional Record, 1126; Statement of Thomas Kuchel, 16 January 1962, Congressional Record, 1962. See also Folder: Portugal Subjects Azores Base 6/12/62-6/19/62, Box 155, NSF, JFKL. Robert C. Albright, "Rusk Defends U.S. Policies Abroad Before Increasing Congressional Criticism," *Washington Post*, 21 December 1961.

105. Letter, Thomas P. O'Neill Jr. to William Fulbright, 23 July 1963, Press Release, Addendum to Part 8, Committee on Foreign Relations, United States Senate, July 24, 1963, Folder: Angola, Box 6, Armstrong Papers.

106. "Holden Roberto, Title?," n.d. [likely 1961], Folder: Angola, Box 6, Armstrong Papers; Houser, *Rain*, 152.

107. See letter, Jonas Savimbi to Mr. Okuma, 12 September 1961, Box 11, RG 8, NCC, PHS.

108. MPLA, Communiqué [on the First National Conference of the MPLA], [n.d.—December 1962], Folder: Angola, Box 6, Armstrong Papers.

109. "Communicado do MPLA sobre a morte de T. Ferreira e outros," 23 November 1961, in Lara, *Amplo Movimento*, 2:201–202.

110. John Marcum, *Conceiving Mozambique* (New York: Palgrave, 2018), 61.

111. Mario de Andrade, "Mario Andrade Speaks," *Spearhead*, January 1963, 23, Folder: Angola, Box 6, Armstrong Papers.

112. Noguiera, conversa com Dean Rusk, 4 May 1962, Athens, Pasta 5, AOS/CO/NE-30, cx 409, TT-PT.

113. Letter, Winifred Armstrong to Mary Robinson, September 12, 1962, Folder: Angola, Box 6, Armstrong Papers.

114. Memcon, Winifred Armstrong with George High, September 16, 1963, Folder: Angola, Box 6, Armstrong Papers.

Chapter 3

1. Telegram, State to Lisbon, 28 July 1962, Box 1814, Central Decimal File, 1960–63, RG 59, NARA.

2. Aide-mémoire to Portuguese Government, Department of State, 8 October 1962, Box 1814, Central Decimal File, 1960–63, RG 59, NARA.

3. Relato de conversa, Noguiera and Rusk, 28 June 1962, in Ministry of Foreign Affairs, Pasta 7, cx 409, AOS/CO/NE-30, TT.

4. Aid Memoire to Portuguese Government, 8 November 1962, Box 1814, CDM 60–63, RG 59, NARA.

5. See telegram, SecState to Lisbon, 26 July 1962, Box 1814, CDF 1960–63, RG 59, NARA.

6. Memo, Henry J. Tasca to Williams, 16 March 1962, CDM 60–63, RG 59, NARA.

7. Letter, Houser to Jose J. Lihuaca, 5 March 1962, Box 79, ACOA.

8. Letter, Robert to Houser, 16 June 1962, Box 79, ACOA. AFL-CIO assistance may have occurred with the input of the Kennedy administration.

9. Letter, Malcolm McVeigh to Houser, 25 March 1966, Box 79, ACOA.

10. The Emergency Relief for Angola drive distributed 115,000 brochures and raised enough to fund the work of a Western doctor in the Congo. ACOA, 1962 Report (New York, 1963), and Houser and Marcum, Joint Press Statement, Overseas Press Club of New York, 1 February 1962, AAA.

11. Memo, "Motivas de atrito nas relações Luso-Americanas," n.d., PAA 288, Processo 922, AHD; "Apontomento," Ministerio dos Negocios Estrangeiros, 10/7/1962, Pasta 4, AOS/CO/NE-30, cx 409, TT.

12. "Resumo dos assuntos, para localização," n.d., PAA 288, Processo 922, AHD.

13. PIDE's attribution of power to ACOA was inconsistent, even accusing it of linking Roberto to Castro's Cuba. SCCIM Informational Bulletin, 19/62, 25 September 1962, SCCIM/A/20/71, TT.

14. Rodrigues Nunes, "Projecção do auxílio americano nas actividades terrroristas," n.d., PAA 288, Processo 922, AHD; SCCI Memo no 45/1963, ND, Pasta: American Committee on Africa and Oficio 4.247/15.009.070 (0), de 31/v/962, Gabinete dos Negocios, extract, n.d. [1962], SCCIM/A/20/71, TT.

15. Noguiera, Conversation with Dean Rusk, 4 May 1962, Athens (transcript signed 14 May 1962), Pasta 5, cx 409, AOS/CO/NE-30, TT.

16. Dean Rusk, As I Saw It (New York: Penguin, 1991), 270.

17. See Meriwether, chapters 5–6; Plummer, In Search of Power, 344.

18. See John Munro, The Anticolonial Front: The African American Freedom Struggle and Global Decolonisation, 1945–1960 (New York: Cambridge University Press, 2017), chapters 5–6.

19. Anderson, Bourgeois Radicals, chapters 2, 5.

20. Max Yergan and Frank Howley, Behind the Terror in Africa/Angola: The Strange American Policy (Pleasantville, NY: Reader's Digest, 1961).

21. See George S. Schuyler, "Views and Reviews," Pittsburgh Courier, 10 March 1962; Schuyler, "Portugal's Salazar: Schuyler's Favorite Dictator," Pittsburgh Courier, 4 December 1965.

22. American Negro Press, "Angolan Leader Says Negro Newsmen Selling Out," Atlanta Daily World, 31 December 1961.

23. Author's translation. Memo, Ponto de Vista relativo a Portugal, from Washington, Selvage and Lee, 25 November 1963, Pasta 40, Box 413, NE-21, Antonio Salazar Archive, Torre do Tombo (Lisbon, Portugal).

24. Houser, Summary of Meeting on May 16 on Afro-American Leadership Conference on American Policy Toward Africa, 22 May 1962, Folder: American Committee on Africa, NAACP Administration 1956–65, General Office File, NAACP Papers, Proquest History Vault.

25. ACOA, Minutes of the Executive Board Meeting, 30 January 1961, Folder 14, Box 2, ACOA, Proquest History Vault.

26. "Press Release," American Negro Leadership Conference on Africa, 4 September 1962, AAA.

27. "Call 100 Top Leaders to 3-Day Summit Meet," Chicago Daily Defender, 19 November 1962.

28. ANLCA, "Resolutions," 13 December 1961, List of Participants, AAA.

29. Associated Press, "U.S. Negroes Urged to Back Africa," Christian Science Monitor, 24 November 1962.

30. Von Eschen, 3. Plummer offers a more nuanced approach, seeing the elite advocates of narrow civil rights as diverging from popular black opinion. Plummer, *Rising Wind*, 304.

31. Associated Press, "U.S. Negroes Urged to Back Africa," *Christian Science Monitor*, 24 November 1962.

32. The title of the conference, "The Role of the Negro Community in United States Policy Toward Africa," reflected the caution of prominent leaders like King, Wilkins, and Young.

33. ANLCA, "Resolutions," 13 December 1961, Section V, AAA.

34. Daniel H. Watts, "American Leadership Conference on Africa," *Liberator*, 3, no. 1 (January 1963): 14. Watts began the article by quoting Eduardo Mondlane's criticism of the African leadership for not fully integrating the civil rights struggle into the anti-imperial struggle.

35. Marcum interview.

36. Schneidman, 52.

37. Memo, "Proposal for a Breakthrough in U.S.-Portuguese Relations in Regard to Africa," Bowles to Secretary, 10 January 1963, 5, Box 1815, Central Decimal File, 1960–63, RG 59, Records of the State Department, NARA.

38. Notes on the audience of the president of the Council (Salazar) and George Ball, 7 September 1963, Pasta 14, cx 409, AOS/CO/NE-30, TT.

39. George Houser, Memorandum on American Negro Leadership Conference on Africa, March 1967, AAA.

40. "The Angola Story: Grim Struggle for Liberation," *Bulletin on African Affairs* 2, no. 113 (August 1962), Folder: Angola, Box 6, Armstrong Papers.

41. Research Memorandum from the Director of the Bureau of Intelligence and Research (Hughes) to Secretary of State Rusk, 5 November 1963, FRUS Africa, 500.

42. Telegram, Pairs to SecState, 31 August 1963, Box 155, NSF, JFKL.

43. Letter, Ian Gilchrist to Dorothy Stoneman, 21 October 1963, Box 79, ACOA.

44. Quoted in Schneidman, 49.

45. See letter, Jonas Savimbi to Mr. Okuma, 12 September 1961, translation, Box 11, RG 8, NCC, PHS.

46. Savimbi also ramped up rhetoric as foreign minister.

47. Telegram, Luanda to SecState, 30 July 1963, Box 3815, CFP 1963, RG 59, NARA.

48. Telegram, SecState to Leopoldville, 16 July 1963, Box 3815, CFP 1963, RG 59, NARA; Winifred Armstrong to Robert A. Lazear, 15 July 1963, Folder: Angola, Box 6, Armstrong Papers.

49. Marcum, 2:90.

50. For an overview of this period, see Guimarães, 62–63, 66; Marcum, vol. 2, chapter 2.

51. Letter, John (Marcum?) to Winifred Armstrong, August 8, 1963, Armstrong Papers, NYPL.

52. Emídio Fernando, *Jonas Savimbi: No Lado Errado da História* (Lisbon: Dom Quixote, 2012), 68–73; Fred Bridgeland, *Jonas Savimbi: A Key to Africa* (New York: Paragon House, 1987), 58–59; Letter, Ian Gilchrist to Houser, 22 January 1964, and Letter, Gilchrist to Houser, 3 January 1964, Box 79, ACOA.

53. Fernando, 79.

54. Guimarães, 78–79; Fernando, 80–83.

55. Letter, Gilchrist to Houser, 14 March 1964, Box 79, ACOA.

56. Letter, Gilbert Jonas to Roberto, 16 October 1964, Box 79, ACOA.

57. Letter, Gilchrist to Houser, 19 September 1964, and Letter, Gilchrist to Houser, early November 1964, Box 79, ACOA.

58. Letter, Houser to Gilchrist, n.d. [July or August 1964], Box 79, ACOA.

59. Letter, Roberto to House, 25 March 1966, Box 79, ACOA.

60. Eduardo Mondlane, "The Struggle for Independence in Mozambique" (1963), 6 and 18–20, available in Aluka Digital Archive; Barry Munslow, *Mozambique: The Revolution and Its Origins* (New York: Longman, 1983), 79–80.

61. Marcelino dos Santos, quoted in Vladimir Shubin, *The Hot "Cold War": The USSR in Southern Africa* (London: Pluto Press, 2008), 121–122. Helen Kitchen, "Conversation with Eduardo Mondlane," *Africa Report* 12, no. 8 (1 November 1967): 31.

62. Interview, Joaquim Chiassano with Sellström, 2 May 1996, in *Liberation in Southern Africa—Regional and Swedish Voices*, ed. Tor Sellström (Uppsala: Nordiska Afrikainstitutet, 2002), 38.

63. Editorial, *Mozambique Revolution* 37 (February 1969). Hereafter, MR.

64. "Memorandum of Scholarship Aid to Eduardo Mondlane Since 1948," 28 March 1957, Box 15, RG 8, NCC, PHS; Kitchen, 31.

65. John Spencer to Richard H. Nolte, Institute of Current World Affairs, "Dr. Eduardo Mondlane,"30 October 1963, Armstrong Papers, NYPL.

66. Eduardo Mondlane, *The Struggle for Mozambique* (New York: Penguin, 1969), 113.

67. José Manuel Duarte de Jesus, *Eduardo Mondlane: Um Homem A Abater* (Coimbra: Almedina, 2010), 79–83; Kitchen, 31.

68. See "2,500 Students to Attend Volunteer Movement Confab," *Atlanta Daily World*, 9 December 1951.

69. Eduardo Mondlane, "Anti-Colonialism in the United States," in *Enquère sur L'anticolonialisme*, ed. Centro de Estudos Políticos (Lisbon: 1957), 188–189; George Houser, phone interview with author, 10 March 2014.

70. Mondlane presented alongside Dr. Albert Schweitzer, the head of the NCC, and U.N. official Ralph Bunche.

71. Duarte de Jesus, *Mondlane*, 78; Eduardo Mondlane, "African Religious Beliefs and the Christian Faith," 19 September 1956, Box 15, RG 8, PHS.

72. John Spencer to Richard H. Nolte, Institute of Current World Affairs, "Dr. Eduardo Mondlane," 30 October 1963, Armstrong Papers, NYPL.

73. Andrew Young Interview, 14 August 2013, Academy of Achievement: https://achievement.org/achiever/andrew-young/#interview.

74. Interview, Sérgio Veira with Sellström, in Sellström, *Regional and Swedish Voices*, 55.

75. This perspective was most pronounced in FRELIMO but also was part of the global vision of Cabral and the MPLA's Neto as well. One MPLA official remembered Neto as "very independent, both in relation to thinking and in the way he was leading the struggle. He wanted to be at a comfortable distance to the countries that could help us militarily, that is the former socialist countries." Interview, Alberto Ribeiro-Kabula with Sellström, in Sellström, *Regional and Swedish Voices*, 27.

76. "African Educators Lecture in America," *African Students' Outlook on America*, June 1962, reproduced in Index, Duarte de Jesus, *Mondlane*, 451–452.

77. Memcom, Edurdo Mondlane with Robert Stephens and Charles W. Grover, 8 February 1962, Box 1814, CDF 60–63, RG 59, NARA. (NARA 8-10 I 323).

78. Kennedy Dictabelts Conversation, 18B.3, Miller Center, http://millercenter.org/presidentialrecordings.

79. Kennedy Dictabelts 18B.3.

80. See Request no. OD 1252G, 27 May 1963, and Program Action File L62-1404, Grant File PA no. 63425, Records of the Ford Foundation, Rockefeller Archives (Sleepy Hollow, NY). Nadja Manghezi, *Meu Coração Está nas Maos de um Negro: Uma História da Vida de Janet Mondlane* (Maputo: Centros de Estudos Africanos, 1999), 237–239; FRELIMO, *The Mozambique Institute* (Dar es Salaam: FRELIMO, June 1967), 3–5.

81. Quoted in John Marcum, "The Politics of Indifference: Portugal and Africa, A Case Study in American Foreign Policy," *Issue* 2, no. 3 (Autumn 1972): 11.

82. Letter, Eduardo Mondlane to George Houser, 3 September 1963, Folder 38, Box 142, ACOA.

83. FRELIMO, press conference, 3 September 1963, Box 142, ACOA.

84. Cabral, Declaração por Ocasião da Independência da Argélia, 1 July 1962, Folder: 04612.063.006, DAC,CC.

85. Quoted in Duarte de Jesus, *Mondlane*, 85–86.

86. CIA, "Anti-Portuguese Campaign in Africa Shifts to Mozambique," 18 December 1964, Box 95, Country File, NSF, LBJL.

87. CIA, "Portuguese Economic Outlook and Its Political Implications," 22 May 1964, Box 203, Country File, NSF, LBJL.

88. Telegram, State to Lisbon, 9 June 1965, Box 203, Country File, NSF, LBJL.

89. There is no record of a response by Kennedy or his successor. Telegram, Cabral to Kennedy, 13 November 1963, Pasta 07075.144.028, DAC, CC. http://casacomum.org/cc/visualizador?pasta=07075.144.028.

90. "While the Portuguese are not rational," Mondlane once argued, "the rest of mankind is." Memo, Director to Governor General of Mozambique, 23 October 1963, Pasta American Committee on Africa, SCCIM/A/20/71, TT.

91. See Mario de Andrade, "Mario Andrade Speaks," *Spearhead*, January 1963, Folder: Angola, Box 6, Armstrong Papers, NYPL.

92. John Spencer to Richard H. Nolte, Institute of Current World Affairs, "Dr. Eduardo Mondlane," 30 October 1963, Folder: Angola, Box 6, Armstrong Papers, NYPL.

93. Mondlane, "The American Negro and the Struggle for Independence in Portuguese Africa," quoted in Daniel H. Watts, "American Leadership Conference on Africa," *Liberator* 3, no. 1 (January 1963): 14.

94. Letter, Houser to Ian Gilchrist, 4 January 1965, Box 79, ACOA.

Chapter 4

1. Raimundo Domingos Pachinuapa, *40 Anniversário II Congresso da Frente de Libertação de Moçambique: Memorias* (Maputo: R. D. Pachinuapa, 2009), 26–28. Kitchen, 32. FRELIMO, "O Segundo Congresso da FRELIMO: Discurso Oficial de Comité Central," 14, Ronald Chilcote Papers, University of Southern California, available in Aluka Digital Archive.

2. Cabral, "Une lumière feconde éclaire le chemin de la lute," 1970, 11, Folder 04602.118, Cabral Archive.

3. Mustafah Dhada, *Warriors at Work: How Guinea Was Really Set Free* (Boulder : University of Colorado Press, 1993), 12–20.

4. Chabal, *Cabral*, chapter 3.

5. "Comunicado do PAIGC analisando a origem e o desenvolvimento da luta na Guiné, e fazendo o balanço de quatro anos de luta," 1963, Folder 07073.132.001, Cabral Archive.

6. John P. Cann, Interview with author, 30 June 2014 (Charlottesville, VA).

7. Munslow, 87, 92–96.

8. Allen Isaacman and Barbara Isaacman, *Mozambique: From Colonialism to Revolution, 1900–1982* (New York: Routledge, 2019), 86–87.

9. CIA, "Anti-Portuguese Campaign in Africa Shifts to Mozambique," 18 December 1964, Box 95, Country File, NSF, LBJL.

10. R. Joseph Parrott, "Tricontinentalism and the Anti-Imperial Project," in Parrott and Lawrence, 30–32.

11. Mondlane, *Struggle for Mozambique*, 212; Cabral, *Revolution*, 13–14; 71–75.

12. Cabral, *Revolution*, 105–107.

13. OAU, Report of the Conciliation Committee, November 1964, Folder 10, Box 89, John Marcum Papers, Stanford University Archives (Stanford, CA).

14. Guimarães, 55–57, 73–75.

15. MPLA, Communiqué [on the First National Conference of the MPLA], [n.d.—December 1962], 1, Folder Angola, Box 6, Armstrong Papers, NYPL.

16. John Darwin, *Britain and Decolonization: The Retreat from Empire in the Postwar World* (London: Palgrave Macmillan, 1988).

17. Amílcar Cabral, "Declaração de Amílcar Cabral à APS sobre a situação na Rodésia do Sul," n.d. [late 1965], Folder: 07064.058.025, DAC, CC.

18. "Notas sobre a Politica Externa Portuguesa," 12 January 1962, Pasta 5, AOS/CO/NE-30B, TT.

19. Telegram, Paris to SecState, 31 August 1963, Box 155, NSF, JFKL.

20. Luís Barroso, *Salazar, Caetano, e o "Reduto Branco"* (Porto: Fronteira de Caos, 2012), 127–129, 233, 353–354.

21. "Washington Talks." The British Cabinet voiced such fears privately, explaining that "the Portuguese might be tempted to respond to tentative South African suggestions of establishing an area of white domination." Conclusions of the Cabinet, 25 April 1961, UKNA, CAB/128/35.

22. Security Council Resolution 217 (1965), S/RES/217(1965), 20 November 1965, United Nations Digital Library.

23. See Luise White, *Unpopular Sovereignty: Rhodesian Independence and African Decolonization* (Chicago: University of Chicago Press, 2015), chapter 5.

24. Memorandum, "Rhodesia," 9 December 1966, 8, UKNA, CAB/129/127. Conclusions of the Cabinet, 13 December 1966, 8, UKNA, CAB/128/41.

25. "Conversation with Ambassador Burger, special envoy of Prime Minster Verwoerd," 31 January 1966, Pasta 12, AOS/CO/NE-30A, TT.

26. Telegram, Lisbon to SecState, 12 August 1969, Box 2441, CFP 1967–69, RG59, NARA.

27. See, for instance, Conclusions of the Cabinet, 21 March 1968, 4, UKNA, CAB/128/43.

28. Memo, Rusk to President, "Request for Appointment for Portuguese Ambassador Garin," 14 May 1966, Box 203, National Security File, Lyndon Baines Johnson Library (Austin, Texas). Hereafter, LBJL.

29. Telegram, Lusaka to SecState, 9 September 1969, Box 2441, CFP 1967–69, RG59, NARA; "The Good Neighbor Policy," reprinted in *African Aims and Attitudes: Selected Documents*, ed. Martin Minogue and Judith Molloy (New York: Cambridge University Press, 1974), 202.

30. Thomas J. Noer, *Soapy: A Biography of G. Mennen Williams* (Ann Arbor: University of Michigan Press, 2006), 293–299.

31. Memo, Robert W. Komer to President Johnson, 19 June 1965, in Nina Davis Howland, *Foreign Relations of the United States, 1964–1968, Volume XXIV: Africa* (Washington, DC: United States Government Printing Office, 1999), 306.

32. See Luise White, *Unpopular Sovereignty: Rhodesian Independence and African Decolonization* (Chicago: University of Chicago Press, 2015), chapter 5, and Richard Mobley, "The Beira Patrol: Britain's Broken Blockade Against Rhodesia," *Naval War College Review* 55, no. 1 (Winter 2002): 63–84.

33. No title (Nogueira conversation with Hendrik Verwoerd), n.d. (likely 1967), Pasta 14, AOS/CO/NE-30A, TT.

34. Airgram, Lisbon to Department of State, "Bases of Portugal's Attitudes and Policies," 14 July 1967, 4, Box 2353, Central Foreign Policy Files, 1967–1969, RG 59, NARA.

35. De Meneses, 601–605; for information on Caetano's role in the *Estado Novo*, see chapter 7. Tom Gallagher, *Portugal: A Twentieth Century Interpretation* (Manchester: Manchester University Press, 1983), 165–170.

36. Edmund Muskie, "African-American Relations in the Seventies: Prospects and Problems," 8 March 1971, Folder 2, Box 506, Gale McGee Papers, American Heritage Center, University of Wyoming (Laramie, Wyoming). Hereafter, GWMP.

37. Apontamento 300, Doc 32, 12 April 1966, Box 12, PS/AMC/01, TT; Kenneth Maxwell, *The Making of Portuguese Democracy* (New York: Cambridge University Press, 1995), 22–29; Airgram, Consul General Lourenço Marques to State Department, 5 March 1968, 10, Box 2345, Central Foreign Policy Files, 1967–1969, RG 59, NARA.

38. Quoted in Thomas Borstelman, *The Cold War and the Color Line: American Race Relations in the Global Arena* (Cambridge, MA: Harvard University Press, 2001), 238.

39. Schneidman, 112.

40. Franco Nogueira, *Diálogos Interditos*, vol. 2 (Lisbon: Intervenção, 1979), 249–252.

41. Anthony Lake, *The "Tar Baby" Option: American Policy Toward Southern Rhodesia* (New York: Columbia University Press, 1976), 124–130.

42. "Paper Prepared by the National Security Council Interdepartmental Group for Africa," 9 December 1969.

43. Minutes of a National Security Council Meeting, 17 December 1969, Document 20 in *Foreign Relations of the United States, 1969–1976, Volume XXVIII: Southern Africa*, ed. Myra Burto (Washington, DC: United States Government Printing Office, 2011). Hereafter, FRUS Africa 1969.

44. See Thomas Noer, "Segregationists and the World: The Foreign Policy of the White Resistance," in *Window on Freedom: Race, Civil Rights, and Foreign Affairs, 1945–1988*, ed. Brenda Gayle Plummer (Chapel Hill: University of North Carolina Press, 2003), 141–162. Donation Form, American Friends of Rhodesia (Nashua, NH), n.d., Folder 1, Box 1, 1040, Hall-Hoag Collection of Extremist and Dissenting Propaganda, Brown University (Providence, RI). Hereafter HH.

45. See, for example, *Rhodesian Commentary* 1, no. 46 (23 October 1967), Box 159, Harry F. Byrd Jr. Papers, University of Virginia Special Collections.

46. E. William Gaedtke, Editorial, "American Friends of Rhodesia" Newsletter, November 1969, HH.

47. American Southern Africa Council, "Peace with Rhodesia," sound disc, 1967.

48. Memo, Ambassador in United States to Secretary of Foreign Affairs, "Americans Friends of South Africa," 5 March 1964, 1/8/1963 to 16/11/1964, 1/33/3; Letter, Avril Malan to William Rusher, n.d. [c. 7 April 1966], 3/9/1964 to 3/5/1966, 1/33/3/1, South African Department of Foreign Affairs Archives (Pretoria, South Africa).

49. James Jackson Kilpatrick, "A Special Study of the Portuguese Provinces: A Place for Pioneers" (AAAA, 1968).

50. Aide-mémoire, "An Account of an Interview with Wayne J. Fredericks," 23 October 1968, Box 23, RG 6, NCC, PHS.

51. While Mondlane did not directly identify the "people on the other side," an African American working on Capitol Hill defined them as "Southern legislators with an 'empathy' for the white Governments of Rhodesia, the Portuguese territories, and South Africa." Joseph R. L. Sterne, "American Negro Leaders Urge Aid to Black Africa," *Sun*, 29 January 1967.

52. George Roberts, "Dar es Salaam," in *Revolutionary State-Making in Dar es Salaam: African Liberation and the Global Cold War, 1961–1974* (Cambridge: Cambridge University Press, 2022), 135–172.

53. Memo, Thomas L. Hughes for Secretary, "The Mozambique Insurgency: Are the Portuguese Gaining the Upper Hand?" 8 April 1969, Folder Pol 23-9 Moz, Box 2353, Central Foreign Policy Files 1967–69, RG 59, NARA.

54. Visit to Washington of Lawrence Henderson and Murray MacInnes, 24 July 1970, Folder 21, Box 23, RG 6, NCC Papers, PHS.

55. National Security Decision Memorandum 38, 28 January 1970, Document 23 in *FRUS Africa 1969*.

56. According to Cann, they were the most utilized 707s in the world. John P. Cann, *Flight Plan Africa: Portuguese Airpower in Counterinsurgency* (Warwick, U.K.: Helion, 2015), 131–132.

57. Telegram, SecState to the Department of State, 4 June 1971, Document 268, in *Foreign Relations of the United States, 1969–1976, Volume XLI: Western Europe 1969–1972*, ed. James E. Miller and Laurie Van Hook (Washington, DC: U.S. Government Printing Office, 2012).

58. "African Issues Before the 92nd Congress," Folder 12, Box 165, Charles Diggs Papers, Moorland-Spingarn Research Center, Howard University, (Washington, DC). Hereafter, CCDP.

59. Schneidman, 121–128.

60. Pamphlet, "Announcing a National Conference on 'The South African Crisis and American Action,'" 21–23 March 1965, Folder: South Africa (Correspondence), Box 52, Donald M. Fraser Papers, Minnesota Historical Society (Saint Paul, Minnesota). Hereafter, DMFP.

61. Letter, Vernon McKay to Fraser, 26 April 1965, Folder: 1965 U.S.-British Parliamentarian Conference, Box 31, DMFP.

62. Draft Letter, McGee to Alan Pifer, n.d. (1970), Folder 3, Box 506, GWMP.

63. Letter, Fraser to O'Hara, 20 April 1966, Folder 630, Box 26, Series VII, Barrett O'Hara Papers, University of Illinois at Chicago. Hereafter BOP.

64. Keys, 76–86.

65. "List of Participants Who Attended Anglo-American Conference on Africa," 1967, Folder 3, Box 506, GWMP (McGee 23_171705); "Biographical Information, Ninth Anglo-American Conference on Africa," 14–18 June 1973, Folder: Ninth Anglo-American Conference on Africa, Box 96, DMFP.

66. Press release, Donald Fraser, "US Needs Firmer Policy in Southern Africa," 29 April 1966, Folder: Rhodesia March 1964–January 1967, Box 36, Series VII, BOP.

67. Letter, Fraser to Jacob Javits, 9 February 1967, Folder: South Africa, Box 55, DMFP.

68. Aide-mémoire, An Account of an Interview with J. Wayne Frederichs [*sic*], 23 October 1968, Box 23, RG 6, NCC Papers.

69. Memo, Houser to Steering Committee, 27 November 1972, Reel IV, ACOA Microfilm.

70. See Letter, McGee to Lockwood, December 21, 1973, Folder 12a, Box 26, WOA, YDL.

71. Letter, Fraser to Benson, 2 December 1966, Folder: Africa, Box 54, DMFP.

72. Letter, McGee to Thomas J. McIntyre, Folder 7, Box 495, GWMP.

73. Letter, Fraser to Paul J. Hanson, 9 October 1967, Folder: South Africa, Box 55, DMFP.

74. Stanley Meisler, "The US Congress and Africa," *Africa Report* 9, no. 8 (August 1964): 3.

75. Letter, Fraser to Collin Gonze, 16 March 1965, Folder: Africa 1963–66, Box 50, DMFP.

76. Paul Delaney, "Rep. Stokes Heads the Black Caucus," *New York Times*, 9 February 1972.

77. Letter, Fraser to Mondlane, 8 June 1967, Folder: Mozambique 1967, Box 55, DMFP.

78. Amílcar Cabral, *The Revolution in Guinea* (New York: Monthly Review Press, 1969), 86.

79. "Entrevista concedida por Amílcar Cabral a Hamed Ali M'Koun," 26 November 1965, Pasta 07064.058.024, DAC, CC.

80. Dhada, Appendix C, Tables 14, 15, and 44.

81. Mondlane, *Struggle for Mozambique*, 163.

82. Eduardo Mondlane, "The War in Mozambique," *Venture* 20, no. 7 (July–August 1968), quoted Munslow, 97.

83. Mondlane, *Struggle for Mozambique*, 173; Interviews with Joaquim Chissano and Janet Mondlane, in *Swedish and Regional Voices*, 28, 41–44.

84. Mondlane, *Struggle for Mozambique*, 172.

85. Robert Maclennan, "Portuguese Africa," 28–31 May 1971, Folder Seventh Anglo-American Conference on Africa, Box 95, DMFP.

86. For a list of medical and educational assistance to the PAIGC, see Dhada, Appendix C, Tables 6–8. China was an early backer but demanded that the PAIGC pick sides in the Sino-Soviet split, pushing Cabral toward the wealthier Soviet Union. Memo, "Subject: Activities of FRELIMO," 18 November 1968, FRELIMO, PT/TT/PIDE/D-A/1/2826-4, TT. "Alliance Against Imperialism," *Mozambique Revolution* 48 (September 1971): 5.

87. See Tor Sellström, *Sweden and National Liberation in Southern Africa*, vol 1. (Uppsala: Nordiska Afrikainstitutet, 1999).

88. Memo, Missão de Onésimo Silveira à Suécia, Escandinávia e Bélgica, 19 August 1968, Pasta 07198.169.151, DAC, CC; Interview, Sietse Bosgra and Trinike Weijdema with author, 13 October 2013, Diebergen, The Netherlands.

89. See House Subcommittee on Africa, "Report on Portuguese Guinea and the Liberation Movement" (Washington, DC: U.S. Government Printing Office, 26 February 1970).

90. Kenneth Carstens, "Report on Visits to Congressmen," 23 June 1967, Box 23, RG 6, NCC, PHS.

91. Gil Fernandes, "A Talk with a Guinean Revolutionary," *Ufahamu* 1, no. 1 (1970): 19.

Chapter 5

1. See letter, William Channel to Duncan Wood, 15 February 1963, Folder: Mozambique and Angola, Box: ISD 1963 Refugee Prog. Overseas, American Friends Service Committee Archives (Philadelphia, PA). Hereafter, AFSC.

2. See British Council of Churches, International Department, "Angola," n.d. [1962], Folder: Angola 1962, Box 11, Series II, RG 8, NCC, PHS.

3. See Margaret Flory, *Moments in Time: One Woman's Ecumenical Journey* (New York: Friendship Press, 1995).

4. "Frontier Internships" CR.33/8/60 (n.d., c 1960), Box 13, RG 86 Margaret Flory Papers, Yale Divinity Library (New Haven, CT). Hereafter, Flory Papers, YDL.

5. "Annual Report: Department of Lay Ecumenical Action of the Division of Ecumenical Relations," 1960, Box 1A, Flory Papers, YDL.

6. Flory, *Moments in Time*, 83.

7. For example, Mondlane spoke at the North American Assembly of African Affairs alongside NCC Africa Committee head Emory Ross, addressed Africa's place in a "turbulent world" at the Evanston Missionary Union in 1954, and joined St. Mark's Methodist Church in Harlem for an Africa symposium in 1959. See Richard J. H. Johnson, "Christians' Unity Help World Need," *New York Times*, 17 June 1952; "Mission Union Will Convene at St. Mark's," *Chicago Daily Tribune*, 21 October 1954; "Symposiums on Africa Set for St. Mark's," *New York Amsterdam News*, 24 October 1959. In 1952 alone, Mondlane attended Methodist Youth Conference Camps in five states and an interdenominational one at Purdue. See Letter, Clerc to Ross, 14 July 1951, and Letter, Mondlane to Ross, 12 December 1952, Box 15, RG 8 Division of Overseas Ministries, NCC, PHS.

8. See "Record of Special Meeting on Angola," 20 June 1961, Box 11, RG 8, NCC, PHS.

9. Andrew Young Interview, 14 August 2013, Academy of Achievement: https://achievement.org/achiever/andrew-young/#interview.

10. Crane, "Eduardo Chivambo Mondlane."

11. Ruth Harris, "Ruth Harris," in *Journeys That Opened Up the World: Women, Student Christian Movements, and Social Justice, 1955–1975* ed. Sara M. Evans (New Brunswick: Rutgers University Press, 2003), 34.

12. Letter, Douglas C. Cook (Director of World Mission of NSCF) to friends, 3 November 1961, Box 11, RG 8, NCC, PHS.

13. Elmira Kendricks Zazombe, "Elmira Kendricks Nazombe," in Evans, 91.

14. Crane, "Eduardo Chivambo Mondlane."

15. Jeanne Audrey Powers, "Jeanne Audrey Powers," in Evans, 57.

16. Pamphlet, "Frontier Internship in Mission," January 1963, Box 13, Flory Papers, YDL.

17. Pamphlet, "Frontier Internship in Mission," n.d. [c. 1964], Box 13, Flory Papers, YDL.

18. Confidential Memo, "Frontier Internship in Mission," n.d. [c. late 1960 or early 1961], Box 13, Flory Papers, YDL.

19. Applications specifically asked interns about participation in social action and protests. Box 15, Flory Papers, YDL.

20. For more on Flory's idea about internationalism, see Margaret Flory and Alice Hageman, *The University, the Church, and Internationalization* (St. Louis: UMHE Publications, 1968), 1.

21. Now Marylee Crofts.

22. David Wiley, Interview with Peter Limb and John Metzler, 20 November 2012 (East Lansing), Interviews in African Studies at Michigan State University: http://www.lib.msu.edu/general/collections/asis/.

23. Wiley interview. Marylee Crofts, Telephone Interview with the Author, 12 June 2013.

24. Pamphlet, "Frontier Internship in Mission," n.d. [c. 1964], Box 13, Flory Papers, YDL.

25. Eduardo Mondlane, "Presidential Message," *Mozambican Revolution* 14 (January 1965).

26. Memo, "The South African Concern of NSCF," n.d. [c. 1964], Private Papers of David Wiley and Christine Root, AAA.

27. Kenneth Carstens, "South African Reality," address given at Nineteenth Ecumenical Student Conference on the Christian World Mission (1964), Box 24, RG 6, NCC PHS.

28. Crane, "Eduardo Chivambo Mondlane."

29. See Mary Dudziak, *Cold War Civil Rights: Race and the Image of American Democracy* (Princeton: Princeton University Press, 2011), chapter 5; John Darwin, *The Empire Project: The Rise and Fall of the British World System* (New York: Cambridge University Press, 2011), 620–621.

30. For a recent justification with an eye toward southern Africa, see Anna Floerke Scheid, "Waging a Just Revolution: Just War Criteria in the Context of Oppression," *Journal of the Society of Christian Ethics* 32, no. 2 (2012): 153–172.

31. Gail Hovey, "Media for the Movement: Southern Africa Magazine," in *No Easy Victories,* ed. William Minter, et al. (Trenton: Africa World Press, 2008), 110; SAC, "Report April 26, 1966" (1966), Box 23, RG 6, NCC, PHS. Gail Hovey Interview. By this point, the Wileys were in Princeton, where David was in graduate school.

32. Gail Hovey Interview. Among the members that came from outside the Christian structure was Janet Hooper, who would join the staff of ACOA in the early 1970s.

33. Robert Maurer, who joined the SAC a few years after its founding, explained in a written letter to the author: "The members of SAC were not 'religious.' Their cohesiveness and longevity was based on their commitment to ending *apartheid,* supporting anti-colonial liberation movements, and so on." This was less true of the original founders, who initially approached southern Africa in terms of a Christian witness, but it became the norm by the end of the decade as radical politics supplanted Christian mission as the major frame informing activism. Robert Maurer, "2015 Response to JP Questions 4 Through 9-1," Correspondence with the Author, 9 April 2015.

34. See the early minutes of the SAC from late 1964 and early 1965 held by the AAA: http://africanactivist.msu.edu/asearch.php?keyword=southern%20africa%20committee.

35. Doug Rossinow, *The Politics of Authenticity* (New York: Columbia University Press, 1998), 1–7; Wini Breines, "'Of This Generation': The New Left and the Student Movement," in *Long Time Gone: Sixties America Then and Now,* ed. Alexander Bloom (New York: Oxford University Press, 2001), 24–29.

36. See Kirkpatrick Sale, *SDS: Rise and Development of Students for a Democratic Society* (New York: Vintage, 1973); Elbaum, *Revolution,* chapter 3.

37. DeBenedetti, 100–102, 124–127.

38. Minutes of Committee on Southern Africa, 20 or 27 November 1964 [date unclear], Private Papers of David Wiley and Christine Root, AAA.

39. Minutes of the Committee on Southern Africa, 18 December 1964, Private Papers of David Wiley and Christine Root, AAA; Bruce Bevelheimer, ed., *SDS National Program 1966* (Ann Arbor, MI: 1966), 5.

40. Letter, Randolph to John Tomlinson, 22 June 1966, Box 23, RG 6 Division of Christian Life and Mission, Series II Department of International Affairs, NCC, PHS.

41. For a timeline of church actions, see "Southern Africa: Chronology of Actions," n.d. [c. 1970], Box 14, RG 6, NCC, PHS.

42. Bill Minter, Telephone Interview with Author, 11 September 2012.

43. The Africa News Service has since become AllAfrica.com.

44. Pamphlet, FIM, "Frontier Internship in Mission," n.d. [c. 1970], Box 13, Folder 76, Margaret Flory Papers, YDL.

45. The word "liberation" entered the FIM questionnaire sometime in the 1960s. See Frontier Internship Program Application, Folder 76a, Box 13, Margaret Flory Papers, YDL.

46. Letter, Eileen Hanson to George Houser, 27 July 1971, Reel III, ACOA Microfilm. Eileen Hanson-Kelly Telephone Interview with the Author, 30 May 2013.

47. Hanson-Kelly Interview.

48. Additional attendees included Carolyn and Charles Wilhelm and David Robinson.

49. William Minter, Interview with the Author; Hovey Interview; Wiley Interview; Hanson-Kelly Interview.

50. No author [Zambia Group], "Strategies for Change in Southern Africa," 1967, Box 23, RG 6, NCC, PHS.

51. [Zambia Group], "Strategies for Change in Southern Africa."

52. ACOA Steering Committee, Special Meeting on Mozambique, 8 December 1969, Folder 26, Box 92, ACOA.

53. "Solidarity Week with the Struggling People of Mozambique," *Sun Reporter*, 26 September 1970.

54. David Wiley, Interview with author, 23 October 2015.

55. David Wiley (?), "Some Hypotheses Concerning the Southern Africa Issue and Wisconsin," n.d. [c. fall 1968], AAA.

56. See MACSA, *Is Southern Africa Wisconsin's Business?* (Madison: MACSA, February 1971), and MACSA, *South Africa and Israel* (Madison: MACSA, October 1971).

57. See, for example, MACSA, "February 4: Day of Solidarity with the People of Angola," n.d. [c. early 1970], AAA; in 1971 alone, MACS worked with the Madison Walk for Development to send between $26,000 and $30,000 to the institute, "Walk Aids Mozambique Institute," *MACSA News* 11 (October 1971).

58. Crofts Interview.

59. MACSA, "Important Meeting: Madison Area Committee on Southern Africa," 6 October [c. fall 1969], MACSA Papers, AAA.

60. Mimi Edmunds, Phone Interview with the Author, 2 July 2013. Edmunds recalls that church members were often more progressive than Peace Corps veterans.

61. The CRV claimed to include two thousand to three thousand Peace Corps alumni alone—about 10 percent of the program to that point. Linda Matthews, "Peace Corps, VISTA Lose Their Luster," *Los Angeles Times*, 7 August 1970.

62. The first CRV General Assembly argued that service abroad led "to a new realization that present day underdevelopment is in many cases perpetuated by the negative and destructive policies of the United States." CRV Generally Assembly I, "Position Paper on the Peace Corps," 15 September 1970, Lynne Weikart Papers, MSU Special Collections.

63. David C. Anderson, "After the Peace Corps, Some Turn Radical," *Wall Street Journal*, 18 March 1970.

64. Ken Pierce, "Salvation, Frustration, Revolution," *Washington Post*, 3 February 1971.

65. Hanson-Kelly Interview.

66. See "General Assembly I," reprinted from *CRV Newsletter* III, no. 7 (October 1969), Carole Collins Papers, MSU Archives.

67. Africa Committee, Committee of Return Volunteers, "Mozambique Will Be Free," 1969, AAA.

68. Nancy Freehafer worked at the Mozambique Institute shortly before returning to join the CRV.

69. Edmunds Interview. Edmunds recalls that Khan and Gil Fernandes "certainly wanted American solidarity, support, so it was relatively easy to meet with them."

70. "National Assembly," *CRV Newsletter* III, no. 7 (October 1969), Carole Collins Papers photo 9059, MSU Archives.

71. Letter, Bunce, Forbes, and Yarwood to [Returnee], 20 February 1967, AAA.

72. The New York chapter planned to create a high-school curriculum on southern Africa. "New York Chapter Activities," Carole Collins Papers, MSU Archives; Leaflet, "A Salute to

Portugal? For the Heart Association? . . . How Heartless," Box 158, ACOA; Lisa Hammel, "Warm Hearts, and Travel, Inspire Ball—and Pickets," *New York Times*, 8 May 1969.

73. Letter, Bunce, Forbes, and Yarwood to [Returnee], 20 February 1967, AAA. "Mozambique Will be Free" was first published in 1969. It introduced radicals to FRELIMO and became one of the CRV's best-selling pamphlets. "Annual Financial Statement, CRV/NY," Carole Collins Papers, MSU Archives.

74. See Elaine Fuller and Trudy Pax, "'Beyond Vietnam' Conference Report" (New York, 1971).

75. Compare to ACOA, "United States and Southern Africa" (New York, 1968), AAA; also Liberation Support Movement, "We Don't Know if Africa Will Become Another Vietnam" (Seattle, 1969), AAA.

76. The dissertation was published as *Mau-Mau from Within: An Analysis of Kenya's Peasant Revolt* (New York: Monthly Review Press, 1968).

77. Ole Gjerstad, Phone Interview with the Author, 2 July 2013.

78. Don Barnett, *With the Guerillas in Angola* (Richmond: LSM Press, 1976), 3–6.

79. Barnett, *With the Guerillas in Angola*, 3–6.

80. LSM, *Spartacus Monimambu*, Interviews in Depth: Angola MPLA series (Richmond: LSM Press, 1973). Barnett's 1968 interview was published in three consecutive issues of the *Guardian* from April 27 to May 11 under the title "In the Liberated Areas of Angola."

81. Ole Gjerstad Interview. The LSM had a branch in Bloomington, IN, around 1970.

82. See entries 1 (Spartacus Monimambu), 3 (Seta Likambuila), and 4 (Paul Jorge) of LSM's Interviews in Depth: Angola MPLA series, and LSM, *Interview with Marcelino dos Santos Vice-President of FRELIMO*, Interviews in Depth: Mozambique, FRELIMO 1 series (Richmond: LSM, 1974).

83. Rick Sterling, Phone Interview with the Author, 19 August 2013.

84. LSM, *MPLA 1970* (Richmond: LSM Press, 1970); LSM, *Getting Hip to Imperialism: ALCAN, Jamaica, and Cabora Bassa* (Richmond, LSM Press, 1971).

85. Rick Sterling Interview.

86. LSM, News Release, 24 November 1973, AAA; Ole Gjerstad Interview.

87. LSM, Press Release, LSM, 16 July 1970, AAA.

88. Rick Sterling Interview. Prominent LSM subscribers included the wife of Greece's prime minister.

89. LSM, News Release, 24 November 1973, AAA. See flyer, "Collect War Surplus for FRELIMO," n.d. [c. 1973].

90. Mailing List, n.d. [1970 or 1971], Folder: Solidarity Conferences Holland 1970–1971, Committee for Freedom in Mozambique, Angola, and Guinea, Bishopsgate Institute (London, United Kingdom). Hereafter, CFMAG.

91. LSM, "1972 Liberation Calendar," n.d. [late 1971], AAA.

92. See "Vietnam Not Only Major War Going On; Wars of Liberation in Africa, Too," *Philadelphia Tribune*, 30 November 1971; Rick Sterling Interview.

93. Anderson, *The Movement in the Sixties*, 195.

94. CRV, "CRV and Southern Africa" (New York, February 1970), AAA.

95. Bill Ayers, *In Fugitive Days* (Boston: Beacon Press, 2001), 157.

96. Letter, Eileen Hanson to ACOA, Field Staff, 16 March 1972, Reel II ACOA Microfilm.

97. Robert Maurer, "2015 Response to JP Questions 4 Through 9-1," Correspondence with the Author, 9 April 2015.

98. Bill Minter Interview.

99. Preliminary Statement, "Dissolution of the Africa Research Group," June 1973, Lyne Weikart Papers, MSU; Schechter Interview; Africa Information Service, "Africa Information Service," 11 September 1972, Carole Collins Collection, AAA.

100. Ole Gjerstad Interview.

101. Edmunds Interview.

Chapter 6

1. Letter, Charles A. Wilhelm for SAC to Robert Bilheimer, 25 July 1966, Box 23, RG 6, NCC, PHS.

2. Memo, Margaret Flory to Bill DuVal, 1 August 1967, Box 23, RG 6, NCC, PHS.

3. No author [Zambia Group], "Strategies for Change in Southern Africa," 1967, Box 23, RG 6, NCC, PHS.

4. Howard Schomer, "Little Church and Big Business," 21 April 1974, Box 14, Howard Schomer Papers, Harvard Divinity Library (Cambridge, MA). Hereafter, Schomer Papers, HDL.

5. Jill K. Gill, *Embattled Ecumenism* (DeKalb: Northern Illinois University Pres, 2011), 208.

6. Gill, 139–140.

7. Gill, 208.

8. Letter, Robert S. Bilheimer to W. E. Grenville-Grey, 7 December 1967, Box 23, RG 6, NCC, PHS.

9. Tim Smith (?), "A Reply to the Gulf Statement of September 10, 1970," Armstrong Papers, NYPL.

10. Letter, Dodge to Marcum, 14 June 1967, Folder 3 Box 90. Marcum Papers, Stanford; Per Hassing, "Ralph Dodge," *Nexus: The Alumni Magazine Boston University School of Theology* 10, no. 1 (November 1966): 25–28: http://www.bu.edu/sth-history/graduates/selected-graduates -1901-2000/ralph-edward-dodge-33-34/.

11. Letter, Houser to Neto, 2 October 1962, Folder 79, Box 5, ACOA.

12. NCC, "Meeting with Regard to South Africa," 8 December 1967, Box 23, RG 6, NCC, PHS.

13. Press Release, United Nations Press Office of Public Information, "Human Rights Expert Group Hears Witness on Angola," 20 June 1970, Box 14, RG 6, NCC, PHS. In the 1970s, MacInnes also occupied an important position with the Toronto Committee for the Liberation of Portugal's African Colonies (TCLPAC).

14. "Background and Discussion Paper on Southern Africa for Consultations Between Representative of the British Council of Churches and the National Council of Churches," September 1966, Box 23, RG 6, NCC, PHS.

15. Meeting of Southern Africa Task Force Minutes, 24 September 1970, Folder 21, Box 23, RG 6, NCC, PHS.

16. NCC, Department of International Affairs, "A Position Paper Concerning Southern Africa," n.d. [c. late 1967], Box 14, RG 6, NCC, PHS.

17. Unpublished article on Mondlane's visit to NCC in February 1967, Folder 6, Box 22, RG 8, NCC, PHS.

18. Letter, Robert S. Bilheimer to W. E. Grenville-Grey, 7 December 1967, Box 23; NCC Memo "Southern Africa: Chronology of Actions," n.d. [c. late 1970 or early 1971], Box 14, RG 6, NCC, PHS.

19. Unpublished article on Mondlane's visit to NCC in February 1967, Folder 6, Box 22, RG 8, NCC, PHS.

20. Letter, Jan Van Hoogstraten to Edward Hawley, 9 August 1967, Box 22, RG 8, NCC, PHS.
21. "U.N. Petitioners—FRELIMO Meeting," 9 November 1967, Box 22, RG 8, NCC, PHS.
22. Letter, Edward Hawley to Jan van Hoogstraten, 28 July 1967, Box 22, RG 8, NCC, PHS.
23. Letter, Ralph Dodge to Juel Nordby, 28 May 1968; Memo, Juel Nordby to Tucker et al., 17 April 1968, Box 23, RG 6, NCC, PHS.
24. See "Summary of Discussion," 3 November 1967, and correspondence between Jan van Hoogstraten and Janet Mondlane, Box 22, RG 8, NCC, PHS.
25. Minter Interview. Ruth Minter spent six months at FRELIMO's request collecting educational material for a textbook, assisted by the FIM.
26. See Minutes, Southern Africa Staff Group, 21 March 1969, and list of participants, "A Working Conference: Our Strategy on Southern Africa," n.d., Box 23, and Memo, to DOM Africa Committee et al., 26 January 1970, Box 14, RG 6, NCC, PHS.
27. Tim Smith, "Reflection and Comments on a Two Month Stint in South Africa," December 1968, Box 23, RG 6, NCC, PHS.
28. Letter, Dodge to Juel Nordby, 28 May 1968, Folder 23, Box 23, RG 6, NCC, PHS.
29. The president of the WEF described a liberal-conservative dichotomy as the reason for the split. Everett L. Cattell, "National Association of Evangelicals and World Evangelical Fellowship," Christianity Today, 29 January 1965.
30. W. B. Blakemore, "Uppsala 1968," n.d. [c. 1968], Folder 428.08.04.10.1-2, Commission of the Churches of International Affairs, World Council of Churches Archives, Ecumenical Centre (Geneva, Switzerland).
31. See Tor Sellström, Sweden and National Liberation in Southern Africa, vol. 1 (Uppsala: Nordiska Afrikainstitutet, 1999), 473–505; Allen J. and Barbara Isaacman, Dams, Displacement, and the Delusion of Development (Athens: University of Ohio Press, 2013), chapter 3.
32. Blakemore, "Uppsala 1968."
33. Programme to Combat Racism [Report of WCC Funding], 1971, 4223.3.15/2, Struggles for Freedom: Southern Africa (Aluka), JSTOR. The MPLA and PAIGC received $25,000, FRELIMO at least $15,000, UNITA and FNLA each $7,500.
34. Letter, Jan van Hoogstraten to Harold F. Miller, 19 January 1968, and Memo, van Hoogstraten to James MacCracken, 19 January 1969, Box 22, RG 8, NCC, PHS.
35. Program, Mondlane Memorial Service, Church Center for the United Nations, 13 February 1969, AAA.
36. Letter, Robert Bilheimer to Gayraud Wilmore, 11 April 1969, Box 23, RG 6, NCC, PHS.
37. Recommendations to the Africa Dept. NCC from Sub-Committee Appointed by the Chairman of the African Dept., 26 May 1970, Box 23, RG 6, NCC, PHS.
38. Letter, Gerhard A. Elston to Bob Bilheimer, 2 October 1969, Box 23, RG 6, NCC, PHS.
39. U.S. Congress, House, Subcommittee on Africa, U.S. Business Involvement in Southern Africa, 92nd Congress, 1st Session, 1971, 94–95.
40. Memo, Murray MacInnes to Members of the Sub-Committee Appointed by the Chairman of the Africa Dept. NCC, 9 July 1970, Box 23, RG 6, NCC, PHS.
41. Proceedings of Consultation on WCC Program to Combat Racism, 22 July 1970, Box 23, RG 6, NCC, PHS.
42. The Church World Services sent medicine to the MPLA's SAM by 1972 and likely earlier.
43. Jim Bristol and Mike Simmons, "Questions for the MPLA Representative Attending Angola Conference," 18 February 1976, General Administration OES (Commes & Orgs to General Lobbying-Policies) 1976, AFSC.

44. "Tentative Criteria for Church Support to the Liberation Movements of Southern Africa," n.d. [c. 1970], Box 23, RG 6, NCC, PHS.

45. "A Working Conference on Our Strategy on Southern Africa," 21 November 1969, Box 23, RG 6, NCC, PHS. SAC members Gail Morlan, Mary McAnally, Tim Smith, and Ken Carstens were all in attendance, as were Gay Wilmore and Mia Adjali.

46. Letter, J. Seymour Flinn to Robert Bilheimer, 9 October 1968, Box 23, RG 6, NCC, PHS.

47. Proceedings of Consultation on WCC Program to Combat Racism, 22 July 1970, Box 23, RG 6, NCC, PHS.

48. Report, "World Justice, Liberation, and Development," Meeting of Church Representatives Organized by NCC, 18–19 February 1971.

49. George Houser (?), "Comment on Prexy's Report to the Board," 25 September 1970, ACOA Microfilm.

50. Hanson-Kelly Interview.

51. Correspondence, Robert Maurer.

52. Minter wrote the ACOA fact sheet on the Azores in 1969.

53. For more on Van Lierop and his work with FRELIMO, see R. Joseph Parrott, "*A Luta Continua*: Radical filmmaking, Pan-African Liberation and Communal Empowerment," *Race and Class* 57, no. 1 (2015): 20–38.

54. Memo, Gary Gappert to George Houser, 31 October 1969, Reel III, ACOA Microfilm.

55. Prexy Nesbitt Interview with Bill Minter, 31 October 1998, *No Easy Victories*: http://www.noeasyvictories.org/interviews/int08_nesbitt.php.

56. Rozell "Prexy" Nesbitt, Interview with the Author, August 2012 (Chicago, IL).

57. Robert Van Lierop, Phone Interview with the Author, 11 October 2014.

58. For a discussion of tricontinentalism and the power of authenticity, see Parrott, "Tricontinentalism," and Ryan Irwin, "Through the Looking Glass," in Parrott and Lawrence, 139–162.

59. Jorge Valentim, Interview with Tor Sellström, in *Swedish Voices*, 35.

60. George Houser, Phone Interview with the Author, 10 March 2014.

61. See memo, Prexy Nesbitt to Staff and Board of ACOA, 14 September 1970, Reel III, ACOA Microfilm.

62. Letter, George Houser to Agostinho Neto, 11 June 1969, Box 79, ACOA.

63. Memo, George Houser to Murray MacInnes, 23 June 1971, Reel III, ACOA Microfilm.

64. Ann Mohr, "American Friends of the Angolan Revolution," January 22, 1970, Armstrong Papers, NYPL.

65. Interview, Cora and Peter Weiss with the Author, 26 March 2014.

66. Memo, Houser to Executive Board, 29 September 1970, Reel III, ACOA Microfilm.

67. Minutes, ACOA Special Executive Board, 8 October 1970, Reel V, Minutes, ACOA Microfilm.

68. Copy of Letter, Peter Weiss to Charles Hightower, 7 August 1970, Reel III, ACOA Microfilm.

69. Lenore Cooley, "Charles C. Diggs, Jr.," Ralph Nader Congress Project (1972), 1 and 12, Folder 16, Box 58, CCDP.

70. See, for example, Committee on Foreign Affairs, Report of Special Study Mission to Southern Africa (Washington, DC: U.S. Government Printing Office, August 10, 1969).

71. Letter, Gary Gappert to Diggs, 8 December 1969; see also Houser to Diggs, 15 July 1969, Folder 6, Box 208, CCDP.

72. See Houser to Diggs, 15 July 1969, Folder 6, Box 208, CCDP.

73. See Folder 10: Africa—Portuguese Territories, Box 208, CCDP. The CFM *News and Notes* was also a source of information.

74. Letter, Houser to Diggs, 11 February 1970, Folder: Portuguese Guinea, Box 191, CCDP.

75. House Subcommittee on Africa, "Report on Portuguese Guinea and the Liberation Movement" (Washington, DC: U.S. Government Printing Office, 26 February 1970), 10–11.

76. Telegram, Cabral to Diggs, 1 January 1971, and Letter, David M. Abshire to Diggs, 23 February 1971, Folder 29, Box 127, CCDP.

77. ACOA, "The United States and Southern Africa: A Position Paper for the 1968 Campaign," 1968, AAA.

78. Prexy Nesbitt to Staff and Board of ACOA, 14 September 1970, Reel III, ACOA Microfilm.

79. Memo, Charles Hightower to George Houser, "Meeting with Congressmen Diggs and Freidel," 23 January 1970, Reel III, ACOA Microfilm.

80. "Complicity of Imperialists," *Mozambique Revolution* 4 (March 1964).

81. PAIGC, "Dix ans après le Massacre de Pidjiguiti," January 1970, Pasta 04602.054, DAC, CC.

82. Memo, Missão de Onésimo Silveira à Suécia, Escandinávia e Bélgica, 19 August 1968, Pasta 07198.169.151, DAC, CC.

83. Interview, Sietse Bosgra and Trinike Weijdema with the Author, 13 October 2013, Diebergen, Netherlands.

84. "The Rome Conference," *Mozambique Revolution* 42 (March 1970): 21.

85. "The Rome Conference," *Mozambique Revolution* 43 (June 1970): 19.

86. "The Rome Conference," *Mozambique Revolution* 44 (September 1970): 13. The Rome meeting inspired subsequent annual conferences to help discuss and coordinate solidarity activities.

87. See, for example, Angola Comité, "Report by the Dutch Angola Comité and Mondlane Foundation," Easter 1972, Folder 2, CFMAG.

88. Memo, Houser to Executive Board, April 1970, Reel III, ACOA Microfilm.

89. Memo, Houser to Executive Board, April 1970, Reel III, ACOA Microfilm.

90. Memo, Van Lierop to Members of the Executive Board of ACOA, 22 February 1972, Reel III, ACOA Microfilm.

91. Memo, George Houser to Steering Committee of WOA, 27 November 1972, Reel IV, ACOA Microfilm.

92. ACOA Executive Board Meeting Notes, 14 September 1970, ACOA, Proquest History Vault; Memo, Robert Van Lierop to Members of the Executive Board of ACOA, 22 February 1972, Reel III, ACOA Microfilm.

93. Both Freehafer and Edmunds were involved with the CRV and the Committee for a Free Mozambique in New York. The CRV dissolved around 1971, transitioning into an anti-imperial collective that included regional working groups like CCLAMG. History of NWRC, n.d., Folder: CAIC, Carole Collins Papers, MSU; Letter, Deb Brewster to Dwight, 20 May 1973, Box 11, New World Resource Center Papers, Chicago History Museum. Hereafter, NWRC.

94. CCLAMG Principles of Support, summer 1973, AAA.

95. Hanson-Kelley Interview.

96. Funding Proposal for the New World Resource Center, n.d., Box 13, NWRC.

97. Beyond prison work, the southern Africa program demanded the majority of funds for the NWRC.

98. Houser to ACOA Officer and Steering Committee, 3 August 1971, Reel III, ACOA Microfilm.

99. Hanson-Kelly Interview

100. NWRC hosted regular events and had a mailing list of five hundred. Attendance at events varied from fifteen to eighty, with forty-five being average, not including traveling shows put on by CCLAMG. NWRC, Funding Proposal? (no first page), n.d. [1973?], Box 13, NWRC.

101. NWRC Literature List, n.d., and NWRC, Southern Africa Literature, n.d., Box 12, NWRC.

102. Hanson-Kelly Interview; Robert McClory, "Pickets Here Demand GE Get Out of South Africa," *Chicago Defender*, 11 May 1974.

103. NWRC, Funding Proposal? (no first page), n.d. [1973?], Box 13, NWRC; Prexy Nesbitt, Report to Executive Committee of ACOA, 16 April 1970, Reel III, ACOA Microfilm.

104. NWRC, Funding Proposal, Box 13, NWRC.

105. Don Barnett, "Principles of the Liberation Support Movement's Anti-Imperialist Work" (Richmond: LSM Press, 1972).

106. In 1973 alone, CCLAMG attended more than ten conferences outside Chicago. NWRC, Funding Proposal? (no first page), n.d. [1973?], Box 13, NWRC.

107. For example, Conference Information (Film Showings), n.d., Box 14, NWRC.

108. "Support Southern African Struggles," *Womankind* 2, no. 2 (October 1972). CCLAMG produced an OMA button that was widely sold in Chicago and used within the MPLA.

109. CCLAMG Overview, 1975?, AAA. Given estimated attendance between thirty and fifty people at each viewing, more than four thousand people saw the film in the year-long period. The CCLAMG continued to show the film dozens of times a year until at least 1977.

110. Memo, William K. Du Val to International Affairs Secretaries, 13 March 1968, Folder 23, Box 23, NCC, PHS.

111. Memo, William K. Du Val to International Affairs Secretaries, 13 March 1968, Folder 23, Box 23, NCC, PHS.

112. Ted Lockwood Interview with David Goodman, 16 November 2004, 7, AAA.

113. Lockwood Interview.

114. The United Methodist Building—once a base for temperance lobbying—was located at First and Maryland.

115. Letter, Ted Lockwood to Peter Weiss, 21 January 1981, Box 2, Series 2, Washington Office on Africa Papers, YDL.

116. Christine Root, Zoom Interview with the Author, 16 March 2021.

117. Interview with Andrew Young, North Georgia, 1981 July 21, Box 140, Item 9, Side 2, Andrew Young Oral History Collection, Tulane University Digital Library: https://digitallibrary .tulane.edu/islandora/object/tulane%3A48390.

118. "Congressional Black Caucus Tells Nixon It Wants Action," *Cleveland Call and Post*, 10 April 1971; "Policy Declaration Released by the Congressional Black Caucus," *Cleveland Call and Post*, 10 June 1972.

119. Senate Foreign Relations Committee, "Executive Agreements with Portugal and Bahrain," 1, 2, 3, February 1972; Edward Kennedy, "Statement on Senate Resolution 214," 4 March 1972, Box 188, ACOA.

120. See Root Interview.

121. See, for example, Letter, Lockwood to Diggs, 20 July 1972, Folder 31, Box 208, CCDP.

122. "Rangel Bills May Halt Chemical War," *Afro-American*, 9 June 1973.

123. Hanson-Kelly Interview.

124. Edmunds Interview.

125. Janet Hooper, "ACOA—Some Options for the Future," 25 January 1974, AAA.

126. Maurice Isserman and Michael Kazin, *The Civil War of the 1960s*, 2nd ed. (Oxford: Oxford University Press, 2004), 174–175.

127. Howard Schomer and A. Donn Kesselheim, "Is Third World Liberation Compatible with One World Culture?" 1970, Box 20, Schomer Papers, HDL.

Chapter 7

1. Melani McAlister, "One Black Allah: The Middle East in the Cultural Politics of African American Liberation, 1955–1970," *American Quarterly* 51, no. 3 (1999): 650.

2. See Von Eschen; Plummer, *Rising Wind.*

3. See Munro.

4. Beveridge worked with the CAA and was close with Alphaeus Hunton. Lowell P. Beveridge Jr., *Domestic Diversity and Other Subversive Activities* (Minneapolis: Mill City Press, 2009), 262–263.

5. See Meriwether, 233–236.

6. "Pulse of New York's Public Life," *New York Amsterdam News*, 2 March 1963.

7. "A Letter from Angola," *Liberator*, August 1961.

8. "Portugal's Defender: George Schuyler of the Pittsburgh [*sic*] Courier," *Liberator*, August 1961.

9. "Two Statements from Angola Explain Position of Major Organizations," *Liberator* 2, no. 2 (February 1962): 2.

10. "Angola Rebel to Speak in Harlem Sunday," *New York Amsterdam News*, 16 December 1961. See Nesbitt, 27–30.

11. Robert Williams, "Let's Meet Violence with Violence," *Afro-American*, 3 February 1962.

12. See Emmett J. Marshal, "For Africa," *Chicago Defender* (daily), 3 July 1961; Laurence Llewellyn, "Well-Traveled," *New York Amsterdam News*, 2 December 1961.

13. This was an aspect of the MPLA-FNLA-UNITA divide, as well as a tactic used by a major PAIGC competitor, François Mendy's Movimento de Libertação da Guiné. See Parrott, "Brother and a Comrade," 251–253.

14. Pan-Africanism and some antiwhite rhetoric was more prominent domestically, though the latter was rare from most CONCP leadership.

15. Douglas L. Wheeler, "A Document for the History of African Nationalism: The Unemo 'White Paper' of 1968, a Student Reply to Eduardo Mondlane's 1967 Paper," *African Historical Studies* 3, no. 1 (1970), 175.

16. See, for instance, L. P. Beveridge Jr. "Apartheid's Allies," *Liberator* 3, no. 12 (December 1963).

17. L. P. Beveridge, "Angola: Portugal's Crime, U.S. Embarrassment," *Liberator* (June 1961), 6.

18. Daniel H. Watts, "American Leadership Conference on Africa," *Liberator* 3, no. 1 (January 1963): 14.

19. Cruse, "Rebellion or Revolution?" Part Two, *Liberator* 3, no. 11 (November 1963): 10.

20. Cabral argued "we can not answer racism with racism." Cabral, *Return to the Source: Selected Speeches of Amilcar Cabral*, ed. African Information Service (New York: Monthly Review Press, 1973), 76.

21. Christopher Tinson, "The Fight for Freedom Must Be Fought on All Fronts: The *Liberator* Magazine and Black Radicalism, 1960–1971," dissertation submitted to the University of Massachusetts Amherst (May 2010), 122.

22. Rolland Snellings, "The New Afro-American Writer," *Liberator* 3, no. 10 (October 1963): 10.

23. Richard Price and Bob Stewart, "Watts, L.A.; a First Hand Report Rebellion Without Ideology," *Liberator* 5, no. 9 (September 1965). In the issue, an article defended Black rights to self-defense, arguing: "Africans through force of arms and mass actions were upsetting white colonial empires," providing some clarification for the Black American question of "how best to survive." Ossie Sykes, "Self Defense a Right and a Necessity," *Liberator* 5, no. 9 (September 1965).

24. Differences with Elijah Muhammad included his lack of interest in Africa. After their split, Malcolm complained that Muhammad never said anything "pro-African." *Malcolm X: The Last Speeches*, ed. Bruce Perry (New York: Pathfinder Press, 1989), 139. See Manning Marable, *Malcolm X: A Life of Reinvention* (New York: Viking, 2011), 270–272.

25. Malcolm was housed with the stateless revolutionary leaders while attending a conference in Cairo.

26. Malcolm X, *Say Brother*, episode 257, WGBH Archive (Boston, MA).

27. Malcolm X, *The Last Speeches*, 167. Malcolm regularly used the Portuguese colonies as examples in his speeches.

28. Marable, 303.

29. Peniel Joseph, "Introduction: Toward a Historiography of Black Power," in *The Black Power Movement: Rethinking the Civil Rights-Black Power Era*, ed. Peniel Joseph (New York: Routledge, 2006), 3.

30. Quoted in Leonard N. Moore, *The Defeat of Black Power* (Baton Rouge: Louisiana State University Press, 2018), 5.

31. See Chapter 2.

32. Meriwether, chapter 7.

33. Peniel Joseph, *Stokely: A Life* (New York: Basic Books, 2014), 223.

34. Joseph, *Stokely*, 223.

35. "A Message from Chairman H. Rap Brown," *Black Panther*, 23 November 1967.

36. Jeffrey O. G. Ogbar, *Black Power: Radical Politics and African American Identity* (Baltimore: Johns Hopkins University Press, 2004), 121. See, for instance, "African Patriotic Armed Struggle Grows in Strength," *Black Panther*, 17 February 1969.

37. One article ran under the title "U.S. Trains African Oppressors," *SOBU Newsletter*, 17 October 1970.

38. "Black Panther Discussion with African and Haitian Liberation Fighters," *Black Panther*, 23 August 1969.

39. Robert Van Lierop, Phone Interview with the Author, 11 October 2014. Prexy Nesbitt, Interview with William Minter, September 2004, *No Easy Victories*: http://www.noeasyvictories.org/interviews/int08_nesbitt.php.

40. It appears Gil Fernandes attended Lincoln in the early 1960s when John Marcum operated the program there, likely gaining English proficiency before studying at New Hampshire. "Lincoln Net Coach Sees Winning Year for Lions," *New Journal and Guide*, 14 April 1962. See also, Gil Fernandes, Interview with John Slade, *Say Brother* 220 (1 February 1972), WGBH Media Archive, Boston, MA. Hereafter, WGBH.

41. Quoted in Martha Biondi, *The Black Revolution on Campus* (Berkeley: University of California Press, 2012), 237.

42. Randall Robinson, *Defending the Spirit: A Black Life in America* (New York, 1998), 65.

43. U.S. Congress, House, Subcommittee on Africa, U.S. Business Involvement in Southern Africa, 92nd Congress, 1st Session, 1971, 133.

44. See chapter 4.

45. Robert Van Lierop, Interview with William Minter, 16 April 2004, New York, *No Easy Victories*: www.noeasyvictories.org/interviews/int07_vanlierop.php. Many African Americans involved in the solidarity movement reference Malcolm X as a major influence. Gene Locke, Interview with the Author, 8 May 2013 (Houston, TX); Interview, Owusu Sadaukai, *Say Brother*, episode 317: *Malcolm X*, 20 February 1974, WGBH.

46. Van Lierop, Interview with Minter.

47. See, "Pan African Solidarity Committee," n.d. [1970?] , and flyer, "These Brothers Died Fighting the Racist System," n.d. [early 1971], Pan African Solidarity Committee P.A.S. Comm, Box 3, Robert Van Lierop Papers, Schomburg Center for Research in Black Culture, New York Public Library. Hereafter, RVLP, NYPL.

48. Robert Van Lierop, untitled Letter, 27 October 1970, P.A.S. Comm, Box 3, RVL, NYPL.

49. Interview with Amiri Baraka, 31 March 1989, Blackside, Inc., *Eyes on the Prize*, Washington University Archives.

50. Amiri Baraka, "Revolutionary Party: Revolutionary Ideology," 31 March 1974, Folder: CAP 1974 (2), 01-001-04.010, Baraka Papers, Proquest.

51. Moore, 63–65, 102–103.

52. Paul Delaney, "Rep. Stokes Heads the Black Caucus," *New York Times*, 9 February 1972.

53. Interview with Amiri Baraka, 31 March 1989, Blackside, Inc., *Eyes on the Prize*, Washington University Archives.

54. Moore, 64–65.

55. "The Black Agenda, The Gary Declaration: Black Politics at the Crossroads" (1972), *BlackPast*: https://www.blackpast.org/african-american-history/gary-declaration-national-black-political-convention-1972/.

56. Amiri Baraka, "Toward the Creation of Political Institutions for All African Peoples," *Black World* (October 1972), 68. CAP reprinted the article as a stand-alone pamphlet.

57. Howard Fuller, Telephone Interview with the Author, 5 July 2013; Nesbitt Interview with the Author. Sadaukai joined Van Lierop temporarily as he filmed for *A Luta Continua*.

58. Open Letter, African Liberation Day, 17 February 1972, ALSC, FBI, 0983437000 HQ15725073 Section 1, Archives Unbound.

59. Fuller Interview with the Author; Letterhead, African Liberation Day Coordinating Committee, n.d. [early 1972], provided to the author by Fuller.

60. Owusu Sadaukai, "Inside Liberation Mozambique," *African World*, 4 March 1972.

61. Sadaukai. Quoting a delegate to the Gary Conference, Sadaukai explained that the goal of the ALD was to show that the "new negro" will "stand up for the right of his people—wherever they are."

62. "Understand the Struggle," *African World*, 27 March 1972.

63. The search for African American unity was half the goal of the ALD. As Gene Locke remembered, "It was easier to adopt that name as a foundation for coalition." Locke Interview.

64. Amiri Baraka, "African Liberation Day," *Black News*, 1 May 1972.

65. Baraka.

66. See, for example, "Understand the Struggle," *African World*, 27 May 1972.

67. "A Goal Worth Reaching," *African World*, 22 January 1972.

68. "African Liberation Day," *Say Brother*, episode 427 (22 May 1975), WGBH.

69. "ALD March Orderly and Enthusiastic," *African World*, 10 June 1972.

70. "African Liberation Day Follow-up Measures," *Black Newark*, 1 July 1972.

71. Komozi Woodard, *A Nation Within a Nation: Amiri Baraka (LeRoi Jones) and Black Power Politics* (Chapel Hill: University of North Carolina Press, 1999), 175.

72. "Potential for Violence in the Major Cities During Summer 1973," 6 April 1973, 12–13, Ex HU 3-1, White House Central Files, Nixon Presidential Library, Yorba Linda, CA.

73. The records of the Portuguese embassy were unavailable during research for my book, so it is difficult to challenge Themido's cavalier dismissal of the ALD. But given the concern he and others showed about the Gulf boycott, official concerns were likely greater. João Hall Themido, *Dez Anos em Washington, 1971–1981* (Lisbon: Dom Quixote, 1995), 98.

74. Memo, Ambassador to Secretary, "Afrika Bevrydingsdag: Washington, D.C.," 2 June 1972, 1/33/3, Department of Foreign Affairs Archives (Pretoria, South Africa). Hereafter, SADFAA. Author's translation.

75. Regular Pan-African columns appeared in the *New York Amsterdam News*, *Chicago Defender*, and *Baltimore Afro-American* and in George Schuyler's old paper, the *Pittsburgh Courier*, which by 1970 had thrown its editorial weight behind the revolutions.

76. Bob Van Lierop, "The Quiet War in Mozambique," *Ebony* 28, no. 4 (February 1973).

77. See Amilcar Cabral, "The Power of Arms," *Black Panther*, 6 September 1969.

78. Cabral, *Revolution in Guinea*, 86.

79. Amílcar Cabral, *Unity and Struggle*, 45.

80. See Alice Robert and Don Barnett, "Rebellion in Angola," *Black Panther*, 14 June 1969.

81. Of special note was *Revolution in Guinea*, published by the Monthly Review Press in English in 1969.

82. See Letter, Lawrence Ferguson to NWRC, 23 April 1973, Folder 5, Box 11, NWRC.

83. Van Lierop Interview with the Author.

84. Eduardo Mondlane, *Struggle for Mozambique*, 123–124.

85. Robert Van Lierop, dir., *A Luta Continua* (Tricontinental Film Center, 1972), 16mm. Copy obtained from Evangelical Lutheran Church in America Library, Chicago, IL.

86. Van Lierop, *A Luta Continua*.

87. Locke Interview.

88. See R. Joseph Parrott, "'A Luta Continua': Radical Filmmaking, Pan-African Liberation, and Communal Empowerment," *Race and Class* 57, no. 1 (July–September 2015): 20–38.

89. See informational announcement, CCLAMG, "African Liberation Support Workshop," 1973?, CCLAMG Materials, Collins Papers, MSU, and advertisement, "Benefit Performance," *Black New Ark*, 1 March 1973; *Say Brother*, episode 306, 15 November 1973, WGBH.

90. Africa Information Service, "A Discussion Guide for *A Luta Continua*," AAA.

91. Sylvia Hill, Interview with William Minter, Washington, DC, 23 September 2003, *No Easy Victories*: www.noeasyvictories.org/interviews/int11_hill.php.

92. Cabral, *Return to the Source*, 76.

93. See various posters in Lincoln Cushing's OSPAAAL Archive, *Docs Populi*: https://www.docspopuli.org/CubaWebCat/gallery-01.html.

94. Raw footage from *Say Brother*, "African Liberation Day Committee Press Conference and Demonstration," n.d., WGBH.

95. Letter, Owusu Sadaukai to Lu Walker, 27 February 1973, Box 1, Southern Africa Collective Collection, NYPL.

96. "Support World Afrikan Liberation," *Black New Ark*, 1 May 1973. More than two thousand people attended the rally. "1000s March in New Ark," *Black New Ark*, 1 June 1973.

97. ALSC, "African Liberation Day—1973, Special Issue," June–July 1973, Greensboro Massacre Digital Collection, University of North Carolina Greensboro; Baxter Smith, "May 26 Protests hit US Role in Africa," *Militant*, 8 June 1973, 14–15. See also reports from FBI offices: ALSC, FBI, 1126832000 HQ15725073 Section 6, Archives Unbound.

98. IFCO Project Analysis, "African Liberation Support Committee," 15 March 1974, African Liberation Day Coordinating Committee, IFCO Collection, Schomburg Center, New York Public Library.

99. "Over 100,000 March on African Liberation Day," *Struggle* 1, no. 5 (July 1973).

100. Thomas Blanton, Telephone Interview with the Author, 2 May 2013.

101. Interview, John Henrik Clarke with Komozi Woodard, n.d. [mid-1980s], Folder: John Henrik Clarke—Oral History, Amiri Baraka Papers, Proquest.

102. The decision was eventually made to allow white participation but to keep the leadership wholly Black.

103. Alice Bonner, "Rallies Support Africans," *Washington Post*, 27 May 1973.

104. "African Liberation Day Marked by a March and Rally in Harlem," *New York Times*, 27 May 1973.

105. Lear Len, "Media Charged with Racism in African Liberation Day Treatment," *Philadelphia Tribune*, 5 June 1973.

106. Goler T. Buthcer et. al. "Congress and American Relations with South Africa," *Issue: A Quarterly Journal of Africanist Opinion* 3, no. 4 (Winter 1973): 54.

107. Telegram, Luanda to SecState, 30 June 1972, Box 2040, Political and Defense, Subject Numeric Files, 1970–1973, RG 59, NARA.

108. Memcon, Sharfudine Khan with David Matthews, 22 June 1972, Box 2491, Political and Defense, Subject Numeric Files, 1970–1973, RG 59, NARA.

109. Bureau of Intelligence and Research, "Portuguese Africa: Growing Western Support for Liberation Movements," 21 August 1972, Box 2040, Political and Defense, Subject Numeric Files, 1970–1973, RG 59, NARA.

110. Telegram, Washington to Lisbon, 2 June 1972, Processo 922, PAA 288, AHD.

111. Memcon, Rui Patricio and Luis Navega with David Newsom and Richard Post, 20 March 1973, Box 2555, Political and Defense, Subject Numeric Files, 1970–1973, RG 59, NARA.

112. Plummer, *In Search of Power*, 344.

113. Munro, chapter 8.

114. Komozi Woodard, "Amiri Baraka, the Congress of African People, and Black Power Politics from the 1961 United Nations Protests to the 1972 Gary Convention," in *The Black Power Movement: Rethinking the Civil Rights–Black Power Era*, ed. Peniel Joseph (New York: Routledge, 2006), 62.

Chapter 8

1. CONCP, "Declaração Geral à Conferência," 20 April 1961, in Lara, *Amplo Movimento*, 2:79.

2. Ted Lockwood Interview with David Goodman, 16 November 2004, 8, AAA.

332 Notes to Pages 192–195

3. William Minter, "Action Against Apartheid," in *Reflections on Protest: Student Presence in Political Conflict* ed. Bruce Douglass (Richmond: John Knox Press, 1968). Several groups and publications associated with Christian churches sided with the NSCF, including the influential *Christianity and Crisis* magazine. For the evolution of ecumenical leftist thinking in the periodical, see Mark Hulsether, *Building a Protestant Left: Christianity and Crisis Magazine, 1941–1993* (Knoxville: University of Tennessee Press, 1999). See George Dugan, "Church Is Leaving Bank as Protest," *New York Times*, 10 February 1969.

4. Briefing Paper, "Corporate Social Responsibility in a Christian Perspective," 13 April 1976, Box 14, Schomer Papers, HDL.

5. See Tim Smith, "Subject: South Africa and the Bank Campaign," n.d. [c. fall 1969], Southern Africa Committee, Collection of David Wiley and Christine Root, AAA.

6. See "Mozambique: Colony of America," *Mozambique Revolution* 10 (September 1964).

7. Memo, ACOA Staff to Steering Committee, 6 June 1969, Box 92, ACOA.

8. Bureau of Mines, *International Petroleum Annual 1968* (Washington, DC: Department of the Interior, 1970), 4. Angolan oil had a low sulfur content, making it attractive to countries worried about air pollution like the United States and Canada.

9. "Imperialist Allies," *Mozambique Revolution* 7 (June 1964).

10. Bureau of Mines, *International Petroleum Annual 1969* (Washington, DC: Department of the Interior, 1971), 8. See also Paul Sheldon, "Statement," U.S. Congress, House, Subcommittee on Africa, U.S. Business Involvement in Southern Africa, 92nd Congress, 1st Session, 1971, 94–95.

11. Tim Smith (?), "A Reply to the Gulf Statement if September 10, 1970," Armstrong Papers, NYPL.

12. ACOA Fact Sheet, "Why We Protest Gulf Oil in Angola," June 1973, AAA. See also Houser, *Rain*, 185.

13. Telegram, Lisbon to SecState, 21 March 1969, Folder: Political Affairs 1/1/67, Box 2436, Central Foreign Policy Files 1967–1969, RG 59, NARA.

14. See "Mozambique: Colony of America," *Mozambique Revolution* 10 (September 1964); "Caetano, Capitalism, Cahora-Bassa," *Mozambique Revolution* 40 (September 1969), 6.

15. ACOA proposed "a public campaign plus resolutions in Congress to get the U.S. government, by Executive Act, to ban Angolan coffee." Letter, Gary Gappert to Diggs, 8 December 1969, Box 208, CCDP.

16. CRV/NY, *Mozambique Will be Free* (New York: CRV, 1969), 23.

17. "Allies in Empire," special issue of *Africa Today* 17, no. 4 (July–August 1970).

18. CRV/NY, *Gulf Oil Corporation: A Report* (New York: CRV, 1970), 2.

19. SAC member Tim Smith first proposed the idea to the NCC. Minutes, Southern Africa Task Force, 19 January 1970; Minutes, Southern Africa Task Force, 23 March 1970, Box 23, RG 6, NCC, PHS.

20. Letter, no author [Houser?] to Eric Peterson, 7 December 1970, Box 79, ACOA.

21. Gail Hovey, Phone Interview with the Author, 9 July 2014.

22. "Gulf Oil Earnings Skidded 15% in Quarter; Protesters Set Off Uproar at Meeting," *Wall Street Journal*, 29 April 1970.

23. Gulf Action Project, "Demands to Be Presented April 28, 1970 at Gulf Stockholders' Meeting," n.d., Private Papers of Gail Hovey (provided to the author).

24. Hovey Interview; Hovey, Journal, 83, Private Papers of Gail Hovey (provided to the author).

25. Philip Greer, "10 Arrested at Gulf Meeting," *Washington Post*, 29 April 1970.

26. Hovey Interview; Hovey, Journal, 83, Private Papers of Gail Hovey (provided to the author).

27. Greer, "10 Arrested at Gulf Meeting"; "Gulf Oil Earnings Skidded 15% in Quarter"; Gulf Action Project, "Demands to Be Presented."

28. The NCC made the distinction between direct assistance and "the problem of generally doing business" in southern Africa. Memo, Robert Bilheimer to Juel Nordby, 13 November 1968, Box 23, RG 6, NCC, PHS.

29. See MACSA, "Solidarity in Worldwide Struggle," n.d. [fall 1970?], AAA; Hanson-Kelly Interview; Conference Report, "Beyond Vietnam," 4 July 1971, Lynne Weikart Collection, MSU.

30. Letter, Janet Hooper to friend, 26 February, 1971, Box 79, ACOA.

31. "Gulf Statement to Trustees Ohio Conference UCC, Columbus, Ohio, September 10, 1970," Folder: Angola, Box 6, Armstrong Papers, NYPL.

32. Resolution, 1970 Annual Meeting of the Ohio Conference of the Church of Christ, in Richard L. Righter, "The Materials of the Gulf Boycott Coalition," Ph.D. diss., Union Institute and University (1976), 6–7.

33. "Gulf Statement to Trustees Ohio Conference UCC."

34. John Marcum, "Comment on the Gulf Statement to Trustees Ohio Conference, The United Church of Christ," September 10, 1970, 2, Folder: Angola, Box 6, Armstrong Papers, NYPL.

35. Smith (?), "A Reply to the Gulf Statement of September 10, 1970."

36. Nicholas von Hoffman, "Taxing Goliath," *Washington Post*, 7 September 1970.

37. Ann-Mary Currier, "Churches Prompted to Restudy Their Plans for Social Activism," *Boston Globe*, 29 August 1970.

38. Minutes, Southern Africa Task Force, 6 November 1970, Box 23, RG 6, NCC, PHS; Arthur H. Lubow, "Presbyterians Lead Proxy Fight over Gulf Involvement in Angola," *Harvard Crimson*, 17 April 1971; Lubow "Ship Passes in Night: Harvard Votes Proxies with Gulf Management," *Harvard Crimson*, 24 April 1971. Wayne State, Charles Diggs's alma mater, was the only school to respond positively to any of the resolutions.

39. "Dear Colleague" Letter from Jonathan B. Bingham, 12 April 1971, Box 127, CCDP.

40. Betty Medsger, "Get Us All into Heaven," *Washington Post*, 15 May 1971.

41. See PALC, "Boycott Gulf," n.d. [c. 1973], Brookline, MA, AAA.

42. Quotes and details from U.S. Congress, House, Subcommittee on Africa, U.S. Business Involvement in Southern Africa, 92nd Congress, 1st Session, 1971, 94, 129, 133.

43. Richard Righter, Phone Interview with the Author, 24 February 2015, excerpts published in R. Joseph Parrott, "The Gulf Boycott Coalition: An Interview with Rev. Richard Righter," *Radical History Review* 134 (May 2019): 169–180.

44. Jeffrey K. Hadden and Charles F. Longino Jr., *Gideon's Gang: A Case Study of Church Social Action* (Philadelphia: Pilgrim Press, 1974), 114–115. The congregation included members who were not religious but participated in the church due to its activism. Righter Interview.

45. See "Selected Bibliography," n.d. (likely summer 1971), in Righter, 13–14. See also, Hadden and Longino, 116. Eileen Hanson attended, representing the CRV.

46. GBC, Press Release, July 1971, in Righter, 12.

47. GBC, "Gulf Boycott: The Best Possible Way to a Breakthrough in Southern Africa," n.d. [c. late 1972], AAA.

48. GBC, Press Release, July 1971, in Righter, 13.

49. "Dayton Bars Gulf Oil Bid in Victory for Activists," *Wall Street Journal*, 9 December 1971.

50. Marylin Bender, "Gulf's Chief Defender," *New York Times*, 7 November 1971.

51. GBC, "Another Vietnam in Africa," n.d. (1972), AAA.

52. CRV, "Gulf Kills Fish, Birds, & Plants . . ." (New York, April 1970), AAA.

53. Jack Hart of the United Electrical Workers of America even addressed the National Anti-Imperialist Coalition in 1973, using Gulf as the centerpiece of his call to action. "U.S. Should Stop Aiding African Slaughter," *Philadelphia Tribune*, 27 November 1973.

54. Righter Interview. Influential liberals John Kenneth Galbraith and Joseph Rauh Jr. joined the advisory board.

55. See "Recent Development in the Gulf Boycott Coalition," 1 June 1972, Box 80, ACOA.

56. Gulf Boycott Coalition News and Notes, September 1973, Box 2, Southern African Support Group, Vivian G. Harsh Collection, Chicago Public Library.

57. Pat Roach, "Gulf Boycott Coalition Response to Gulf Building Bombing," 20 June 1974, Box 2, Southern Africa, Harsh Collection.

58. U.S. Congress, House, Subcommittee on Africa, U.S. Business Involvement in Southern Africa, 92nd Congress, 1st Session, 1971, 131.

59. For a fuller explanation of the founding of the PALC and the Harvard protest, see R. Joseph Parrott, "Boycott Gulf! Angolan Oil and the Black Power Roots of American Anti-Apartheid Organizing," *Modern American History* 1, no. 2 (2018): 195–220.

60. Jeff Greenfield, "Stocks as Tools for Social Change," *New York Times*, 16 April 1972.

61. Willard Johnson, Phone Interview with the Author, 22 August 2014; Jim Winston, Phone Interview with the Author, 20 May 2014.

62. "The African Liberator," 19 May 1972, ALSC, FBI, 1126832000 HQ15725073 Section 4, Archives Unbound.

63. SOBU [YOBU] News Service, "Positive Action Steps for Black Community," *African World*, 8 July 1972.

64. PALC, "1971 National and State Gulf Product Distribution Breakdown," 8 June 1972, 1126832-000——157-HQ-25073——Section 4. 6/8/72–11/21/72. African Liberation Support Committee. FBI Library. Archives Unbound.

65. Robinson to Diggs, 9 August 1972; Letter, Robinson to Lucius Walker, 9 August 1972, Private Papers of Brenda Randolph (formerly Robinson). Hereafter BRP.

66. See, for example, Letter, Randall Robinson to Marshall Brown, 31 March 1971, BRP.

67. Randall Robinson et. al, "Dear Friend," n.d. [1973?], AAA.

68. Letter, PALC to Brother/Sister, 9 March 1973; Letter, Nteta, Robinson, and Winston to Brother/Sister, 27 April 1973, BRP. The full-page advertisement appeared in *Jet* in the 31 May 1973 issue. *Ebony* appeared in the fall.

69. Various Questionnaires Responses, Labeled Packet #2, n.d., BRP. Memo, PALC to State and Local Organizers, 15 May 1973, BRP.

70. See PALC Advertisement, *Ebony* (August 1973), 11.

71. Memo, PALC to State and Local Organizers, 27 July 1973, BRP.

72. Robinson and Winston to William Ferry, 6 December 1972, BRP.

73. Letter, Randall Robinson to General Mwesi Chui, 31 July 1972, BRP.

74. Pat Roach, "Gulf Boycott Coalition Response to Gulf Building Bombing," 20 June 1974, Box 2, Southern Africa, Vivian G. Harsh Collection, Chicago Public Library. Other cities with shared organizing included Philadelphia, Washington, Toronto, and Birmingham.

75. Robinson and Winston to William Ferry, 6 December 1972, BRP; Barbara Brown, Telephone Interview with the Author, 3 February 2014.

76. Barbara Brown Interview; Richard Clapp, "A Brief History of the Boston Coalition for the Liberation of Southern Africa," African Activist Archive, 2004; Richard Clapp, Phone interview with the Author, 28 May 2015.

77. For example, the Black Panthers. See Bloom and Martin, 301–302.

78. James Cassell, "James Cassell . . . and Africa," *Philadelphia Tribune*, 21 October 1972. The MPLA also discouraged tourism in Portugal and the importation of Angolan coffee.

79. See Agostinho Neto, "Messages to Companions in the Struggle," LSM, December 1972; LSM, Interviews in Depth series, Angola #4: *Paulo Jorge*, March 1973, AAA; Don Barnett and Roy Harvey, *The Revolution in Angola: MPLA Life Histories and Documents* (Indianapolis: Bobbs-Merrill, 1972).

80. Letter, Richard Leonard to Charles Cook, 18 January 1973, Box 79, ACOA. ACOA was his primary agent.

81. Letter, no name [Houser?] to Agostinho Neto, 11 March 1971, Box 79, ACOA.

82. Gulf Advertisement, *Ebony* (August 1973), 128. See, for example, "The OIC and Gulf," *Forward Times* (Houston), 5 May 1973.

83. Telegram, Lisbon to SecState, 10 November 1971, Box 2040, Political and Defense, Subject Numeric Files, 1970–1973, RG 59, NARA.

84. Telegram, Washington to Lisbon, 25 April 1972, Processo 922, PAA 288, AHD.

85. Letter, Gary Gappert to Diggs, 8 December 1969, Box 208, CCDP.

86. Tim Smith, "Response to Memo by Dr. H. Schomer," n.d. [c. December 1972], bms 551/22, Schomer Papers, HDL.

87. "A Discussion with Amílcar Cabral, PAIGC," *Southern Africa* 3, no. 3 (March 1970): 8.

88. "Firms Queried on Africa Deals," *Baltimore Afro-American*, 27 January 1973; Letter, Houser to Friends, n.d. [c. December 1972], Box 79, ACOA Papers; "Oil Company Told to Halt Angola Plans," *Baltimore Afro-American*, 30 December 1972.

89. GBC, "Proposal for Funding," 1974, Box 80, ACOA.

90. See, for example, Memo Barbara to Diggs, Re: Tim Smith Conversation, 18 April 1973, Folder: U.S. Business Involvement in Southern Africa, Box 320, CCDP.

91. "Legislative and Judicial Strategies Workshop," 26 May 1973, Folder: May 22, Box 224, CCDP.

92. Andrew Young, Remarks to the Atlanta Press Community, 19 January 1976, Folder: Speeches, Box 70.8, AJYP.

93. "Portugal Bid for U.S. Aid in Africa Reported," *Los Angeles Times*, 14 November 1973.

94. One Kennedy staffer referred to the first ALD as "one of the most outstanding, most well-organized, most exceptional demonstrations the city has ever seen," though he noted additional demonstrations would be needed to maintain congressional attention. Goler Butcher et al., "Congress and American Relations with Southern Africa," *Issue* 3, no.4 (Winter 1973), 58.

95. Andrew Young, Excerpt of Remarks to ADA, 19 May 1973, Folder: Speeches, Box 70.6, AJYP.

96. Memorandum, Government of United States to Government of Portugal, n.d. [late 1973], in *Foreign Relations of the United States, 1969–1976, Volume E-15, Part 2: Document on Western Europe, 1973–1976*, ed. Kathleen B. Rasmussen (Bureau of Public Affairs, State Department, 2014), online: https://history.state.gov/historicaldocuments/frus1969-76ve15p2/d128.

97. When discussing the matter with Kissinger, Foreign Minister Rui Patricio commented that he knew the secretary of state was "very much concerned about Congressional opinion and public opinion" concerning the request. Memcon, 17 December 1973, in *FRUS 1969–1976, Volume E-15, Part 2,* online: https://history.state.gov/historicaldocuments/frus1969-76ve15p2/d130.

98. See Memo, Leslie Yate to Bob Boetcher, "Discussion of U.S. NATO Commanders on Use of Azores During Last Year's Middle East War," 10 April 1974, Box 165, CCDP; Memorandum, Director of Policy Planning Staff for Kissinger, 8 March 1974, *FRUS 1969–1976, Volume E-15, Part 2,* online: https://history.state.gov/historicaldocuments/frus1969-76ve15p2/d131.

99. Quoted in Cedric Johnson, *Revolutionaries to Race Leaders: Black Power and the Making of African American Politics (Minneapolis: University of Minnesota Press, 2007),* 72.

100. "Long Live May Day and African Revolution Day," *Unity and Struggle,* May/June 1977.

101. See, for example, Revolutionary Worker's League, "ALSC and Black Liberation Movement," Draft, n.d. [c. 1975], Series IX: African Liberation Support Committee, Amiri Baraka Papers.

102. Amiri Baraka, "The National Black Assembly and the Black Liberation Movement," *Black World,* March 1975, 22–25.

103. FBI Memo, Chicago to Washington, 16 March 1973, ALSC, FBI, 1126832000 HQ15725073 Section 6, Archives Unbound.

104. See *Say Brother,* episode 264: *African Liberation Day,* WGBH.

105. For information on Sangumba and the UNITA approach to mestiços, see Leon Dash, "Black Roots in Angola: In Search of a Classless Society," *Washington Post,* 26 December 1973.

106. Letter, Jorge Sangumba to Mailk Chaka, 15 November 1973, File: African Liberation Day Coordination Committee, Box 22, Interreligious Foundation for Community Organizing Papers, NYPL. UNITA also criticized the Black African Neto for marrying a white Portuguese woman.

107. Leon Dash, "Rebel Chief Lives 'Where the Fight Is,'" *Washington Post,* 25 December 1973; Bridgeland, 93.

108. "Minutes of the Executive Council," Institute of Positive Education, 21–22 September 1972, Folder: Congress of African People (01.001.013.011), Amiri Baraka Papers.

109. Florence Tate and Jake-Ann Jones, *Sometimes Farmgirls Become Revolutionaries* (Baltimore: Black Classics Press, 2021), 203.

110. See Simon Anekwe, "May Proclaimed African Liberation Month," *New York Amsterdam News,* 19 May 1973; "'Africa Is at War' Writer Tells Group," *New Pittsburgh Courier,* 9 June 1973.

111. See Leon Dash, "Rebel Bands Roam at Will in Portuguese Territory," *Washington Post,* 23 December 1973; Dash, "Black Roots in Angola."

112. Guimarães was among the most active Angolans in the Gulf boycott campaign, with speaking engagements sometimes arranged through ACOA.

113. Memo, Lucius Walker to Owusu Sadauki, 18 April 1973, Folder: Requests to visit Mozambique, Box 3, RVL, NYPL.

114. ALSC, "Report on UNITA Tour," 1 February 1974, ALSC, FBI, 1126832000 HQ15725073 Section 13, Archives Unbound.

115. "Victory Is Certain in Angola—MPLA," *African World,* 19 February 1972.

116. Prexy Nesbitt, "[Organizing] Outrage into Action: A Brief Discussion of U.S. Anti-Apartheid and African Solidarity Work, Then and Now," unpublished paper, presented at the International Conference on a Decade of Freedom: Celebrating the Role of the International Anti-Apartheid Movement (Durban, South Africa, 13 October 2004).

117. Marable, *Race Reform and Rebellion*, 135.

118. FBI Memo, Cincinnati to Washington, 2 July 1973, ALSC, FBI, 1126832000 HQ15725073 Section 9, Archives Unbound.

119. Abdul Alkalimat and Nelson Johnson, "Toward the Ideological Unity of the African Liberation Support Committee: A Response of Criticisms of the ALSC Statement of Principles" (Greensboro, NC: ALSC International Steering Committee, 1974), 1.

120. Alkalimat and Johnson, "Toward the Ideological Unity of the African Liberation Support Committee," 8–9.

121. "Carmichael Returns from Africa Sojourn," *Milwaukee Star*, 5 June 1971.

122. Haki Madhubuti, "Enemies: From the Left and the Right," in ALSC, FBI, 1126832000 HQ15725073 Section 13, Archives Unbound.

123. Omowale Luthuli, Telephone Interview with the Author, 27 April 2013.

124. Luthuli Interview; Nesbitt Interview with the Author.

125. Memo, Cincinnati FBI to Director, 14 May 1974, in ALSC, FBI, 1126832000 HQ15725073 Section 14, Archives Unbound.

126. Phil Hutchings, "Report on the ALSC National Conference," *Black Scholar*, July–August 1974, 51.

127. Margaret Tarter, "The Politics of African Liberation Organizations," *Bay State Banner* (Boston), 7 July 1977. See also Cedric Johnson, "From Popular Anti-Imperialism to Sectarianism: The African Liberation Support Committee and Black Power Radicals," *New Political Science* 15, no. 4 (December 2003): 492–493.

128. "1st Draft of General CAP Summation of National ALSC 1972–1975," Folder: African Liberation Support Committee 1975, 01.001.05.022, Baraka Papers.

129. For a concise overview of the Carnation Revolution in English, see Kenneth Maxwell, *The Making of Portuguese Democracy* (New York: Cambridge University Press, 1995), 27–29, 55–63.

130. Stephanie Urdang, Skype Interview with the Author, 1 May 2014.

131. Prexy Nesbitt, Interview with the Author, 1 September 2012 (Chicago, IL).

132. Charles Diggs, Questions Submitted to the State Department, 24 May 1974, Folder May 20–24, Box 226, CCDP.

133. Schneidman, chapter 4.

134. Tiago Moreira de Sá, *Os Estados Unidos e a Descolonização de Angola* (Alfragide: Dom Quixote, 2011), 96–100; Maxwell, 102–104, 122.

135. See Poster, ALSC, "A Luta Continua: Azania, Namibia, Zimbabwe," early 1976, Oakland, CA; South Africa Catalyst Project, *A Luta Continua*, 4, Amherst, MA, AAA.

136. Harry Amana, "Philadelphia Angola Backers to March on Gulf Oil Offices," *Philadelphia Tribune*, 7 February 1976, 3.

137. Cabral, *Unity and Struggle*, 261.

138. Meetings in New York at United Nations, 23 September–9 August 1974, Folder: 23–27 September, Box 226, CCDP.

139. Draft, African Liberation Day Statement, 25 May 1975, Folder: 20–24 May Box 226, CCDP.

Chapter 9

1. UPI, "200 Protests U.S. Role in Angola," *Washington Post*, 20 January 1976.

2. Robert David Johnson, *Congress and the Cold War* (New York: Cambridge University Press, 2005), chapters 5–7; Julian Zelizer, *Arsenal of Democracy* (New York: Basic Books, 2010), 256–264.

3. Thomas M. Franck and Edward Weisband, *Foreign Policy by Congress* (New York: Oxford University Press, 1979), 3; Campbell Craig and Fredrik Logevall, *America's Cold War: The Politics of Insecurity* (Cambridge, MA: Belknap Press of Harvard University Press, 2009), chapter 8.

4. Margaret E. Keck and Kathryn Sikkink, *Activists Beyond Borders* (Ithaca: Cornell University Press, 1998), 119.

5. Though authors discuss organizing around Portuguese Africa, none link it to popular opposition to Angola in 1975 nor the role it played expanding U.S. interest in southern Africa. See Francis Njubi Nesbitt, *Race for Sanctions: African Americans Against Apartheid, 1946–1994* (Bloomington: Indiana University Press, 2004); Donald R. Culverson, *Contesting Apartheid: U.S. Activism, 1960–1967* (Boulder: Westview Press, 1999).

6. Jeremi Suri, *Power and Protest: Global Revolution and the Rise of Détente* (Cambridge, MA: Harvard University Press, 2005). Congress receives little mention despite its efforts promoting withdrawal from Vietnam.

7. John A. Lawrence, *The Class of '74: Congress After Watergate and the Roots of Partisanship* (Baltimore: Johns Hopkins University Press, 2018), chapters 5–6; Johnson, *Congress and the Cold War*, chapter 6.

8. Elizabeth Drew, *Senator* (New York: Simon and Schuster, 1978), 18.

9. Barbara J. Keys, *Reclaiming American Virtue: The Human Rights Revolution of the 1970s* (Cambridge, MA: Harvard University Press, 2014), chapter 4.

10. Frank Ferarri/Jane Jacqz, "Report of the Kinshasa Conference of African and American Representatives," 4 September 1975, Folder: Speeches, Box 70.7, Andrew J. Young Papers, Auburn Avenue Research Library on African American Culture and History (Atlanta, GA). Hereafter, AJYP.

11. Anne Forrester Holloway, "International Economic Policy," September 1976; see also Policy Position Paper, International Economic Policy, n.d., Folder: Position Statements International Economics, Box 68.3, AJYP.

12. Letter, Clark to Bernard O'Dell, 26 September 1975, Folder: FR-2, Box 42, Richard C. Clark Papers, University of Iowa (Iowa City, IA). Hereafter, RCCP.

13. Dick Clark, Radio Show, 5 September 1975, Folder: 1975 Radio Show Scripts, Box 117, RCCP.

14. Johnson, *Congress and the Cold War*, 186.

15. "Foreign Affairs," n.d., Folder: John V. Tunney Extra Copies, Carton 3, John V. Tunney Papers, University of California (Berkeley, CA). Hereafter, JVTP.

16. The NCC testified in favor of a New International Economic Order. Letter, John Sparkman to Gale McGee, 20 March 1976, Folder 7, Box 547, GWMP.

17. Andrew Young, "Congressional Reform," Statement to Atlanta Press Club, 27 September 1972, Folder: Speeches, Box 70.5, AJYP.

18. Transcript, Andrew Young Oral History, LBJL, 28.

19. See, for instance, Tunney, Statement, 21 April 1971, Folder: Peace Demonstrations, Carton 3; Tunney, Remarks to San Jose Rotary, 13 October 1976, Folder: unlabeled, Carton 7, JVTP.

20. Letter, Clark to Dennis Murphy, 24 April 1975, Folder: FR-1, Box 42, RCCP. See also, press clipping, "Pro and Con: Abandon Angola to Russia?" *U.S. News and World Report*, 1976, Folder: Angola, Box 50, RCCP.

21. Transcript, Andrew Young Oral History, LBJ Library, 29. See also Andrew Young, Excerpts of Remarks to NAACP National Convention, 5 July 1973, Folder: Speeches, Box 70.6, AJYP.

22. Interview transcript, Julius Nyerere with Jonathan Power, n.d. [c. 1979], Folder: South Africa, Box 118.9, AJYP.

23. Andrew Young, Transcript of talk to Council of Foundations, 13 May 1976.

24. Johnson, *Congress and the Cold War*, chapters 5–6.

25. "A More Perfect Union," n.d. [c. 1975], Folder: Interviews, Box 64.5, AJYP.

26. Known as *cooperantes*, these Western volunteers joined Eastern bloc citizens to help FRELIMO and many of its most important domestic institutions, including the Ministry of Education, the Ministry of Information, and the National Institute of Cinema. They included several longtime activists mentioned in previous chapters, including Bill Minter of MACSA, Ole Gjerstad of the LSM, and Sam Barnes of the CRV.

27. See chapter 2 for discussion on Kissinger's views on the developing world in foreign policy.

28. Henry Kissinger, *The Years of Renewal* (New York: Simon and Schuster, 1999), 799.

29. CIA Information Cable, 9 June 1975, Document 107, in *Foreign Relation of the United States, 1969–1976, Volume XXVIII: Southern Africa*, ed. Myra Burton (Washington, DC: United States Government Printing Office, 2011). Hereafter, *FRUS, 1969–1976*.

30. For Ford's political difficulties, see Zelizer, *Arsenal of Democracy*, 256–264.

31. Memorandum for Records, 5 June 1975, Document 106, *FRUS, 1969–1976*.

32. Telegram, Kinshasa to Secstate, 22 July 1975, Box 7, Presidential Country Files for Africa, Gerald R. Ford Presidential Library (Ann Arbor, MI). Hereafter, GRFL. See also Angola Section, *FRUS, 1969–1976*.

33. Memorandum for Record, 8 August 1975, Document 123, *FRUS, 1969–1976*. Document 201; Memorandum of Record, 14 November 1975, Document 137, in *FRUS, 1969–1976*.

34. Telegram, Kinshasa to SecState, 24 June 1975, Box 10, IFM (Institutional Meetings File), U.S. National Security Council, GRFL.

35. Minutes of National Security Council Meeting, 27 June 1975, Document 113, *FRUS, 1969–1976*.

36. Diggs's Subcommittee on Africa would become the Subcommittee on Resources, Food, and Energy; he remained chair but with a much broader range of issues to cover.

37. Clark credited the CBC, singling out Andrew Young, with leading the transformation in Africa policy. Dick Clark, Draft "U.S. Africa Policy at a Crossroads," n.d. [1979], Folder: U.S. Africa Policy at a Crossroads, Box 142. RCCP.

38. Richard F. Fenno Jr. *Senators on the Campaign Trail: The Politics of Representations* (Norman: University of Oklahoma Press, 1996), 11–112.

39. Quoted in Robert David Johnson, "The Unintended Consequences of Congressional Reform: The Clark and Tunney Amendments and U.S. Policy Toward Angola," *Diplomatic History* 27, no. 2 (2013): 223.

40. WOA, "What Can We Expect from the New Congress?" 22 November 1972, Box 6, Southern Africa Support Group, Vivian G. Harsh Collection, Chicago Public Library.

41. Dick Clark, Phone Interview with the Author, 25 September 2012.

42. Franck and Weisband, 228–229.

43. Dick Clark, "Angola: A Story of My Personal Involvement," 8 April 1982, Box 143, RCCP. Though poorly attended—Biden was often the only other person there—the hearings were pivotal for Clark and his staff.

44. Dick Clark Interview. Clark could not remember when his association with them first began.

45. Allen Isaacman was close to FRLEIMO, a MACSA member, and later taught in free Mozambique. Willard Johnson of MIT was active in the Boston ALSC and acted as a mentor to Randall Robinson and the PALC.

46. "U.S. Policy Toward Southern Africa," Hearings Before the Subcommittee on African Affairs of the Committee on Foreign Relations, June–July 1975 (Washington, DC, 1976), 43.

47. "U.S. Policy Toward Southern Africa," 79.

48. "U.S. Policy Toward Southern Africa," 103.

49. For John Marcum's relationship with Roberto and domestic activities in the early 1960s, see chapters 1–2.

50. "U.S. Policy Toward Southern Africa," 93.

51   "U.S. Policy Toward Southern Africa," 235.

52. "U.S. Policy Toward Southern Africa."

53. "U.S. Policy Toward Southern Africa," 500.

54. Memo, Clark to John Sparkman, 27 June 1975, Folder: FR 1-3, Box 42, RCCP.

55. Kissinger, *Years of Renewal*, 802. Telecon, Hyland and Kissinger, 23 December 1975, Kissinger Papers, Library of Congress. Frank Church claimed that not even he had been fully briefed until "after the fact." "Senate's Aim: Get Us out of Angola," *New York Post*, 16 December 1975.

56. Memorandum for the Record, 8 August 1975, Document 123, in *FRUS, 1969–1976*.

57. John Stockwell, *In Search of Enemies: A CIA Story* (New York: W. W. Norton and Company, 1978), 227–228; Dick Clark Interview.

58. Dick Clark Interview. Dick Moose was famously hostile to Kissinger, who commented: "He's gone so far he doesn't even like me." Memorandum for the Record, 8 August 1975, Document 123, in *FRUS, 1969–1976*.

59. The U.S. embassy in Kinshasa requested guidance from Kissinger about how much it could reveal to the congressional delegation. Telegram, Kinshasa to SecState, 13 August 1975, Box 7, Presidential Country Files for Africa, GRFL; Stockwell, 227–228.

60. Clark recalled the meeting being "most helpful to my later efforts to end United States covert involvement in Angola." Telegram, Clark to Dos Santos, 26 October 1976, Folder FR 1-3 Africa, Box 50, RCCP.

61. Dick Clark Interview.

62. Dick Clark Interview.

63. Memo, J. H. A. Buekes to the Secretary of Foreign Affairs, 30 January 1976, USA Relations with SA, vol. 32, 1/33/3, SADFAA.

64. Leslie H. Gelb, "U.S., Soviet, China Reported Aiding Portugal, Angola," *New York Times*, 25 September 1975.

65. Gleijeses, 165–272.

66. See Pamela J. Banks, "Angolan Lib Forces Battle Towards Nov 11 Independence," *Baltimore Afro-American*, 8 November 1975.

67. Letter, McGee to Mark Hoffman, 2 February 1976, Folder 5, Box 549, GWMP.

68. Johnson, *Unintended Consequences*, 226. The *Washington Post* went on record supporting "modest open" assistance.

69. Johnson, Congress, 209–221.

70. 121 Congressional Record, 94th Congress, 1st Session, pp16699 (3 June 1975).

71. Johnson, "Unintended Consequences," 226.

72. John W. Lewis Jr., "Say U.S. Involvement in Angola Could Lead to Another Vietnam," *Atlanta Daily World*, 4 December 1975. Memo, HSC to CCD, Meeting with Ted Lockwood et al. of the Washington Office on Africa, 1 October 1975, Box 300, CCDP. WOA reached out to Diggs at the beginning of October and encouraged him to look deeper into the Angola issue, specifically the shipment of arms through Zaire.

73. Untitled notes [Havana Meeting?], n.d. [May 1976?], Box 44, Washington Office on Africa Papers, Yale Divinity Library (New Haven, CT). Hereafter, WOA, YDL.

74. "National Working Conference to Be Held in Madison," *MACSA News* 52 (September 1975); "Ballot [for the selection of the steering committee of the coalition on the liberation of southern Africa]," Box: 1975 PED, AFSC Archive.

75. "Minutes of October 13 Plenary Session on National Coordination at Working Conference on Southern Africa at Madison, Wisconsin," 13 October 1975, AFSC Archive.

76. "Minutes of October 13 Plenary."

77. Houser, *Rain*, 291.

78. See Episcopal Churchmen for South Africa, "USA—South Africa Allies in Angola War," 29 November 1975; Bay Area Namibia Action Group, "Legislative Action Alert," n.d. [likely November or December 1975], Box 44, WOA, YDL.

79. "Conversation with Lou Gerber," 10 December [1975], Box 44, WOA, YDL.

80. Statement of Edgar Lockwood Before Subcommittee of International Food, Resources, and Energy of the House Committee on International Relations, 5 November 1975, AAA.

81. Gleijeses, 294–305.

82. See Jamie Miller, "Yes, Minister: Reassessing South Africa's Intervention in the Angolan Civil War, 1975–1976," *Journal of Cold War Studies* 15, no. 3 (Summer 2013): 4–33.

83. Gleijeses, 308–326.

84. Memo, Hal Horan to Brent Scowcroft, 15 December 1975, Box 5, Presidential Country Files for Africa, GRFL.

85. George Houser, "Communism and the War in Angola," *New York Times*, 14 December 1975.

86. "The Robert MacNeil Report: Angola," 19 December 1975, NewsHour Productions, American Archive of Public Broadcasting (GBH and the Library of Congress), Boston, MA, and Washington, DC, accessed August 13, 2023, http://americanarchive.org/catalog/cpb-aacip -507-vh5cc0w75k.

87. Press clipping, "Pro and Con: Abandon Angola to Russia?" *U.S. News and World Report*, 1976, Folder: Angola, Box 50, RCCP.

88. Telcon, Barry Schweid with Henry Kissinger, 8 December 1975, Kissinger Telcons. When asked about possible covert operations in Angola, Kissinger said, "There is nothing."

89. Stockwell, 230; Dick Clark Interview.

90. Johnson, "Unintended Consequences," 227–228.

91. See Chapter 4.

92. "Portugal Bid for U.S. Aid in Africa Reported," *Los Angeles Times*, 14 November 1973.

93. Letter, Tunney to Californian, December 1975, Folder: Views on Angolan War 1975, Carton 2, JVTP.

94. Dana Adams Schmidt, "Covert Actions Pits Congress Vs. Kissinger," *Christian Science Monitor*, 19 December 1975.

95. Additional funds were badly need, as money had run dangerously low. Memorandum for Record, 21 November 1975, Document 139, in *FRUS, 1969–1976*.

96. Spencer Rich, "Angola Aid Plan Returned to Ford," *Washington Post*, 19 December 1975.

97. Franck and Weisband, 53.

98. Spencer Rich, "Senate Bars Angola Aid," *Washington Post*, 20 December 1975.

99. "The Robert MacNeil Report: Angola."

100. "Weicker Hits Policy in Angola," *Hartford Courant*, 18 December 1975, and WOA, "Previous Statements by Senators on Angola," n.d. [c. 1981], Box 15, WOA, YDL.

101. Spencer Rich, "Senate Moves to Bar Aid," *Washington Post*, 18 December 1975.

102. "The Robert MacNeil Report: Angola."

103. "The Robert MacNeil Report: Angola."

Chapter 10

1. William F. Buckley, Jr., "The Bad Guys in Angola," *Los Angeles Times*, 19 December 1975.

2. Theodore Draper, "Appeasement and Détente," *Commentary* 61:2 (February 1976), 38.

3. "The Robert MacNeil Report; Angola," 19 December 1975, NewsHour Productions, American Archive of Public Broadcasting (WGBH and the Library of Congress), Boston, MA and Washington, DC, accessed August 13, 2023, http://americanarchive.org/catalog/cpb-aacip -507-vh5cc0w75k.

4. See James F. Dinwiddie, "Russians in Angola: Threat to Whom?" *Christian Science Monitor*, 31 December 1975.

5. "Kissinger's No-Win Policy in Angola," *Human Events* 35, no. 52 (27 December 1975).

6. Jules Witcover, "Reagan Starts '76 Bid in N.H.," *Washington Post*, 6 January 1976.

7. Richard Bergholz, "Reagan Opens N.H. Drive, Says He Won't Force Taxes," *Los Angeles Times*, 6 January 1976.

8. "Reagan Tough on Angola," *Sun*, 11 January 1976.

9. William F. Buckley, "A Question of Answers," *Newsday*, 10 January 1976.

10. See Patrick J. Sloyan, "Reagan's Answers Still Need Solutions," *Newsday*, 6 February 1976.

11. Memorandum for Records, 11 December 1975, Document 147, in *FRUS, 1969–1976*.

12. "Senate Decision to Cut Off Additional Funds," 19 December 1975, National Security Adviser Presidential Country Files for Africa, Angola (1), GRFL.

13. "Congress Divided over Angola Aid," *Washington Post*, 27 December 1975; after the Senate vote, a resolution expressing a nonbinding sense of the House that the U.S. should stay out of Angola received 140 signatures—nowhere near a majority. Spencer Rich, "Senate Bars Angola Aid," *Washington Post*, 20 December 1975.

14. Congressional Record, Senate 94th Congress, First Session, 41619 (18 December 1975).

15. "Sparkman Doubts Angola Aid Ban," *Washington Post*, 11 January 1976.

16. Diggs, "A Report from the OAU Meeting on Angola, Addis Ababa," 11 January 1976, Folder: Angola, Box 193, CCDP.

17. Diggs, Press Statement on Angola, 11 January 1976, Folder: Angola, Box 193, CCDP.

18. Letter, Tunney to Dick Clark, 28 January 1976, Folder: African Affairs, Carton 2, JVTP.

19. Mary McGrory, "The Lunacy of Our Role in Angola," *Boston Globe*, 20 December 1975.

20. Andrew Young, Remarks to the Atlanta Press Community, 19 January 1976, Folder: Speeches, Box 70.8, AJYP.

21. The Ethiopian conference chair said, "The struggle for Angola is for the body and soul of Africa." Diggs, "A Report from the OAU Meeting on Angola."

22. David B. Ottoway, "Rep. Diggs Hits Ford on Angola," *Washington Post*, 12 January 1976.

23. Harrington, Young, Harking, et al. to Colleague, 16 January 1976, Leon and Leppert Files, Box 1, Angola; Letter, Ted Lockwood, 15 January 1976, Box 44, WOA Paper, YDL.

24. George M. Daniels, "Americans May Be Close to Seeing African Events as They Are," *Baltimore Afro-American*, 24 January 1976.

25. "Policy over Angola Is Examined by CBS," *New York Times*, 17 December 1975.

26. Memo, J. H. A. Beukes to the Secretary of Foreign Affairs, 2 January 1976, US Relations with SA, vol. 32, 1/33/3, SADFAA.

27. "Fighter Brigade to Aid MPLA," *New York Amsterdam News*, 24 January 1976.

28. See "Call for National Unity in Angola—Superpowers Try to Partition Angola with Civil War," *Unity and Struggle* V, no. 1 (January 1976): 1.

29. "Roy Innis Replies to Critics on Angola War," *New York Amsterdam News*, 6 March 1976; Leon Dash, "Black Vets Recruited: Unit Organizing for Angola War 200 Area Black Veterans Ready to Fight in Angola," *Washington Post*, 27 January 1976.

30. Florence L. Tate with Jake-Ann Jones, *Sometimes Farmgirls Become Revolutionaries* (Baltimore: Black Classics Press, 2021), 202.

31. Advertisement, ACOA, "Angola . . . A New Vietnam?" *New York Times*, 18 January 1976.

32. "Summary of CCLAMG's Work," n.d. [March or April 1977], Carole Collins Papers, Michigan State University Special Collections (East Lansing, MI).

33. Letter, Wiley to Dick Clark, 16 March 1976, Folder: Angola, Box 50, RCCP.

34. See Campaign for a Democratic Foreign Policy and Center for National Security Studies, "CIA War in Angola," 5 January 1976, Box 5, Southern Africa Support Group, Harsh Collection; letters to President Ford, White House Central File, CO, Box 6, CO 7 Angola, GRFL; CR—House, 94th Congress, Second Session 1040 (27 January 1976), 1045–1046.

35. William Chapman, "Activists of the 60s Reappear, with Angola Aid as Target," *Washington Post*, 25 January 1976.

36. Letter, Deborah Huntington to WOA, 7 January 1976; Report, Clergy and Laity Concern, January 1976 [early], Box 44, WOA, YDL.

37. Announcement and handwritten note, "Protest at U.S. and Soviet Missions," 24 December 1975, Box 44, WOA, YDL.

38. Nesbitt Interview; Angola Solidarity Coalition, "Angola Solidarity Rally," January 1976, AAA. Thomas L. Dabney, "Support for Angola Urged in Norfolk," *Norfolk Journal and Guide*, 10 January 1976. See also C. Gerald Fraser, "Small Groups of Blacks in U.S. Focusing on Angola," *New York Times*, 14 December 1975. More than four hundred people showed up at an MPLA rally in Boston as late as February. "Faneuil Hall," *Harvard Crimson*, 9 February 1976.

39. "1,000 Here March Against U.S. Role in Angola," *New York Times*, 18 January 1976.

40. Memo, J. B. Shearar to Secretary of Foreign Affairs, 4 March 1976, SA Public Relations Activities in the United States, vol. 5, 1/33/3/1, SADFAA. Author's translation.

41. Robert P. Hey, "Congress May Ban Angola Aid," *Christian Science Monitor*, 6 January 1976. Quoted in Dana Adams Schmidt, "Congress Waits Impatiently to Press Angola Curbs," *Christian Science Monitor*, 23 January 1976.

42. Ford to Albert, 27 January 1976, Max Friedersdorf Files, Box 10, Angola, GRFL.

43. "Angolans Lobby for U.S. Aid," *Washington Post*, 29 January 1976.

44. CR—House, 94th Congress, Second Session 1040 (27 January 1976), 1045–1046.

45. CR—House, 94th Congress, Second Session 1040 (27 January 1976), 19.

46. George Mahon, "Statement on the Angola Amendment to the Defense Bill," 26 January 1976, Box 1, Loen and Leppert Files, GRFL.

47. Ford prepared for other allies to back the anti-communists, including Saudi Arabia and Iran. Cuban exiles openly planned travel to Angola to fight Castro's forces, with the United States likely aiding them covertly. Informational Bulletin, Jon Howe to Vice President, 4 January 1976, Box 13, Series 19, Papers of Vice President Nelson A. Rockefeller, Rockefeller Archives (Sleepy Hollow, NY).

48. Memo, Granger and Janke to Scowcroft, "Overt Funding," 16 January 1976, Box 1, Presidential Country Files for Africa, GRFL.

49. Kissinger, *Years of Renewal*, 832; See, for instance, David Binder, "Congressmen Tell of Irritation over Covert U.S. Angola Aid," *New York Times*, 13 December 1975.

50. "Transcript of Goldwater/Ford Conversation in Oval Office," n.d. [late January 1976], Howard H. Callaway Files, Box 1, Memoranda, GRFL.

51. Dana Adams Schmitt, "Kissinger Expected to Seek Overt Aid for Angola Action," *Christian Science Monitor*, 29 January 1976.

52. Harry Amana, "Philadelphia Angola Backers to March on Gulf Oil Offices," *Philadelphia Tribune*, 7 February 1976.

53. Daryl Lembke, "Recruiting for Angola War Opposed," *Los Angeles Times*, 13 February 1976.

54. Letter, Elizabeth S. Genne to Ford, 26 January 1976, White House Central File, CO, Box 6, CO 7 Angola, GRFL.

55. Telcon, Henry Kissinger and Brent Scowcroft, 6 January 1976, National Security Archive.

56. Telegram, Washington to FCO, 26 February 1976, FCO 082/641, Folder: Henry Kissinger, UKNA; Telegram, Washington to FCO, 5 February 1976, National Security Archive.

57. "Sen. Weicker Defends Stand on Angola Aid," *Hartford Courant*, 12 February 1976; Anthony Lewis, "The Politics of Patriotism," *New York Times*, 16 February 1976.

58. Memo, J. B. Shearar to Secretary of Foreign Affairs, 3 March 1976, S.A. Public Relations Activities in the United States, vol. 5, 1/33/3/1, SADFAA.

59. William F. Buckley Jr. "Assigning the Blame for U.S. Reversals," *Newsday*, 6 April 1976.

60. "Rumsfeld Says Congress Won't Repeat Angola Action," *Boston Globe*, 15 February 1976.

61. Jon Nordheimer, "Reagan, in Direct Attack, Assails Ford on Defense," *New York Times*, 5 March 1976.

62. William F. Buckley Jr. "Does Angola Really Matter," *Newsday*, 21 February 1976.

63. Dana Adams Schmidt, "Congress Waits Impatiently to Press Angola Curbs," *Christian Science Monitor*, 23 January 1976.

64. "Defense Turnabout on the Hill," *Baltimore Sun*, 21 March 1976.

65. Charles Diggs, Statement to National Black Political Assembly, 18=20 March 1976, Folder: Democratic Party Foreign Affairs, Box 110, CCDP.

66. "Report Prepared by the Working Group on Angola," 2 April 1976, Document 162, in *FRUS, 1969–1976*.

67. Memo, Les Janka to Brent Scowcroft, 18 May 1976, Box 4, NSC Press and Congressional Liaison Staff, National Security Adviser Files, GRFL.

68. Andrew Young, "The Promise of U.S. Africa Policy . . . ," *Washington Post*, 17 May 1976.

69. "Ford, Reagan in Texas Showdown Today," *Washington Post*, 1 May 1976; Kenneth Reich, "Reagan Sweeps Texas Primary," *Los Angeles Times*, 2 May 1976.

70. "Behind the Reagan Surge," *Wall Street Journal*, 10 May 1976.

71. Sean Byrnes, *Disunited Nations: U.S. Foreign Policy, Anti-Americanism, and the Rise of the New Right* (Baton Rouge: Louisiana State University Press, 2021), 3.

72. See James Mann, *Rise of the Vulcans* (New York: Penguin, 2004), chapter 4; Julian Zelizer, *Arsenal of Democracy* (New York: Basic Books, 2010), chapters 11–12; Sean Byrnes, *Disunited Nations: US Foreign Policy, Anti-Americanism, and the Rise of the New Right* (Baton Rouge: Louisiana State University Press, 2021).

73. Ernest W. Lefever, "The Paralysis of Power," *New York Times*, 18 January 1976

74. Norman Podhoretz, "Making the World Safe for Communism," *Commentary* 61, no. 4 (April 1976): 39.

75. South African Broadcasting Corporation (SABC), "Senator Clark: A Change of Heart?" 8 December 1976, Folder: Africa Trip—newspaper articles, Box 50, RCCP.

76. SABC, "Senator Clark and Southern Africa," 11 November 1976, Folder: Africa Trip—newspaper articles, Box 50, RCCP.

77. Quoted in David Mutch, "Europe Worries About America," *Christian Science Monitor*, 23 February 1976. See also NSSM 238—U.S. Policy Toward Persian Gulf (3 of 3), Institutional Files, National Security Council, GFL, Clements; John Saar, "Foreign Minister Apprehensive After Angola," *Washington Post*, 14 May 1976.

78. Margaret Thatcher, Speech at Kensington Town Hall ("Britain Awake"), 19 January 1976, Margaret Thatcher Foundation: https://www.margaretthatcher.org/document/102939.

79. William Cotterell, "Dean Rusk Favors U.S. Aid to Combat Reds in Angola," *Atlanta Daily World*, 1 January 1976.

80. Interview with Jeane Kirkpatrick, CNN's *The Cold War*, episode 19, Transcript, National Security Archive: https://nsarchive2.gwu.edu/coldwar/interviews/episode-19/kirkpatrick1.html.

81. Committee on the Present Danger, "Common Sense and Common Danger," 11 November 1976.

82. Keys, chapter 5.

83. Bayard Rustin and Carl Gershman, "Africa, Soviet Imperialism, and the Retreat of American Power," *Commentary* (October 1977): 35, 41.

84. Rustin and Gershman, "Africa, Soviet Imperialism, and the Retreat of American Power."

85. Ernest W. Lefever, *Amsterdam to Nairobi: The World Council of Churches and the Third World* (Washington, DC: Ethics and Public Policy Center, 1979).

86. Keys, chapter 5.

87. Letter, John Sparkman to Gale McGee, 20 March 1976, Folder 7, Box 547, GWMP.

88. Memo, Grace to Hayakawa, 19 May 1978, Folder: Africa, Box 193, S.I. Hayakawa Papers, Hoover Institution (Stanford, CA). Hereafter, SIHP.

89. See, for example, Robert Moss, "On Standing Up to the Russians in Africa," *Policy Review* (1978): 109.

90. Jonas Savimbi, "Mensagem de esperança e de fé para o ano de 1979," December 1978, in *Primeiro o Angolano, Aegundo o Angolano ... Angolano Sempre: Os Discursos do Dr. Jonas Malheiro Savimbi ed. Esteves B. I. Pena (Lisbon: Gepmi, 2019),* 44.

91. Resolution 416, 58th National Convention of the American Foreign Legion, 24–26 August 1976, Folder: FR 1-3, Box 59, RCCP.

92. Moss, "On Standing Up to the Russians in Africa,"109.

93. George M. Houser, "Report of the Havana Seminar," 25–29 February 1976, African Activist Archive, Michigan State University. The Congressional Black Caucus had been invited but declined to attend, a decision based largely on ongoing discussions about how African American legislators should treat Cuba.

94. James E. Bristol, "Report on Seminar on Angola," February 1976, AAA.

95. Marjorie Boehm, "Report of Angolan Seminar Held in Havana," March 1976, AAA.

96. See, for instance, "Group Urges Recognition of Angola," *Baltimore Afro-American*, 6 March 1976.

97. Dick Clark, "Opening Statement for February 6 Subcommittee Hearings," 6 February 1976, Folder: Angola, Box 72, RCCP. See Charles Diggs, "Angola: Why Washington Should Recognize Luanda," 24 March 1976, Box 300, CCDP.

98. Interview transcript, Julius Nyerere with Jonathan Power, n.d. [c. 1979], Folder: South Africa, Box 118.9, AJYP.

99. See, for example, Kenneth Gibson, "A Necessary United States Policy for Africa," 21 September 1976, Folder FR 1-3 Africa, Box 50, RCCP.

100. Young, "The Promise of U.S. Africa Policy . . . ."

101. Draft, "The Caucus of Black Democrats U.S. Policy Toward Africa," 12 April 1976, Box 300, CCDP.

102. See Tunney, Draft Statement on Rhodesia, 29 April 1976, Folder: African Affairs, Carton 2, JVTP.

103. Bud Day, "Reflections on Intensive Southern Africa Programming in Chicago, April 1977," 25 April 1977, Folder: Program Other, Box: PED Program Resources Southern Africa 1977, AFSC.

104. Draft, "The Caucus of Black Democrats U.S. Policy Toward Africa," 28 April 1976, Box 300, CCDP.

105. Undated notes [c. 1976], Folder 8, Box 44, WOA, YDL.

106. Memo, David Sogge to Earle Edwards, 7 June 1976, Box PED Program Resources Southern Africa Speakers Services 1976, AFSC.

107. Memo, Jim Bristol, Mike Simmons, and David Sogge, "Questions for MPLA Representatives Attending Angola Conference," 18 February 1976, Folder: ID Africa Programs 1976; Memo, Earl Edwards and David Sogge, Southern Africa Program, 7 June 1976, Folder: PED Southern Africa 1976, Box PED Program Resources Southern Africa Speakers Services 1976, AFSC.

108. Speech, Tunney, "Toward a New Africa Policy," n.d. [c. mid-1976], Folder: African Policy, Carton 7, JVTP.

109. Memo, Steven F. McDonald to William Richardson, 22 December 1976, Folder: Africa Trip, Box 50, RCCP.

110. Telegram, Lusaka (for Clark) to SecState, 11 November 1976, Folder: Africa Trip, Box 50, RCCP.

111. Dick Clark, "U.S. Africa Policy at a Crossroads," n.d. [1979], Folder: U.S. Africa Policy at a Crossroads, Box 142, RCCP.

112. Charles Diggs, Statement to National Black Political Assembly, 18–20 March 1976, Folder: Democratic Party Foreign Affairs, Box 110, CCDP.

113. Zoom Interview, Brewster Rhoads with the Author, 9 April 2024.

114. See Letter, Coalition for a New Foreign and Military Policy, 15 February 1977, AAA; Roger Peace, *A Call to Conscience: The Anti-Contra War Campaign* (Amherst: University of Massachusetts Press, 2012), chapters 3–4.

115. Diggs, "A Report from the OAU Meeting on Angola."

116. One poll concluded, "The potential black constituency for US policy toward South Africa is not a figment of the imagination of black leaders." Carnegie Endowment for International Peace, "The Results and Political Implications of a Public Opinion Poll on American Attitudes Toward South Africa," n.d. [c. 1977], Folder: South Africa, Box 118.9, AJYP.

117. "The African-American Participants in the African-American Conference," n.d. (November 1976), Folder: African-American Institute Congress, Box 53.1, AJYP.

118. David L. Hostetter, *Movement Matters: American Antiapartheid Activism and the Rise of Multicultural Politics* (New York: Routledge, 2006), chapter 3.

119. Crocker Snow Jr., "Our Own Tug-of-War on Angola," *Boston Globe*, 2 January 1976.

120. Van Gosse, "Unpacking the Vietnam Syndrome," in *The World the Sixties Made*, ed. Van Gosse and Richard Moser (Philadelphia: Temple University Press, 2008), 111.

121. Zelizer, 264.

Conclusion

1. See Zelizer, 264.

2. Thomas Borstelmann, *The 1970s: A New Global History from Civil Rights to Economic Inequality* (Princeton: Princeton University Press, 2012), 190.

3. See Doug Rossinow, *The Reagan Era: A History of the 1980s* (New York: Columbia University Press, 2015); Sean Wilentz, *The Age of Reagan: A History, 1974–2008* (New York: Harper Perennial, 2009); Robert O. Self, *All in the Family: The Realignment of American Democracy Since the 1960s* (New York: Hill and Wang, 2012).

4. Daniel T. Rodgers, *Age of Fracture* (Cambridge, MA: Belknap Press of Harvard University Press, 2011), prologue. I hint at a global explanatory factor missed by Rodgers: namely, decolonization and reaction against it.

5. Petra Goedde, *Politics of Peace: A Global Cold War History* (New York: Oxford University Press, 2019), 10.

6. See Brian S. Mueller, *Democracy's Think Tank: The Institute for Policy Studies and Progressive Foreign Policy* (Philadelphia: University of Pennsylvania Press, 2001), 42.

7. See Wells, 580; Farber, 264; Bloom, 4; Maurice Isserman, *If I Had a Hammer: The Death of the Old Left and the Birth of the New Left* (Urbana: University of Illinois Press, 1987), 219–244.

8. See Frank Gerits, *The Ideological Scramble for Africa: How the Pursuit of Anticolonial Modernity Shaped a Postcolonial Order, 1945–1966* (Ithaca: Cornell University Press, 2023), introduction.

9. Ian Tyrell and Jay Sexton, "Whither Anti-Imperialism in a Postcolonial World?" In *Empire's Twin*, ed. Tyrell and Section (Ithaca: Cornell University Press, 2015), 223.

10. This also explains why the period fits uneasily within historiographies of peace movements, since revolts against stubborn imperialism challenged nonviolent traditions of social justice. See Jay Winter, *Dreams of Peace and Freedom: Utopian Movements in the 20th Century* (New Haven: Yale University Press, 2006), chapter 5; David Cortright's otherwise excellent study of peace movements almost wholly avoids the thorny topic of decolonization, Cortright, *Peace: A History of Movements and Ideas* (New York: Cambridge University Press, 2008).

11. Memo, Houser to Executive Board, April 1970, Reel III, Microfilm Records of the American Committee on Africa, Part I: ACOA Executive Committee Minutes and National Office Memoranda, 1952–1975.

12. Poster, ALSC (Oakland, CA), "*A Luta Continua*: Azania, Naimbia, Zimbabwe," Inkworks Press, AAA.

13. See Memo, "Sub-Saharan Africa," NLC-128-7-3-1-8, RAC, Jimmy Carter Library (Atlanta, GA). Hereafter, JCL.

14. Memo, U.S. U.N. to SecState, 27 April 1978, NLC-24-110-2-3-7, RAC, JCL.

15. Aaron Donaghy, *The Second Cold War: Carter, Reagan, and the Politics of Foreign Policy* (Cambridge University Press: 2021), 1–17.

16. See, Memo, North-South to David Aaron, 23 June 1980, NLC-10R-30-1-4-3, RAC, JCL; Press Release, 14 August 1979, Box 13, Chronological Files, White House Press Office, Presidential Papers, JCL.

17. Letter, Tsongas to the President, 22 June 1978, Box 218, Office of Congressional Liaison Beckel, Presidential Papers, JCL.

18. Memo, Cyrus Vance to the President, 27 December 1977, NLC 128-13-3-17-4, RAC, JCL; Memo, Tom Thornton to Brzezinski, 10 April 1978, NLC-24-97-9-11-7, RAC, JCL.

19. S.I. Hayakawa, "Press Conference on His Trip to Africa," 8 June 1978, Folder Press Conferences, Box 194, SIHP; Memo, Zbigniew Brzezinski to the President, 29 October 1979, NLC 126-19-29-1-9, RAC, JCL.

20. Weekly Report, North-South to Brzezinski, 10 January 1980, NLC-24-110-8-11-2, RAC, JCL.

21. Richard C. Clark, *Iowa and the World: Memoirs of Senator Dick Clark* (State College, PA: Editions Enlaplage, 2017), chapter 11.

22. Notably, the Reagan administration recognized the limits Congress continued to place on executive action and crafted policies to push back against legislative critics. Malcolm Byrne, *Iran-Contra: Reagan's Scandal and the Unchecked Abuse of Presidential Power* (Lawrence: University Press of Kansas, 2014), 14.

23. See Lara Pawson, *In the Name of the People: Angola's Forgotten Massacre* (London: I. B. Tauris, 2014), introduction.

24. Qualifying Lydia Walker, Lusophone African solidarity hints that transnational networks did not fully disappear after independence; rather, reduced asymmetries of power meant that newly sovereign parties no longer relied solely on transnational advocates to negotiate their interests in the United States or Western Europe. Where power disparities continued and/or problems operated outside official channels, such as covert U.S. assistance for UNITA, the MPLA and FRELIMO continued collaborating with advocates. See Lydia Walker, *States-in-Waiting: A Counternarrative of Global Decolonization* (New York: Cambridge University Press, 2024), 5, 140–141.

25. Western *cooperantes* worked with FRELIMO in media, healthcare, and education, for example.

26. See Samuel Moyn, *Last Utopia: Human Rights in History* (Cambridge, MA: Belknap Press of Harvard University Press, 2010), chapter 3.

27. Barbara Keys, *Reclaiming American Virtue: The Human Rights Revolution of the 1970s* (Cambridge, MA: Harvard University Press, 2014), chapters 4–5.

28. Richard Clapp, Interview with the Author, 28 May 2015; Richard Clapp, "A Brief History of the Boston Coalition for the Liberation of Southern Africa," 2004, African Activist Archive.

Other groups included the evolution of *Southern Africa News* from the Mozambique Project and the origins of the ZANU Support Committee in the Norfolk, VA, protest of Portugal at the International Azalea Festival honoring NATO in 1972.

29. See "Change Investment Policy," *Harvard Crimson*, 19 November 1977; Jesse M. Fried, "A Long and Winding Road," *Harvard Crimson*, 15 September 1983.

30. Sifiso Mxolisi Ndlovu, "The ANC and the World," in *The Road to Democracy in South Africa*, ed. SADET, vol. 1 (Pretoria: UNISA Press, 2010), 505.

31. See Christabel Gurney, "The 1970s: The Anti-Apartheid Difficult Decade," *Journal of South Africa Studies* 35, no. 2 (June 2009), 471–487.

32. Joseph Jordan, "The 1970s," in *No Easy Victories*, ed. William Minter et al. (Trenton: Africa World Press, 2008), 123.

33. Locke Interview; Wiley Interview.

34. Coletta A. Youngers, *The Washington Office on Latin America: Thirty Years of Advocacy for Human Rights, Democracy, and Social Justice* (Washington, DC: Washington Office on Latin America, 2006), 12.

35. Joseph Eldridge, Telephone Interview with the Author, 19 May 2014.

36. Eldridge interview.

37. Brewster Rhoads, Zoom Interview with the Author, 9 April 2024; Elridge interview.

38. See Christine Root, draft article for *Guardian*, 16 March 1981, Folder 109, Box 15, WOA, YDL.

39. Covert Operations Task Force phone tree, n.d. [1980/1?], Folder 109, Box 15, WOA, YDL.

40. Youngers, 16, 28.

41. Mickey Leland, "The United States and El Salvador: Statement of the Congressional Black Caucus" (Washington, DC: Congressional Black Caucus, 1981).

42. See Arnson, 108–112; Edward Walsh, "House Democratic Leaders Promise to Fight Two Rebel Aid Proposals," *Washington Post,* 21 February 1986.

43. See Christian Smith, *Resisting Reagan: The U.S. Central America Peace Movement* (Chicago: University of Chicago Press, 1996), chapter 4, 261; Roger Peace, *A Call to Conscience: The Anti-Contra War Campaign* (Amherst: University of Massachusetts Press, 2012), chapter 3.

44. Smith, 175.

45. Smith, chapter 11.

46. Arnson, 60–67.

47. See Peace, chapter 7.

48. See Paul Adler, *No Globalization Without Representation: U.S. Activists and World Inequality* (Philadelphia: University of Pennsylvania Press, 2021), parts IV and VI.

INDEX

Illustrations are indicated by page numbers followed by *fig*.

Abernathy, Ralph, 177
Abreu Padrón, Lázaro, 203*fig.*
Abzug, Bella, 223
ACOA. *See* American Committee on Africa (ACOA)
Ad-Hoc Coalition for a New Foreign Policy, 272
Adjali, Mia, 324n45
Adoula, Cyril, 68
AFL-CIO, 46, 62, 201, 285
Africa Affairs Institute (AAI), 93–94
Africa Information Service, 128, 184
African Americans: Africanists, 167–68, 170, 173; African liberation and, 15, 63–67, 172–74, 177–84; Africa policy and, 273, 347n116; CONCP and, 163–64, 166, 172; domestic politics and, 65–66, 165, 167–69; leftist anti-imperialism and, 164–65; legislators, 157–58, 289; Mondlane and, 164, 166; NCC and, 141; Pan-African solidarity movement, 63–64, 143, 162–69, 172–73, 178–80, 182–84, 186–89; political organizing, 174–80; Portuguese propaganda campaigns, 63–64; racial solidarity appeals, 164–66, 169, 175, 177–82, 329n63; socialist ideology and, 186; voting rights, 157; youth activists, 126–28. *See also* Black activists
African American Students Foundation, 26, 95*fig.*
Africa News Service, 116, 319n43
African Information Service, 213
African liberation: American solidarity activists, 2–5, 9–15, 112–13, 271–73,

300n32; anti-communist alliances, 4, 6–7, 38, 54, 106, 145, 165, 232, 234, 236, 247, 249, 255, 258, 260–62, 265, 268; authentic ideology and, 125, 141, 144, 162, 189; Black Power movement and, 170–72, 188–89; civil rights movement and, 63–65, 143–44; grassroots organizing and, 3–5, 7, 9–15, 46–51, 58, 174; guerrilla wars, 78, 80–82; Gulf Oil boycott, 200–202, 203*fig.*, 204–9; partisanship in, 211–16; public diplomacy and, 10, 57, 299n20; public narratives, 37–38, 44; rhetorical use of, 55, 66, 123, 165; transnational collaboration, 4–11, 13–14, 162–63, 300n32; tripartite struggles, 211–13. *See also* Lusophone liberation; self-determination
African Liberation Day (ALD): Angolan intervention activism, 254; Black agenda and, 15, 162–63; Black unity and, 177–80, 329n63; Congress and, 175, 208, 335n94; expansion of audiences, 185–88; grassroots organizing and, 187–88; Gulf Oil boycott, 204–5; ideological divide, 215–16; multiracial alliances, 208, 211; Pan-Africanism and, 162, 174, 188; political organizing, 162–63, 187–88; Portuguese downplaying of, 180, 330n73; regional demonstrations, 185–87; Sadaukai and, 176–77, 329n61; socialist ideology and, 186; transnational solidarity, 176, 283; tricontinentalism and, 209; Washington demonstration, 178–79, 179*fig.*, 180, 186; white participation in, 186, 331n102

African Liberation Support Committee
(ALSC): African liberation and, 174, 183,
185, 191, 211; ALD and, 174, 181, 184,
204; Black identity and, 185–86, 204, 212;
Gulf Oil boycott, 204; leftist ideology, 190,
209–10; Marxist ideology, 214–15; multiracial alliances, 205, 210–11, 214–15;
socialist-nationalist divide, 214–17,
280–81; UNITA and, 212–13, 215–16
African National Congress (ANC), 46, 88,
193, 288
African nationalism: African American
support, 63–67, 166, 172–74, 177–84;
American solidarity activists, 3–4, 10,
13–16, 46–47, 50–51, 93, 102, 106,
110–27, 131–32, 206fig., 320n69; Black
press and, 180–81; Cold War fears, 23–24,
30, 35, 52–53; decolonization and, 20–21,
64; diplomacy and, 37, 97–100; European organizing, 37–38, 48; humanitarian outrage, 45, 58, 61–63; ideological
competition, 56–58; leftist organizing,
38–39; militarization of, 26, 28, 43, 59,
75, 111, 136; modernity and, 21, 40, 279;
New Left Internationalism and, 5, 12,
16, 106, 190, 229; public narratives, 37,
46–49, 52–53; racial fears and, 52–53;
religious mobilization, 46–49, 61–62,
106–13, 120; rise of, 19–20, 23; transfer
of power, 218–19; transnational appeals,
25–28, 35, 37, 43–44, 65, 73, 77–78, 280;
tricontinentalism and, 82–83, 146, 186,
189; U.S. support for, 29–35, 77–78; youth
activists and, 106, 110–16, 119–23. See
also African liberation; Lusophone Africa;
self-determination
African Nationalist Pioneer Movement, 165
African Party for the Independence of
Guinea and Cabo Verde. See PAIGC
African Studies Association, 256
African World, 172, 184
Africa Research Group, 128
Africa Today, 25, 194
Albert, Carl, 257
ALD. See African Liberation Day (ALD)
Algeria: decolonization, 64; Egyptian allies,
37; FLN and, 26, 28, 37, 281; France and,
29; FRELIMO and, 2; independence of,
30; military assistance for revolutionaries,
80; revolution in, 34, 75, 281

Algerian Front de Libération Nationale
(FLN), 26, 28, 37, 281
Alkalimat, Abdul, 214, 216
All-Africa's People Conference (1960), 41
Allende, Salvador, 228
A Luta Continua, 176–77, 182–84, 186,
210–11, 255, 329n57
American-African Affairs Association
(AAAA), 90
American Committee on Africa (ACOA):
African nationalism and, 25, 27–28,
35, 37, 45, 47, 77, 93, 96, 101, 129–30,
146–47, 172–73, 280, 286; Angolan
intervention activism, 241–43; Angolan
self-determination and, 57, 61; anti-
apartheid movement and, 25, 114; Black
self-determination and, 64–65; CCLAMG
and, 151–52, 154–55; civil rights movement and, 25, 27; congressional internationalists and, 241–43, 272; FNLA and,
143; FRELIMO and, 3, 100; generational
friction in, 144–49; grassroots organizing and, 15, 45–46, 63, 102, 155, 255;
Gulf Oil boycott, 191, 194–96, 199–200;
humanitarian aid, 61–62; as informational
clearinghouse, 97, 129–30, 150–51, 255;
institutional transformation, 133, 142–52,
154–56, 160; international education
program, 50, 62; issue-based alliances,
200, 216, 280; Kennedy administration
and, 29–30, 67; liberalism, 27–28, 44, 115,
302n33; lobbying efforts, 47, 96–97, 144,
155–56; militant liberation and, 111, 132;
MPLA and, 44, 135, 145, 269, 284; NCC
and, 47, 96, 145; New Left ideas, 5, 10,
150; nonviolent principles, 27, 111; Portuguese criticism of, 62, 310n13; propaganda campaigns, 47, 52, 54; Roberto and,
26–28, 31, 35, 44–45, 62, 145–46; SAC
and, 114–15; solidarity movement, 144,
150, 152; transnational collaboration, 65,
93, 102, 145–48, 150–51; UPA nationalists
and, 26–27, 27fig., 31, 44; U.S. foreign
policy and, 14, 59, 235; youth activists,
14–15, 106, 126, 129–31, 143–50, 152,
172, 280
American Friends Service Committee
(AFSC), 141, 242, 256, 269–71
American Negro Leadership Conference on
Africa (ANLCA): African nationalism

and, 59, 64–67, 91, 180; domestic goals, 65–66, 162, 167; Pan-African collaboration, 77

Americans for Democratic Action, 46, 201, 256

Americans for Freedom, 267

Anderson, George, 67

Anglo-American Conference on Africa, 93–94

Angola: Cold War strategies, 15, 32; leftist organizing, 38–39; liberation campaign, 2–3, 25–26, 38, 211; Luanda uprising, 28–29, 44–45, 302n36; March 1961 rebellion, 20, 24, 27, 31, 51–52, 56, 59, 135; MPLA and, 40, 57; NATO arms in, 45, 48, 50–51; nonpartisan approach to, 211–13; Portuguese repression in, 28–29, 31, 45–46, 48, 50–52, 57, 61, 135; Portuguese settlers in, 22, 300n6; U.S. arms in, 50–52, 63, 307n64, 307n66; U.S. foreign policy, 12, 50–51, 244; U.S. support for gradual self-determination, 30–34, 61; youth activists, 123

Angola (post-1974): aftermath of military coup, 217–20, 231; communist support for, 231, 233, 240–46, 250–51, 266fig., 283–84, 344n47; Congress and, 235–38, 340n59; FNLA-UNITA coalition, 231, 233, 237–39, 253; leftist-nationalist government in, 223–24; MPLA and, 218–19, 223–25, 231, 233, 236–40, 244, 250, 253, 260, 266, 269–70; nationalist factions in, 218–19, 231–32, 232fig., 233, 237–39; solidarity movement, 239–43; South African involvement, 238, 244, 253–54, 260, 269; superpower competition in, 253; transfer of power, 217–20, 225, 231, 237–39; U.S. intervention in, 15, 223–26, 233–62, 269; Vietnam analogy, 15, 240–41, 243, 247, 249, 255–57, 274

Angola Comité (AC), 127, 147, 149

Angolan Refugee Assistance Service. See Serviço de Assistência aos Reugiados de Angola (SARA)

Angolan Revolutionary Government in Exile, 68

Angolan Women's Organization. See Organização da Mulher de Angola (OMA)

ANLCA. See American Negro Leadership Conference on Africa (ANLCA)

anti-apartheid movement: ACOA and, 25, 114; anti-imperialism and, 282; congressional collaboration, 13, 289; divestment campaigns, 281, 288; expansion of self-determination struggle, 288–89, 349n28; human rights rhetoric, 288; mobilization difficulties, 193; New Left Internationalism and, 11, 287–89; public diplomacy and, 299n20; Soweto uprisings, 271, 288; youth activists and, 111, 114–15

Anti-Apartheid Movement, U.S.A., 224fig.

anti-communism: African Americans and, 63; anti-imperialism and, 265; Cold Warriors and, 228–29, 241, 249–51, 257–58, 260–62, 264–65, 267–68, 285; human rights rhetoric, 265; New Right and, 257, 263–67; Portuguese appeals, 6, 38, 54; pro-Rhodesian lobbying, 90; Roberto and, 35, 41, 57; Southern segregationists, 90, 263; UNITA and, 266fig., 267–68; U.S. foreign policy, 90, 233–34, 241, 244–45, 247, 249, 258, 264; white minority regimes, 90–91; White Redoubt and, 79, 282

anti-imperialism: anti-communism and, 265; Black agenda for, 15, 64–65, 162–65; Black Power and, 10, 143, 171, 175–76; challenges to nonviolent principles, 347n10; Gulf Oil boycott, 191; Marxist activism, 125–26; national debates and, 159–60; New Left Internationalism and, 144, 150, 279, 294–95; race and, 163, 166; radical solidarity, 115, 163–65; religious groups and, 134; SDS and, 114; solidarity movement, 290–91; transnational collaboration, 4, 6–7; tricontinentalism and, 7–9, 146, 184; youth activists and, 115, 119–21, 146, 282

anti-interventionism: Black activists, 254–55, 259; Cold Warrior opposition, 249–50, 257–60, 262–63, 265–68, 282; congressional internationalists and, 223–26, 234–60, 342n13; New Left Internationalism and, 240–41, 245, 248–52, 261, 263–64, 267–68, 270, 273–74; public support for, 255–59; solidarity movement, 241–48, 253–57; Vietnam War as repudiation of, 240–41, 243, 247, 249, 255–58 anti-war movement: anti-imperialism and, 10, 282; Central American, 294; decolonization and, 347n10; leftist organizing, 5, 278; New Left Internationalism and, 10, 294; nonviolent principles, 347n10; U.S. legislation, 11; youth activists and, 113–14, 119, 123–24, 127. *See also* Vietnam War

Antunes, José Freire, 303n50

Armed Forces Movement (MFA), 218

Armstrong, Winifred, 58

Asia: anti-imperialism, 41, 144, 152; Cold War dictatorships, 279; decolonization and, 23, 139; self-determination, 19–20, 31, 50, 143; tricontinentalism and, 7, 9; U.S. foreign policy, 95, 114, 228. *See also* Global South; Vietnam War

Ayers, Bill, 127

Azores islands: Portugal and, 19–21, 87; as U.S. strategic asset, 55–56, 60, 92, 155, 158–59, 209

Babu, Mohamed, 76*fig.*

Baldwin, James, 64

Ball, George, 45, 67, 77

Baraka, Amiri: African liberation and, 181, 188; ALD and, 177; Black Power movement, 174; CAP and, 186, 204; LSM and, 127; Malcolm X and, 174; Maoism and, 175, 216; Pan-Africanism, 178; political organizing, 174–78, 181; Third World Marxism, 210; UNITA and, 255; *Unity and Struggle*, 184

Barnes, Sam, 339n26

Barnett, Don, 124–25, 321n80

Barroso, Luís, 85

Beeman, Josiah, 198

Belgian Congo. *See* Congo (Republic of)

Bender, Gerald, 236

Bender, Thomas, 13

Beveridge, Lowell P., Jr., 164, 327n4

Biden, Joe, 231, 234, 237–38

Biko, Steve, 272

Bingham, Jonathan, 230

Biondi, Martha, 172

Black activists: African nationalism and, 65, 163–65, 170–72, 177–78, 211–13, 273; anti-imperialism and, 168, 215–16; anti-interventionism and, 254–55, 259; Cold War trade-offs, 128; domestic politics

and, 65–66; FRELIMO and, 14, 172; Gulf Oil boycott, 15, 191, 202, 204; issue-based alliances, 216; leftist ideology and, 181–82, 209, 213–15; LSM and, 126–27; MPLA and, 213, 254–55; multilevel collaboration, 175–76; multiracial alliances, 128, 209–14; New Left ideas, 213; Pan-Africanism and, 162–69, 172–73, 178–79; partisanship and, 211–16; radical politics and, 163–65, 170–72; re-Africanization and, 39; revolutionary ideology, 165, 168, 170, 328n23; Roberto and, 164–65; transnational solidarity, 66, 176, 189; tricontinentalism and, 141, 205, 209–11, 213; UNITA and, 255. *See also* African Americans

Black Arts Movement, 167, 174

Black Coalition Against U.S. Intervention in Angola, 259

Black Convention Movement, 273

Black identity: Africa in, 230; ALD organizing, 163; communitarianism, 174; liberation parties, 166; Pan-Africanism and, 174, 182; racialized presumptions, 162; radical internationalism, 163, 170; transnational, 66, 180–81; UNITA and, 166, 212–13, 327n13; unity goals, 169, 177, 185

Black nationalism: Baraka and, 174; global inequality and, 169; New Left and, 185, 209; racial unity and, 185, 214–15; rejection of white communists, 167, 215; socialist ideology and, 163; UNITA and, 212, 215. *See also* African nationalism

Black Panther (newspaper), 127, 171, 203*fig.*

Black Panthers, 170–72, 181

Black politics: African American organizing, 174–76; African liberation and, 189, 191, 204; African solidarity movement, 163–64, 170, 176; CBC and, 158, 229; class in, 214; internationalism and, 173; legislators, 157–58, 289; nation-building, 175; tricontinentalism and, 176

Black Power: African liberation and, 170–72, 188–89; anti-imperialism and, 10, 143, 171, 175; deference to African leadership, 170–71; growth of, 119; impact of Malcolm X on, 170–71, 173; independent leadership, 202; internationalism and, 170; leftist ideology and, 141, 181–82;

LSM and, 127; New Left Internationalism and, 10, 143, 192; Pan-Africanism and, 173, 181; self-determination and, 174; transnational collaboration, 162, 164, 173; tricontinentalism and, 141, 205

Borstelmann, Thomas, 277

Boston Coalition for the Liberation of Southern Africa, 288, 348n28

Boumediene, Houari, 76*fig.*

Bowles, Chester, 29

Bragança, Aquino de, 76*fig.*

Brockett, E. D., 195–96

Brockway, Fenner, 48, 306n41

Brown, Elaine, 259

Brown, Rap, 171

Brzezinski, Zbigniew, 283–84

Buckley, William, Jr., 250–51, 260

Bundy, McGeorge, 29, 77

Burton, John, 257

Butcher, Goler, 156, 158

Byrd Amendment, 155, 158, 270, 284

Byrnes, Sean, 263

Cabo Verde, 22–23, 39, 218, 231

Cabral, Amílcar: anti-imperialism and, 146, 208, 215–16; armed revolution, 75; assassination of, 184; Black leaders and, 180–82, 184; Carmichael and, 171; Cold War neutrality, 312n75; CONCP and, 41, 43, 150, 211; congressional testimony, 148; diplomatic ambitions, 149; Gulf Oil boycott, 195; MAC and, 305n13; Marxist ideology, 181, 210; MPLA and, 40; nationalist movements, 39–40, 81; Nordic support for, 100; PAIGC and, 39–40, 57, 71, 76*fig.*, 98*fig.*, 100, 106; Pan-Africanism, 171; Portuguese attempt to capture, 92; re-Africanization, 39; *Return to the Source*, 184; revolutionary theory, 39–40, 180–81, 184–85; on the Rhodesian UDI, 84; social and economic improvements, 9, 97–98, 98*fig.*, 176, 181, 317n86; on transfer of power, 219; tricontinentalism and, 7, 168, 210, 298n12; on U.S. arms, 77, 313n89; "Weapon of Theory" speech, 83; youth activists and, 146, 160

Cabral, João, 41, 43, 48, 56

Cabral, Luís, 285

Caetano, Marcello: assumption of power, 87, 91; Estado Novo and, 315n35; Estado Social, 87; lusotropicalism and, 87; military coup against, 217, 254; Nixon and, 89; Western appeals, 149

Camacho, Martin, 52–54, 56

Campaign for a Democratic Foreign Policy, 224*fig.*

Cann, John P., 316n56

Carey, W. Sterling, 223

Carmichael, Stokely (Kwame Ture), 170–71, 214–15

Carstens, Kenneth, 111–13, 135–36, 138, 324n45

Carter, Jimmy, 283–85

Carver, John, 157

Casa dos Estudantes do Império (House for Colonial Students), 39, 71

Case, Clifford, 237

Casey, William J., 265

Castro, Fidel, 215

Catholic Worker movement, 256

CCLAMG. *See* Chicago Committee for the Liberation of Angola, Mozambique, and Guinea (CCLAMG)

Central Intelligence Agency (CIA): Angolan intervention, 233–34, 236; Black activist suspicion of, 143; covert operations, 231, 237–38; denial of Angolan intervention, 245; Roberto and, 32, 89, 238–39; on Salazar regime, 76–77; Savimbi and, 225, 238; southern Africa, 220; undermining radical groups, 148

Chabal, Patrick, 81

Chase Manhattan Bank, 114–15, 136, 192–93

Chicago Committee for African Liberation, 283

Chicago Committee for the Liberation of Angola, Mozambique, and Guinea (CCLAMG): ACOA and, 151–52, 154–55; Angolan intervention activism, 242–43; anti-imperialism, 152, 154; Black activists, 154; CRV and, 325n93; educational outreach, 152, 154–55; Gulf Oil boycott, 194; ideological flexibility, 155; liberation struggle film, 154, 326n109; MPLA and, 255, 269; NWRC and, 152, 154–55, 326n100; solidarity movement, 155; southern Africa policy, 270; WOA and, 159

Chile, 154, 228, 240, 243, 268, 273, 281

Chitunda, Jeremias, 247, 255
Christian church: African nationalism and,
110; international engagement, 107–8,
115–16; NCC and, 46; pacifism and, 27,
111–12; social justice and, 73, 116, 132;
South African divestment, 115; on waging
just wars, 112; youth activists, 109–13,
319n33. *See also* Protestant church
Church, Frank, 231, 340n55
Church World Services (CWS), 137, 323n42
civil rights movement: ACOA and, 25, 27;
Africanists, 167; African liberation and,
63–65, 143–44; anti-colonialism, 47, 63;
Black internationalism, 108; Cold War
ideology and, 65–66; communist accusations against, 53; grassroots organizing
and, 114; nonviolence, 170; pro-Angola
sentiment, 46
Clark, Dick: Africa Group, 94; African
policy and, 234–35, 339n37; African self-
determination, 157–58, 271–72, 285; anti-
interventionism, 237–43, 245–49, 253,
261, 262*fig.*, 340n60; Congressional hearings on Angola, 235–38, 340n59; interim
Angolan government and, 237–38; MPLA
and, 262*fig.*, 269; New Left Internationalism, 225, 227, 240; North-South divide
and, 228; opposition to Vietnam War, 231;
social justice and, 208; Subcommittee on
Africa, 234–37
Clark Amendment, 243, 247–49, 257–58,
260, 267, 284–85, 293
Clarke, John Henrik, 186
Cleaver, Eldridge, 171
Clergy and Laity Concerned, 224*fig.*, 256
Coalition for a New Foreign and Military
Policy (CNFMP), 291, 293
Coalition for a New Foreign Policy (CNFP),
269, 272–73
Coalition to Stop Funding the War, 272
Colby, William, 234, 237–38, 252
Cold War: advocacy networks, 225–26;
anti-communism, 90, 106, 224, 226,
228–29, 249, 264–65, 267–68; civil rights
movement and, 65–66; containment
strategies, 3–4, 7–8, 52, 58, 224, 226,
264–65, 268; decolonization, 6, 20, 23–24,
36, 38, 50; fears of nationalism, 23–24,
30, 35; global allies, 132, 264; Global
South and, 6, 8, 20–21, 29–30, 36; liberal

internationalism, 7, 224, 237–41, 245,
247–49; liberalism, 59, 63, 65, 77; party
allegiances, 263; pro-Western stability, 34,
53, 58–59; reactionary regime support,
4, 225–26; Soviet expansion fears, 241,
250–52, 257, 260–61, 263–67; U.S. foreign
policy and, 3–6, 8, 12–13, 30, 32, 249–50;
U.S. interventionism, 100, 129, 142, 234,
241, 249–50
Collins, Cardiss, 2, 229
Commission on World Mission, 107
Committee for a Free Mozambique, 325n93
Committee for a Unified Newark, 174
Committee for the Present Danger, 265
Committee of Returned Volunteers (CRV):
critique of U.S. system, 122, 320n62;
educational outreach, 123, 128, 320n72;
Gulf Oil boycott, 194–96; Lusophone self-
determination and, 123–24; membership
of, 122; Mozambique self-determination
and, 123; *Mozambique Will Be Free*, 123,
321n73; New Left Internationalism,
123–24; new radicalism and, 123–24, 131;
NWRC and, 152; Peace Corps alumni in,
320n61; transition to collective, 325n93
communism: African nationalism and, 40;
anti-imperialism and, 28; Mozambique
and, 3; radicalism and, 7, 30; religious
outreach, 134, 139; Soviet Union and, 20.
See also anti-communism; Cold War
Comprehensive Anti-Apartheid Pact, 294
CONCP. *See* Conferência das Organizações
Nacionalistas das Colónias Portuguesas
(CONCP)
Condesse, José, 126
Conferência das Organizações Nacionalistas
das Colónias Portuguesas (CONCP):
African Americans and, 163–64, 166,
172; anti-imperialism, 41, 279, 295; anti-
Portuguese resistance, 38, 41, 43; armed
revolution, 75, 81–83, 88, 98, 111, 118;
authoritarianism and, 285; Black Power
and, 180–81; Dar es Salaam conference,
76*fig.*; Eastern bloc alliances, 41, 88;
European alliances, 41, 43; formation of,
14, 38–39, 41, 45; FRAIN and, 305n13;
FRELIMO and, 60, 71–72; gender equity,
154; grassroots diplomacy and, 16, 102,
280–81, 295; Guinea-Bissau leadership,
231; issue-based alliances, 189, 280; leftist

organizing, 39, 169, 181; Luanda uprising, 44–45; *A Luta Continua*, 182–84, 186, 255–56; MPLA and, 39, 83, 145, 213; multiracial alliances, 205; New Left Internationalism and, 172, 277, 279–81; PAIGC and, 39, 71; Pan-Africanism and, 168, 181; propaganda campaigns, 44, 180; religious mobilization, 49, 105; revolutionary liberation, 88, 97–98, 102, 105, 172; social and economic improvements, 98–99; socialism and, 43–44, 60, 132, 190; social relations and, 79–80; solidarity movement, 41, 100, 102, 105–6, 126, 131, 144–45, 149–51, 160, 181, 211, 255–56, 271; transnational appeals, 37–38, 44, 59, 77, 79, 97, 281, 286; tricontinentalism and, 83, 114, 144, 166, 279; UPA and, 38; U.S. lobbying, 101; Western aid for, 99–100

Congo (Democratic Republic). *See* Zaire

Congo (Republic of): crisis in, 24, 30, 55, 164; FNLA and, 70; GRAE and, 68; Houser in, 61–62; independence of, 23; nationalist struggles and, 77; Roberto and, 24–25, 43, 69; UPA and, 29, 44, 59

Congregation of Reconciliation, 199, 333n44

Congressional Black Caucus (CBC): African policy, 234, 270, 339n37; African self-determination, 158, 176, 187; anti-interventionism, 253, 261; call for defunding Portugal, 188; call for divestment, 202; Diggs and, 2–3, 158, 175, 229; foreign policy and, 229–30, 346n93; Global South and, 229–30; Gulf Oil boycott, 191; North-South divide and, 228; recognition of MPLA, 284

Congress of African Peoples (CAP): ALD and, 177; Angolan intervention activism, 242; Baraka and, 174–75, 204, 210, 212; Black nation-building, 175; Gulf Oil boycott, 204; Maoism and, 175, 210, 213, 216, 255; multiracial alliances, 215; tricontinentalism and, 176; UNITA and, 212, 255

Congress of Racial Equality (CORE), 25, 46, 97, 114, 242, 259

Connelly, Matthew, 6–7, 37

Cook, Carlos, 165

Cortright, David, 347n10

Council for Christian Social Action, 157

Council for Freedom in Portugal and the Colonies, 48

Council on African Affairs, 63, 164, 302n33

Cox, Courtland, 254

Craig, Campbell, 8

Crane, Anne, 117*fig.*

Crane, Henry "Hank," 109, 111–13, 115, 117, 117*fig.*

Cronkite, Walter, 254

Cruse, Harold, 167, 170

Cruz, Viriato da, 69

CRV. *See* Committee of Returned Volunteers (CRV)

Cuba: Cabral and, 184; involvement of exiles in Angola, 344n47; leftist revolts in, 80, 82; PAIGC and, 148; support for FRELIMO, 99; support for MPLA, 224, 231, 233, 241–42, 250, 266*fig.*, 269, 284; tricontinentalism and, 7, 83, 146; U.S. foreign policy and, 346n93; youth activists and, 106

Culver, John, 94, 227, 231, 234, 238, 240, 285

Dash, Leon, 213

Davidson, Basil, 43, 182, 212

Davis, Angela, 177, 179, 195

Davis, Jennifer, 194, 235

D.C.-Chile Solidarity Committee, 224*fig.*

De Andrade, Mário Pinto, 39–41, 44, 57, 305n13

DeBenedetti, Charles, 114

decolonization: African nationalism and, 20–21, 64; Cold War and, 6, 20, 23–24, 32, 36, 38, 50, 74, 77, 263; European alliances and, 60–61; Global South and, 4, 6–7, 9, 13, 279; Johnson administration and, 86; Kennedy administration and, 14, 29–32, 34–37, 45, 49–51, 57, 59, 73; liberal internationalism and, 7, 132, 280; New Right and, 265–66; peace movements and, 347n10; Portuguese narratives, 37, 53, 58–59; public diplomacy and, 37–38, 299n20; religious mobilization, 108, 132–34, 139; transformative effect of, 6; transnational collaboration, 11, 38; U.S. foreign policy and, 4, 11, 30–31, 60–61, 295; White Redoubt impact, 80, 84, 88, 93; youth activists and, 111, 132, 280

De Gaulle, Charles, 34–35

Dellinger, David, 195, 223

Dellums, Ron, 229, 289

Democratic Party of Angola, 68

Denmark, 100, 245
Dhada, Mustafah, 98
Diggs, Charles C., Jr., 95*fig.*; ACOA and,
    147–48; Africa Group and, 94, 97, 100;
    African nationalism and, 101, 162, 175,
    249, 271; Angolan intervention, 241,
    243, 253–54, 261; Black organizing and,
    187, 273; Cabral and, 100, 148; CBC
    and, 2–3, 158, 175, 188, 229, 234, 253;
    decolonization lobby, 96–97; demand to
    defund Portugal, 188; Gulf Oil boycott,
    199, 202, 204–5; House Subcommittee on
    African Affairs, 97, 100–101, 146, 339n36;
    Lusophone transfer of power, 219–20,
    241; on military coup in Portugal, 218;
    mobilization against White Redoubt, 14,
    94–97; New Left Internationalism and,
    225, 227, 261; political organizing and,
    175–77, 179, 235; resignation of, 285; sol-
    idarity movement and, 121, 272; support
    for MPLA, 253–54, 269; WOA and, 158,
    341n72; youth activists and, 121, 147–48
diplomacy: African nationalists, 13–14, 27,
    37, 80, 97–100; Black African identity and,
    166, 180; Black participation in, 65–66;
    CONCP and, 176, 219, 280–81; Global
    South and, 229–30; grassroots, 4, 13, 16,
    80, 286, 295; Lusophone organizing, 3,
    6–7; New Left Internationalism and, 278,
    294–95; Salazar government, 37–38, 57,
    86, 299n20; shuttle, 261; UNITA and, 70,
    255; White Redoubt and, 88
Dirksen, Everett, 54
Dodge, Ralph, 46, 135–38
Donaghy, Aaron, 283
Dorsey, B. R., 196, 200
Dos Santos, Marcelino: CONCP and, 55,
    71; European alliances, 41, 43; FRELIMO
    and, 76*fig.*, 91, 125; leftist organizing, 40,
    305n13; Marxist rhetoric, 91, 125; re-
    Africanization and, 39; Swedish activism,
    149; UDENAMO and, 40, 71
Douglas, Emory, 203*fig.*
Draper, Theodore, 250
DuBois, W. E. B., 164, 170

Edmunds, Mimi, 123, 130, 152, 154, 160,
    320n60, 320n69, 325n93
Eisenhower, Dwight, 24, 30, 32, 34
Elbrick, Burke, 45, 67

Eldridge, Joseph, 291
El Salvador, 282, 293
Emergency Relief for Angola drive, 310n10
Episcopal Peace Fellowship, 256
Estado Novo (New State): anti-colonial
    condemnations, 43; Caetano and, 315n35;
    colonial policies, 22–23, 28–30; luso-
    tropicalism, 33; multi-continental state,
    81; neo-mercantilist strategy, 22; PIDE
    repression, 21, 23–24; U.S. foreign policy,
    28, 30, 32. *See also* Portugal
Estado Social, 87
Ethics and Foreign Policy Center, 267
Europe: alliance with Portugal, 34–35, 37,
    44–45; CONCP alliances, 41, 43; defense
    of colonialism, 31, 34–35; political
    pressure on Portugal, 48–49; Southern
    nationalism and, 2–3, 6, 19–20, 23
European Economic Community, 217

Fanon, Frantz, 26, 43, 298n12
Farmer, James, 46, 64–65
Featherstone, David, 300n32
Fellowship of Reconciliation, 25, 256
Fernandes, Gil: African nationalism and,
    102; American solidarity activists, 184,
    205, 320n69; CONCP and, 146; Lincoln
    University and, 100, 172, 328n40; PAIGC
    and, 152
Figueiredo, Elísio de, 245, 250, 254
FIM. *See* Frontier Internship in Mission
    (FIM)
First, Ruth, 217
Fletcher, Bob, 176
FLN. *See* Algerian Front de Libération
    Nationale (FLN)
Flory, Margaret: FIM and, 109–10, 115–17;
    Mondlane and, 108; NSCF and, 107; pro-
    independence activism, 109, 113, 129,
    133, 138; religious internationalism and,
    109–10, 115, 129, 318n20; transformation
    of church missions, 107–10; youth activ-
    ists and, 107–10, 116–17, 133, 138
FNLA. *See* Frente Nacional de Libertação de
    Angola (FNLA)
Fonseca, Amália, 76*fig.*
Ford, Gerald: Angolan intervention,
    15, 223–26, 233–35, 244, 252–53,
    257–60, 265, 344n47; conservative
    anti-communists and, 258; denial of

intervention, 245–46; détente and, 252; military funding for Angola, 246, 252, 258–59; public anti-interventionism, 256–57, 259; solidarity movement and, 277; southern Africa policy, 249, 251, 258; on Tunney Amendment, 257

Ford Foundation, 74, 99

France: African nationalists in, 40; decolonization of Algeria, 26, 29; leftist support for nationalists, 99; liberation campaigns, 28; support for Portugal, 31, 34–35, 45, 51

Fraser, Donald M.: Africa Group and, 94–95, 100; African nationalism and, 101, 285; decolonization lobby, 96–97; human rights and, 94, 96, 158, 230, 293; WOA and, 158; youth activists and, 121

Freedom Information Service, 242

Freehafer, Hanson, 123

Freehafer, Nancy, 123, 152, 194, 320n68, 325n93

Frente de Libertação de Moçambique (FRELIMO): African Liberation Day protests, 12; American solidarity activists, 123, 127, 131, 137; armed revolution, 78, 80–83, 85, 111, 217; Black nation-building, 175, 211; Cold War neutrality and, 74, 312n75; CONCP and, 60, 71–72; *cooperantes* and, 339n26, 348n25; CRV and, 123; Eastern bloc alliances, 80–81, 99, 217; grassroots diplomacy, 4, 12; leadership crisis, 91; liberation campaign, 2–3, 6, 71, 74–75; *A Luta Continua*, 176–77, 182–84, 329n57; Mondlane and, 14, 60, 65, 72, 100, 111–12; Mozambique Institute and, 74, 99, 211; Mozambique leadership, 231; propaganda campaigns, 123; religious allies, 112, 140; social and economic improvements, 82, 98–99; socialist allies, 2, 4, 9, 71, 82, 99; socialist nationalism and, 73–74, 106; Soviet communism and, 286; transnational appeals, 72, 100, 139–41, 149, 166, 177, 348n24; tricontinentalism and, 7–8, 80–81, 114; Western aid for, 99–100, 286

Frente Nacional de Libertação de Angola (FNLA): ACOA and, 145–46; Angolan leadership struggles, 231, 233, 237–39, 257; collapse of, 75, 83; formation of, 68; leadership crisis, 69–70; MPLA and, 231; racialist rhetoric, 68, 311n46; recognition

of, 68; Roberto and, 68–69, 232, 232*fig.*, 236, 239; South African support for, 244; UNITA and, 231, 233, 237–39; U.S. support for, 83, 233, 236, 239, 257; Zairean aid, 233–34, 237, 239

Frente Revolucionária Africana para a Independência Nacional das colónias portuguesa (FRAIN), 305n13

Freyre, Gilberto, 33

Friends of the Filipino People, 224*fig.*

Frontier Internship in Mission (FIM): Global South relationships, 110, 115; institutional impact, 110, 115, 132; regional organizing, 120–21; youth activists and, 109–10, 115–17, 120–21, 133

Fuller, Howard. See Sadaukai, Owusu

Fulton, James, 198

Galbraith, John Kenneth, 334n54

Garvey, Marcus, 179

Gary Convention (1972), 175–78, 189, 216, 329n61

GBC. See Gulf Boycott Coalition (GBC)

Gelb, Leslie, 239, 246

Gerit, Frank, 279

Gibson, Kenneth, 210

Gilchrist, Ian, 70

Gill, Jill K., 134

Gjerstad, Ole, 124, 339n26

Global North: decolonization and, 6, 20, 129; defining, 300n32; Global South relations, 106, 139, 248; Southern nationalism and, 7–8; youth activists and, 112

Global South: anti-imperial alliances, 6–7, 105, 279–81; Cold War and, 6, 8, 20–21, 29–30, 36; decolonization and, 4, 6–7, 9, 13, 20; defining, 300n32; development assistance, 227–28; diplomacy and, 229–30; Global North relations, 106, 139, 248; New Left Internationalism and, 125, 129, 281–82; postcolonial societies in, 6–8; religious internationalism, 110, 318n20; religious involvement in, 14–15, 107; self-determination and, 9, 15, 20, 23, 229, 277; Soviet influence in, 265, 266*fig.*; superpower competition in, 20, 36–37, 139, 274; tricontinentalism and, 82, 129; U.S. foreign policy and, 3–16, 248, 263, 284, 298n16; U.S. imperialism in, 109, 114, 121–22; youth activists and, 106

Goa, 19, 22–23, 43, 55–56
Goedde, Petra, 10, 277
Goldwater, Barry, 258–59
Gonçalves, Vasco, 2
Gosse, Van, 274
Govêrno Revolucionário de Angola no
    Exílio (GRAE), 68
grassroots organizing: ACOA and, 15,
    45–46, 102, 155; African liberation
    and, 11–15, 46–51, 58, 174; ALD and,
    187–88; Angolan intervention, 255–57;
    anti-apartheid movement, 287–89; anti-
    imperialism, 279; decentralization and,
    15, 191, 267; economic activism, 192–93;
    Gulf Oil boycott, 191, 194–96, 199–200;
    legislative branch, 11–12; New Left
    Internationalism and, 12, 14–15, 194–95,
    293–94; New Right and, 267–68; policy
    awareness, 157, 159; religious mobiliza-
    tion, 15, 46–49; social justice and, 105;
    social revolution and, 101–2; solidarity
    movement, 128–29, 159, 271; transna-
    tional collaboration, 6–7, 11, 46–49; U.S.
    foreign policy, 11–12, 47, 50–51, 80, 105,
    272, 282, 299n24
Guebuza, Armando, 121
Guevara, Che, 123, 184, 215
Guimarães, Abel, 207, 213, 336n112
Guinea-Bissau: armed struggles in, 60,
    79–81, 86; coup of 1980, 285; indepen-
    dence of, 231; leftist organizing, 41; lib-
    eration campaign, 2–3, 38, 71, 81; NATO
    arms in, 81; PAIGC and, 75, 80–81, 218;
    Portuguese settlers in, 22, 300n6; social-
    ism and, 60, 82
Guinea-Conakry, 41, 80–81, 92, 98fig.
Gulf Action Committee, 195
Gulf-Angola Committee, 199
Gulf Boycott Coalition (GBC): African
    Americans and, 202; African liberation
    and, 200–201; grassroots organizing and,
    199–202, 204–5, 334n54; New Left goals,
    201; PALC and, 205
Gulf Oil boycott: ACOA and, 191, 194–96,
    199–200; African liberation and, 200–202,
    203fig., 204–9; Angolan students, 213,
    336n112; anti-capitalist critique, 197–98;
    anti-imperialism and, 191; Black activists
    and, 15, 186, 191, 202, 204–5, 207; CRV
    and, 194–96; decentralization and,

202, 209; grassroots organizing and,
    199–202, 204–5, 207, 334n74; ideological
    differences, 191; MPLA and, 205, 207,
    211; New Left Internationalism and, 200;
    religious mobilization, 191, 196–200, 208;
    SAC and, 195–96; shareholder activism,
    195–97; solidarity movement, 191–200,
    202, 204–9, 219; targeting of gas stations,
    196, 199–200; tricontinentalism and, 209;
    unions and, 195, 201, 334n53; university
    divestment, 202, 204, 207; youth activists
    and, 121, 136
Gulf Oil Company: defense of overseas
    record, 196, 199, 207; disruption of
    shareholder meeting, 195–97; funding of
    Portuguese military, 194, 197; operations
    in Angola, 88, 185, 191, 193–200, 205–8;
    rebuttal of boycott campaign, 207; South-
    east Asian operations, 200; UCC critique
    of, 197–99

Hamilton, Lee, 261, 265
Hands Off Angola rally, 223, 224fig., 225
Hanson, Eileen, 116, 117fig., 122, 143, 151,
    154
Hare, Nathan, 177
Hart, Jack, 334n53
Harvard University, 202, 204, 288, 334n59
Haskell, Floyd, 231
Hatcher, Richard, 175
Height, Dorothy, 65
Heritage Foundation, 267–68
Herskovits, Melville, 72
High, George, 58
Hightower, Charles, 144, 146–48, 173, 199,
    202
Hill, Sylvia, 183
Hooper, Janet MacLaughlin, 133, 143, 152,
    160, 319n32
Horne, Gerald, 302n33
Houser, George: ACOA and, 25, 27, 29, 61,
    70, 142–44, 147, 151, 156; Africa advisory
    council, 29, 62; African nationalists and,
    77–78; on ANLCA, 67; anti-colonial alli-
    ances, 144; grassroots organizing and, 63,
    150, 159, 280; on intervention in Angola,
    237, 244–45; Mondlane and, 75; MPLA
    and, 305n23; NCC and, 47; pacifism and,
    143; political lobbying, 97; religious mobi-
    lization, 129; Roberto and, 44, 145–46,

211; testimony to Congress, 158, 235; UPA nationalists and, 26–27, 27*fig.*

Hovey, Gail, 117*fig.*, 120, 195

Howley, Frank, 53–54, 308n79

Hughes-Ryan Act, 237

Hultman, Tami, 116

human rights: African liberation and, 74; anti-apartheid movement, 288; anti-communist rhetoric, 265, 287; Carter and, 283; Fraser and, 94, 96, 158, 230, 293; FRELIMO and, 72; global reformism and, 227–28; global social justice, 287; internationalism and, 241; Latin American solidarity, 291; New Left Internationalism and, 228, 277, 287; religious mobilization, 134, 139; southern Africa policy, 262, 270; U.S. foreign policy and, 283–84, 287

Humphrey, Hubert, 25, 46, 239, 241, 247, 263

Hunton, Alphaeus, 327n4

IA Feature, 231, 237, 252, 270, 272

imperialism: Black activists and, 168, 214–16; capitalist, 122, 144, 164, 176, 183; economic and cultural, 7; Franco-British defense of, 31, 34; Portuguese defense of, 3, 22, 28, 33–34, 56, 63; race and, 163, 166; Soviet, 213, 250, 265, 268; tricontinentalism and, 169, 181; U.S. and, 82, 109, 122, 126–27, 171, 176, 198, 228; Western, 83–84, 105, 120, 122. *See also* anti-imperialism

India, 19, 22–23, 43, 55–56

Innis, Roy, 242

Institute for Policy Studies, 278, 293

institutional transformation: ACOA and, 142–52, 156, 160; divestment of stocks, 115, 132, 196, 202, 204, 288; Global South relationships, 135–36, 160–61; Gulf Oil boycott, 197, 202; multigenerational alliances, 133, 135, 137–38; NCC and, 132–42, 155–56; New Left Internationalism and, 268–69, 282; religious, 28, 107, 113; solidarity movement, 159–60; transnational worldviews, 274; Vietnam War and, 192; youth activists and, 15, 110, 115, 131–35, 137–40, 148–52, 154, 160

Irish, Paul, 156, 199

Isaacman, Allen, 121, 235–36, 340n45

Isaacman, Barbara, 121

Isserman, Maurice, 160

Javits, Jacob, 252

Jesuit Conference, 224*fig.*

Johnson, Lyndon: Lusophone Africa policy, 59, 75–77, 86, 89; Mozambique Institute funding cuts, 99; opposition to minority rule, 86; Rhodesian embargoes, 90, 93, 95; Vietnam War and, 192

Johnson, Nelson, 214

Johnson, Robert David, 228

Johnson, Willard, 340n45

Jones, LeRoi. *See* Baraka, Amiri

Jordan, Joseph, 289

Jorge, Paulo, 207

Joseph, Peniel, 170–71

Karenga, Maulana, 174

Kaunda, Kenneth, 25, 86, 238

Kazin, Michael, 160

Keck, Margaret, 11, 225

Kennedy, Edward "Ted": Africa Group and, 94, 96; ALD and, 335n94; anti-intervention in Angola, 238; Global South relationships, 289; New Left Internationalism and, 225; pro-Africa sentiment, 158, 208–9

Kennedy administration: African policy and, 66–67; anti-colonial lobbying, 47; arms policy in Angola, 51; Cold War fears, 35–36, 50; European opposition, 35, 45; Portuguese offensive in Angola, 45, 54–55; Portuguese relations, 59–62, 66–68, 74

Kennedy, John F.: assassination of, 59, 67, 75, 77; Cabral communication on napalm bombs, 77, 313n89; decolonization and, 14, 29–32, 34–37, 45, 49–51, 58–59; Peace Corps and, 107; retreat from pro-African position, 56–59, 64, 66–69, 76; Roberto and, 26, 29, 32, 57

Kennedy, Robert, 74–75

Kenyatta, Jomo, 232*fig.*

Keys, Barbara, 11, 227, 265, 287

Khan, Sharfudine: African American support, 172; American solidarity activists, 119–21, 123, 126–27, 152, 184, 205, 320n69; appeals to religious leaders, 137; CONCP and, 146; FRELIMO and, 100, 123, 127, 154; *A Luta Continua*, 182–83; PASC and, 173; UN lobbying, 100; U.S. lobbying, 187

Kilpatrick, James J., 90
King, Martin Luther, Jr., 25, 63, 65, 108,
    169–70
Kirkpatrick, Jeane J., 265
Kissinger, Henry: Angola leadership and,
    233; covert operations and, 237, 240,
    340n59; denial of intervention, 245,
    247, 341n88; détente and, 226, 250–52;
    great-power politics, 227; on IA Feature,
    237; intervention in Angola, 237–38,
    253, 259, 340n59; majority rule negotia-
    tions, 261–62; reactionary regimes, 261;
    regional stability and, 88–89; relations
    with Portugal, 89, 209, 336n97; southern
    Africa policy, 231–33, 258, 339n27; suspi-
    cion of the MPLA, 236; transfer of power
    in Portugal, 218–19, 232
Knopf, Jeffrey W., 12
Kramer, Reed, 116

Lake, Anthony, 89
Lara, Lucio, 43
Latin America: anti-imperialism, 152;
    Cold War interventionism, 273, 279;
    peace movements, 294; Reagan-era
    interventions, 11, 13, 291, 293; solidarity
    movement, 291, 293; tricontinentalism,
    7, 9, 144
Lefever, Ernest, 263–65, 267
leftist organizing: anti-colonialism, 39; Black
    activists and, 181–82, 209, 213–15; Black
    anti-imperialism, 164–65; collabora-
    tive relationships, 5; CONCP and, 41,
    169, 181; global equality and, 105–6;
    Lusophone African nationalism, 4, 8–10,
    15, 37–40, 44–45, 188; MPLA and, 255;
    nationalist philosophies, 40; partisan
    competition, 56–58; re-Africanization
    and, 39; solidarity movement, 45, 124–28,
    282–83; tricontinentalism and, 7, 141. See
    also New Left Internationalism
Leland, Mickey, 289, 293
Liberation Committee for Africa (LCA),
    164–67, 170
Liberation Support Movement (LSM):
    African liberation and, 124–27; authentic
    political movements and, 153fig.; Black
    activists and, 127, 213; Gulf Oil boycott,
    196, 199, 207; information dissemi-
    nation, 125–26, 207; life histories of

revolutionaries, 125, 158, 207; Marxist
    ideology and, 124–26, 128–29; MPLA
    and, 213; solidarity movement, 124–29,
    131, 154, 182
Liberator, 164–67, 171
Lincoln University, 50, 62, 66, 100, 172, 236,
    328n40
Locke, Dawolu Gene, 214
Locke, Gene, 289, 329n63
Lockwood, Edgar "Ted," 156–57, 159, 192,
    235, 243, 254, 278
Logevall, Fredrik, 8
LSM. See Liberation Support Movement
    (LSM)
Lumumba, Patrice, 23–24, 63, 164, 184
Lusophone Africa: colonial policies, 9,
    20–24; decolonization and, 20–21, 50,
    279; economic activism, 193; expulsion of
    missionaries, 47, 54; map of, 42fig.; non-
    state actors, 37; Portuguese repression in,
    3, 24, 28, 33, 38; propaganda campaigns,
    52–58; revolutionary diplomacy, 3–4; uni-
    versity students, 39, 50, 62, 66, 304n2; U.S.
    relations with, 283–84. See also Estado
    Novo (New State); Portugal
Lusophone liberation: Black solidarity and,
    163–64, 174, 176, 178, 180, 185, 189, 208;
    CONCP and, 81, 83, 189; congressional
    advocates, 11–12; guerrilla wars, 75, 78,
    80–82, 212, 260, 284; leadership struggles,
    211–13; leftist organizing, 9–10, 37–40,
    106, 132, 154, 274; New Left Interna-
    tionalism and, 106, 191–92, 229, 278–82;
    religious mobilization, 106–7, 131, 135,
    141; revolutionary diplomacy, 3, 6–7, 14;
    self-determination, 28–29, 44, 50, 58–59,
    81, 83; transnational collaboration, 14,
    23–24, 162, 211; tricontinentalism and,
    7–8, 105–6; U.S. support for, 5–6. See also
    African liberation; solidarity movement

MAC. See Movimento AntiColonialista
    (MAC)
Machel, Samora, 2, 91, 100, 238
MacInnes, Murray, 135–36
Macmillan, Harold, 20, 34, 49, 55, 85
Madhubuti, Haki, 215
Madison Area Committee on Southern
    Africa (MACSA): Angolan intervention
    activism, 242–43; anti-imperialism and,

121, 154; congressional internationalists and, 235, 242; coordination of activism, 121–22, 126–27, 242–43; educational outreach, 121, 152, 172; Gulf Oil boycott, 196; multiracial alliances, 128; New Left Internationalism and, 121, 123, 125, 129; research activities, 121, 128
Madison Conference, 242–43, 255
Mahon, George, 257
Makunga, Stella, 212
Malcolm X Liberation University, 176–77
Mandela, Nelson, 272, 281, 288
Maoism, 69, 175, 212, 216, 255
Marable, Manning, 169, 213
Marcum, John: ACOA and, 29, 50, 65, 236; Angolan nationalism and, 69, 236; defense of MPLA, 236; Gulf Oil boycott, 197; humanitarian aid to SARA, 61–62; Lincoln University and, 62, 328n40; revolutionary ideology, 147; Roberto and, 236, 340n49
Marxism: African liberation and, 119; ALSC and, 214; Black nationalist critique, 215; New Left Internationalism and, 8; PAIGC and, 40; Pan-Africanism and, 167; political and economic reform, 279; Third World, 210; tricontinentalism and, 7; youth activists and, 125–26, 128–29
Maurer, Robert, 120, 319n33
Mboya, Tom, 25, 29, 281
McAlister, Melani, 163
McAnally, Mary, 324n45
McClellan, John, 238, 246
McCloy, John, 74
McGee, Gale, 94, 96, 158, 235, 240, 265
McGhee, George C., 265
McKay, Vernon, 93
McVeigh, Malcolm, 47, 50, 54, 62, 111
Meany, George, 46
Mendy, François, 57, 327n13
Meridian Hill (Malcolm X) Park, 179fig.
Meriwether, Jim, 63
Minter, Ruth Brandon, 115–17, 117fig., 120–21, 138, 323n25
Minter, William "Bill": aid to independent nations, 339n26; Christian internationalism, 115–16; educational outreach, 143, 194; FIM and, 116–17, 120; MACSA and, 121; Mozambique Institute, 138; SNCC and, 115; on U.S. involvement in

Lusophone colonies, 194; Zambia Group, 117, 117fig.
missionaries: African nationalists and, 25, 46, 106–7, 111; education of African children, 39, 72; Eurocentric paternalism, 107, 110, 132, 138, 142; ideological diversity, 141; nonviolent principles, 111; reports of Portuguese atrocities, 46–48, 50–51, 62, 108; Salazar expulsion of, 47, 54; White Redoubt and, 135; youth activists and, 109–11
Mobutu Sese Seko, 232–33, 237–39, 258
Mondlane, Eduardo: African American relations, 164, 166–67; anti-colonial solidarity, 73; armed revolution, 74–75, 78, 111–12, 115, 137; assassination of, 91, 96, 132, 140, 184; Christian ties, 72–73, 108–9, 112, 135–36, 158; coalition-building, 149; FRELIMO and, 14, 60, 65, 72, 76fig., 78, 82, 100, 105, 111–12, 115–16; grassroots organizing and, 15, 311n34; leftist organizing, 105; liberation campaign, 95–96; Marxist ideology and, 181; as model nationalist, 74; nonviolent principles, 73–75, 108, 111–12; political lobbying, 60, 97, 99; religious mobilization, 108–9, 132, 135–37; social justice and, 73–74, 98, 182; solidarity movement and, 131; transnational appeals, 66, 71–75, 77, 119, 127, 160, 166; United Nations and, 72, 164, 166; Western culture and, 72–74; on white minority regime solidarity, 91, 316n51; youth activists and, 108, 112, 115–16, 146, 318n7
Mondlane, Janet, 82, 97, 100, 108, 116, 149, 166
Moniz, Júlio Botelho, 30, 303n50
Montero, Frank, 26
Moose, Dick, 238, 340n58
Moran, Mark, 253
Moreira, Adriano, 61, 303n50
Morlan, Don, 116–17, 117fig.
Morlan, Gail, 116–17, 117fig., 120, 135–36, 138, 324n45
Morse, Bradford, 94
Movement for Colonial Freedom (MCF), 48
Movement for the Liberation of São Tomé and Príncipe, 218
Movimento AntiColonialista (MAC), 305n13

Movimento das Forças Armadas (MFA), 218
Movimento de Libertação da Guiné, 327n13
Movimento Popular de Libertação de
Angola (MPLA): ACOA and, 44, 145;
American solidarity activists, 10, 12, 124,
132, 242–43, 255–56, 269, 281; Angolan
leadership struggles, 218–19, 225, 231,
233, 237–40, 260; anti-imperialism, 213;
armed revolution, 83; authoritarianism and, 285; Cold War neutrality and,
312n75; CONCP and, 39, 83, 145, 213;
Congressional delegation and, 238; Cuban
aid for, 224, 231, 233, 241–42, 250, 257,
269, 284; formation of, 40; government of,
223; Gulf Oil boycott, 205, 207, 335n78;
liberation campaign, 3, 6, 44, 231; Luanda
uprising, 45, 302n36; Marxism and, 126;
mestiço leadership, 40, 57, 68–69, 212;
national identity and, 40–41; Neto and,
232fig.; New Left Internationalism and,
145, 267; presence in the U.S., 255; recognition of, 269–70, 284; religious humanitarian aid for, 141, 323n42; socialism and,
40, 56; Soviet communism and, 223–24,
231, 233, 245–46, 250–51, 253, 257, 269,
284, 286; transnational appeals, 44, 49,
140, 211, 306n48, 348n24; tricontinentalism and, 8; UPA and, 45, 56–57; U.S.
foreign policy and, 16, 223–26, 233–45;
U.S. opposition to, 238–39
Mozambican National Resistance (REN-
AMO), 286
Mozambique: armed struggles in, 60,
79–82, 85–86, 92; Cahora Bassa Dam, 88,
139; FRELIMO and, 71, 81–82, 85, 218;
guerrilla wars, 81–82; independence of,
1–3, 231; liberation campaign, 2–3, 38,
71, 81–82, 176, 182; Portuguese settlers
in, 22, 300n6; socialism and, 60, 82; youth
activists and, 123
Mozambique Institute, 74, 82, 99, 101, 138,
211, 320n68
Mozambique Liberation Front. See Frente de
Libertação de Moçambique (FRELIMO)
Mozambique Project, 349n28
Mozambique Will Be Free, 123, 321n73
MPLA. See Movimento Popular de Libertação de Angola (MPLA)
Muhammad, Elijah, 168, 328n24
Mulcahy, Ed, 245

Munro, John, 164, 189
Muskie, Edmund, 87

Nascimento, Lopo do, 262fig.
Nasser, Gamal Abdel, 23
National Anti-Imperialist Coalition,
334n53
National Association for the Advancement
of Colored People (NAACP), 63, 65, 97,
114
National Black Political Convention, 174
National Conference of Black Lawyers, 269
National Council of Churches (NCC):
ACOA and, 47, 96, 145; African nationalism and, 47–48, 93, 95, 133–34, 141–42;
anti-imperialism and, 134, 136; concern with military operations, 136–37;
corporate responsibility, 192–93, 333n28;
foreign policy and, 263–64; FRELIMO
and, 137, 141; global racial equality and,
134–35, 141–42; grassroots organizing
and, 46, 102; Gulf Oil boycott, 195, 197;
institutional transformation, 132–42,
155–56; lobbying efforts, 47, 155–56;
Mondlane and, 72, 108, 137, 322n19; New
Left Internationalism, 10, 190; New Right
critique of, 267; nonviolent principles,
136; peace and, 46–47; Roberto and,
302n30; southern Africa investment, 133,
136, 138, 156; southern Africa strategy,
136–37; youth activists and, 10, 15, 113,
115, 131, 133–38, 141–42
National Council of Negro Women, 65
National Democratic Union of Mozam-
bique. See União Democrática Nacional
de Moçambique (UDENAMO)
National Liberation Front of Angola. See
Frente Nacional de Libertação de Angola
(FNLA)
National Mobilization for Justice and Peace
in Central America and Southern Africa,
294
National Security Council (NSC), 244, 258
National Security Study Memorandum
(NSSM), 89
National Student Christian Federation
(NSCF), 107–9, 111–12, 332n3
National Union for the Total Independence
of Angola. See União Nacional para a
Independência Total de Angola (UNITA)

National Union of Angolan Students, 207

Ndlovu, Sifiso Mxolisi, 288

Nehru, Jawaharlal, 23, 55

Nelson, Bill, 245

Nesbitt, Prexy: ACOA and, 143–45, 148, 151; Africa Information Service, 128; on Carnation Revolution, 217; CCLAMG and, 152, 154; MPLA and, 145, 212–13, 215; solidarity movement, 162

Neto, Agostinho: Angolan leadership and, 232*fig.*; Cold War neutrality, 312n75; Gulf Oil boycott, 195, 207; imprisonment of, 48; leftist organizing, 40, 305n13; mestiço leadership and, 69; MPLA and, 40, 76*fig.*, 238; re-Africanization, 39; religious mobilization, 135; solidarity activists, 124

New Left Internationalism: activist collaborations, 291, 292*fig.*, 293–94; African Information Service, 184; African liberation and, 5, 12, 16, 106, 190–92, 229, 278–82; anti-apartheid movement, 11, 287–89; anti-imperialism and, 144, 150, 279, 294–95; anti-interventionism and, 240–41, 245, 248–52, 261, 263–64, 267–68, 270, 273–74; authentic political movements and, 141, 144–45, 153*fig.*, 281; Black Power and, 10, 143, 192; CONCP and, 172, 277, 279–81; decentralization and, 9–11, 280–81, 286, 291; Global South and, 125, 129, 281–82; grassroots organizing and, 12, 14–16, 194–95, 293–94; Gulf Oil boycott, 200–201; human rights and, 228, 277, 287; institutionalizing, 268–69, 274–75, 289; MPLA and, 145, 267; North-South divide and, 190, 196, 198, 226–28; participatory democracy and, 13, 119, 200, 278, 295; radicalism and, 161, 278–79; religious institutions and, 142, 293–94; self-determination and, 11, 263, 277; solidarity movement, 9–10, 132, 189–91, 196, 200–201, 277–79, 290–91, 293–94; transnational collaboration, 5–6, 9–10, 278; tricontinentalism and, 8–9, 146, 160, 190, 279, 300n32; U.S. foreign policy and, 5–6, 9–12, 15, 155–56, 190, 225–29, 231, 235, 240, 245–47, 249, 278, 284–85; youth activists and, 113–14, 119, 122–24, 129, 146, 151, 160

New Mobilization Committee to End the War in Vietnam (New Mobe), 127, 294

New Right: anti-communism and, 257, 263–68, 277, 282; attacks on Clark Amendment, 267–68; attacks on détente, 251–52, 263–64; conservative coalitions, 90, 263–66, 277; evangelical churches, 290; foreign policy and, 15–16, 257, 263–66; grassroots organizing and, 267–68; human rights rhetoric, 265, 267; interventionism and, 15–16, 263–68, 274; UNITA and, 267–68

Newsom, David, 188

Newton, Huey P., 177

New World Resource Center (NWRC), 152, 154–55, 293–94, 326n100

Nicaragua, 285, 293–94

Nixon, Richard: ALD demonstrations and, 180; Azores agreement, 158; détente and, 226; power politics, 88–89; relations with Portugal, 79, 89, 92, 97, 101; southern Africa policy, 88–89, 91–93, 95–96, 197, 209; Tar Baby Option, 89; Watergate and, 226–27; White Redoubt and, 89–90

Nkrumah, Kwame: African nationalism and, 23, 25, 36; Black activists and, 182; Carmichael and, 171; Malcolm X and, 168; Pan-Africanism and, 26, 167, 171; Roberto and, 36, 67

Nogueira, Franco, 57, 61, 88–89, 303n50

nonviolence: ACOA and, 27, 143; anti-imperialism and, 347n10; Christian church and, 111–12, 136; Gandhian, 73, 108, 112; limitations on state violence, 112; Mondlane and, 73–75, 108, 111–12

North American Anti-Imperialist Coalition, 154

North Atlantic Treaty Organization (NATO): Angolan self-determination, 31, 34–35; Azores agreements, 55–56, 60; Kennedy administration and, 31, 34–35; Lusophone Africa and, 19; Portugal and, 20–21, 30–31, 37, 44, 81, 83; use of weapons in Lusophone Africa, 45, 48, 50–51, 81, 83

Northern Rhodesia. *See* Zambia (Northern Rhodesia)

Norway, 99–100, 245

NSCF. *See* National Student Christian Federation (NSCF)

Nteta, Chris, 202

NWRC. *See* New World Resource Center (NWRC)

Nyasaland (Malawi), 66, 84

Nyerere, Julius, 25, 71, 167, 170, 176, 181, 230, 238

O'Brien, E. D., 307n71

Office of Social Ministries, 224*fig.*

OMA. *See* Organização da Mulher de Angola (OMA)

O'Neill, Thomas P. "Tip," 56

Organização da Mulher de Angola (OMA), 154

Organization of African Unity (OAU), 68, 83, 145, 253

Organization of Afro-American Unity, 168

Overseas Companies of Portugal, 307n72

PAIGC. *See* Partido Africano da Independência da Guiné e Cabo Verde (PAIGC)

PALC. *See* Pan-African Liberation Committee (PALC)

Palme, Olof, 100

Pan-Africanism: African Americans and, 63–64, 143, 162–69, 172–73, 178–79, 181–84, 187–89; ANLCA and, 77; anti-imperialism and, 143–44, 184; Black press and, 330n75; CONCP and, 168, 181; foreign policy and, 299n24; liberation parties, 166, 327n14; Marxist rhetoric, 167; political organizing and, 162; radical Black solidarity, 143, 162–69, 174, 214–15; socialist ideology and, 163, 171, 186; solidarity movement, 162–64; transnational collaboration, 172–73; tricontinentalism and, 184–85

Pan-African Liberation Committee (PALC): activist allies, 205; African liberation and, 205; Black activists and, 204; grassroots organizing and, 204–5; Gulf Oil boycott, 202, 203*fig.*, 204; Harvard protest, 202, 204, 334n59; multiracial alliances, 202, 205, 210–11; tricontinentalism and, 210–11

Pan-African Solidarity Committee (PASC), 173

Partido Africano da Independência da Guiné e Cabo Verde (PAIGC): American solidarity activists, 12, 132; armed revolution, 75, 80–83, 217; Black nation-building, 175; Cabo Verde leadership, 231; CONCP and, 39; Eastern bloc alliances, 80, 217, 317n86; formation of, 39–40; mestiço leadership, 57; national identity and, 40–41; postcolonial modernization, 40; racial tensions in, 285; social and economic improvements, 82, 97–98, 98*fig.*, 317n86; socialism and, 9, 40, 71, 82, 106; Soviet aid for, 80, 317n86; struggle in Guinea-Bissau, 71; transnational appeals, 77, 139–40, 149, 166, 177; tricontinentalism and, 7–8, 80–81; U.S. lobbying, 100

Partido Democrático de Angola, 68

PASC. *See* Pan-African Solidarity Committee (PASC)

Patricio, Rui, 336n97

Peace Corps, 107, 109, 118, 122, 320n61

peace movements. *See* anti-war movement

Pereira, Theotonio, 303n50

PIDE (Polícia Internacional e de Defesa do Estado), 21, 23–24, 87, 310n13

Plummer, Brenda Gayle, 63, 65, 188, 311n30

Podhoretz, Norman, 264–65

Popular Movement for the Liberation of Angola. *See* MPLA

Portugal: African colonies, 2–3, 19–21, 42*fig.*; arms embargo, 208; British relations with, 85–86, 88, 314n21; Carnation Revolution, 217, 219, 254, 337n129; civilizing mission, 33, 39, 53; colonial policies, 9, 20–24, 28–29; decolonization, 1–3, 6, 38; economic boycotts, 192; Estado Social, 87; European alliances, 34–35, 37, 44, 48–49; European Economic Community, 217; Gulf Oil operations, 88, 191, 193–95, 197–99, 332n8; loss of Goa, 55–56; lusotropicalism, 33, 53, 87, 303n63; military coup, 217–19; multiracial imperialism, 53, 63; NATO and, 20–21, 30–31, 37, 44, 51, 60, 81, 83; order and hierarchy in, 21–22, 45, 91; propaganda campaigns, 52–59, 63–64, 307n71, 307n72; public diplomacy, 37–38, 57, 86, 299n20; regional stability and, 34, 53, 58–59, 61; relations with South Africa, 85–87, 314n21; Rhodesia and, 85–86; transfer of power in, 218–19; U.S. intervention in, 218–19, 232, 239; U.S. relations with, 3–4, 11–12, 14, 29, 31, 45,

56, 61, 79, 85–89, 91–92, 209, 233–36;
U.S. sale of Boeing 707s, 92, 148, 316n56;
warfare in Angola, 48, 50–52; White
Redoubt, 14, 42*fig.*, 80, 88–92, 97. *See also*
Estado Novo (New State); Lusophone
Africa
Portuguese Africa. *See* Lusophone Africa
Portuguese-American Committee on For-
eign Affairs (PACFA), 52–54
Powell, Adam Clayton, 25, 50, 170
Presbyterian Commission on Religion and
Race, 140
Presbyterian Southern Africa Task Force, 141
propaganda campaigns: anti-colonial
violence, 52–53; anti-white racism, 52–53;
civilizing mission, 33, 53; Cold War fears,
52–54, 58; CONCP and, 41, 44; Portuguese anti-liberation, 52–59, 307n71,
307n72; Portuguese courting of African
Americans, 63–64; pro-Portuguese colonialism, 52–59, 92; Protestant churches
and, 46–48, 50, 52; Rhodesia and, 90–91;
White Redoubt, 90–91, 93, 95–96, 102
Protestant church: ACOA and, 28, 62;
African nationalism and, 108, 135; anti-
colonialism, 46–47; condemnation of Portugal, 48–49; decline of, 290; economic
activism, 192–93, 197, 332n3; ethical
guidelines, 156; Eurocentric engagement,
107–8, 138; Global South relationships,
133, 135–36; grassroots organizing and,
15, 46–49; Gulf Oil boycott, 195, 197; leftist organizing, 332n3; propaganda campaigns, 46–48, 50, 52; reconsideration of
missions, 107–8; tensions with Portugal,
24, 47; youth activists and, 107–9. *See also*
Christian church; missionaries; religious
internationalism

racial equality: African liberation and, 105,
171; anti-imperialism and, 163, 166; Black
identity and, 163, 170; internationalist
critique, 168–69; lusotropicalism and,
53; NCC and, 134–35, 141; New Left
Internationalism, 5; religious mobilization, 139–40; transnational collaboration,
63–65, 73, 141–42, 174; youth activists
and, 112–14, 132
radicalism: African liberation and, 74, 82,
160; anti-imperialism, 152, 154; Black

solidarity and, 65–67, 162–65, 168,
170–72, 176, 189, 191–92, 213, 229; CIA
undermining of, 148; communist fears, 7,
30; Gulf Oil boycott, 194–95; internationalism and, 163, 189; New Left Internationalism and, 161, 278–79; Pan-Africanism,
205; religious, 106–30, 136, 143–44, 150;
solidarity movement, 105, 185; youth
activists and, 113–16, 119, 123–25, 131,
150, 167–68, 191–92, 213, 229
Randolph, A. Philip, 25, 64–66, 115
Randolph, Brenda, 202
Rangel, Charles, 158
Rauh, Joseph, Jr., 334n54
Reagan, Ronald: aid to Nicaraguan Contras,
285, 293–94; Angolan intervention,
251–53, 259, 262; anti-communism and,
225, 251–52, 260, 262–63, 274; attacks
on Ford, 251, 260, 263; foreign policy
and, 251, 260, 262–64; Latin American
interventions, 11, 13, 291, 293; New Right
and, 268; push-back against Congressional limits, 248n22; on Rhodesia, 262–63;
South African relations, 87, 225, 294
religious internationalism: divestment of
stocks, 115, 134, 196; FIM and, 109–10,
115–17, 120; Flory and, 109–10, 115, 129,
318n20; Global South ideas, 141; Gulf Oil
boycott, 191, 197–200; Latin American,
293; New Left Internationalism, 142,
293–94; paternalism, 132, 138, 142; progressivism, 290; youth activists, 109–11,
115, 128–29, 141, 151; Zambia Group, 15,
117, 117*fig.*, 118–20
Republic of New Afrika, 170
Resistência Nacional Moçambicana (REN-
AMO), 286
revolution: anti-imperialism and, 7–8, 72,
144; Black Power and, 170–75, 180–81;
Cabral and, 39–40, 180–81, 184–85;
global allies, 6, 9–10, 26, 62; Mondlane
and, 75, 108, 135; multilevel diplomacy,
10, 26; Pan-Africanism and, 164–65;
practical vision of, 180–81, 185; religious
support for, 106–12; Roberto and, 67–70,
165; social, 98–99, 101, 132, 182; tricontinentalism and, 7, 41, 80–81, 105–6,
160; women's liberation and, 212. *See also*
African liberation
Rhoads, Brewster, 273, 291

Rhodesia: British relations with, 85–86; Byrd Amendment, 155, 158, 270, 284; grassroots organizing and, 267, 283; independence of, 84, 113; Johnson embargo, 90, 93, 95; Portugal and, 85–86; propaganda campaigns, 90–91; self-determination, 261; UDENAMO and, 40; UDI and, 14, 79–80, 84–86, 90, 93, 134; U.S. relations with, 86, 90, 155, 262–63, 284; White Redoubt, 14, 42*fig.*, 84–85, 90

Ribeiro, Margarida Calafate, 22

Righter, Richard, 199, 201

Roach, Patricia, 199–201

Roberto, Holden: ACOA and, 26–28, 31, 35, 44–45, 62, 145–46; African American activists and, 164–65; Angolan leadership and, 232, 232*fig.*; anti-communism, 28, 32, 35–36, 41, 57, 302n30; Bakongo ethnocentrism, 26, 37–38, 41, 44, 59, 69, 236; CIA and, 32, 89, 225, 238–39; Congo mobilization, 43; executive branch aid, 225, 239; FNLA and, 68–70, 145–46; grassroots organizing and, 45–46; intracolonial network, 57; leadership struggles, 68–70; March 1961 rebellion, 24, 28, 31; MPLA and, 14, 69–70; nationalism and, 24–25, 32; propaganda campaigns, 44; racist rhetoric, 57, 70; rejection of MPLA union, 56–57; transnational alliances, 35, 66; UPA and, 26, 31–32, 35, 37–38, 41, 56, 59–60, 67; U.S. lobbying, 14, 26, 28–29, 31–32, 37, 51, 302n30

Robinson, David, 112, 117*fig.*, 319n48

Robinson, Randall: African liberation, 173, 202, 205; anti-apartheid movement, 202, 205; Gulf Oil boycott, 172–73, 204–5; MPLA and, 212; PALC and, 216, 340n45; TransAfrica lobbying, 173, 205, 216, 273, 284

Rodgers, Daniel T., 277, 347n4

Rodrigues, Luís Nuno, 303n50

Rome Conference (1970), 149, 154, 325n86

Root, Christine "Chris," 156–57, 159

Ross, Emory, 318n7

Rossinow, Doug, 114

Rostow, Eugene, 265

Rumsfeld, Donald, 260

Rusher, William, 90

Rusk, Dean: African policy, 45, 66; Angolan intervention and, 264–65; on Angola self-determination, 30; ANLCA and, 66–67; on European interests in Africa, 32, 60; Kennedy administration and, 29, 47; Portuguese propaganda campaigns and, 57–58; Roberto and, 68; Salazar and, 62, 86

Rustin, Bayard, 64, 266

SAC. *See* Southern Africa Committee (SAC)

Sadaukai, Owusu: ALD and, 176–77, 179, 329n61; Carmichael on, 214; Gulf Oil boycott, 204; liberation campaign, 177, 185, 188; *A Luta Continua*, 329n57; tricontinentalism and, 210

Salazar, Antonio de Oliveira: Azores agreements, 55–56, 60; on civilizing mission, 33, 39; colonial policies, 22–24, 31; Congressional defense of, 54–55; Estado Novo (New State) and, 21–22, 32–33; European alliances, 34–35, 37, 44; NATO and, 20, 30, 55, 60; Operation Viriato, 51; propaganda campaigns, 52–53, 58, 307n71, 307n72; repression of missionaries, 47, 54; U.S. relations with, 30–35, 59–62, 67–68, 76–77; violent response to Angolan revolt, 36, 50–52; White Redoubt and, 14, 84–86

Samuel Rubin Foundation, 290

Sangumba, Jorge, 212–13, 336n105

Santos, José Eduardo dos, 238

São Tomé, 22

SARA. *See* Serviço de Assistência aos Reugiados de Angola (SARA)

Savimbi, Jonas: Angolan leadership, 232*fig.*; anti-communism and, 268; Black identity and, 212–13, 215, 242; CIA and, 225, 238; GRAE and, 68; Maoism and, 69, 212; Ovimbundu nationalism, 68–69, 211–12; racialist rhetoric, 68, 311n46; Roberto and, 231; South African connections, 238; UNITA and, 69–70, 145, 166, 211–13, 238; UPA and, 55, 57; U.S. support for, 284, 286

Schlesinger, Arthur, 62

Schuyler, George, 53–54, 63–64, 330n75

Scowcroft, Brent, 259

SDS. *See* Students for a Democratic Society (SDS)

self-determination: ACOA and, 25; African liberation campaigns, 3–5, 9, 14, 20, 28–29, 44, 50, 58–59, 81, 83; Black Power

and, 163, 175; decolonization and, 279–
80; defensive use of force, 112; democracy
and, 27–28; Global South and, 9, 15, 20,
23, 229, 277; New Left Internationalism
and, 277; Rhodesia/Zimbabwe, 261, 284;
Western support for, 4, 30–34, 73
Selvage and Lee, 52–54, 64, 307n72
Serviço de Assistência aos Reugiados de
Angola (SARA), 62, 70
Sexton, Jay, 279
Shabazz, Betty, 173, 177
Sheldon, Paul, 198–99
Shultz, George, 265
Sikkink, Kathryn, 11, 225
Sinclair, John, 291
Smith, Christian, 294
Smith, Ian, 90, 272
Smith, Jackie, 13
Smith, John Coventry, 196
Smith, Mark, 172
Smith, Tim: African liberation and, 136, 138;
Gulf Oil boycott, 195, 197, 208, 332n19;
NCC and, 138; SAC and, 120, 135,
324n45, 332n19; UCC Council for Chris-
tian Social Action, 138, 157, 192–93, 195
Snellings, Rolland, 167–68, 170, 173–74
Snow, Crocker, Jr., 274
socialism: anti-imperialism and, 7; CONCP
and, 43–44, 60; FRELIMO and, 2, 4, 9, 71,
73–74, 82, 99, 106; military liberation, 4,
9; MPLA and, 40, 56; PAIGC and, 9, 40,
71, 82, 106; tricontinentalism, 41
social justice: African communalism and,
73; Black international, 108; Christian
ethics and, 73, 116; CONCP and, 102;
global racial equality and, 73, 112–13;
grassroots organizing and, 105; human
rights politics, 287; New Left Internationalism and, 5; nonviolent principles,
347n10
solidarity movement: ACOA and, 144, 150,
152; activist collaborations, 291, 292fig.,
293–94; African Americans and, 65, 162–
63, 189; African self-determination, 3–4,
10, 13–16, 46–47, 50–51, 93, 102, 106,
110–22, 158, 164–65, 175, 189, 270–73,
277, 282–83, 293–94; aid to independent
nations, 231, 339n26; Angolan intervention activism, 241–48, 253–57, 269, 281;
anti-capitalism, 168–69; anti-imperialism,

290–91; Black African identity and,
166, 204, 327n13; CONCP and, 41, 100,
102, 105–6, 126, 131, 144–45, 149–51,
160; congressional collaboration, 15, 97,
223–26, 235, 241–42, 248, 254; decentralization and, 9–10, 15, 159–60, 191,
209, 216, 272; dedication to action, 160;
foreign policy strategies, 118–19; Global
South perspectives, 12; grassroots organizing and, 128–29, 159, 271; Gulf Oil
boycott, 191–202, 203fig., 204–9; human
rights rhetoric, 287; impact of Malcolm X
on, 329n45; institutional collaborations,
131–32; Latin American, 291, 293–94;
leftist organizing, 45, 124–28, 282–83;
lobbying efforts, 155–56; multiracial
alliances, 127–28, 184, 205, 209–10,
214–15, 217; New Left Internationalism,
9–10, 132, 190–91, 196, 200–201, 277–79,
290–91, 293–94; Pan-Africanism, 162–69,
172–80; radical politics and, 14, 113–16,
119, 123–25; religious mobilization, 45,
105; socialism and, 186; transnational
collaboration, 41, 155, 189, 223, 278,
281, 285–86; tricontinentalism and, 163,
209–10; youth activists and, 105, 112–28,
159–60, 320n69; Zambia Group, 15, 117,
117fig., 118–20, 122, 124, 128
Soumialot, Gaston, 76fig.
South Africa: anti-apartheid movement,
13, 25, 193, 287–88; boycotts, 192–93;
constructive engagement policy, 87;
divestment campaigns, 281, 288; grassroots organizing and, 283; involvement
in Angola, 238, 244, 253–54, 260; public
support for anti-interventionism, 256–57;
relations with Portugal, 85–87, 314n21;
resistance to majority Black rule, 30,
88; Sharpeville Massacre, 48, 111, 114,
164; Soweto uprisings, 271, 288; UNITA
support, 238, 244, 247, 254; U.S. complicity with, 109, 114, 121; U.S. lobbying,
238–39; U.S. relations with, 88, 114, 264,
267; White Redoubt, 14, 42fig., 80, 85
southern Africa: ALD demonstrations, 180;
anti-communist appeals, 90–91; British
colonialism, 22, 79, 84; CIA in, 220; Congressional hearings, 235–36; missionary
ties, 106–7; propaganda campaigns, 96;
solidarity movement, 114–15, 127, 220,

southern Africa (*continued*)
270–73; U.S. alliance with Portugal,
85–87; U.S. foreign policy, 118, 261, 270,
283, 338n5; U.S. relations with, 88–90;
white minority regimes, 6, 79, 88–90;
White Redoubt, 14, 79, 84–85, 88, 95;
youth organizations, 120–22. *See also*
Lusophone Africa
Southern Africa, 113, 120, 128
Southern Africa Committee (SAC): ACOA
and, 114–15; African nationalism and,
120, 133, 319n33; anti-apartheid movement, 114–15, 319n33; Chase campaign,
114–15, 192; Christian witness, 319n33;
Committee of Conscience Against Apartheid, 114–15; formation of, 112; global
justice and, 112–13; Gulf Oil boycott,
195–96, 332n19; institutional transformation, 133; leftist organizing, 128; NCC
and, 134; New Left and, 113; religious ties,
142; SDS and, 114; solidarity movement,
154; youth activists and, 112–14, 117, 120,
126, 131. *See also* University Christian
Movement (UCM)
Southern Rhodesia. *See* Rhodesia
Soviet Union: aid to PAIGC, 80, 317n86;
anti-Soviet Afghans, 13, 225; détente and,
226, 250; Global South and, 265, 266*fig.*;
MPLA and, 223–24, 231, 233, 245–46,
250–51, 253, 257, 266*fig.*, 269, 284; power
politics and, 89; U.S. fears of expansion,
241, 250–52, 257, 260–61, 263–67
Sparkman, John, 237–38, 253
Spiegel, Marianne, 235, 238
Spínola, António de, 218
Sterling, Rick, 125–26
Stewart R. Mott Foundation, 290–91
Stockwell, John, 237
Student Conference on the Christian World
Mission, 107, 111
Student Nonviolent Coordinating Commit-
tee (SNCC), 115, 170
Students for a Democratic Society (SDS),
113–15, 192, 210
Students Organized for Black Unity (SOBU),
171–72, 181, 204
Suri, Jeremi, 226
Sutton, Percy, 187
Sweden, 99–100, 139, 149, 245
Symington, Stuart, 230, 240

Tambo, Oliver, 46, 121
Tanzania, 2, 64, 71, 74, 80–82, 99, 101
Tate, Florence, 242
Thatcher, Margaret, 264
Themido, João Hall, 330n73
Third World: anti-imperialism, 154, 176,
210; independence movements, 23, 152;
interventionism and, 100, 161, 268; Marx-
ism in, 210; political organizing, 174–75;
religious missions in, 107, 109, 197, 267;
revolution and, 40–41, 129, 146; U.S. for-
eign policy, 262–63. *See also* Global South
Third Worldism, 300n32
Thomas, Norman, 25
Thörn, Håkan, 13
Till, Emmet, 94
Touré, Ahmed Sékou, 92
Touré, Askia M., 167
Touré, Sékou, 171
TransAfrica, 173, 205, 216, 273, 284, 286
transnational collaboration: African liberation, 4–11, 23, 43–44, 65, 73, 77–78,
162–63, 280–82, 286, 300n32; anti-
Portuguese, 38; CONCP and, 37–38, 44;
congressional, 11–12, 282; independent
governance and, 286, 348n24; solidarity
movement, 189, 223, 278, 281, 285–86
tricontinentalism: African nationalist
struggles, 7–8, 80–83, 186, 189; American
solidarity activists, 7–9, 123, 146; anti-
imperialism and, 7–9, 146, 184; authentic
political movements, 144, 324n58; Black
activists and, 141, 205, 209–11, 213;
CCLAMG and, 152; CONCP and, 83,
114, 144, 166; FRELIMO and, 7–8, 80–81,
114; Global South and, 82, 129; Gulf Oil
boycott and, 209; leftist critique and, 7,
141; multiracial alliances, 210–11; neocolonialism and, 82; New Left Internationalism and, 8–9, 146, 160, 190, 300n32;
Pan-Africanism and, 184–85; socialism
and, 41; solidarity movement, 163,
209–10; Third Worldism and, 300n32;
U.S. and, 9, 298n18; youth activists and,
123, 146, 160
Tsongas, Paul, 284
Tucker, Theodore, 140, 302n30
Tunney, Gene, 246
Tunney, John V.: Africa Group and, 94;
African self-determination and, 157,

208–9, 285; anti-interventionism, 238, 245–47, 253, 258, 261; Cold War rhetoric, 229, 271; foreign policy and, 228–29; New Left Internationalism and, 225; solidarity movement and, 15

Tunney Amendment, 246–49, 253, 257, 293

Ture, Kwame. *See* Carmichael, Stokely

Tutu, Desmond, 281

Tyrell, Ian, 279

UDI. *See* Unilateral Declaration of Independence (UDI)

União Democrática Nacional de Moçambique (UDENAMO), 40, 71

União dos Povos de Angola (UPA): ACOA and, 27*fig.*, 31, 44; anti-Portuguese resistance, 29, 38, 51; Bakongo-dominated, 37–38, 41, 44, 56, 67; CONCP and, 38; MPLA and, 45, 56–57; religious aid for, 107; Roberto and, 26, 31–32, 35, 37–38, 41; self-determination, 46; U.S. lobbying, 37

União Nacional para a Independência Total de Angola (UNITA): African American support, 213; ALSC support for, 212–13, 215–16; Angolan leadership struggles, 231, 233, 237–39, 247; anti-communism, 255, 267–68; Black identity and, 166, 212–13, 215, 327n13; Black nationalist support, 145–46, 211, 255, 259; Chinese aid for, 70; FNLA and, 231, 233, 237–39; guerrilla wars, 145, 212, 260, 268, 284; liberation of Angola, 211–13; Maoism and, 212; mestiço leadership, 336n105; MPLA and, 213, 231; Savimbi and, 69–70, 145, 166, 211–13, 232*fig.*, 238; South African support for, 238, 244, 247, 254; U.S. support for, 233, 247, 255, 266*fig.*, 267, 284–86, 348n24

Unilateral Declaration of Independence (UDI): Anglo-American response to, 93–94; anti-decolonization, 79, 84; NCC opposition, 134; propaganda campaigns, 90; White Redoubt and, 14, 79–80, 84–86

Union of Angolan Peoples. *See* União dos Povos de Angola (UPA)

Union Theological Seminary, 109, 112, 115

UNITA. *See* União Nacional para a Independência Total de Angola (UNITA)

Unitarian Universalist Association, 293

United Auto Workers, 46, 224*fig.*

United Church of Christ (UCC): African nationalism and, 138, 157; Angola missionaries, 135, 197; anti-capitalist critique, 197–98; Congregation of Reconciliation, 199, 333n44; corporate social responsibility, 193; Gulf Oil boycott, 195, 197–200; Smith and, 138, 157, 192–93, 195, 197

United Farm Workers, 201

United Kingdom: African colonies, 22, 79, 84; anti-colonial movement, 43, 48–49, 306n41; CONCP and, 43, 48; condemnation of Indian rebellion, 55–56; decolonization and, 38; Labour Party, 44, 48–49; liberation campaigns, 28; pro-Portuguese propaganda, 55; relations with Portugal, 31, 34–35, 43, 85–86, 88, 314n21; religious mobilization, 48–49; Rhodesia and, 84–86; support for MPLA, 49; transnational liberation efforts, 43–45; U.S. foreign policy and, 50

United Nations: ACOA and, 25, 144; decolonization appeals, 23–26, 35; development assistance, 227; Estado Novo and, 22; Franco-British colonialism, 31, 34; Global South membership, 24; postcolonial societies in, 7; Security Council for Angolan self-determination, 31–32; substate actors and, 25

United Presbyterian Church, 196, 198

United States: African nationalist diplomacy in, 3–4, 10, 13, 49–50; African solidarity movement, 3–4, 206*fig.*; anti-communist appeals, 4, 6, 26, 28; Cold War and, 20–21, 23–24, 58; complicity in southern Africa, 109, 114, 121–22; conservative fear of declining power, 251–53; pro-Portuguese propaganda, 52–59, 308n79; pro-Rhodesian lobbying, 90; public support for anti-interventionism, 255–59; racial fears and, 52–53; relations with Portugal, 3–4, 11–12, 14, 29, 31, 56, 61, 79, 85–89, 91–92; relations with South Africa, 87–88, 114, 264, 267; religious mobilization, 46–49, 61–62, 310n10; UN vote for Angolan self-determination, 31–32, 54. *See also* U.S. Congress; U.S. foreign policy

University Christian Movement (UCM), 117

UPA. *See* União dos Povos de Angola (UPA)

Urdang, Stephanie, 217

U.S. Congress: Africa Group and, 94–95, 97, 100–101; African American legislators, 157–58; African liberation and, 271–72; Africa policy, 147–48, 158–59, 208–9, 223–30, 234–35, 269–70; Angolan anti-interventionism, 223–26, 234–58, 342n13; Clark Amendment, 243, 247–49, 257–58, 260, 267, 284–85, 293; coalitions in, 12–13; Cold War criticism, 230–31; conservative anti-communists, 6, 15, 60, 114, 209, 249–51, 255, 257, 260–61, 285; decolonization lobby, 96–97; defense of Salazar, 54–55, 58; delegation to Angola, 237–38; funding for Angola, 223, 245–46, 252, 261; grassroots organizing and, 11–12, 208–9, 271–73; Hughes-Ryan Act, 237; New Left Internationalism and, 5, 12, 15, 225–31, 235, 237–38, 240, 246–47, 249, 252, 270, 284–85; North-South divide and, 226–28, 253, 264, 275; pro-liberation sentiment, 92–97, 100–101; pro-Portuguese propaganda, 92; South African lobbying, 238–39; transnational networks, 12–13, 282; Tunney Amendment, 246–49, 253, 257, 293; Vietnam War and, 230–31, 338n6. *See also* Congressional Black Caucus (CBC)

U.S. foreign policy: advocacy networks, 225–26; African liberation campaigns, 2–5, 76–80, 188–89; African stability concerns, 30, 34–35, 53, 88–89, 91, 95; Angolan intervention, 15, 223–26, 233–62; Angolan self-determination, 60–61; anti-communism, 90, 233–34, 241, 244–45, 247, 249–50, 258, 264; arms exports, 50–52, 307n64, 307n66; Azores lease, 55, 92; backlash against anti-interventionists, 249–50, 282; Black agenda for, 64–65, 273; Cold War interventionism, 100, 129, 142, 228, 234, 241, 249–51, 255, 257, 283, 285; Cold War liberalism, 59, 63, 65, 77; decolonization and, 4, 11, 30–33; détente and, 226, 250–51, 264; domestic politics, 8, 13, 190–91, 207–11; Eurocentric engagement, 230, 278, 282; European opposition, 34–35; executive branch and, 11, 13, 59, 282, 293, 299n24; Global South and, 3–16, 20, 36–37, 139, 248, 253, 284, 298n16; grassroots organizing and, 11–12, 50–51, 80, 282, 299n24; majority rule

negotiations, 261–62; New Left Internationalism and, 5–6, 9–12, 15, 155–56, 190, 225–31, 240, 245, 249–50, 278; New Right and, 15–16, 263; pan-African internationalism, 299n24; Portuguese relations, 3–4, 45, 188, 209, 233–36; pro-African, 59, 86–87, 92; religious critique of, 134; Rhodesia and, 86, 284; southern Africa, 118, 261, 283, 338n5; Soviet Union and, 260–61; support of reactionary regimes, 118, 127, 154, 178, 194, 225–26, 239, 241, 244–45, 261; Vietnam War and, 8, 86–87, 93, 101, 114, 226; youth activists and, 109, 118, 122–23, 127, 148

Vance, Cyrus, 283–84

Van Hoogstraten, Jan, 140

Van Lierop, Robert: ACOA and, 143–44, 150–52, 173; Africa Information Service, 128, 184; FRELIMO and, 154, 173, 324n53; *A Luta Continua*, 176–77, 182–83, 210, 329n57; MPLA and, 212; NAACP and, 147, 173; Pan-Africanism, 143–44, 186; revolutionary action and, 173; solidarity movement, 162; testimony to Congress, 158

Vietnam War: congressional opposition, 230–31; détente and, 250–51; grassroots organizing and, 274; institutional policy and, 192; liberal internationalism and, 224; NCC opposition, 134; protests against, 4, 9, 113–14, 127, 281; as repudiation of interventionism, 240–41, 243, 247, 249, 255–57, 264–65; U.S. foreign policy and, 8, 86–87, 93, 101, 226; youth activists and, 122, 127

Von Eschen, Penny, 65

Walker, Lucius, 177

Walker, Lydia, 348n24

Walters, Ronald, 223, 224*fig.*, 254

War on Want, 49, 306n48

War Resisters League, 201, 256

Washington Office on Africa (WOA): activist collaborations, 291, 292*fig.*, 293; African liberation and, 156, 208, 271, 286; ALSC and, 216; Angolan intervention activism, 241–44, 256; congressional collaboration, 158–59, 234–35, 241–43, 246, 257, 272–73; Covert Operations

Task Force, 292*fig.*, 293; information dissemination, 158–59, 240, 257; MPLA and, 269, 284; New Left Internationalism and, 155–57; on Zaire arming of FNLA, 341n72

Washington Office on Latin America (WOLA), 291, 293

Watts, Daniel H.: on African leadership, 311n34; African nationalism and, 66; ANLCA and, 66, 167; impact on Black Power, 170; internationalism, 169, 188; LCA and, 164, 168, 188; Pan-Africanism, 166

Weicker, Lowell, 246

Weijdema, Trinike, 149

Weiss, Cora, 26, 95*fig.*, 146, 223, 290

Weiss, Peter, 26, 146, 293

Westad, Odd Arne, 6

Wheeler, Douglas, 236

White Redoubt: Anglo-American response to, 14, 93–94; anti-communist defense, 79, 282; anti-decolonization, 14, 79, 84–85; Cold War and, 268; grassroots organizing and, 90, 289; nationalist struggles, 42*fig.*, 79–80; Nixon and, 89–90, 92; Portugal and, 14, 84–86, 88–92, 97; propaganda campaigns, 90–91, 93, 95–96, 100, 102; Rhodesian UDI and, 14, 79–80, 84–86; Southern segregationists and, 90, 96, 316n51; state violence and, 112; U.S. lobbying, 90–91, 93, 95–96, 144, 155, 316n51; white minority regimes, 79–80, 84, 88–90

Wiest, Dawn, 13

Wiley, David, 110–13, 117, 117*fig.*, 120–21, 254, 256, 289

Wiley, Marylee Crofts, 110–13, 117, 117*fig.*, 120–22

Wilhelm, Carolyn, 117*fig.*, 319n48

Wilhelm, Charles, 117*fig.*, 319n48

Wilkins, Roy, 65–66

Williams, G. Mennen "Soapy," 29, 45, 49–50, 62, 86

Williams, Robert F., 165

Wilmore, Gayraud, 140–41, 324n45

Wilson, Harold, 85

Winston, Jim, 204

WOA. *See* Washington Office on Africa (WOA)

Wolpe, Howard, 289

women's movement, 154, 212

Women's Strike for Peace, 224*fig.*, 256

Woodard, Komozi, 179, 189

World Council of Churches (WCC): African nationalism and, 142; CONCP and, 140; Consultation on Race Relations in Southern Africa, 111; global ecumenism, 138–39; Programme to Combat Racism, 140; racial equality and, 139–40; support for liberation movements, 48, 139; Uppsala conference, 139

World Evangelical Alliance, 138, 323n29

Wu, Judy, 10

X, Malcolm: assassination of, 169, 184; Baraka and, 174; Black unity goals, 169, 177; deference to African leadership, 170; impact on Black Power movement, 170–71, 173, 329n45; internationalist critique, 168–69; Nation of Islam, 168; Pan-Africanism and, 168–69; rights-based discourse, 169; scientific socialism and, 214; split from Muhammad, 168, 328n24; Van Lierop and, 143

Year of Africa, 19, 43

Yergan, Max, 63, 90, 308n79

YOBU. *See* Youth Organized for Black Unity (YOBU)

Young, Andrew: African policy, 225, 227, 268, 339n37; Angolan intervention and, 253–54; Angolan self-determination and, 283–84; civil rights movement, 73, 157; on Cold War critics, 231; Congressional Black Caucus, 229–30; on Gandhian nonviolence, 73, 108; on majority rule negotiations, 262; Mondlane and, 73, 108, 157; MPLA and, 269–70; New Left Internationalism and, 224; self-determination and, 229, 283; social justice and, 208; as U.N. ambassador, 283, 285

Young, Robert J. C., 298n12

Young, Whitney, 65

youth activists: ACOA and, 126, 129–31, 143–46, 150; African nationalism and, 106, 110–16, 119–30; African revolutionaries and, 121, 124; anti-apartheid, 111, 114–15; anti-imperialism, 115, 119–21, 146; anti-war movement, 113–14, 119, 123–24, 127; CONCP and, 145; CRV

youth activists (*continued*)
and, 122–23, 320n61, 320n62, 320n68; decolonization and, 111, 280; educational outreach, 113, 119–26; FIM and, 109–10, 115–17; Freedom Summer, 111; grassroots organizing and, 105–6, 120–21, 157; Gulf Oil boycott, 195–96; institutional transformation, 15, 115, 131–46, 148–52, 154, 160; Marxist analysis, 125–26, 128–29; Mondlane and, 108, 115–16, 318n7; multigenerational alliances, 131, 133, 135, 137–38; NCC and, 10, 15, 133–36; New Left Internationalism and, 113–14, 119, 122–23, 129, 146, 151, 160; racial solidarity, 112–14, 128, 132; radical solidarity, 113–16, 119, 123–25, 131; regional organizing, 121–26; religious mobilization, 105–13, 115, 122, 128–29, 141, 151, 318n19, 320n60; SAC and, 112–13; socialist nation-building, 118; solidarity movement, 112–28; triconti-nentalism and, 123, 146, 160; U.S. foreign policy and, 109, 118, 122–23, 127, 148; WOA and, 156–57; Zambia Group, 15, 117, 117*fig.*, 118–20, 122, 124

Youth Against Fascism and War, 127
Youth Organized for Black Unity (YOBU), 171, 176, 210, 213, 215

Zaire, 231–33, 237, 258
Zambia (Northern Rhodesia), 84, 86, 119, 233
Zambia Group: African liberation and, 133; anti-imperialism and, 122, 144; decen-tralized solidary movement, 118–19, 122, 127; institutional reform, 133; leftist organizing, 124, 127–28; membership of, 117*fig.*; multigenerational alliances, 133; religious ties, 119, 133, 135–36, 142; youth activists and, 15, 116–20, 122, 124, 127–28, 138, 147, 280
ZANU Support Committee, 349n28
Zelizer, Julian, 274
Zimbabwe, 261, 284. *See also* Rhodesia

ACKNOWLEDGMENTS

The project that informs this book evolved over more than a decade, transforming from a diplomatic history of the end of Portuguese empire in Africa to a transnational study encompassing a variety of actors and competing visions of foreign affairs. On this journey, I accrued a debt to many scholars, archivists, activists, and friends. I worked with wonderful scholars at the University of Texas, including my committee: Toyin Falola, Jeremi Suri, Minkah Makalani, and the late Barbara Harlow. Mark Lawrence deserves special praise as an ideal adviser and gracious collaborator. I have been fortunate to join an incredibly supportive community at the Ohio State University. I want to thank all my colleagues, particularly Jennifer Siegel, David Steigerwald, Mitch Lerner, Christopher Nichols, Lydia Walker, Peter Hahn, Alice Conklin, Robert McMahon, Joan Flores-Villalobos, Theodora Dragostinova, Yiğit Akin, Bartow Elmore, Peter Mansoor, Zachary Matusheski, and Dorry Noyes. In addition, many incredible scholars have helped me conceptualize parts of this project over the years via conferences, correspondence, and conversation. There are too many to list, but special thanks go to Ryan Irwin, Aurora Almada e Santos, Ronald Williams II, Charles Thomas, Jeremy Friedman, Christopher Dietrich, Sarah Snyder, Bradley Simpson, James Meriwether, Russell Rickford, Natalia Telepneva, Miguel Bandeira Jerónimo, Carl P. Watts, Frank Gerits, Alexander Marino, Robert Rakove, Paul Adler, Amanda Joyce Hall, and Simon Stevens. I also want to thank Bob Lockhart for serving as a thoughtful editor, and everyone at University of Pennsylvania Press who helped assemble this book.

The exploration and evaluation of grassroots social organizing and its political influence is difficult due to the decentralized, ephemeral nature of these movements, so I am enormously grateful to the wonderful archivists who have preserved rare material and to the many people willing to share memories. I am indebted to everyone who spoke with me on this project, notably William Minter, Gail Hovey, Stephanie Urdang, Brenda Randolph, and David Wiley, whose memories, expertise, and connections were invaluable. Lincoln

Cushing, with his DocsPopuli website, is among the richest resources in the world on radical posters and ephemera. And this research project would have been impossible without the African Activist Archive Project at Michigan State and the world's two most responsive emailers: Richard Knight and Chris Root.

This project benefited from generous financial and technical assistance from several organizations. These include the John F. Kennedy Library, the Gerald R. Ford Library, the Lyndon B. Johnson Library and Foundation (and their wonderful staffs), the Council for European Studies at Columbia University, the Society for Historians of American Foreign Relations, the New York Public Library, the Black Metropolis Research Consortium, WGBH, the Clements Center for National Security, the Center for European Studies at the University of Texas, the John L. Warfield Center at the University of Texas, the UT Department of History, the Miller Center at the University of Virginia (with thanks to Melvyn Leffler, Brian Balogh, and Marc Selverstone), the International Securities Studies Program at Yale (special thanks to Paul Kennedy and the staff), and the Mershon Center for National Security at Ohio State.

Finally, I could not imagine completing, or even undertaking, this work without the support of good friends and encouraging family. I was particularly fortunate to complete my graduate studies within multiple communities that made a potentially isolating experience adventurous and fun. Many are mentioned above, and more should be here, but I will add special thanks to Cacee Mabis, Jason Morgan, Michelle Paranzino, Helen Pho, Matt Bunn and our inconsistent fantasy league, David Conrad, Sundara Vadlamudi and the entire Crown & Anchor crew, Amanda Behm, Wen-Qing Ngoei, and all my coconspirators at Yale ISS. Of course, I owe the greatest thanks to my family: my parents for their unending support and enthusiasm; Julie for her patience and consistent, incredible thoughtfulness; and Austin for the reminders to put the past aside for a bit to appreciate little moments in the present.

www.ingramcontent.com/pod-product-compliance
Lightning Source LLC
Chambersburg PA
CBHW031536260326
41914CB00032B/1828/J